PEANUTS
ALL-STARS

Charles M. Schulz

Ballantine Books
New York

A Ballantine Books Trade Paperback Original

Copyright © 2006 United Feature Syndicate, Inc.

Published in the United States by Ballantine Books,
an imprint of The Random House Publishing Group,
a division of Random House, Inc., New York.

BALLANTINE and colophon are registered trademarks of Random House, Inc.

The comic strips in this book were originally published in newspapers worldwide.

ISBN 0-345-47982-3

Printed in the United States of America

www.ballantinebooks.com

2 4 6 8 9 7 5 3 1

Design by Diane Hobbing of Snap-Haus Graphics

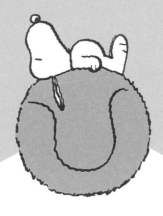

PEANUTS ALL-STARS

Basketball

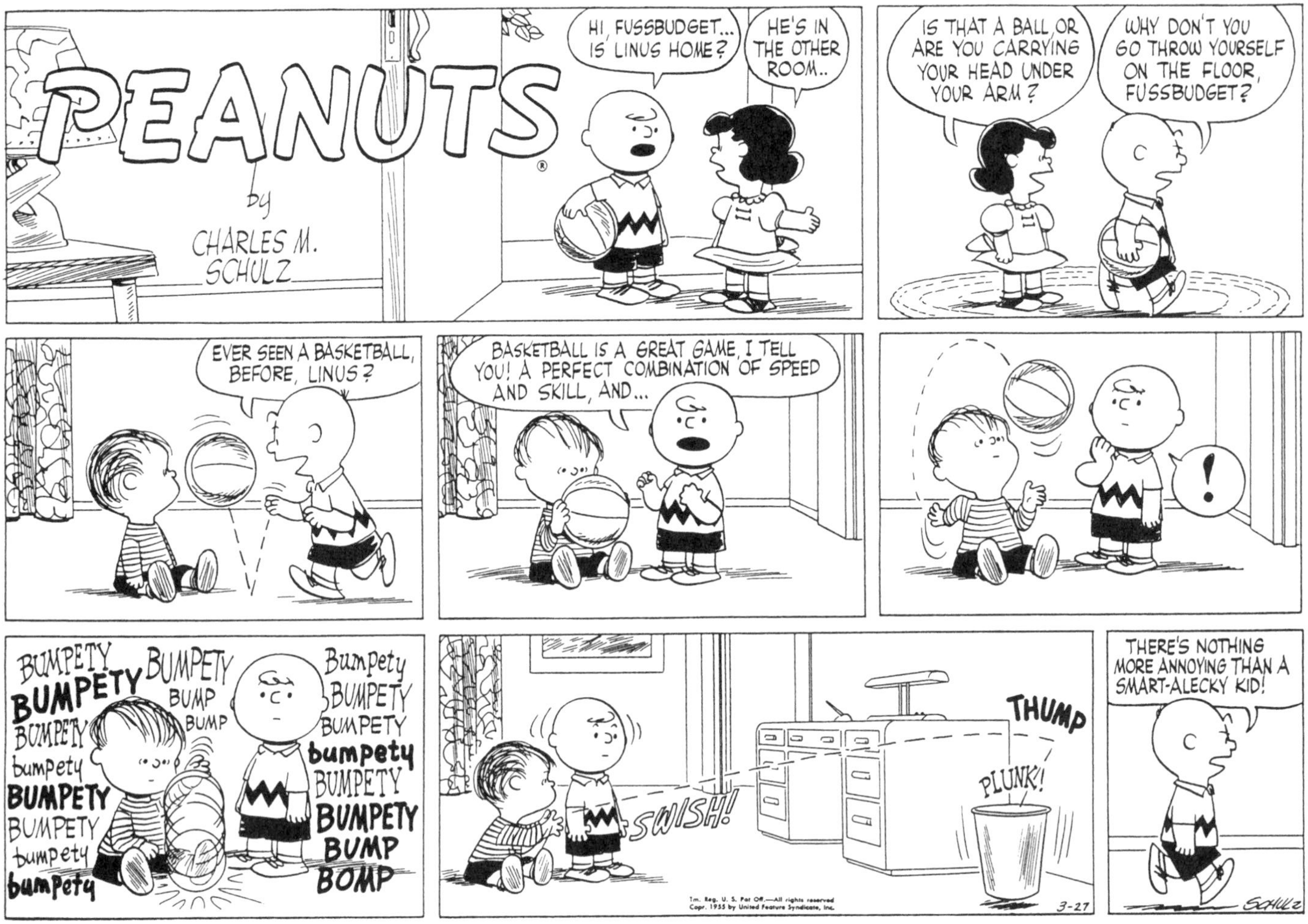
PEANUTS
by CHARLES M. SCHULZ
HI, FUSSBUDGET... IS LINUS HOME?
HE'S IN THE OTHER ROOM..
IS THAT A BALL, OR ARE YOU CARRYING YOUR HEAD UNDER YOUR ARM?
WHY DON'T YOU GO THROW YOURSELF ON THE FLOOR, FUSSBUDGET?
EVER SEEN A BASKETBALL, BEFORE, LINUS?
BASKETBALL IS A GREAT GAME, I TELL YOU! A PERFECT COMBINATION OF SPEED AND SKILL, AND...
!
BUMPETY BUMPETY BUMPETY bumpety BUMPETY BUMPETY bumpety bumpety
BUMPETY BUMP BUMP
Bumpety BUMPETY BUMPETY bumpety BUMPETY BUMPETY BUMP BOMP
SWISH!
THUMP
PLUNK!
Tm. Reg. U. S. Pat. Off.—All rights reserved
Copr. 1955 by United Feature Syndicate, Inc.
3-27
THERE'S NOTHING MORE ANNOYING THAN A SMART-ALECKY KID!
SCHULZ

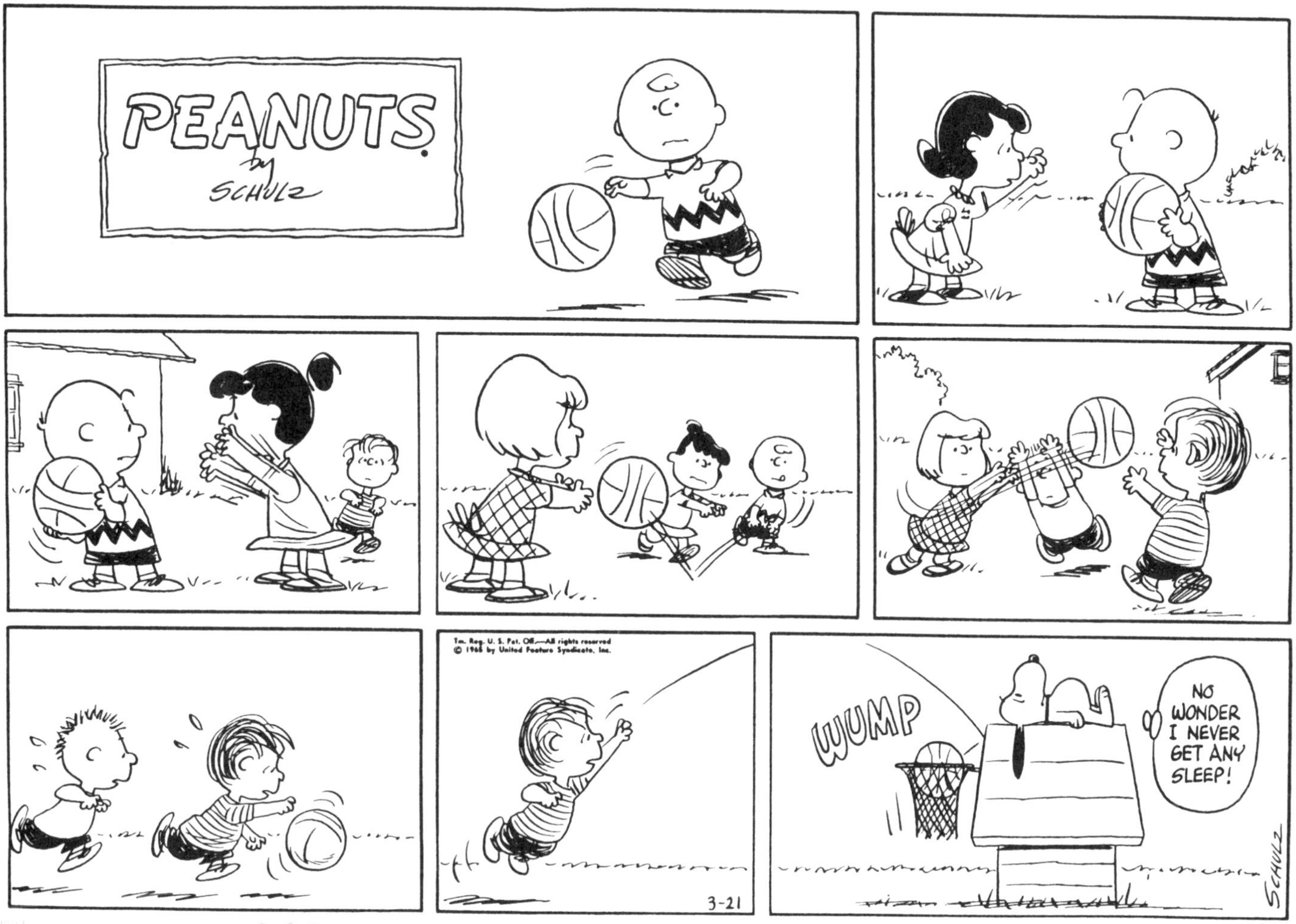
PEANUTS
by SCHULZ
Tm. Reg. U. S. Pat. Off.—All rights reserved © 1965 by United Feature Syndicate, Inc.
3-21
WUMP
NO WONDER I NEVER GET ANY SLEEP!
SCHULZ

PEANUTS
Tm. Reg. U.S. Pat. Off.—All rights reserved
© 1973 by United Feature Syndicate, Inc.
9-21
SCHULZ

PEANUTS
!
Tm. Reg. U.S. Pat. Off.—All rights reserved
© 1973 by United Feature Syndicate, Inc.
9-22
SSSSSS!!
SCHULZ

PEANUTS

MY DAD USED TO PLAY ON A BASKETBALL TEAM IN HIGH SCHOOL...

HE SAID HE CAN'T REMEMBER EVER LOSING A GAME....

THEY MUST HAVE HAD A GREAT TEAM..

NO, HE HAS A TERRIBLE MEMORY!

THAT'S A NEAT LOOKING BASKET-BALL, CHUCK
THE ONE THEY GAVE US GIRLS TO PLAY WITH ISN'T HALF THAT GOOD
9-26
YOU'RE NOT AGAINST WOMEN'S SPORTS ARE YOU, CHUCK?
SIGH
© 1979 United Feature Syndicate, Inc.

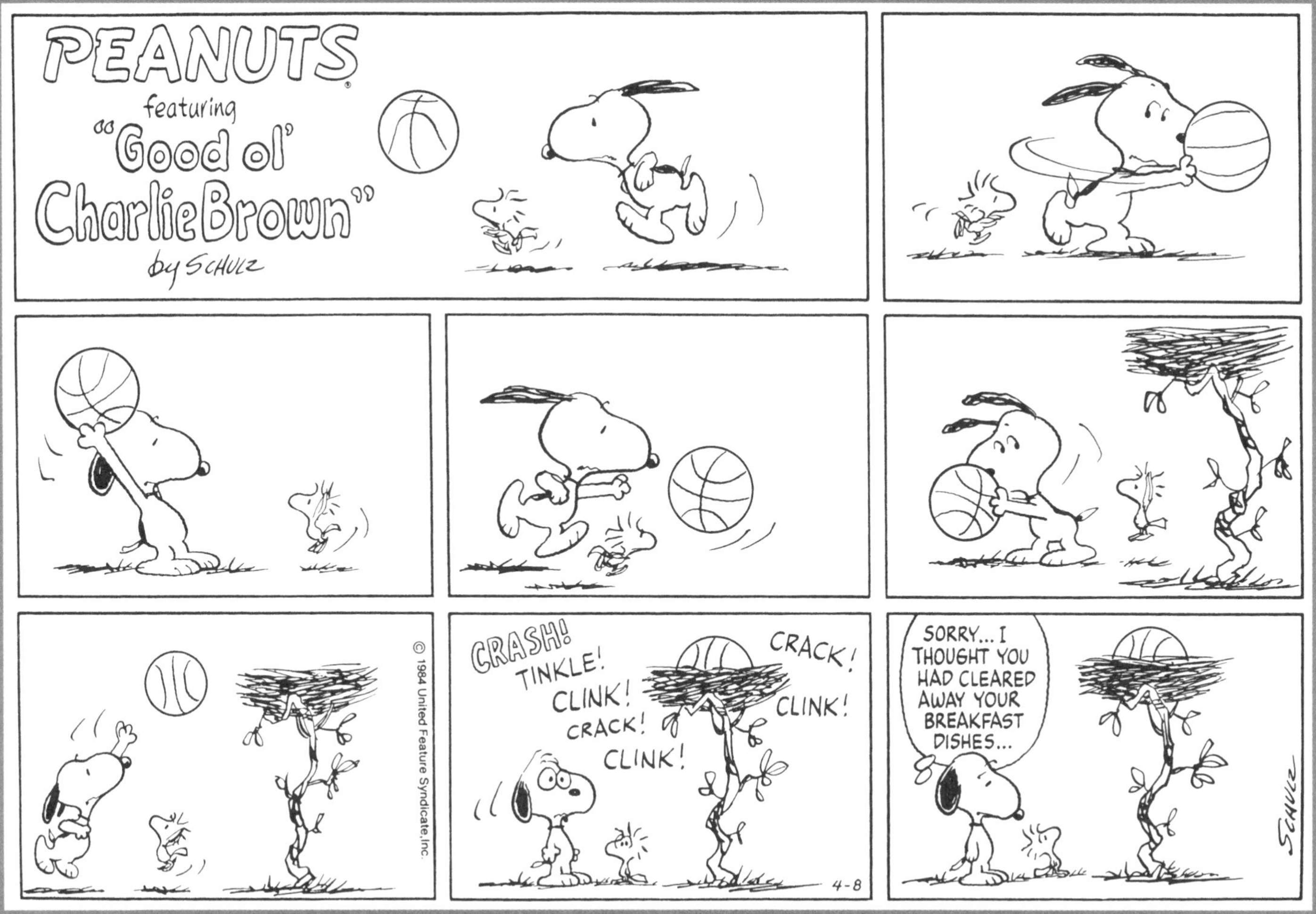
PEANUTS
featuring
"Good ol' CharlieBrown"
by SCHULZ
© 1984 United Feature Syndicate, Inc.
CRASH!
TINKLE!
CLINK!
CRACK!
CLINK!
CRACK!
CLINK!
4-8
SORRY... I THOUGHT YOU HAD CLEARED AWAY YOUR BREAKFAST DISHES...
SCHULZ

FIRST WE'LL SHOOT A FEW BASKETS..
10-4
© 1984 United Feature Syndicate, Inc.
THEN WE'LL PLAY A LITTLE ONE-ON-ONE..
OR MAYBE ONE-ON-ONE-FOURTH...
SCHULZ

PEANUTS
featuring
"Good ol' Charlie Brown"
by SCHULZ
?
© 1985 United Feature Syndicate, Inc
8-25
SCHULZ

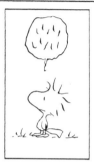

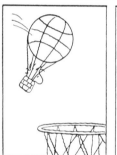

I'M GONNA TRY OUT FOR THE GIRL'S BASKETBALL TEAM
YOU HAVE A LOT TO LEARN...
© 1985 United Feature Syndicate, Inc.
I'VE ALREADY LEARNED SOMETHING...
9-14
YOU DON'T PUT THE KNEEPADS ON OVER YOUR HEAD..
SCHULZ

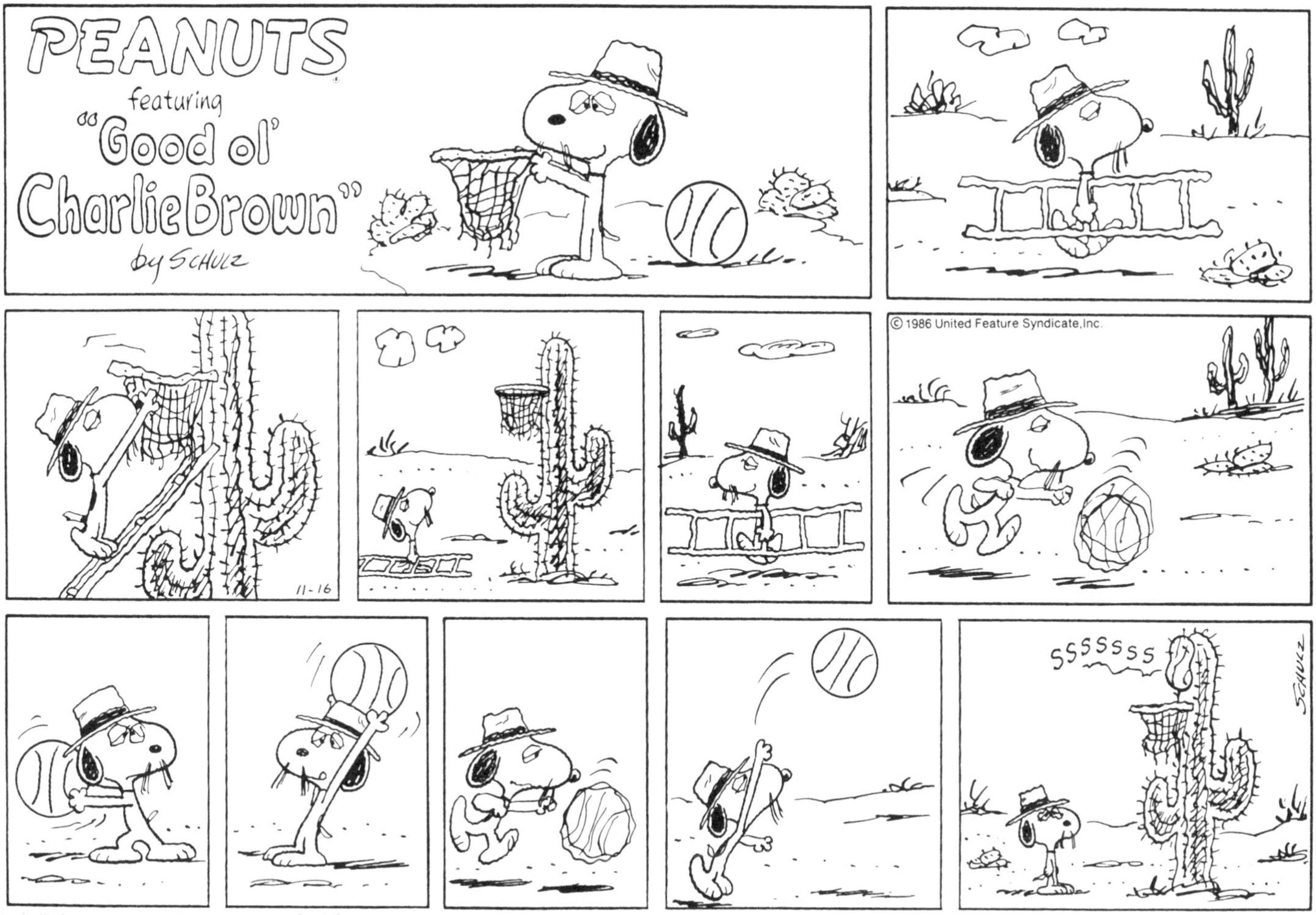
PEANUTS
featuring
"Good ol' Charlie Brown"
by SCHULZ
11-16
© 1986 United Feature Syndicate, Inc.
SSSSSSS
SCHULZ

5-14
THERE'S NO HURRY, I GUESS, BUT LET ME KNOW WHEN I CAN HAVE YOUR SUPPER DISH...
© 1990 United Feature Syndicate, Inc.

RATS!
© 1993 United Feature Syndicate, Inc.
NO MATTER HOW HARD YOU TRY, YOU CAN'T DRIBBLE A TUMBLEWEED!
SCHULZ
3-6

OKAY, SHOOT!
7-29
© 1993 United Feature Syndicate, Inc.
YOU DIDN'T SAY, "NICE TRY"
SCHULZ

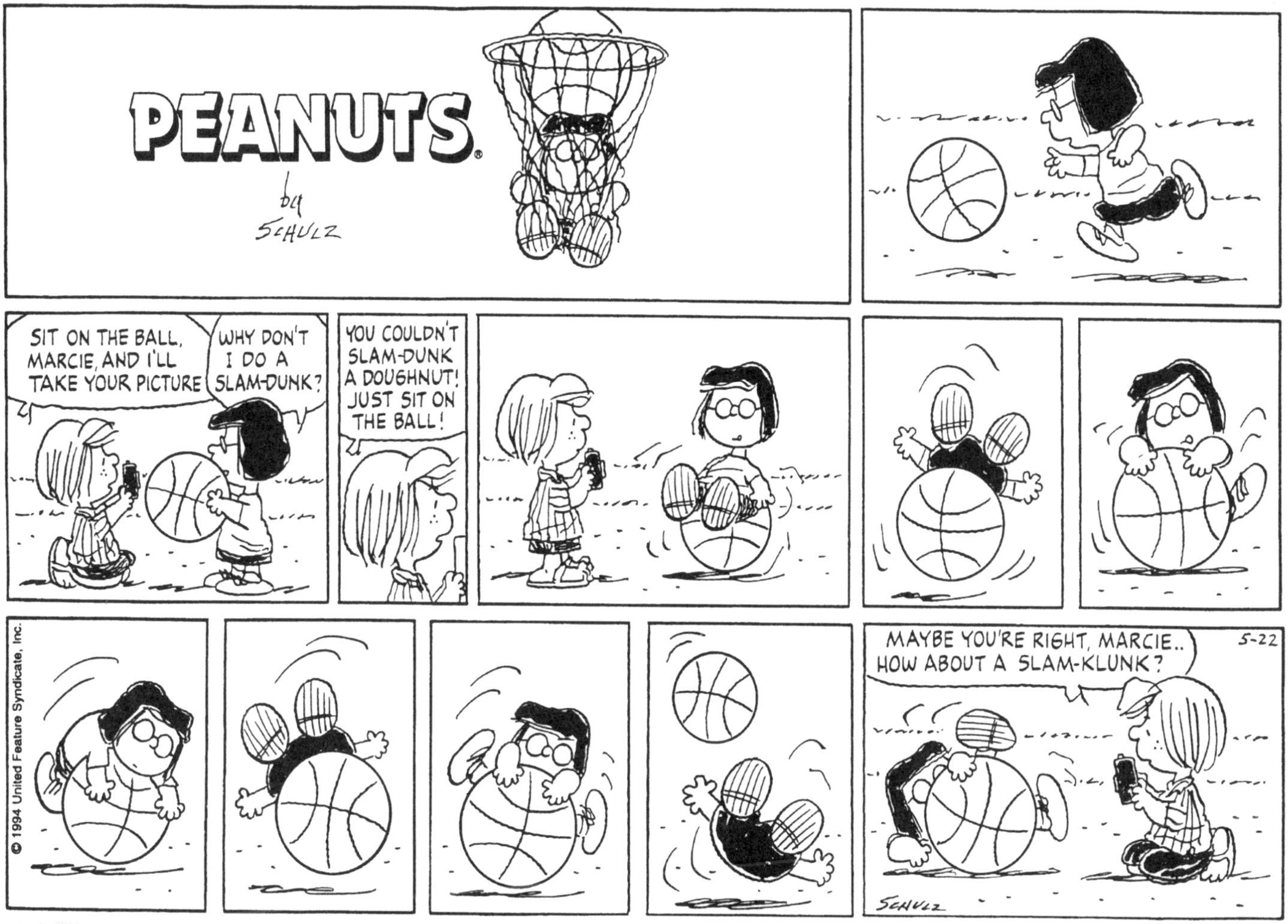
PEANUTS
by SCHULZ
SIT ON THE BALL, MARCIE, AND I'LL TAKE YOUR PICTURE
WHY DON'T I DO A SLAM-DUNK?
YOU COULDN'T SLAM-DUNK A DOUGHNUT! JUST SIT ON THE BALL!
© 1994 United Feature Syndicate, Inc.
5-22
MAYBE YOU'RE RIGHT, MARCIE.. HOW ABOUT A SLAM-KLUNK?
SCHULZ

7-28
THIS IS HOW WE SHOOT BASKETS, RERUN
SEE, WE BOUNCE THE BALL A COUPLE OF TIMES TO GET OUR RHYTHM..
THEN WE FLIP IT THROUGH THE BASKET!
© 1994 United Feature Syndicate, Inc.
WHY?
SCHULZ

© 1994 United Feature Syndicate, Inc.
8-16
SCHULZ

8-23
© 1994 United Feature Syndicate, Inc.
DON'T BE DISCOURAGED.. I'M NEW AT THIS..
SCHULZ

8-30
© 1994 United Feature Syndicate, Inc.
WE DON'T HAVE TO DO THIS, YOU KNOW..

9-1
© 1994 United Feature Syndicate, Inc.
WELL, I'LL SAY THIS FOR YOU.. YOU'RE VERY PATIENT..
SCHULZ

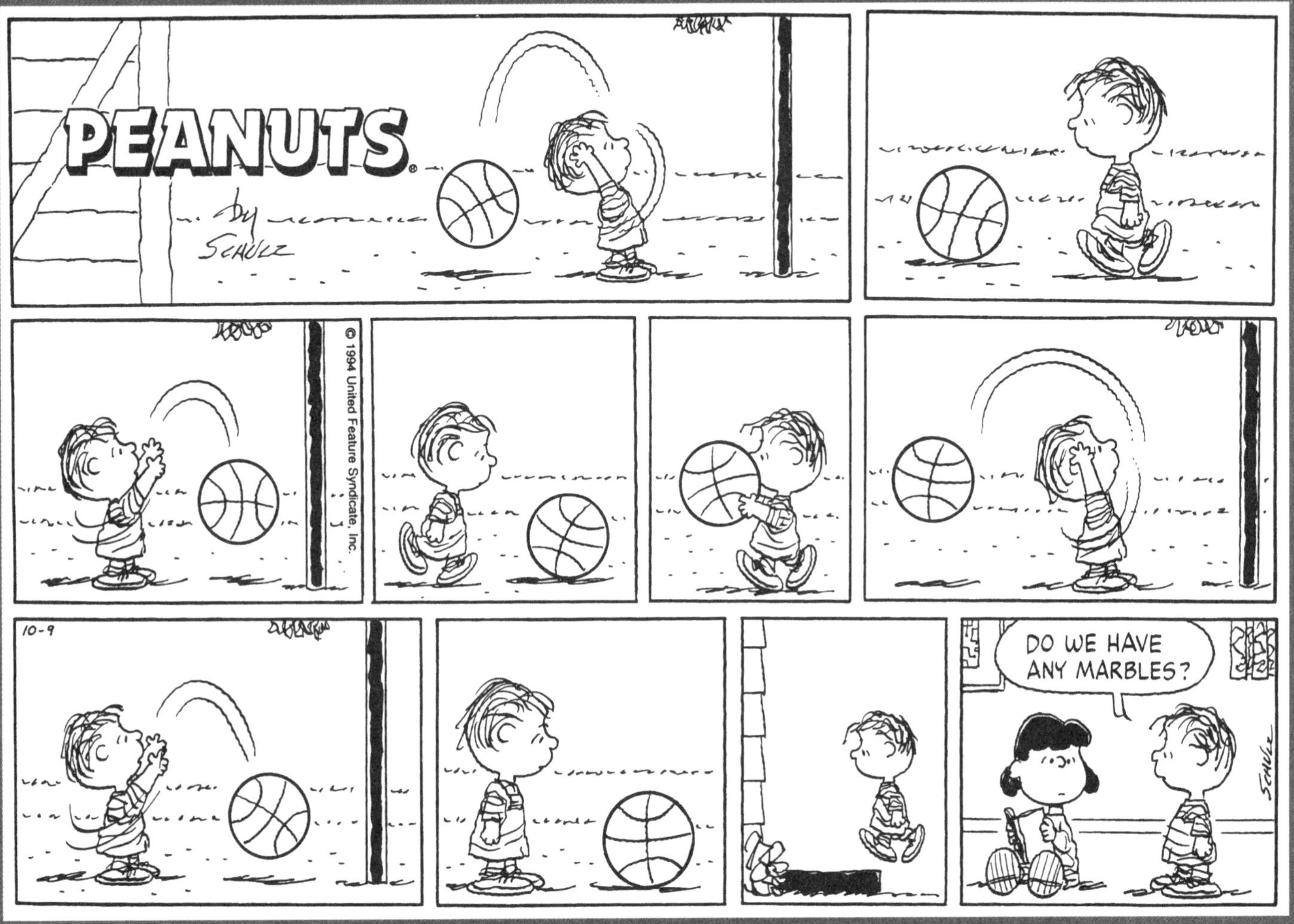
PEANUTS
by SCHULZ
© 1994 United Feature Syndicate, Inc.
10-9
DO WE HAVE ANY MARBLES?
SCHULZ

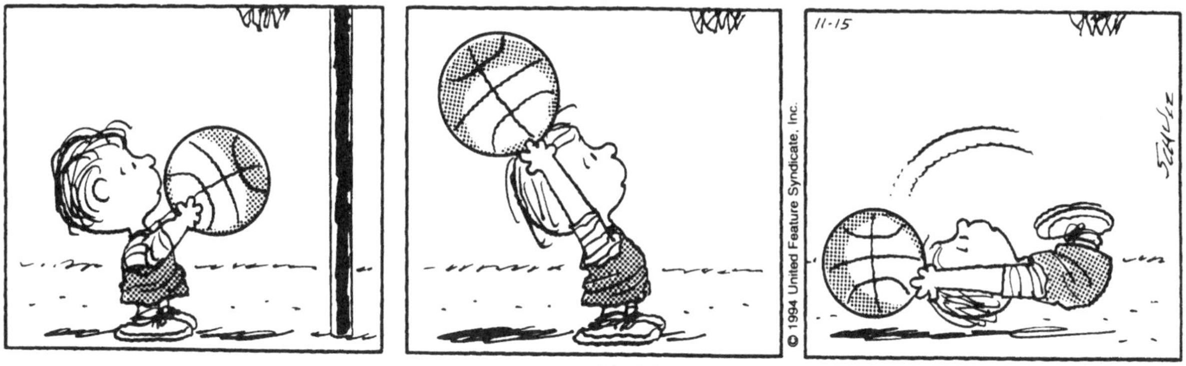
11-15
© 1994 United Feature Syndicate, Inc.
SCHULZ

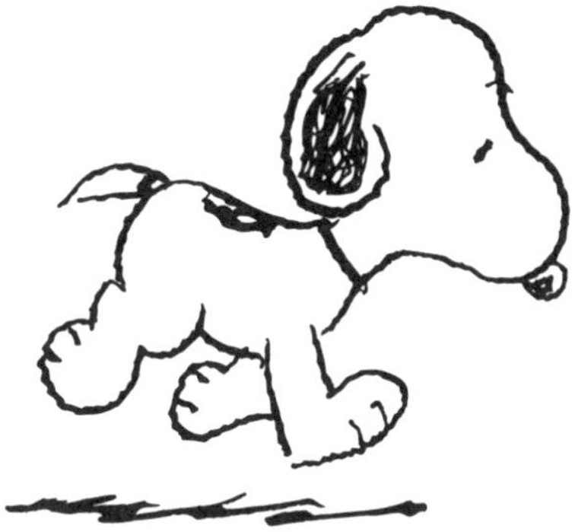

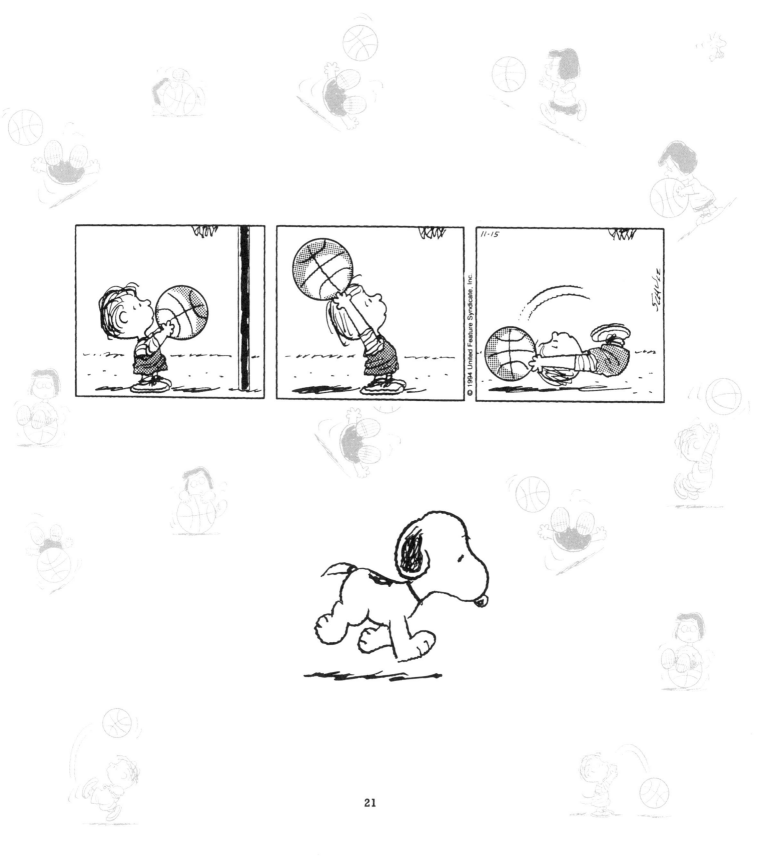

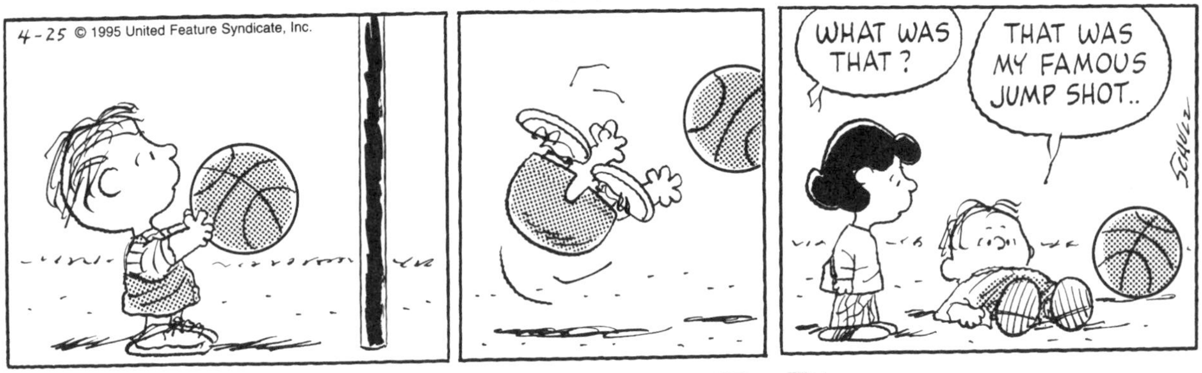
4-25 © 1995 United Feature Syndicate, Inc.
WHAT WAS THAT ?
THAT WAS MY FAMOUS JUMP SHOT..
SCHULZ

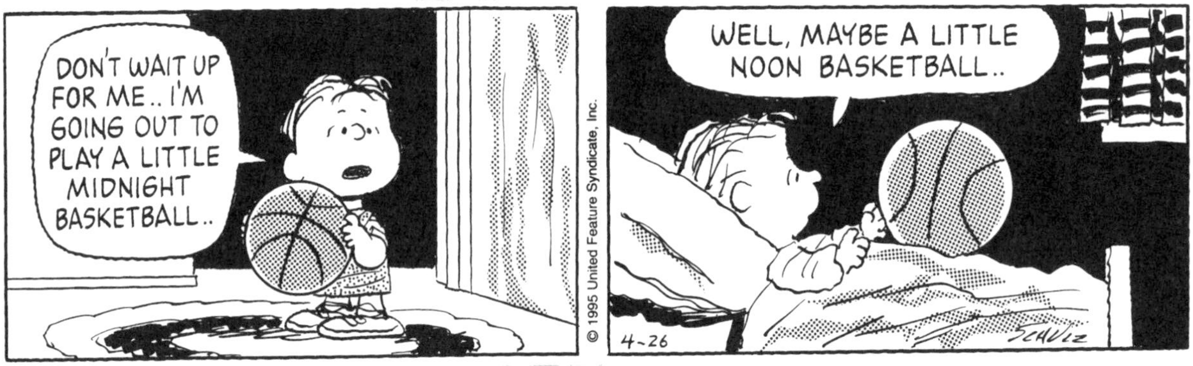
DON'T WAIT UP FOR ME.. I'M GOING OUT TO PLAY A LITTLE MIDNIGHT BASKETBALL..
© 1995 United Feature Syndicate, Inc.
4-26
WELL, MAYBE A LITTLE NOON BASKETBALL..
SCHULZ

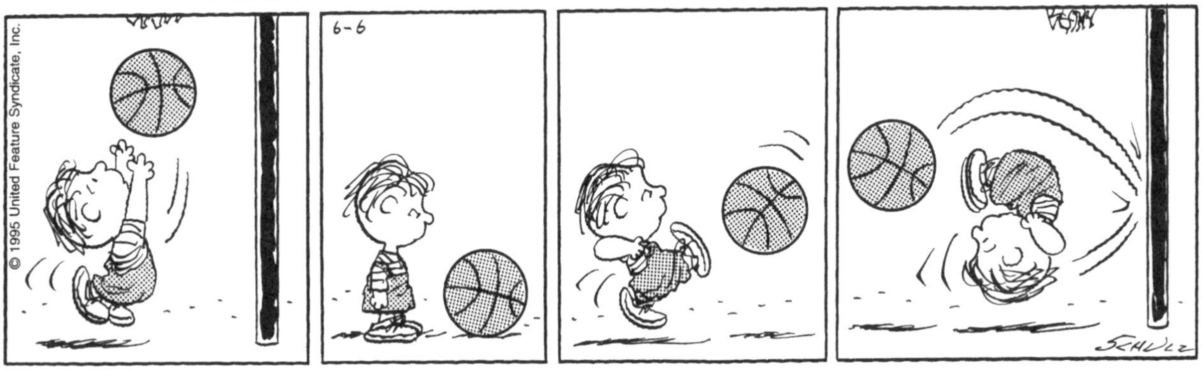
© 1995 United Feature Syndicate, Inc.
6-6
SCHULZ

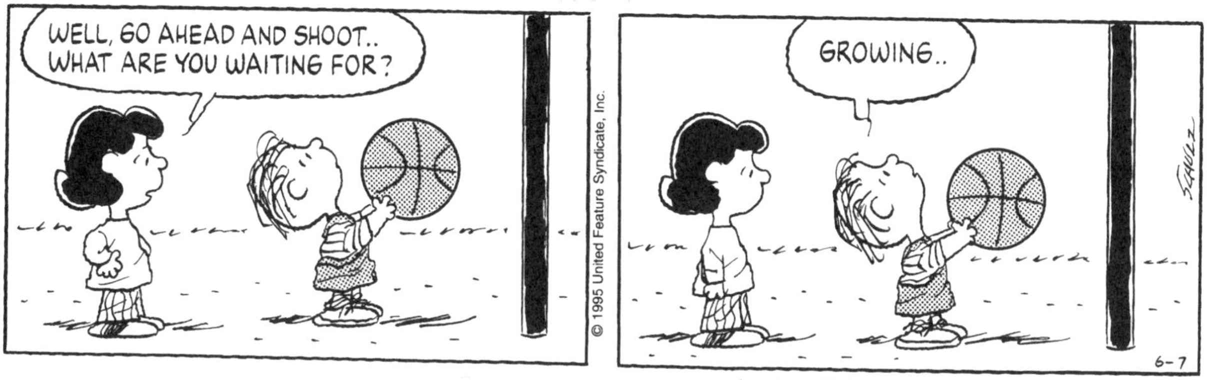
WELL, GO AHEAD AND SHOOT.. WHAT ARE YOU WAITING FOR?
© 1995 United Feature Syndicate, Inc.
GROWING..
SCHULZ
6-7

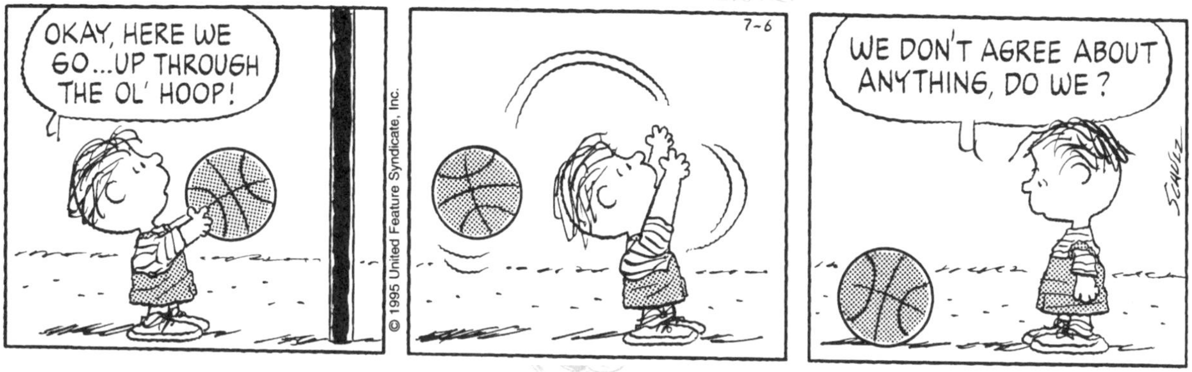
OKAY, HERE WE GO...UP THROUGH THE OL' HOOP!
© 1995 United Feature Syndicate, Inc.
7-6
WE DON'T AGREE ABOUT ANYTHING, DO WE?
SCHULZ

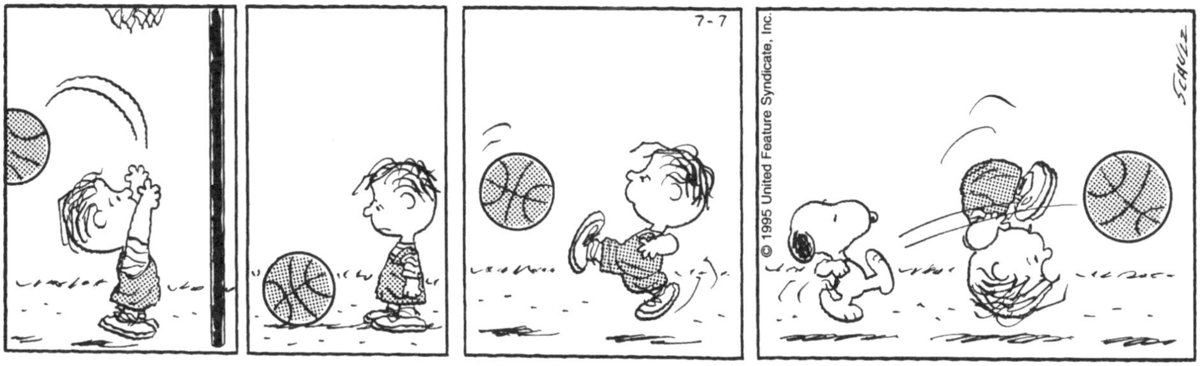
7-7
© 1995 United Feature Syndicate, Inc.
SCHULZ

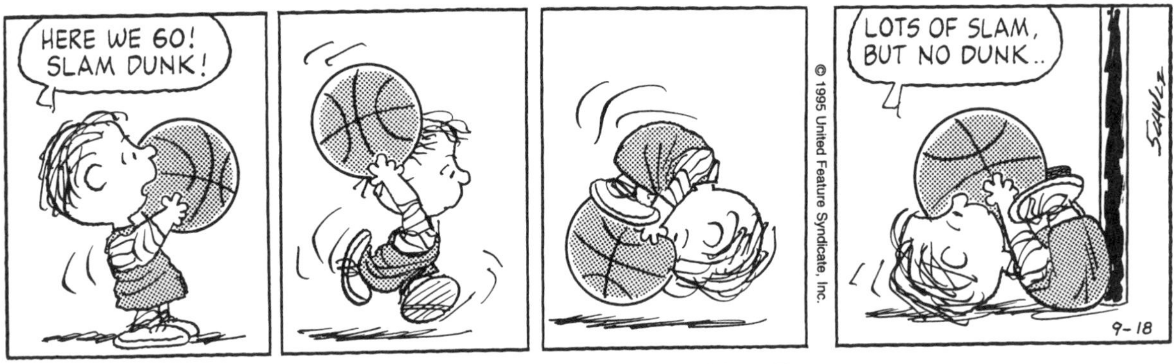
HERE WE GO! SLAM DUNK!
LOTS OF SLAM, BUT NO DUNK..
SCHULZ
9-18

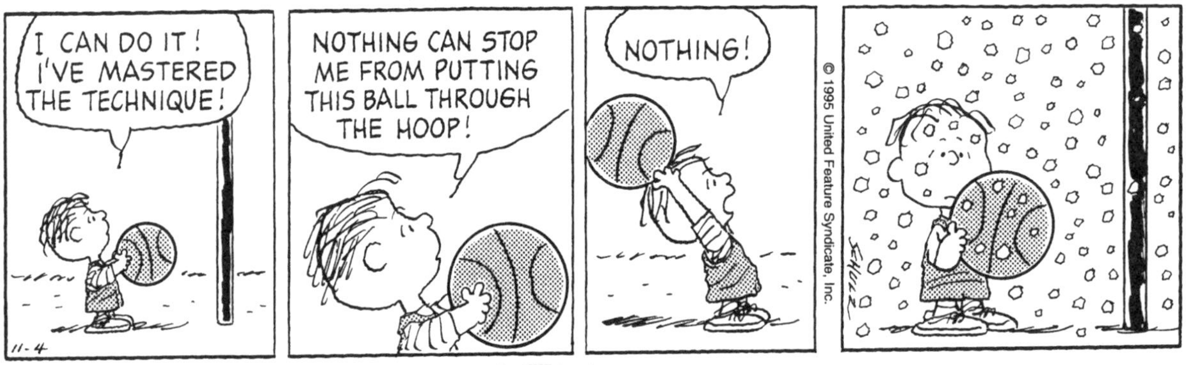
I CAN DO IT! I'VE MASTERED THE TECHNIQUE!
11-4
NOTHING CAN STOP ME FROM PUTTING THIS BALL THROUGH THE HOOP!
NOTHING!
SCHULZ

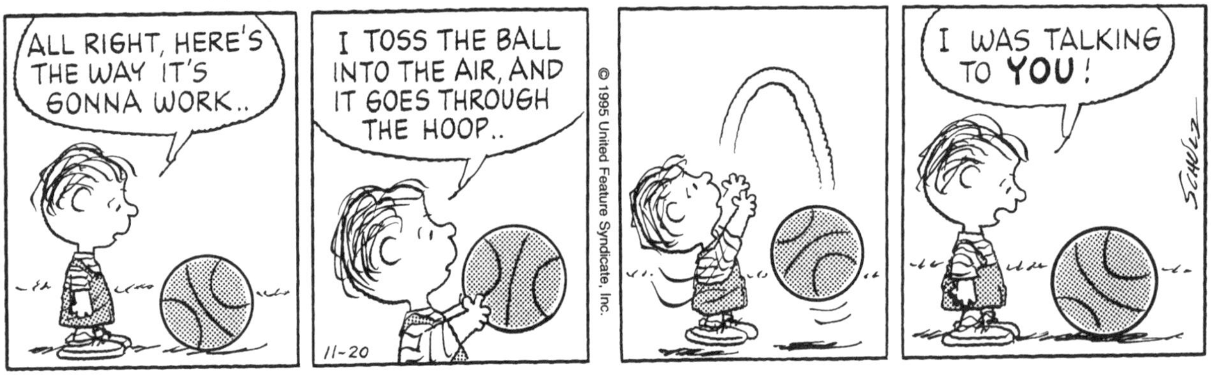
ALL RIGHT, HERE'S THE WAY IT'S GONNA WORK..
I TOSS THE BALL INTO THE AIR, AND IT GOES THROUGH THE HOOP..
11-20
I WAS TALKING TO **YOU**!
SCHULZ

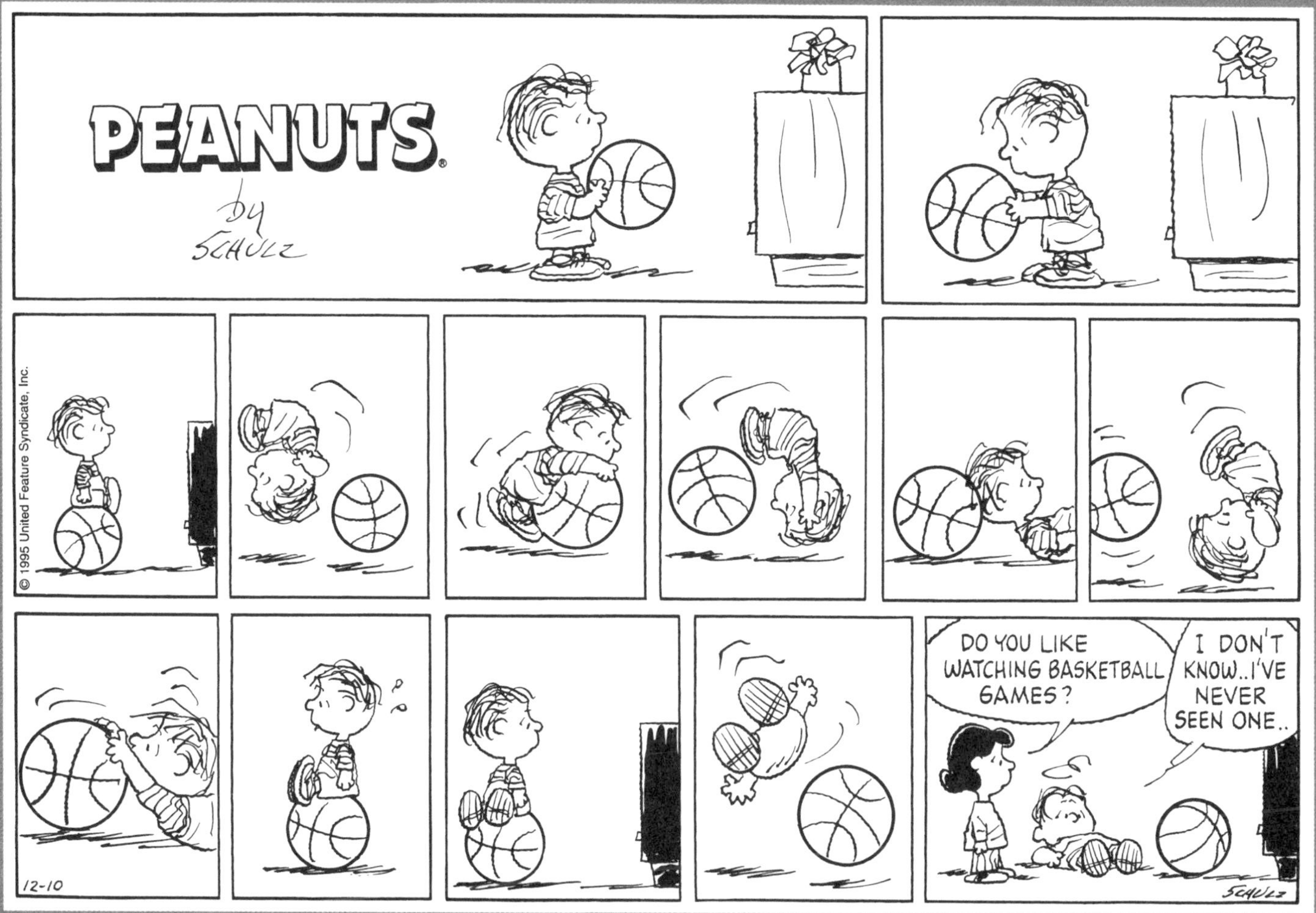
PEANUTS
by SCHULZ
© 1995 United Feature Syndicate, Inc.
12-10
DO YOU LIKE WATCHING BASKETBALL GAMES?
I DON'T KNOW..I'VE NEVER SEEN ONE..
SCHULZ

THE SCORE IS TIED! THREE SECONDS TO PLAY!
HE TURNS! HE SHOOTS!
© 1996 United Feature Syndicate, Inc.
1-22
SORT OF.. MORE OR LESS..
SCHULZ

YOU SHOOT, AND I'LL GO UP FOR THE REBOUND..
1-24
BONK!
© 1996 United Feature Syndicate, Inc.
THAT WAS THE REBOUND..
SCHULZ

© 1996 United Feature Syndicate, Inc.
8-9
SCHULZ

8-22
www.unitedmedia.com
© 1996 United Feature Syndicate, Inc.
WHAT DID YOU STOP FOR?!
SCHULZ

UP YOU GO! SLAM DUNK! THROUGH THE HOOP! GO! GO! GO!
8-23
www.unitedmedia.com
YOU TALK TO IT! IT NEVER LISTENS TO ME!
© 1996 United Feature Syndicate, Inc.
WOOF!
SCHULZ

www.unitedmedia.com
© 1996 United Feature Syndicate, Inc.
BANG!
SCHULZ
9-25

1-6-97
© 1996 United Feature Syndicate, Inc.
HERE'S A LIST OF THE ATHLETES' NAMES..ALL YOU HAVE TO DO IS FORGE THEIR SIGNATURES..YOU CAN START WITH THE BASKETBALLS..
SCHULZ

WHAT'S THIS? THIS ISN'T A BASKETBALL PLAYER'S AUTOGRAPH!
I DON'T DO FAKE AUTOGRAPHS..THAT'S MY DAD'S NAME... HE'S A BARBER..
www.unitedmedia.com
A FAMOUS BARBER?
© 1996 United Feature Syndicate, Inc.
TELL HIM TO AUTOGRAPH A BARBER POLE! WE COULD SELL IT!
SCHULZ
1-7-97

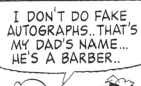

1-11-97
YOU JUST DON'T UNDERSTAND, DO YOU?
© 1996 United Feature Syndicate, Inc.
www.unitedmedia.com
SCHULZ

www.unitedmedia.com
3-15
© 1997 United Feature Syndicate, Inc.
SCHULZ

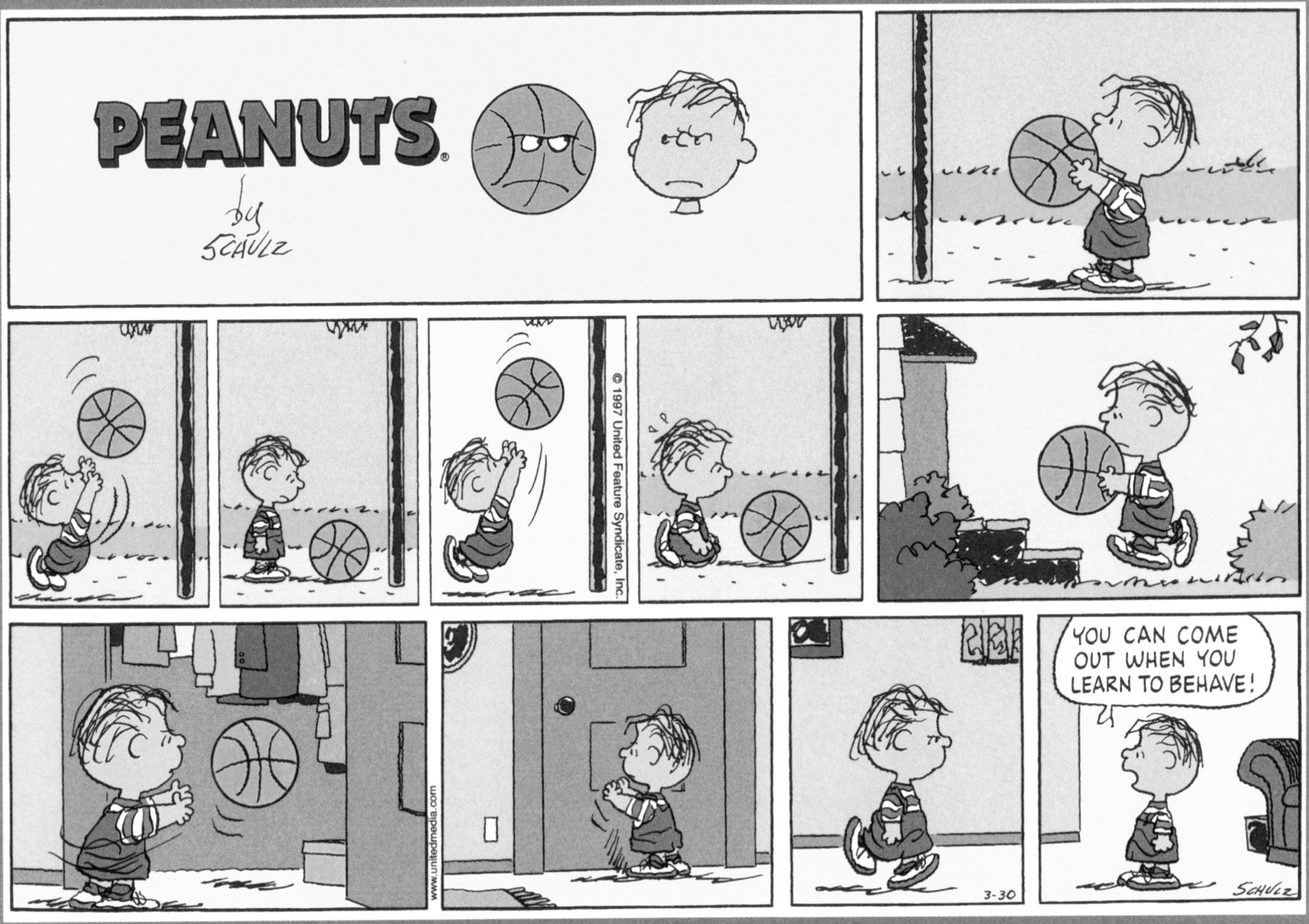
PEANUTS
by SCHULZ
© 1997 United Feature Syndicate, Inc.
www.unitedmedia.com
3-30
YOU CAN COME OUT WHEN YOU LEARN TO BEHAVE!
SCHULZ

AAUGH!!
WHAT'D YOU DO THAT FOR?!
I DIDN'T MEAN TO.. IT WAS A DOG THING..
4-3
www.unitedmedia.com
© 1997 United Feature Syndicate, Inc.
SCHULZ

BONK!
I HIT YOU ON THE HEAD SO I THINK THAT MEANS YOU GET A FREE SHOT...
BONK!
7-4
www.unitedmedia.com
© 1997 United Feature Syndicate, Inc.
SCHULZ

THE GOVERNMENT'S "MIDNIGHT BASKETBALL" PROGRAM HAS STILL TO REACH SOME OUTLYING AREAS..
7-9
© 1997 United Feature Syndicate, Inc.
SCHULZ

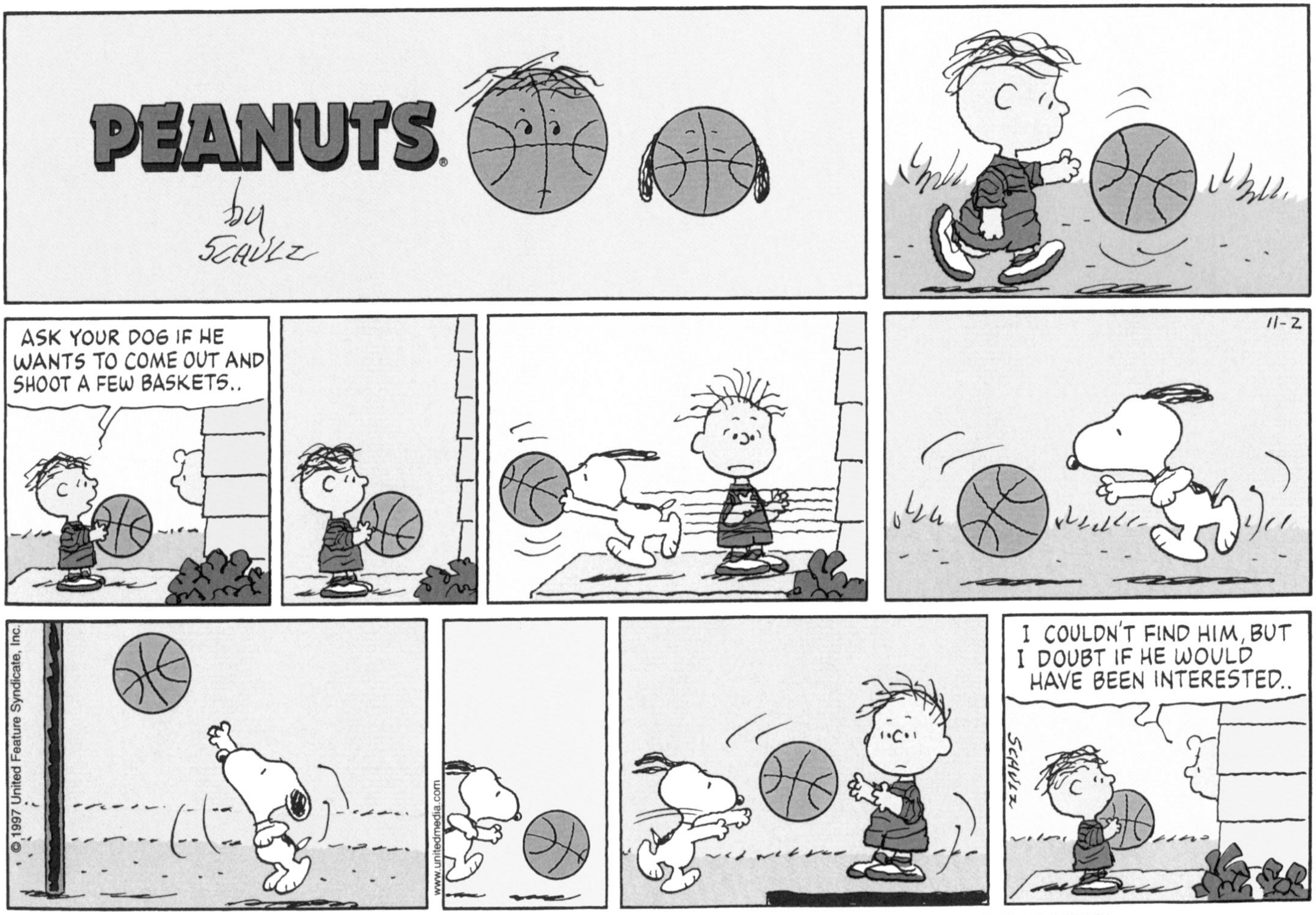
PEANUTS®
by SCHULZ
ASK YOUR DOG IF HE WANTS TO COME OUT AND SHOOT A FEW BASKETS..
11-2
© 1997 United Feature Syndicate, Inc.
www.unitedmedia.com
SCHULZ
I COULDN'T FIND HIM, BUT I DOUBT IF HE WOULD HAVE BEEN INTERESTED..

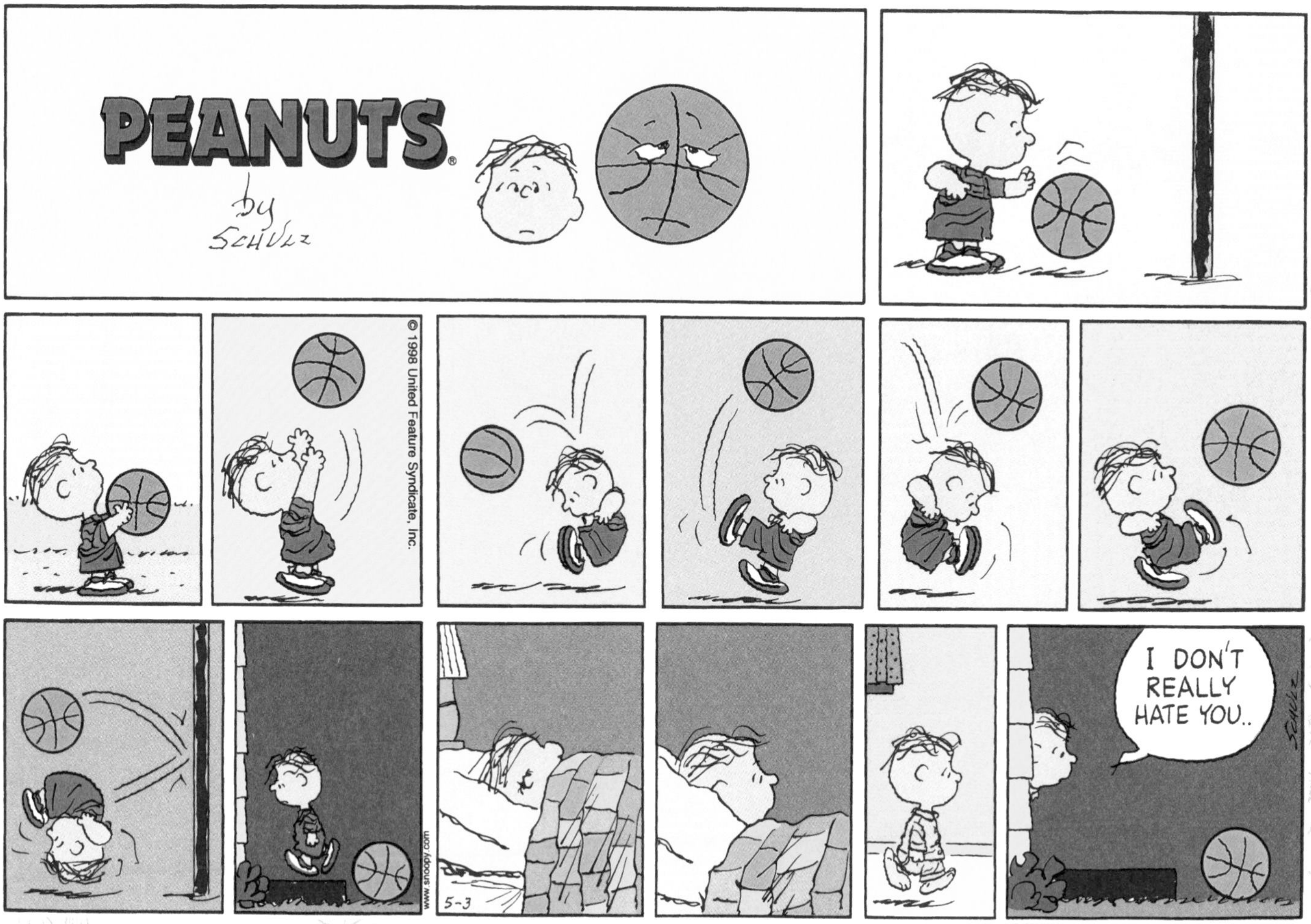

PEANUTS
by SCHULZ
© 1998 United Feature Syndicate, Inc.
www.snoopy.com
5-3
I DON'T REALLY HATE YOU..
SCHULZ

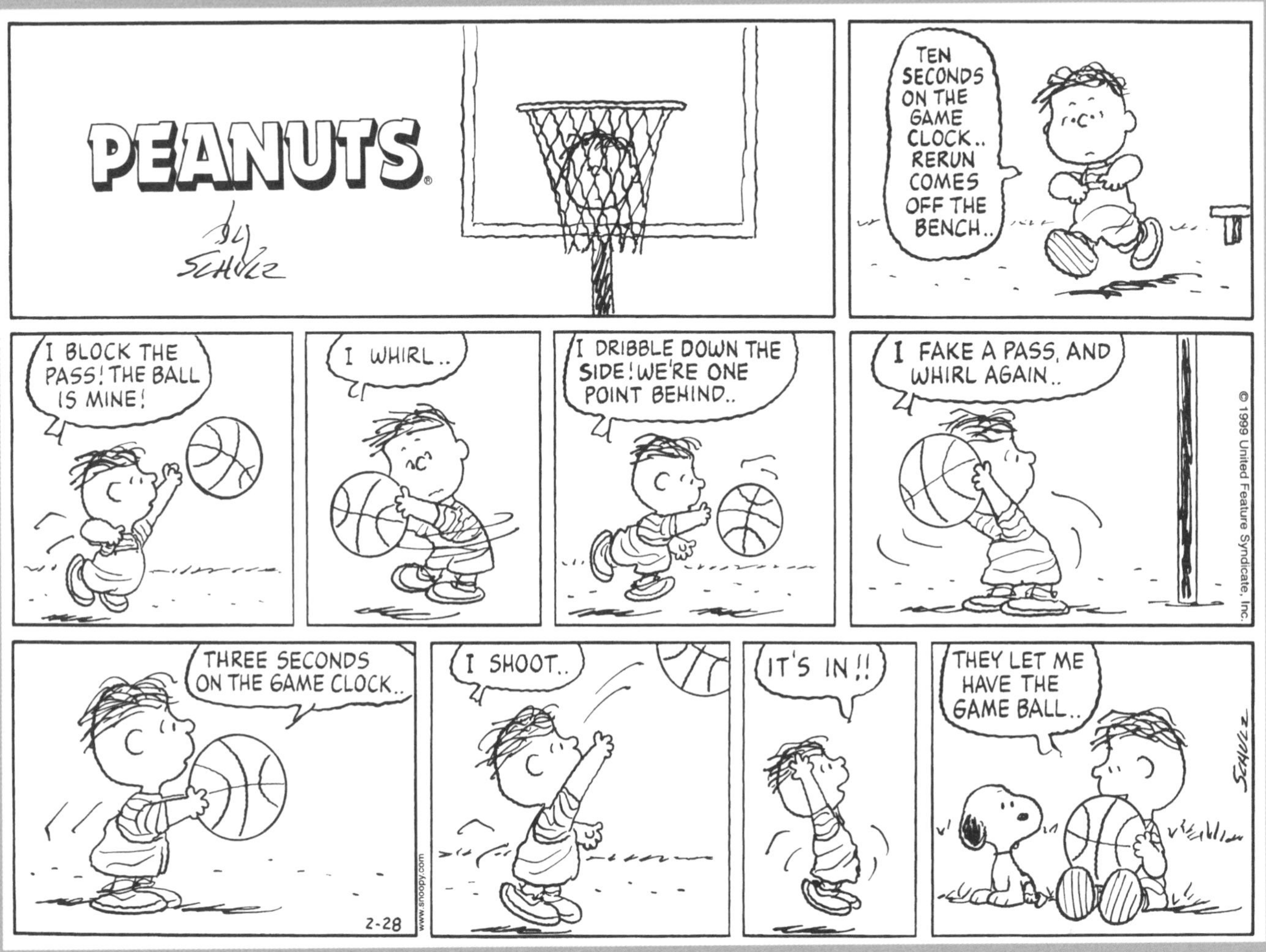
PEANUTS
SCHULZ
TEN SECONDS ON THE GAME CLOCK.. RERUN COMES OFF THE BENCH..
I BLOCK THE PASS! THE BALL IS MINE!
I WHIRL..
I DRIBBLE DOWN THE SIDE! WE'RE ONE POINT BEHIND..
I FAKE A PASS, AND WHIRL AGAIN..
© 1999 United Feature Syndicate, Inc.
THREE SECONDS ON THE GAME CLOCK..
2-28
www.snoopy.com
I SHOOT..
IT'S IN!!
THEY LET ME HAVE THE GAME BALL..
SCHULZ

6-17
LET ME ASK YOU SOMETHING...
DO YOU KNOW WHY WE'RE OUT HERE?
www.snoopy.com
© 1999 United Feature Syndicate, Inc.
SCHULZ

SO WHEN YOU GET OLDER, MAYBE I'LL TAKE YOU TO A NICE WARM GYMNASIUM..

© 1999 United Feature Syndicate, Inc.

Football

...AND THEN I GRABBED A FORWARD PASS....
..AND RAN NINETY YARDS FOR A TOUCHDOWN!
OR AT LEAST I MIGHT HAVE...
BUT THEY WOULDN'T LET ME IN THE GAME!
11-16
Copr. 1950 by United Feature Syndicate, Inc.
SCHULZ

"PEANUTS"
HE'LL KICK MY HAND! I JUST KNOW HE WILL!
I CAN'T GO THROUGH WITH IT!
Copr. 1951 by United Feature Syndicate, Inc.
?
YOU DIDN'T KICK THE BALL, CHARLIE BROWN... WHY DIDN'T YOU KICK IT?
11/14
SCHULZ

PEANUTS
by
CHARLES M. SCHULZ
ALL YOU HAVE TO DO IS HOLD THE BALL, LUCY... THEN I'LL COME RUNNING UP, AND KICK IT...
I DON'T KNOW IF THIS IS SUCH A GOOD IDEA
?
!
WHOMP
I WAS AFRAID YOUR SHOES MIGHT BE DIRTY, CHARLIE BROWN... I DON'T WANT ANYONE WITH DIRTY SHOES KICKING MY NEW FOOTBALL...
DON'T EVER DO THAT AGAIN! DO YOU WANT TO KILL ME ?! THIS TIME HOLD IT TIGHT!
HERE WE GO!
?
!
THUMP
I HELD IT REAL TIGHT, CHARLIE BROWN...
I'M NOT GOING TO GET UP.... I'M GOING TO LIE HERE FOR THE REST OF THE DAY...
11-16
Tm. Reg. U. S. Pat. Off.—All rights reserved ©Copr. 1952 by United Feature Syndicate, Inc.
SCHULZ

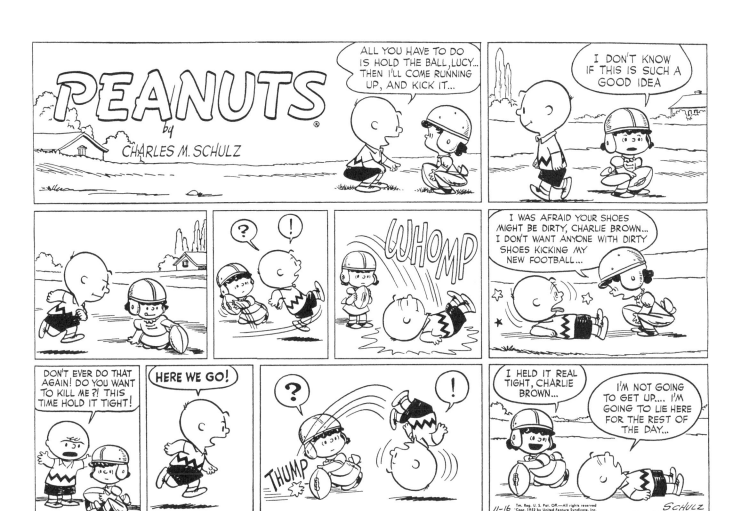

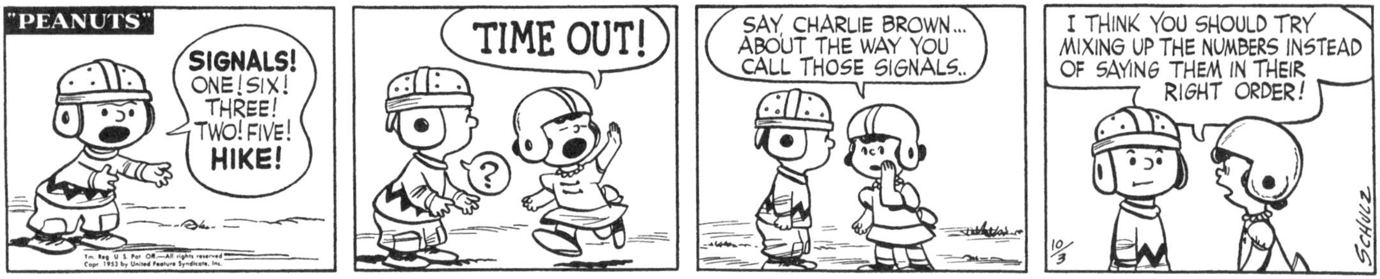
"PEANUTS"
SIGNALS! ONE! SIX! THREE! TWO! FIVE! HIKE!
Tm. Reg. U. S. Pat. Off.—All rights reserved Copr. 1953 by United Feature Syndicate, Inc.
TIME OUT!
?
SAY, CHARLIE BROWN... ABOUT THE WAY YOU CALL THOSE SIGNALS..
I THINK YOU SHOULD TRY MIXING UP THE NUMBERS INSTEAD OF SAYING THEM IN THEIR RIGHT ORDER!
10/3
SCHULZ

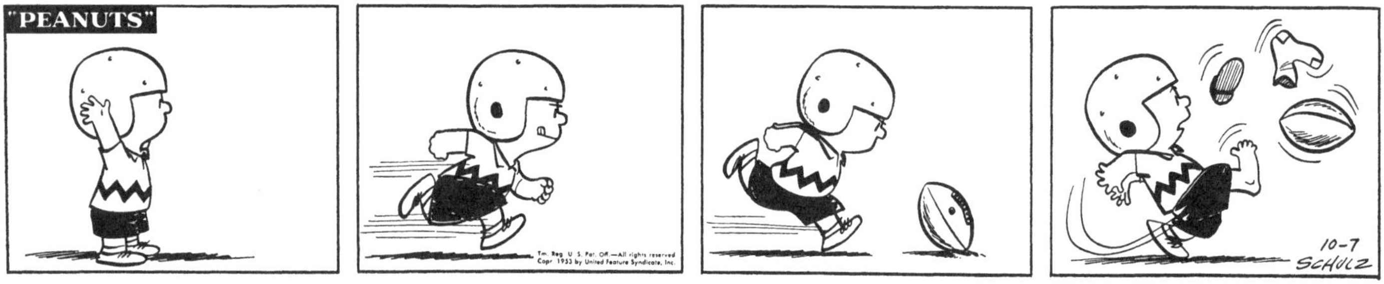
"PEANUTS"
Tm. Reg. U. S. Pat. Off.—All rights reserved Copr. 1953 by United Feature Syndicate, Inc.
10-7
SCHULZ

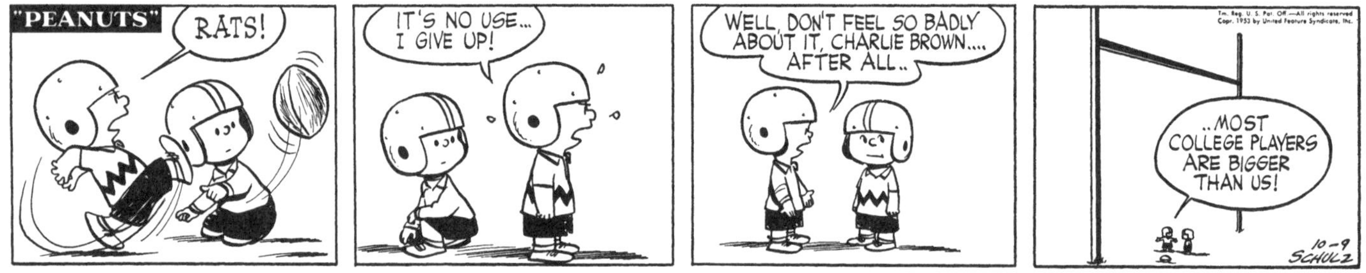
"PEANUTS"
RATS!
IT'S NO USE.. I GIVE UP!
WELL, DON'T FEEL SO BADLY ABOUT IT, CHARLIE BROWN.... AFTER ALL..
Tm. Reg. U. S. Pat. Off.—All rights reserved Copr. 1953 by United Feature Syndicate, Inc.
..MOST COLLEGE PLAYERS ARE BIGGER THAN US!
10-9
SCHULZ

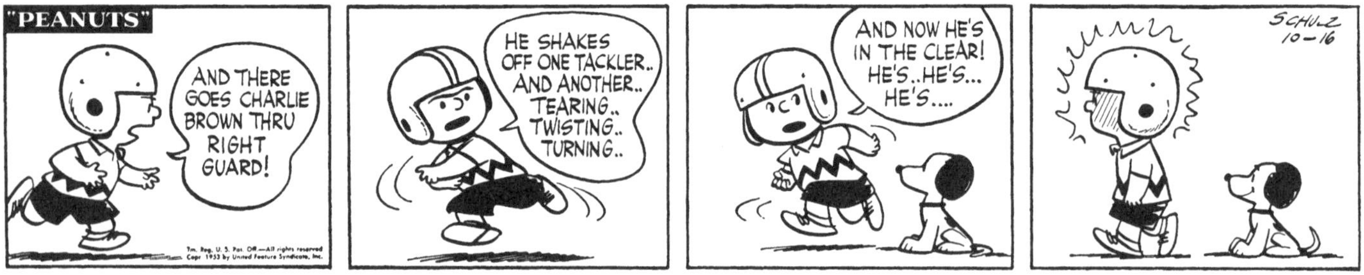
"PEANUTS"
AND THERE GOES CHARLIE BROWN THRU RIGHT GUARD!
Tm. Reg. U. S. Pat. Off.—All rights reserved Copr. 1953 by United Feature Syndicate, Inc.
HE SHAKES OFF ONE TACKLER.. AND ANOTHER.. TEARING.. TWISTING.. TURNING..
AND NOW HE'S IN THE CLEAR! HE'S..HE'S... HE'S....
SCHULZ 10-16

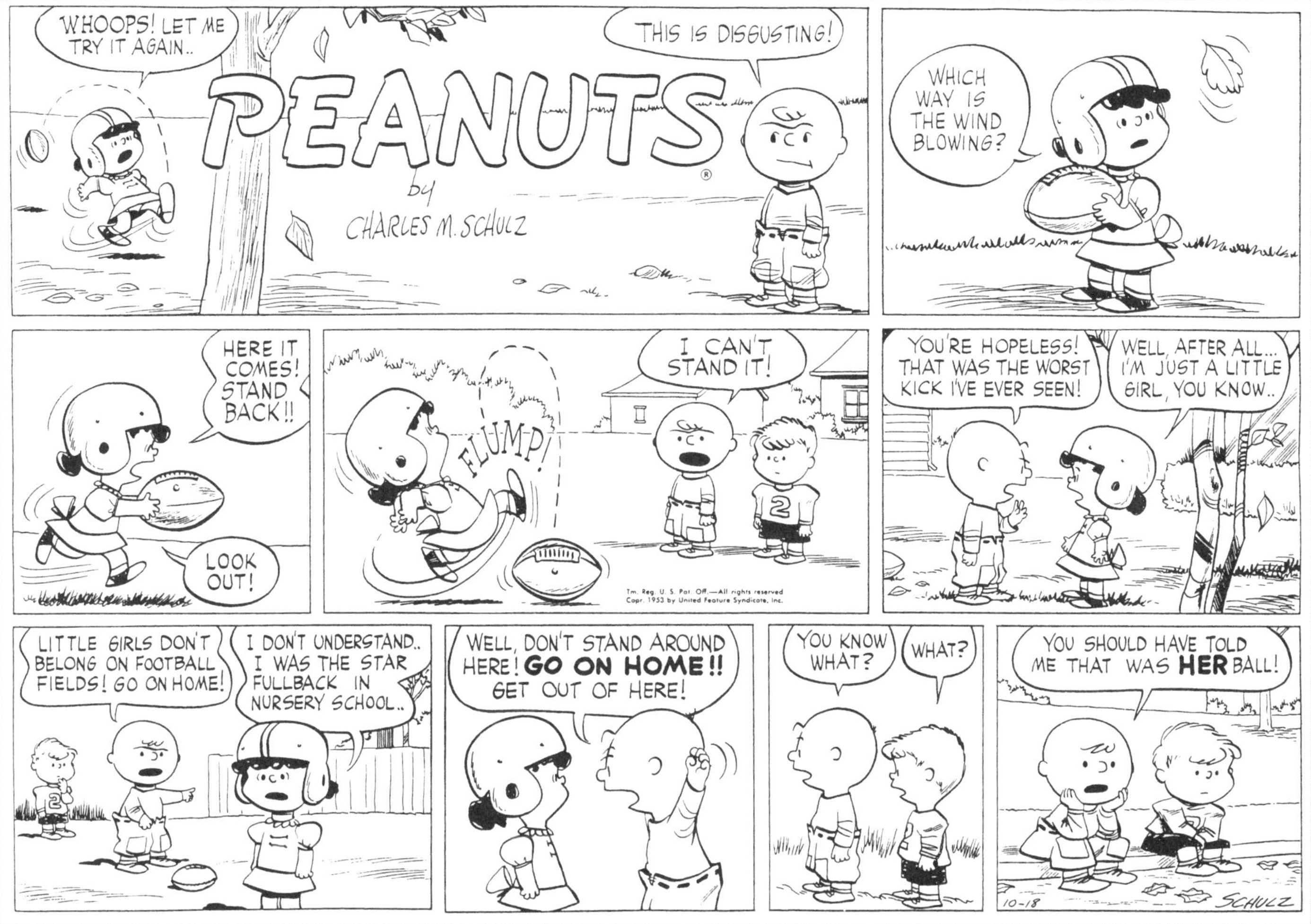
WHOOPS! LET ME TRY IT AGAIN..
PEANUTS
by CHARLES M. SCHULZ
THIS IS DISGUSTING!
WHICH WAY IS THE WIND BLOWING?
HERE IT COMES! STAND BACK!!
LOOK OUT!
FLUMP!
I CAN'T STAND IT!
Tm. Reg. U. S. Pat. Off.—All rights reserved
Copr. 1953 by United Feature Syndicate, Inc.
YOU'RE HOPELESS! THAT WAS THE WORST KICK I'VE EVER SEEN!
WELL, AFTER ALL... I'M JUST A LITTLE GIRL, YOU KNOW..
LITTLE GIRLS DON'T BELONG ON FOOTBALL FIELDS! GO ON HOME!
I DON'T UNDERSTAND.. I WAS THE STAR FULLBACK IN NURSERY SCHOOL..
WELL, DON'T STAND AROUND HERE! GO ON HOME!! GET OUT OF HERE!
YOU KNOW WHAT?
WHAT?
YOU SHOULD HAVE TOLD ME THAT WAS HER BALL!
10-18
SCHULZ

"PEANUTS"
THUMP!!
?
?
POW
O.K., MEN...FIRST DOWN.. TEN TO GO...
11-9
SCHULZ

"PEANUTS"
?
THUMP
WHEW!
I GUESS THAT JUST GOES TO SHOW WHAT CAN HAPPEN IF YOU DON'T KEEP MOVING..
9-3
SCHULZ

"PEANUTS"
A NEW FOOTBALL, CHARLIE BROWN?
UH, HUH...WHY DO YOU SUPPOSE IT'S WHITE?
THAT'S FOR NIGHT GAMES..
WELL, NOW, THAT'S WHAT I CALL STUPID!
I'M NOT ALLOWED TO STAY UP AFTER SEVEN O'CLOCK!
10-22
SCHULZ

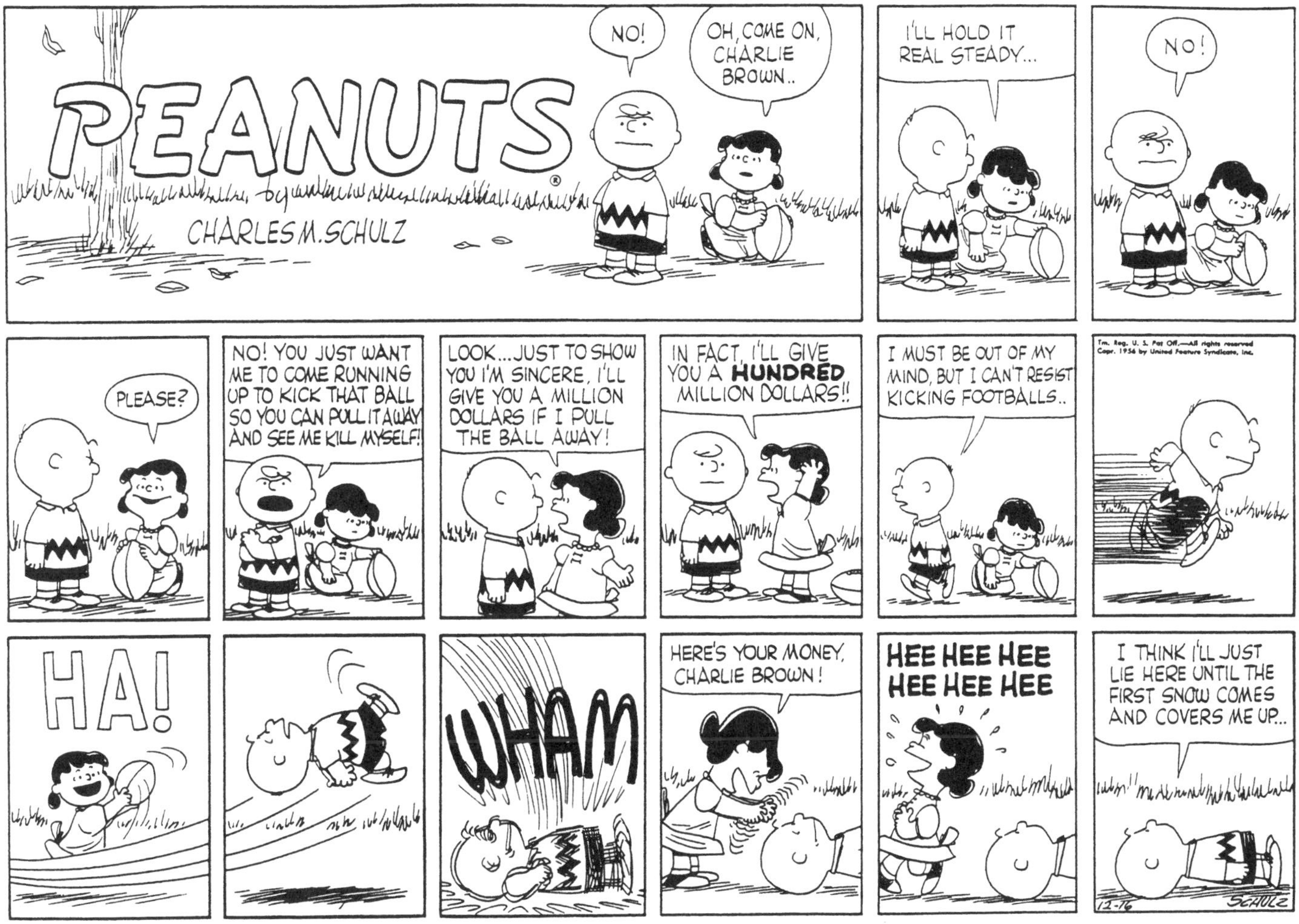
PEANUTS
by CHARLES M. SCHULZ
NO!
OH, COME ON, CHARLIE BROWN..
I'LL HOLD IT REAL STEADY...
NO!
PLEASE?
NO! YOU JUST WANT ME TO COME RUNNING UP TO KICK THAT BALL SO YOU CAN PULL IT AWAY AND SEE ME KILL MYSELF!
LOOK...JUST TO SHOW YOU I'M SINCERE, I'LL GIVE YOU A MILLION DOLLARS IF I PULL THE BALL AWAY!
IN FACT, I'LL GIVE YOU A **HUNDRED** MILLION DOLLARS!!
I MUST BE OUT OF MY MIND, BUT I CAN'T RESIST KICKING FOOTBALLS..
Tm. Reg. U. S. Pat. Off.—All rights reserved
Copr. 1956 by United Feature Syndicate, Inc.
HA!
WHAM
HERE'S YOUR MONEY, CHARLIE BROWN!
HEE HEE HEE HEE HEE HEE
I THINK I'LL JUST LIE HERE UNTIL THE FIRST SNOW COMES AND COVERS ME UP...
12-16
SCHULZ

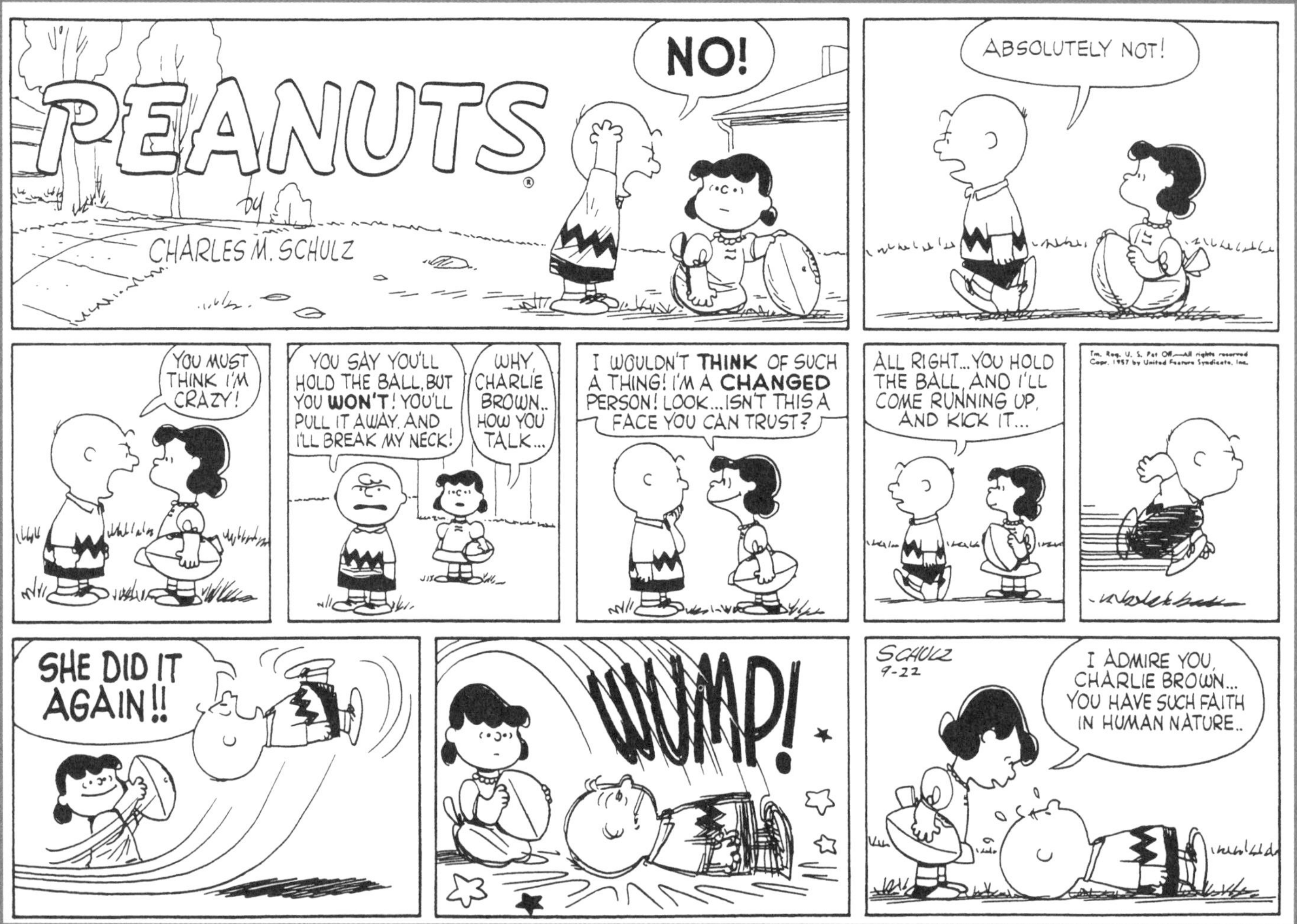
PEANUTS®
by CHARLES M. SCHULZ
NO!
ABSOLUTELY NOT!
YOU MUST THINK I'M CRAZY!
YOU SAY YOU'LL HOLD THE BALL, BUT YOU **WON'T**! YOU'LL PULL IT AWAY, AND I'LL BREAK MY NECK!
WHY, CHARLIE BROWN.. HOW YOU TALK...
I WOULDN'T **THINK** OF SUCH A THING! I'M A **CHANGED** PERSON! LOOK...ISN'T THIS A FACE YOU CAN TRUST?
ALL RIGHT...YOU HOLD THE BALL, AND I'LL COME RUNNING UP, AND KICK IT...
Tm. Reg. U. S. Pat Off.—All rights reserved Copr. 1957 by United Feature Syndicate, Inc.
SHE DID IT AGAIN!!
WUMP!
SCHULZ 9-22
I ADMIRE YOU, CHARLIE BROWN... YOU HAVE SUCH FAITH IN HUMAN NATURE..

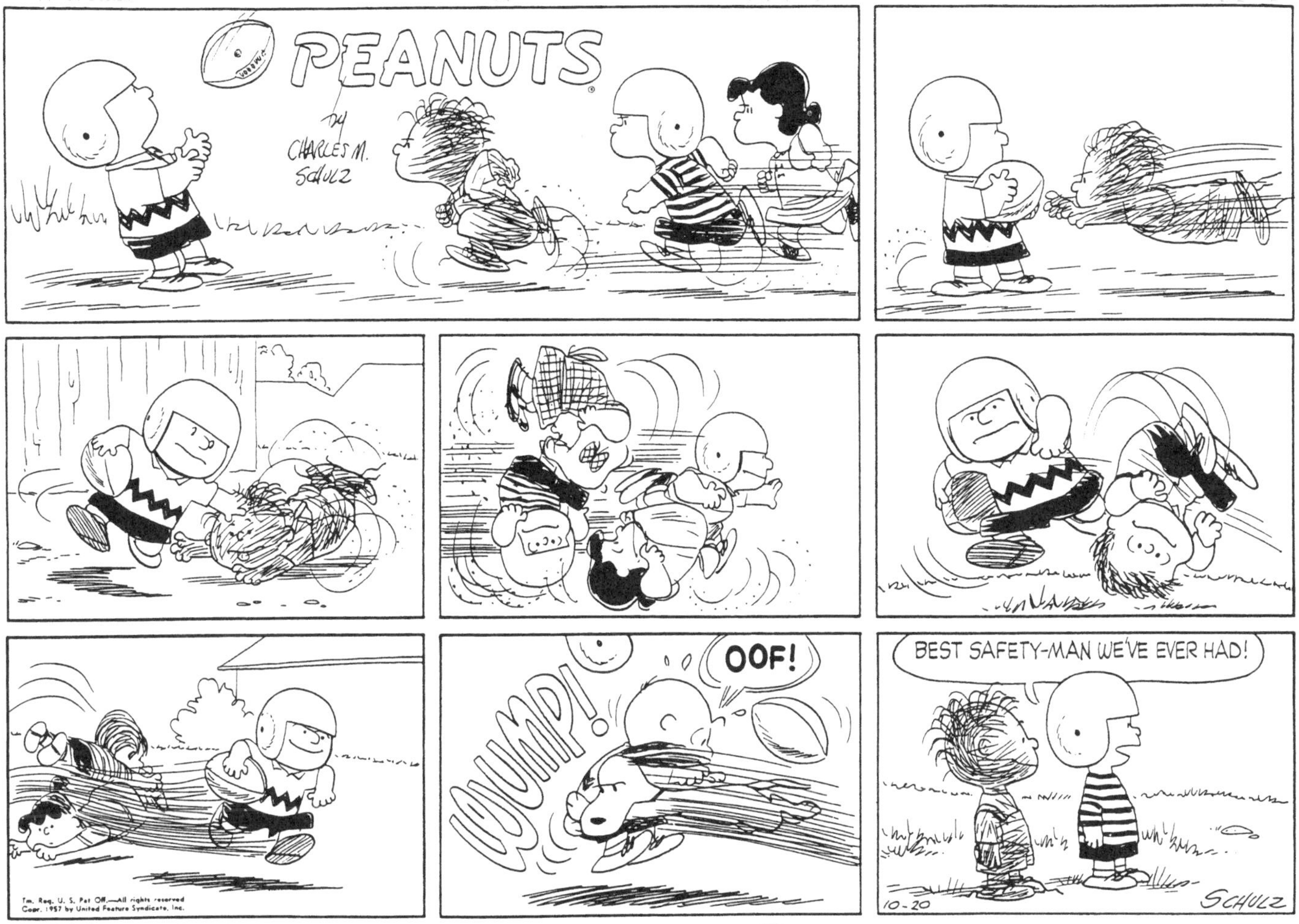
PEANUTS
by CHARLES M. SCHULZ
WUMP!
OOF!
BEST SAFETY-MAN WE'VE EVER HAD!
Tm. Reg. U. S. Pat. Off.—All rights reserved
Copr. 1957 by United Feature Syndicate, Inc.
10-20
SCHULZ

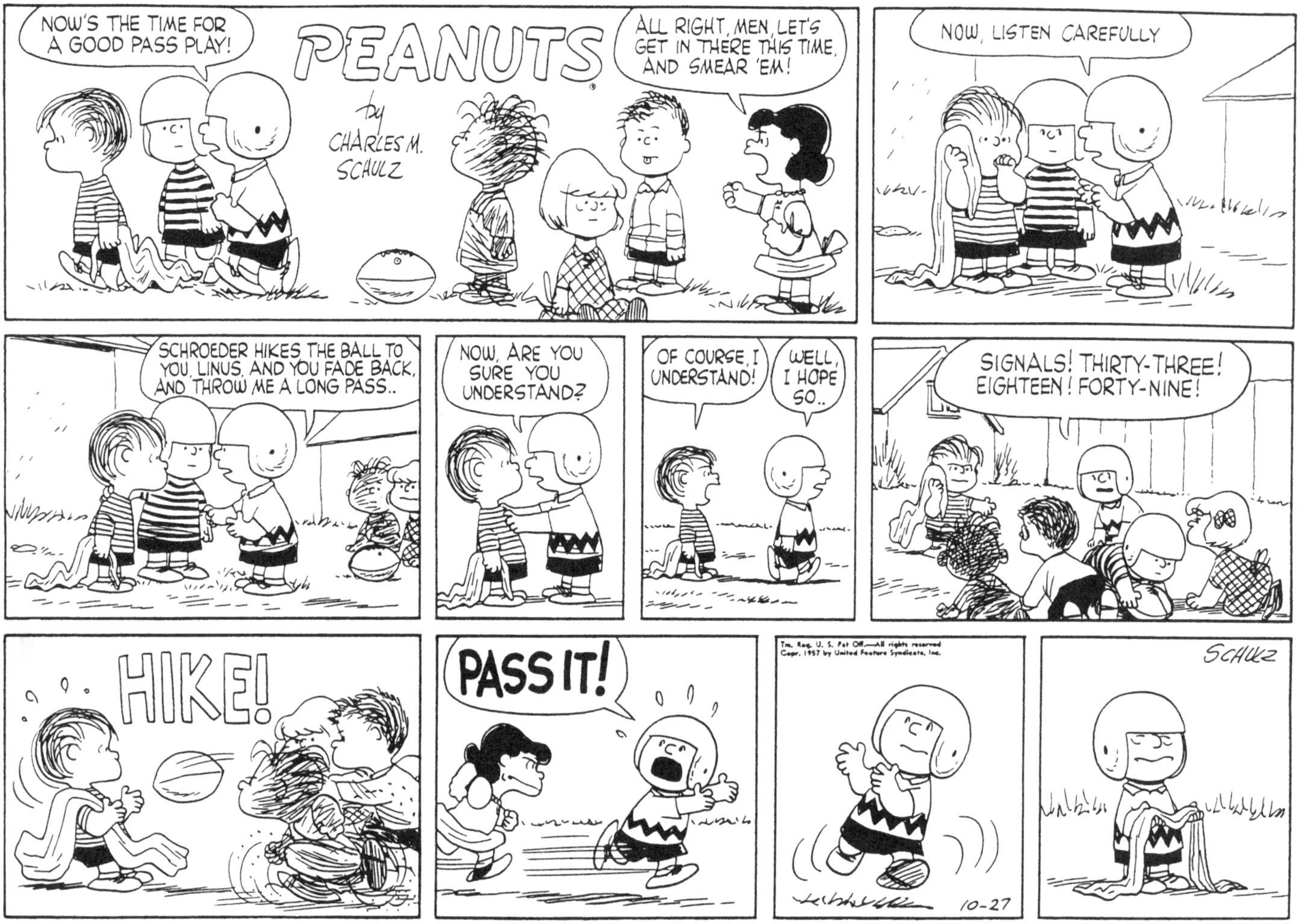
NOW'S THE TIME FOR A GOOD PASS PLAY!
PEANUTS
by CHARLES M. SCHULZ
ALL RIGHT, MEN, LET'S GET IN THERE THIS TIME, AND SMEAR 'EM!
NOW, LISTEN CAREFULLY
SCHROEDER HIKES THE BALL TO YOU, LINUS, AND YOU FADE BACK, AND THROW ME A LONG PASS..
NOW, ARE YOU SURE YOU UNDERSTAND?
OF COURSE, I UNDERSTAND!
WELL, I HOPE SO..
SIGNALS! THIRTY-THREE! EIGHTEEN! FORTY-NINE!
HIKE!
PASS IT!
Tm. Reg. U. S. Pat Off.—All rights reserved Copr. 1957 by United Feature Syndicate, Inc.
10-27
SCHULZ

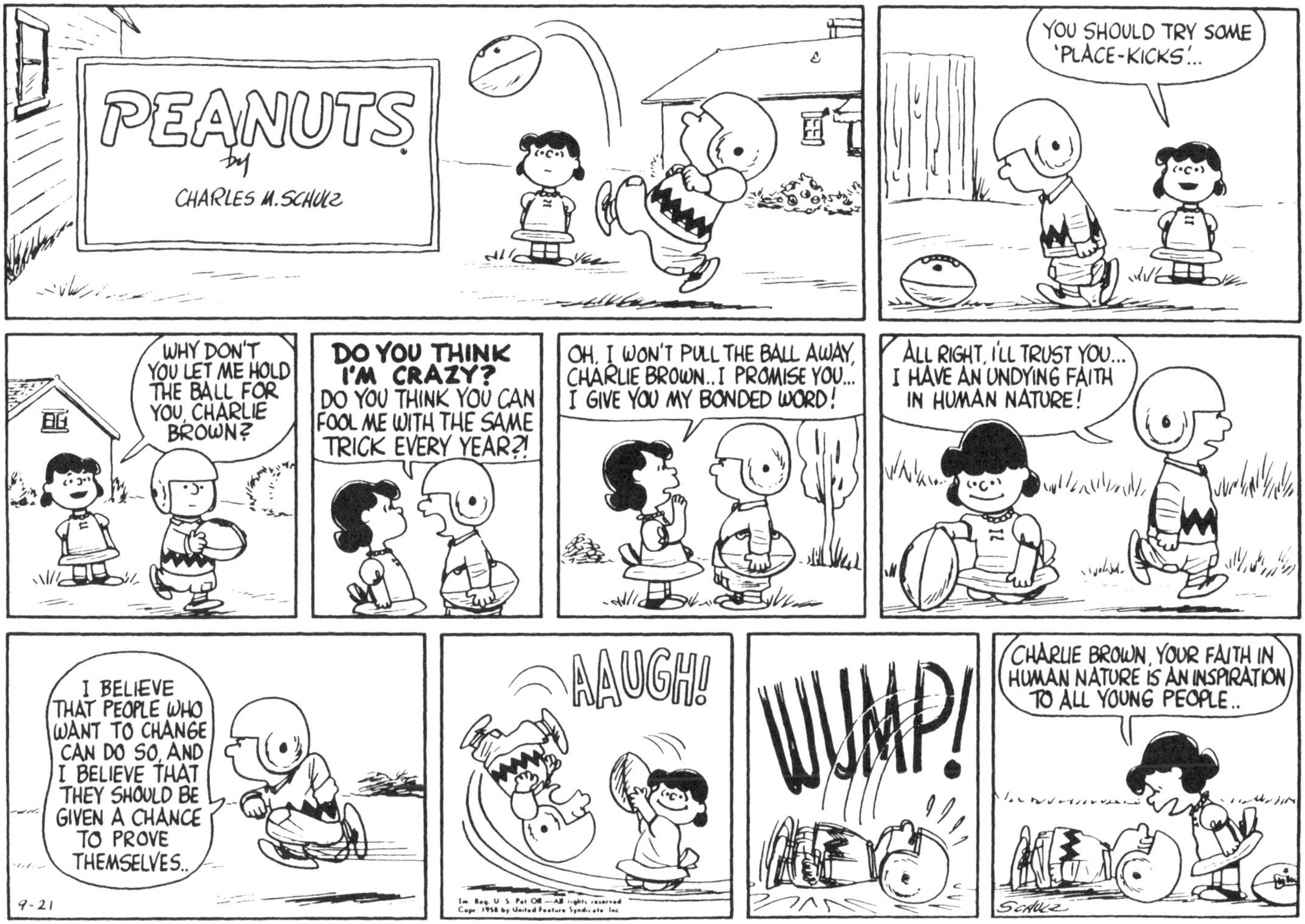
PEANUTS
by
CHARLES M. SCHULZ
YOU SHOULD TRY SOME 'PLACE-KICKS'...
WHY DON'T YOU LET ME HOLD THE BALL FOR YOU, CHARLIE BROWN?
DO YOU THINK I'M CRAZY? DO YOU THINK YOU CAN FOOL ME WITH THE SAME TRICK EVERY YEAR?!
OH, I WON'T PULL THE BALL AWAY, CHARLIE BROWN.. I PROMISE YOU... I GIVE YOU MY BONDED WORD!
ALL RIGHT, I'LL TRUST YOU... I HAVE AN UNDYING FAITH IN HUMAN NATURE!
I BELIEVE THAT PEOPLE WHO WANT TO CHANGE CAN DO SO, AND I BELIEVE THAT THEY SHOULD BE GIVEN A CHANCE TO PROVE THEMSELVES..
9-21
AAUGH!
Tm. Reg. U.S. Pat. Off.—All rights reserved
Copr. 1958 by United Feature Syndicate Inc
WUMP!
CHARLIE BROWN, YOUR FAITH IN HUMAN NATURE IS AN INSPIRATION TO ALL YOUNG PEOPLE..
SCHULZ

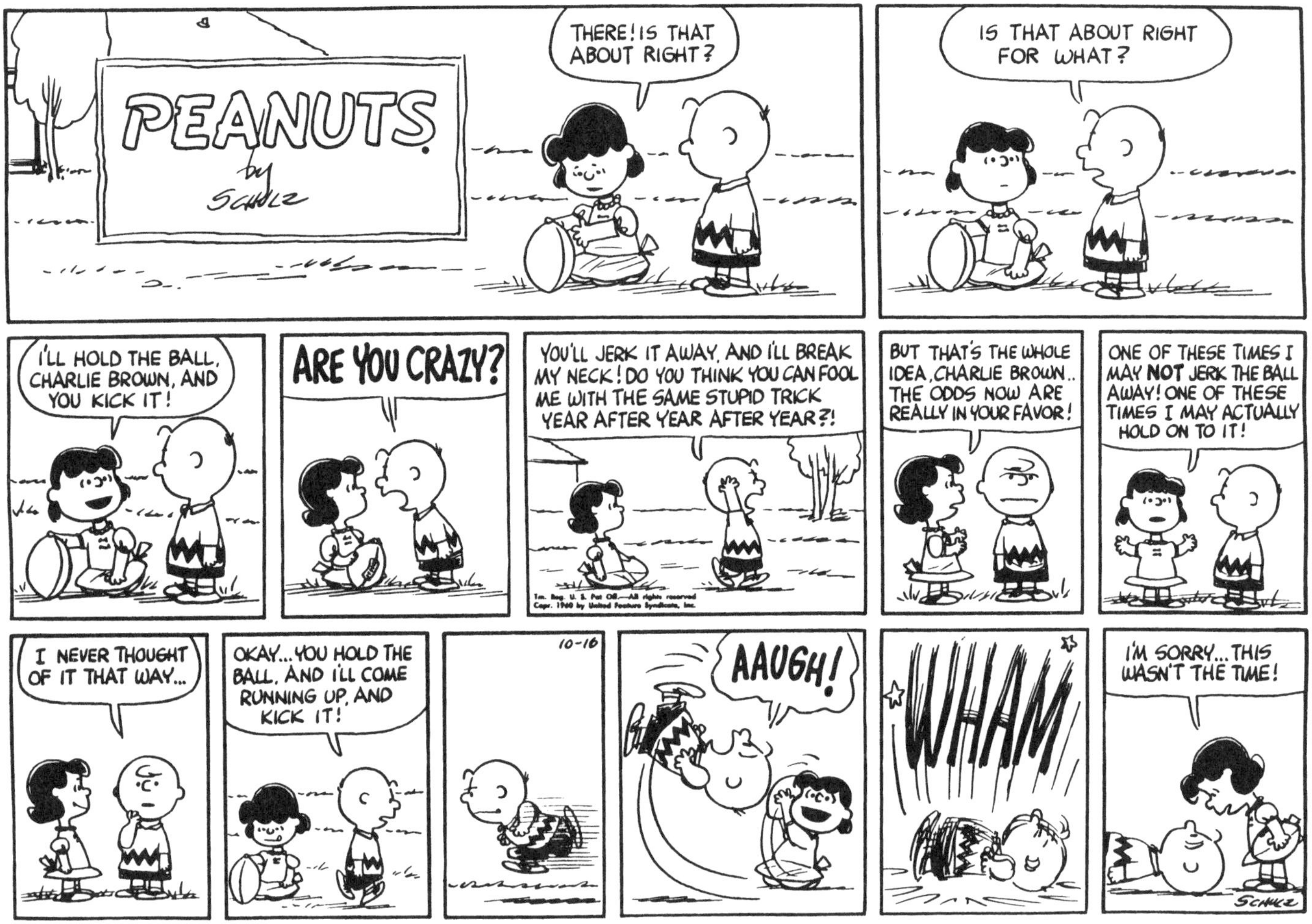
PEANUTS
by SCHULZ
THERE! IS THAT ABOUT RIGHT?
IS THAT ABOUT RIGHT FOR WHAT?
I'LL HOLD THE BALL, CHARLIE BROWN, AND YOU KICK IT!
ARE YOU CRAZY?
YOU'LL JERK IT AWAY, AND I'LL BREAK MY NECK! DO YOU THINK YOU CAN FOOL ME WITH THE SAME STUPID TRICK YEAR AFTER YEAR AFTER YEAR?!
Tm. Reg. U. S. Pat Off.—All rights reserved
Copr. 1960 by United Feature Syndicate, Inc.
BUT THAT'S THE WHOLE IDEA, CHARLIE BROWN.. THE ODDS NOW ARE REALLY IN YOUR FAVOR!
ONE OF THESE TIMES I MAY NOT JERK THE BALL AWAY! ONE OF THESE TIMES I MAY ACTUALLY HOLD ON TO IT!
I NEVER THOUGHT OF IT THAT WAY...
OKAY... YOU HOLD THE BALL, AND I'LL COME RUNNING UP, AND KICK IT!
10-16
AAUGH!
WHAM
I'M SORRY... THIS WASN'T THE TIME!
SCHULZ

PEANUTS
THAT'S ODD...
LAST NIGHT I LEFT MY FOOTBALL IN THE BACK YARD, AND THIS MORNING IT'S IN THE **FRONT** YARD...
VERY PECULIAR...
12/13
THE "MAD PUNTER" STRIKES AGAIN!
PUNT!
Tm. Reg. U. S. Pat Off.—All rights reserved
Copr. 1960 by United Feature Syndicate, Inc.
SCHULZ

PEANUTS
I DIDN'T TAKE YOUR STUPID OL' FOOTBALL!
WELL, SOMEBODY DID!
12-14
SOMEBODY'S BEEN KICKING IT ALL OVER THE NEIGHBORHOOD, AND I'D LIKE TO KNOW...
WUMP
Tm. Reg. U. S. Pat Off.—All rights reserved
Copr. 1960 by United Feature Syndicate, Inc.
THE "MAD PUNTER" HAS STRUCK AGAIN!
SCHULZ

PEANUTS
IT'S FANTASTIC!
ONE MINUTE MY FOOTBALL IS IN THE FRONT YARD, AND THE NEXT MINUTE SOMEBODY HAS PUNTED IT INTO THE BACK YARD
BUT **WHO**? THERE'S ISN'T A **HUMAN BEING** IN SIGHT!
12-15
HEE HEE HEE HEE HEE HEE
Tm. Reg. U. S. Pat. Off.—All rights reserved
Copr. 1960 by United Feature Syndicate, Inc.
SCHULZ

PEANUTS
MOM SAYS COME ON IN FOR SUPPER..
Tm. Reg. U. S. Pat. Off.—All rights reserved
Copr. 1960 by United Feature Syndicate, Inc.
12-19
PUNT
?? ?
THE "MAD PUNTER" STRIKES AGAIN!
SCHULZ

PEANUTS
Tm. Reg. U. S. Pat. Off.—All rights reserved
Copr. 1960 by United Feature Syndicate, Inc.
YOU SAY YOU LEFT YOUR FOOTBALL IN THE BACKYARD LAST NIGHT?
UH HUH... AND THEN, ABOUT TEN O'CLOCK, I WOKE UP, AND I COULD HEAR SOMEONE PUNTING IT ALL OVER THE YARD
BUT WHO IN THE WORLD WOULD BE PUNTING A FOOTBALL AROUND AT TEN O'CLOCK AT NIGHT?
I CAN'T IMAGINE!
12/20

PEANUTS
12-21
PUNT
Tm. Reg. U. S. Pat. Off.—All rights reserved
Copr. 1960 by United Feature Syndicate, Inc.
HAVE YOU SEEN MY FOOTBALL, CHARLIE BROWN? IT SEEMS TO HAVE DISAPPEARED
YOURS, TOO?
THE "MAD PUNTER" HAS STRUCK AGAIN!
IS THERE NO STOPPING THIS FIEND? WILL HE NEVER BE CAUGHT?
SCHULZ

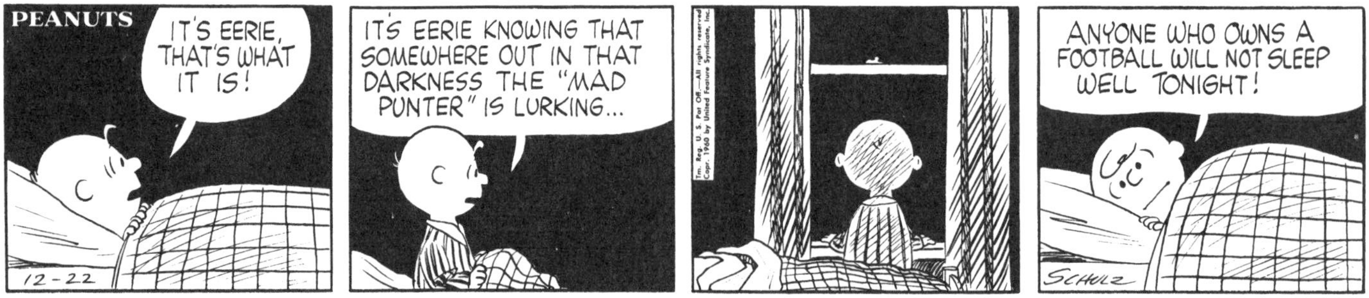
PEANUTS
IT'S EERIE, THAT'S WHAT IT IS!
IT'S EERIE KNOWING THAT SOMEWHERE OUT IN THAT DARKNESS THE "MAD PUNTER" IS LURKING...
Tm. Reg. U. S. Pat. Off.—All rights reserved
Copr. 1960 by United Feature Syndicate, Inc.
ANYONE WHO OWNS A FOOTBALL WILL NOT SLEEP WELL TONIGHT!
12-22
SCHULZ

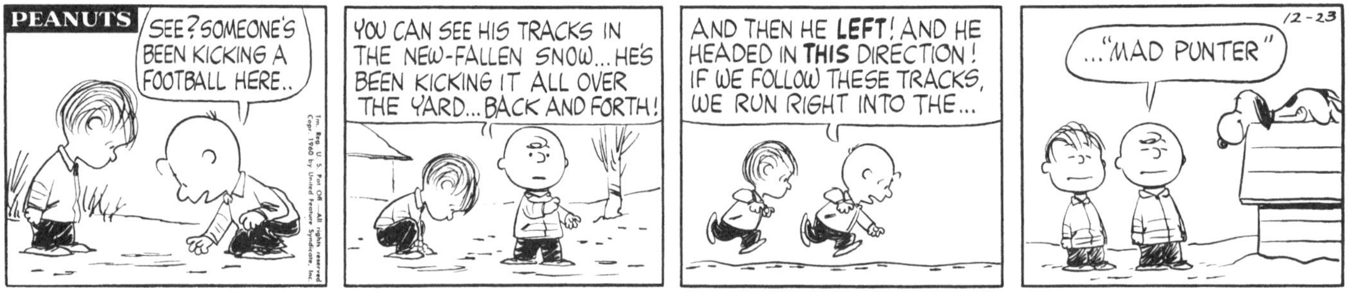
PEANUTS
SEE? SOMEONE'S BEEN KICKING A FOOTBALL HERE..
Tm. Reg. U. S. Pat. Off.—All rights reserved
Copr. 1960 by United Feature Syndicate, Inc.
YOU CAN SEE HIS TRACKS IN THE NEW-FALLEN SNOW... HE'S BEEN KICKING IT ALL OVER THE YARD... BACK AND FORTH!
AND THEN HE **LEFT**! AND HE HEADED IN **THIS** DIRECTION! IF WE FOLLOW THESE TRACKS, WE RUN RIGHT INTO THE...
12-23
..."MAD PUNTER"

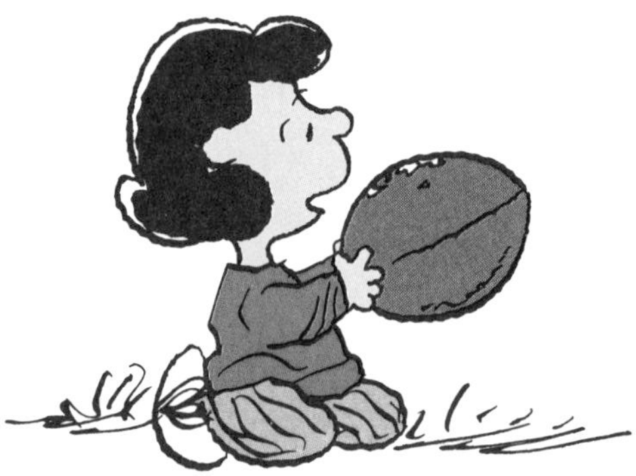

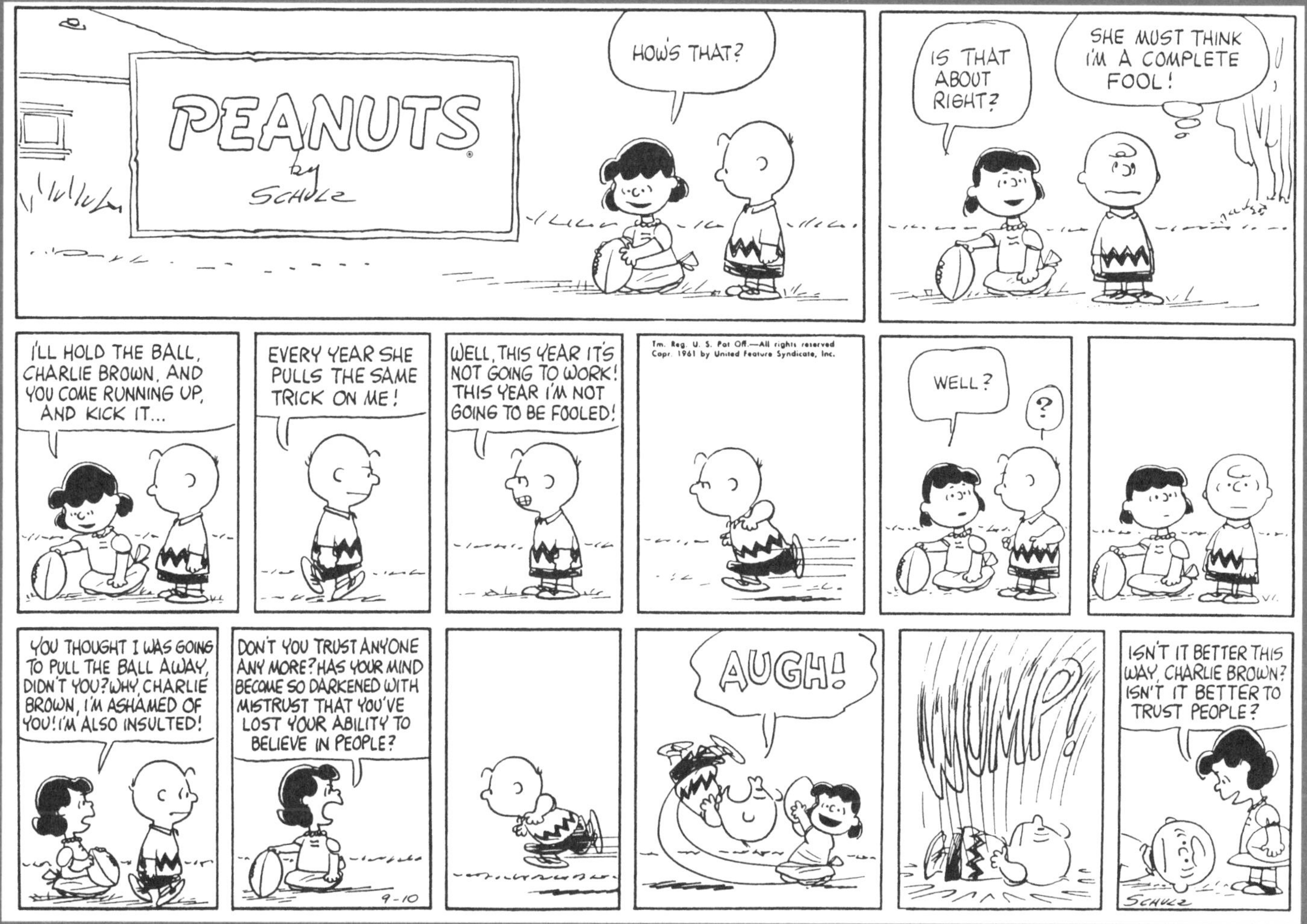
PEANUTS
by SCHULZ
HOW'S THAT?
IS THAT ABOUT RIGHT?
SHE MUST THINK I'M A COMPLETE FOOL!
I'LL HOLD THE BALL, CHARLIE BROWN, AND YOU COME RUNNING UP, AND KICK IT...
EVERY YEAR SHE PULLS THE SAME TRICK ON ME!
WELL, THIS YEAR IT'S NOT GOING TO WORK! THIS YEAR I'M NOT GOING TO BE FOOLED!
Tm. Reg. U. S. Pat Off.—All rights reserved Copr. 1961 by United Feature Syndicate, Inc.
WELL?
?
YOU THOUGHT I WAS GOING TO PULL THE BALL AWAY, DIDN'T YOU? WHY, CHARLIE BROWN, I'M ASHAMED OF YOU! I'M ALSO INSULTED!
DON'T YOU TRUST ANYONE ANY MORE? HAS YOUR MIND BECOME SO DARKENED WITH MISTRUST THAT YOU'VE LOST YOUR ABILITY TO BELIEVE IN PEOPLE?
9-10
AUGH!
WUMP!
ISN'T IT BETTER THIS WAY, CHARLIE BROWN? ISN'T IT BETTER TO TRUST PEOPLE?
SCHULZ

PEANUTS
Tm. Reg. U. S. Pat Off.—All rights reserved
Copr. 1962 by United Feature Syndicate, Inc.
9-10
STOP GRINNING AT ME!
SCHULZ

PEANUTS
Tm. Reg. U. S. Pat Off.—All rights reserved
Copr. 1962 by United Feature Syndicate, Inc.
9-15
PUNT
THAT'S THE CLOSEST I'LL EVER COME TO KICKING A PIG!
SCHULZ

PEANUTS
Tm. Reg. U. S. Pat Off.—All rights reserved
Copr. 1962 by United Feature Syndicate, Inc.
9-22
FIELD GOAL!
SCHULZ

PEANUTS
Tm. Reg. U. S. Pat. Off.—All rights reserved Copr. 1962 by United Feature Syndicate, Inc.
9-24
PUNT!
PURE SATISFACTION!
SCHULZ

PEANUTS
Tm. Reg. U. S. Pat. Off.—All rights reserved Copr. 1962 by United Feature Syndicate, Inc.
9-26
PUNT!
THAT ALWAYS MAKES ME FEEL GOOD!
MANY PSYCHIATRISTS RECOMMEND PUNTING VERY HIGHLY...
SCHULZ

PEANUTS
Tm. Reg. U. S. Pat. Off.—All rights reserved Copr. 1962 by United Feature Syndicate, Inc.
THE "MAD PUNTER" STRIKES AGAIN!
THAT ISN'T "PUNTING"... THAT'S "KICKING-OFF"!
11-17
SIGH
SCHULZ

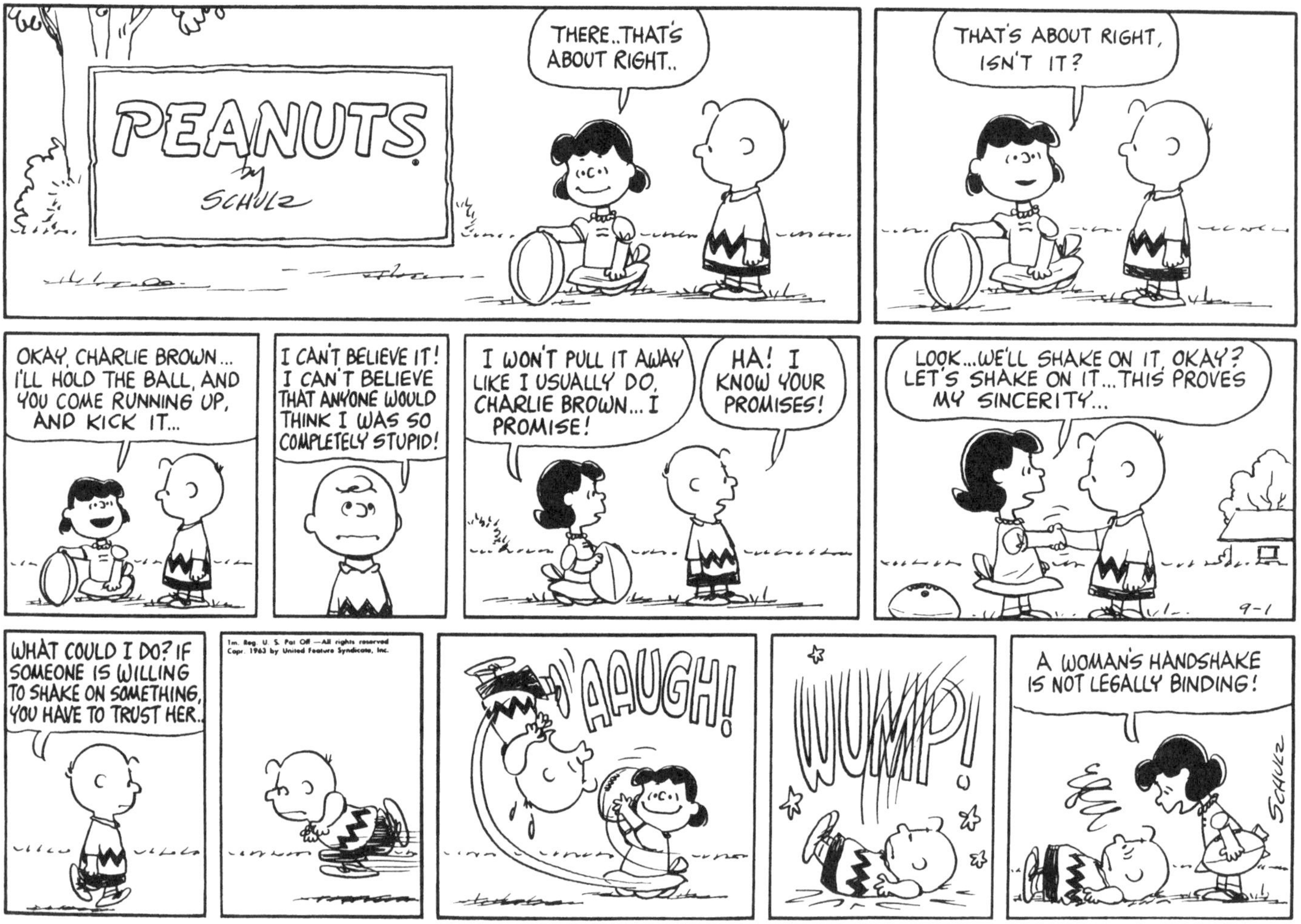
PEANUTS
by SCHULZ
THERE..THAT'S ABOUT RIGHT..
THAT'S ABOUT RIGHT, ISN'T IT?
OKAY, CHARLIE BROWN... I'LL HOLD THE BALL, AND YOU COME RUNNING UP, AND KICK IT...
I CAN'T BELIEVE IT! I CAN'T BELIEVE THAT ANYONE WOULD THINK I WAS SO COMPLETELY STUPID!
I WON'T PULL IT AWAY LIKE I USUALLY DO, CHARLIE BROWN... I PROMISE!
HA! I KNOW YOUR PROMISES!
LOOK...WE'LL SHAKE ON IT, OKAY? LET'S SHAKE ON IT... THIS PROVES MY SINCERITY...
9-1
WHAT COULD I DO? IF SOMEONE IS WILLING TO SHAKE ON SOMETHING, YOU HAVE TO TRUST HER..
Tm. Reg. U. S. Pat. Off.—All rights reserved
Copr. 1963 by United Feature Syndicate, Inc.
AAUGH!
WUMP!
A WOMAN'S HANDSHAKE IS NOT LEGALLY BINDING!
SCHULZ

PEANUTS
Tm. Reg. U. S. Pat Off.—All rights reserved
Copr. 1963 by United Feature Syndicate, Inc.
WHOP!
10-22
I LOVE TOUCH FOOTBALL!
SCHULZ

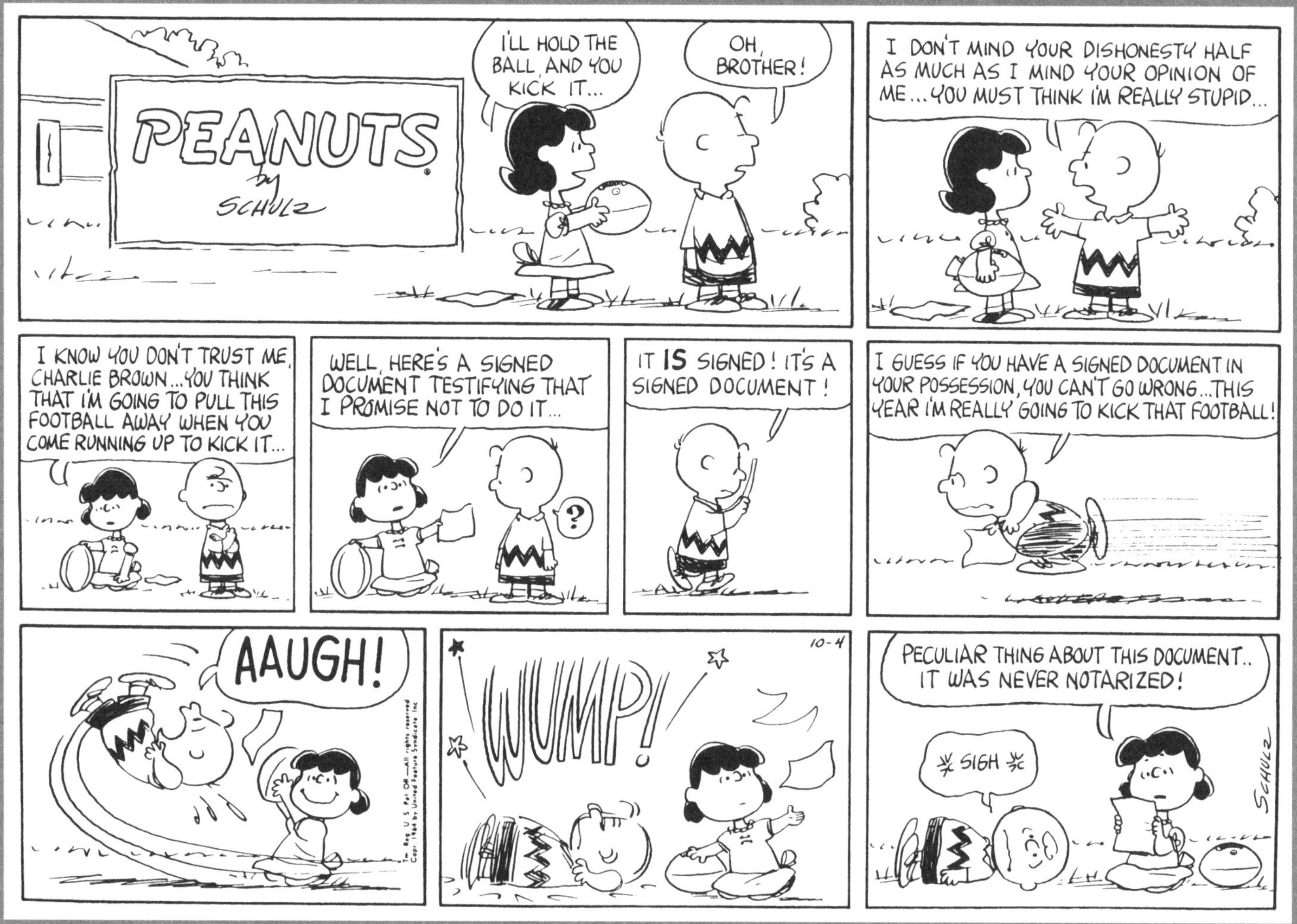
PEANUTS
by SCHULZ
I'LL HOLD THE BALL, AND YOU KICK IT...
OH, BROTHER!
I DON'T MIND YOUR DISHONESTY HALF AS MUCH AS I MIND YOUR OPINION OF ME... YOU MUST THINK I'M REALLY STUPID...
I KNOW YOU DON'T TRUST ME, CHARLIE BROWN...YOU THINK THAT I'M GOING TO PULL THIS FOOTBALL AWAY WHEN YOU COME RUNNING UP TO KICK IT...
WELL, HERE'S A SIGNED DOCUMENT TESTIFYING THAT I PROMISE NOT TO DO IT...
?
IT IS SIGNED! IT'S A SIGNED DOCUMENT!
I GUESS IF YOU HAVE A SIGNED DOCUMENT IN YOUR POSSESSION, YOU CAN'T GO WRONG...THIS YEAR I'M REALLY GOING TO KICK THAT FOOTBALL!
AAUGH!
Tm. Reg. U. S. Pat. Off.—All rights reserved
Copr. 1964 by United Feature Syndicate, Inc.
10-4
WUMP!
PECULIAR THING ABOUT THIS DOCUMENT.. IT WAS NEVER NOTARIZED!
SIGH
SCHULZ

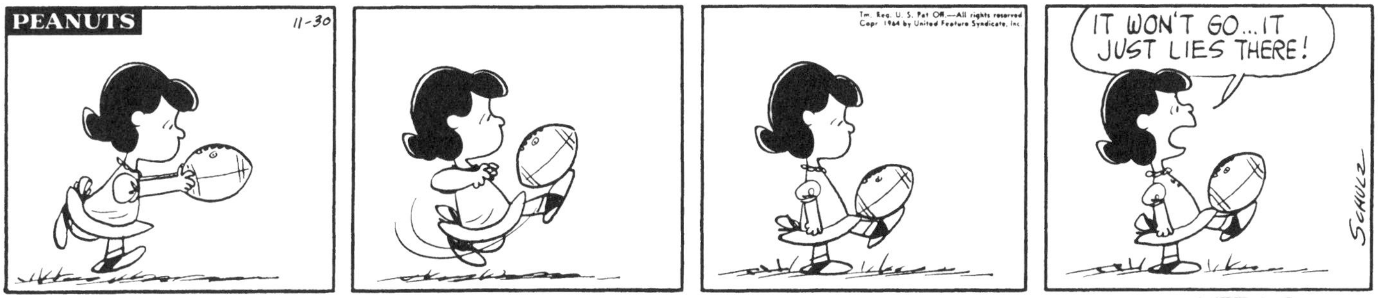
PEANUTS
11-30
Tm. Reg. U. S. Pat. Off.—All rights reserved
Copr. 1964 by United Feature Syndicate, Inc.
IT WON'T GO...IT JUST LIES THERE!
SCHULZ

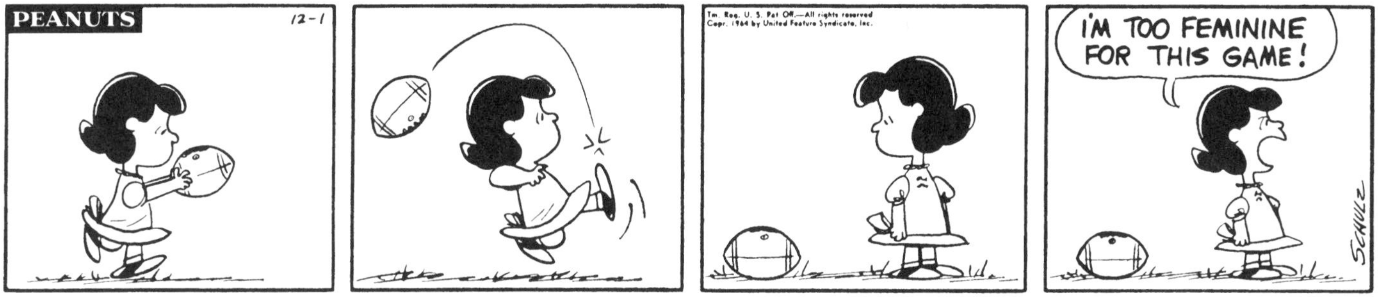
PEANUTS
12-1
Tm. Reg. U. S. Pat. Off.—All rights reserved
Copr. 1964 by United Feature Syndicate, Inc.
I'M TOO FEMININE FOR THIS GAME!
SCHULZ

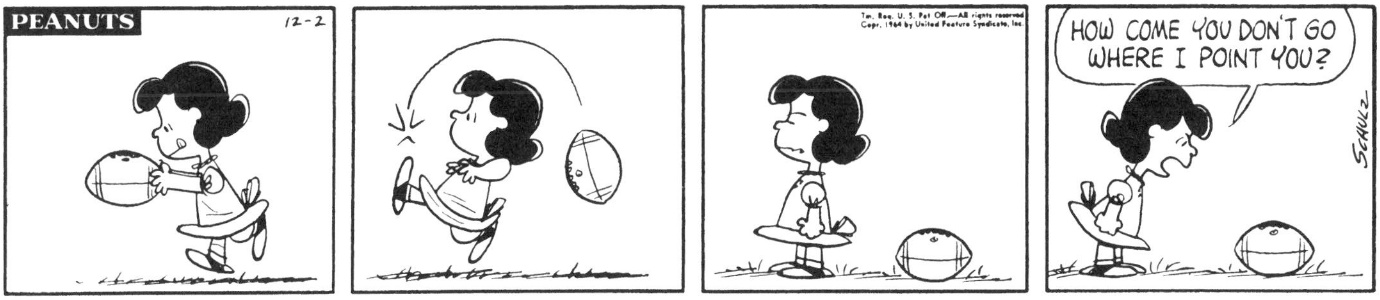
PEANUTS
12-2
Tm. Reg. U. S. Pat. Off.—All rights reserved
Copr. 1964 by United Feature Syndicate, Inc.
HOW COME YOU DON'T GO WHERE I POINT YOU?
SCHULZ

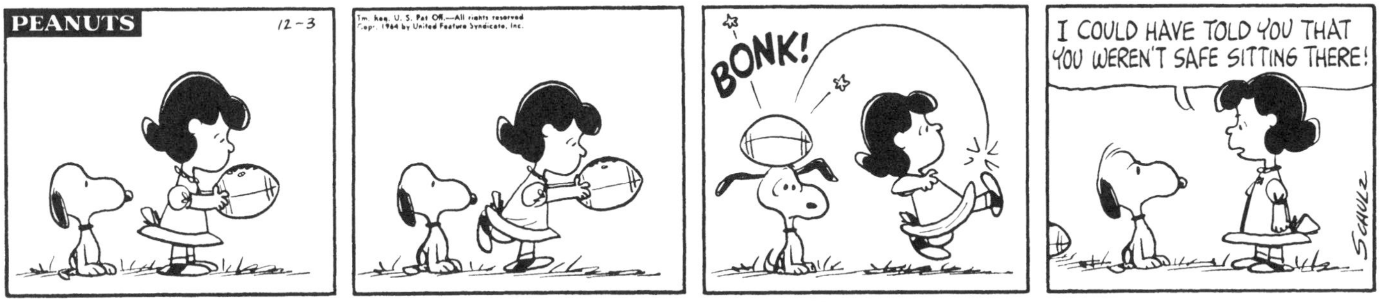
PEANUTS
12-3
Tm. Reg. U. S. Pat. Off.—All rights reserved
Copr. 1964 by United Feature Syndicate, Inc.
BONK!
I COULD HAVE TOLD YOU THAT YOU WEREN'T SAFE SITTING THERE!
SCHULZ

PEANUTS
12-4
BOOT!
Tm. Reg. U. S. Pat. Off.—All rights reserved
Copr. 1964 by United Feature Syndicate, Inc.
HOW HUMILIATING!
SCHULZ

PEANUTS
12-5
Tm. Reg. U. S. Pat. Off.—All rights reserved
Copr. 1964 by United Feature Syndicate, Inc.
DON'T LOOK AT ME LIKE THAT, OR I'LL LET ALL YOUR AIR OUT!
SCHULZ

PEANUTS
10-16
Tm. Reg. U. S. Pat. Off.—All rights reserved
© 1965 by United Feature Syndicate, Inc.
RATS!
MY PROBLEM IS I CAN NEVER FIND TWENTY-ONE OTHER BEAGLES
SCHULZ

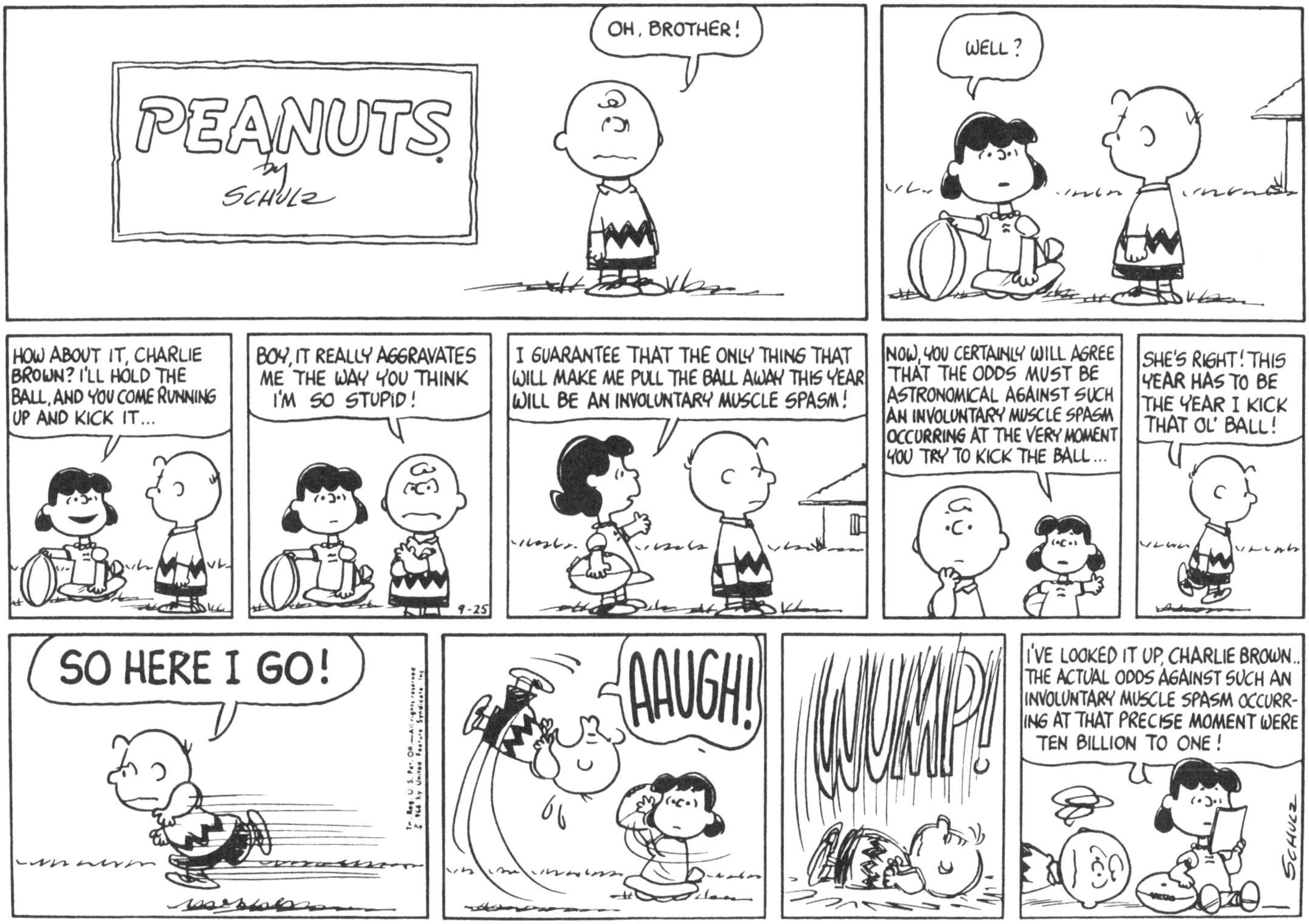
PEANUTS
by SCHULZ
OH, BROTHER!
WELL?
HOW ABOUT IT, CHARLIE BROWN? I'LL HOLD THE BALL, AND YOU COME RUNNING UP AND KICK IT...
BOY, IT REALLY AGGRAVATES ME THE WAY YOU THINK I'M SO STUPID!
9-25
I GUARANTEE THAT THE ONLY THING THAT WILL MAKE ME PULL THE BALL AWAY THIS YEAR WILL BE AN INVOLUNTARY MUSCLE SPASM!
NOW, YOU CERTAINLY WILL AGREE THAT THE ODDS MUST BE ASTRONOMICAL AGAINST SUCH AN INVOLUNTARY MUSCLE SPASM OCCURRING AT THE VERY MOMENT YOU TRY TO KICK THE BALL...
SHE'S RIGHT! THIS YEAR HAS TO BE THE YEAR I KICK THAT OL' BALL!
SO HERE I GO!
Tm. Reg. U. S. Pat. Off.—All rights reserved © 1966 by United Feature Syndicate, Inc.
AAUGH!
WUMP!
I'VE LOOKED IT UP, CHARLIE BROWN.. THE ACTUAL ODDS AGAINST SUCH AN INVOLUNTARY MUSCLE SPASM OCCURRING AT THAT PRECISE MOMENT WERE TEN BILLION TO ONE!
SCHULZ

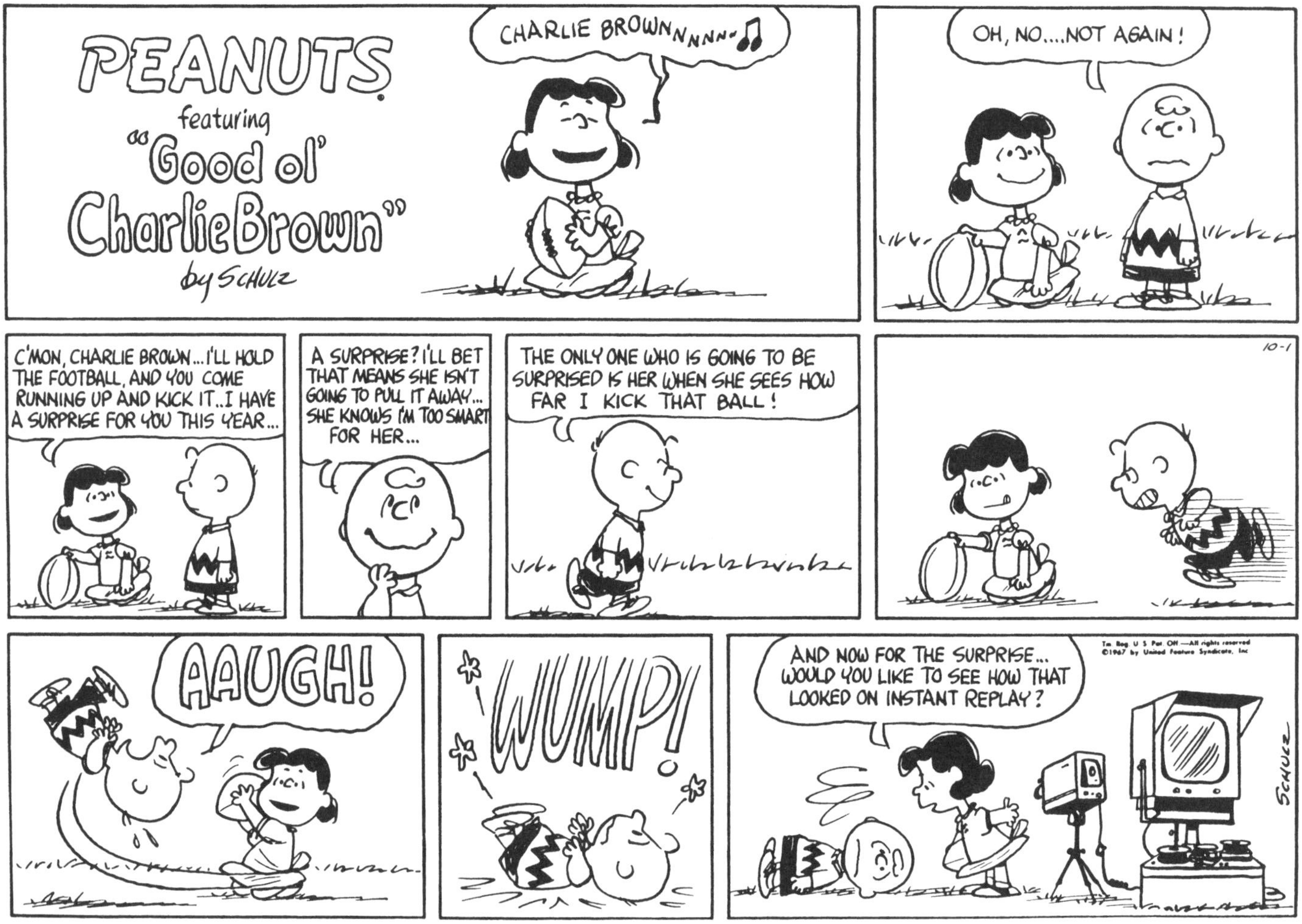
PEANUTS featuring "Good ol' Charlie Brown" by SCHULZ
CHARLIE BROWNNNNN
OH, NO....NOT AGAIN!
C'MON, CHARLIE BROWN...I'LL HOLD THE FOOTBALL, AND YOU COME RUNNING UP AND KICK IT..I HAVE A SURPRISE FOR YOU THIS YEAR...
A SURPRISE? I'LL BET THAT MEANS SHE ISN'T GOING TO PULL IT AWAY... SHE KNOWS I'M TOO SMART FOR HER...
THE ONLY ONE WHO IS GOING TO BE SURPRISED IS HER WHEN SHE SEES HOW FAR I KICK THAT BALL!
10-1
AAUGH!
WUMP!
AND NOW FOR THE SURPRISE... WOULD YOU LIKE TO SEE HOW THAT LOOKED ON INSTANT REPLAY?
Tm Reg U S Pat Off —All rights reserved ©1967 by United Feature Syndicate, Inc
SCHULZ

PEANUTS
Tm. Reg. U. S. Pat. Off.—All rights reserved ©1967 by United Feature Syndicate, Inc.
10-19
BOOT!
OKAY, NOW YOU KICK IT BACK...
YOU'RE KIDDING!
SCHULZ

PEANUTS
10-20
BOOT!
Tm. Reg. U. S. Pat. Off.—All rights reserved ©1967 by United Feature Syndicate, Inc.
WHAT'S SO EXCITING ABOUT THE KICKOFF?
SCHULZ

PEANUTS
DON'T ASK ME TO PLAY FOOTBALL ANY MORE!
WHY NOT?
Tm. Reg. U.S. Pat. Off.—All rights reserved © 1967 by United Feature Syndicate, Inc.
I HAVE NO DESIRE TO SUSTAIN A KNEE INJURY THAT MIGHT PLAGUE ME THROUGHOUT THE REMAINDER OF MY YEARS!
10-21
I FEEL GUILTY FOR NOT HAVING CONSIDERED THAT
SCHULZ

PEANUTS
PUNT!
9-21
Tm. Reg. U.S. Pat. Off.—All rights reserved © 1968 by United Feature Syndicate, Inc.
I WAS WONDERING WHAT WAS INSIDE IT...
SCHULZ

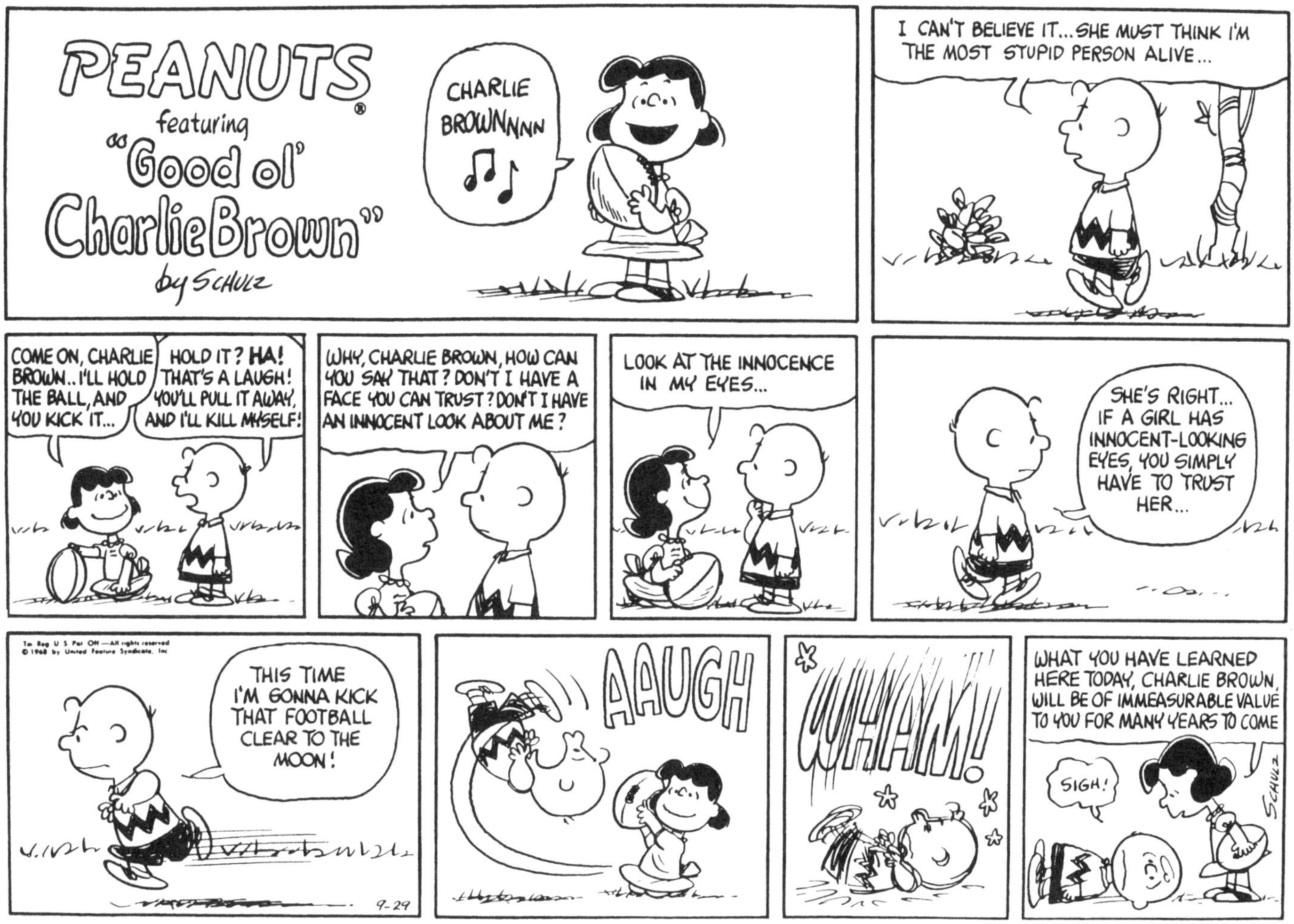
PEANUTS
featuring "Good ol' CharlieBrown"
by SCHULZ
CHARLIE BROWNNNN
I CAN'T BELIEVE IT...SHE MUST THINK I'M THE MOST STUPID PERSON ALIVE...
COME ON, CHARLIE BROWN..I'LL HOLD THE BALL, AND YOU KICK IT...
HOLD IT? HA! THAT'S A LAUGH! YOU'LL PULL IT AWAY, AND I'LL KILL MYSELF!
WHY, CHARLIE BROWN, HOW CAN YOU SAY THAT? DON'T I HAVE A FACE YOU CAN TRUST? DON'T I HAVE AN INNOCENT LOOK ABOUT ME?
LOOK AT THE INNOCENCE IN MY EYES...
SHE'S RIGHT... IF A GIRL HAS INNOCENT-LOOKING EYES, YOU SIMPLY HAVE TO TRUST HER...
Tm Reg U S Pat Off —All rights reserved © 1968 by United Feature Syndicate, Inc
THIS TIME I'M GONNA KICK THAT FOOTBALL CLEAR TO THE MOON!
9-29
AAUGH
WHAM!
WHAT YOU HAVE LEARNED HERE TODAY, CHARLIE BROWN, WILL BE OF IMMEASURABLE VALUE TO YOU FOR MANY YEARS TO COME
SIGH!
SCHULZ

PEANUTS
Tm. Reg. U.S. Pat. Off.—All rights reserved © 1968 by United Feature Syndicate, Inc.
BONK!
I HATE THE KICK-OFF!
SCHULZ
10-12

PEANUTS
FOURTEEN! TWENTY-THREE! NINE!
9-16
HIKE!
Tm. Reg. U.S. Pat. Off.—All rights reserved © 1969 by United Feature Syndicate, Inc.
I'M NOT GETTING ANY PASS PROTECTION!
SCHULZ

PEANUTS
Tm. Reg. U.S. Pat. Off.—All rights reserved © 1969 by United Feature Syndicate, Inc.
YOU SHOULD ORGANIZE A FOOTBALL TEAM, CHUCK..
9-17
THEN I COULD BRING MY TEAM OVER TO SLAUGHTER YOU... WE'D MANGLE YOU..WE'D STOMP ON YOU, AND CRUSH YOU AND TRAMPLE YOU INTO THE GROUND!
GET YOUR TEAM ORGANIZED, CHUCK...WE'LL PLAY NEXT WEEK
THAT'S JUST WHAT I NEED... SEVEN DAYS TO LIVE!
SCHULZ

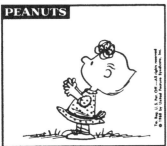

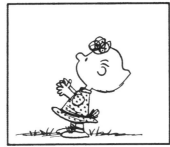

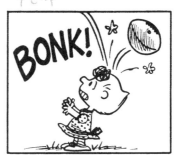

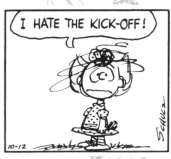

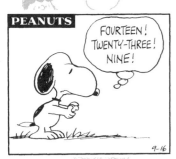

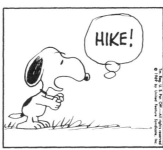

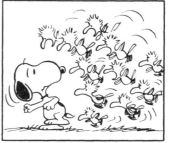

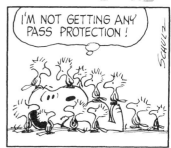

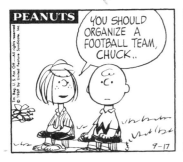

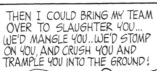

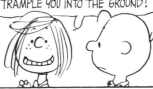

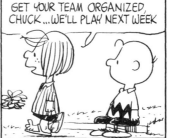

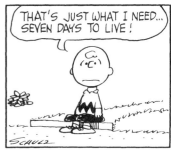

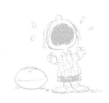

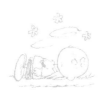

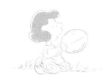

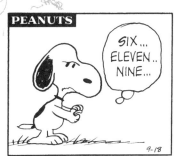

PEANUTS
SIX... ELEVEN.. NINE...
9-18
THIRTY-THREE...
Tm. Reg. U. S. Pat. Off.—All rights reserved © 1969 by United Feature Syndicate, Inc.
THUNK!
A LITTLE OFFSIDE THERE, MAC!
SCHULZ

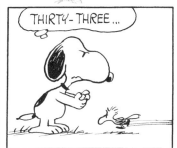

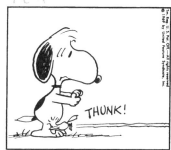

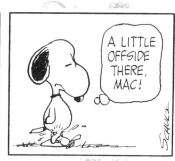

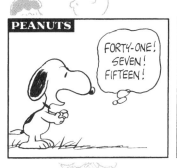

PEANUTS
FORTY-ONE! SEVEN! FIFTEEN!
Tm. Reg. U. S. Pat. Off.—All rights reserved © 1969 by United Feature Syndicate, Inc.
9-20
MY CENTER HAS DIFFICULTY GETTING THE BALL BACK...
SCHULZ

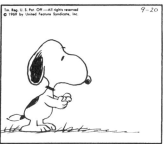

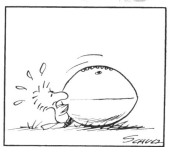

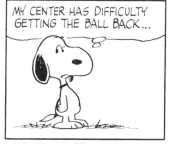

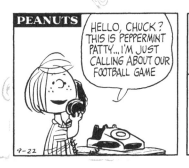

PEANUTS
HELLO, CHUCK? THIS IS PEPPERMINT PATTY...I'M JUST CALLING ABOUT OUR FOOTBALL GAME
9-22
OUR TEAM HAS BEEN PRACTICING LIKE MAD... COUNTDOWNS, PASS PATTERNS, RED-DOGGING...YOU KNOW, THAT SORT OF THING...
Tm. Reg. U. S. Pat. Off.—All rights reserved © 1969 by United Feature Syndicate, Inc.
HOW'S YOUR TEAM DOING?
WELL, WE'VE JUST ABOUT GOT THE BALL INFLATED...
SCHULZ

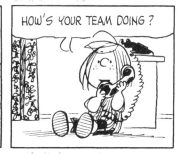

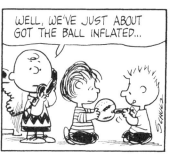

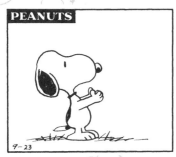

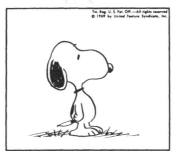

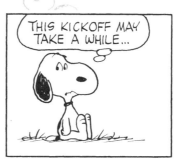

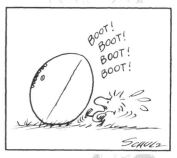

PEANUTS
Tm. Reg. U. S. Pat. Off.—All rights reserved © 1969 by United Feature Syndicate, Inc.
THIS KICKOFF MAY TAKE A WHILE...
BOOT! BOOT! BOOT! BOOT!
9-23
SCHULZ

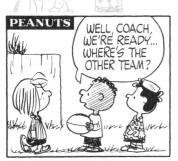

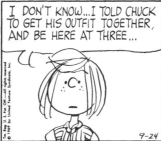

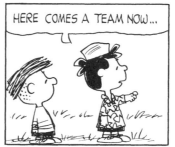

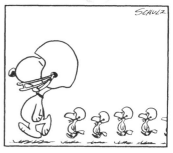

PEANUTS
WELL, COACH, WE'RE READY... WHERE'S THE OTHER TEAM?
I DON'T KNOW...I TOLD CHUCK TO GET HIS OUTFIT TOGETHER, AND BE HERE AT THREE...
Tm. Reg. U. S. Pat. Off.—All rights reserved © 1969 by United Feature Syndicate, Inc.
9-24
HERE COMES A TEAM NOW...
SCHULZ

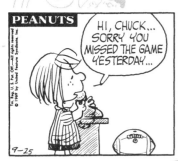

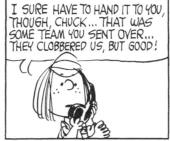

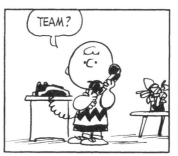

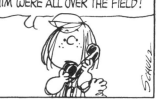

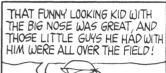

PEANUTS
Tm. Reg. U. S. Pat. Off.—All rights reserved © 1969 by United Feature Syndicate, Inc.
HI, CHUCK... SORRY YOU MISSED THE GAME YESTERDAY...
9-25
I SURE HAVE TO HAND IT TO YOU, THOUGH, CHUCK... THAT WAS SOME TEAM YOU SENT OVER... THEY CLOBBERED US, BUT GOOD!
TEAM?
THAT FUNNY LOOKING KID WITH THE BIG NOSE WAS GREAT, AND THOSE LITTLE GUYS HE HAD WITH HIM WERE ALL OVER THE FIELD!
SCHULZ

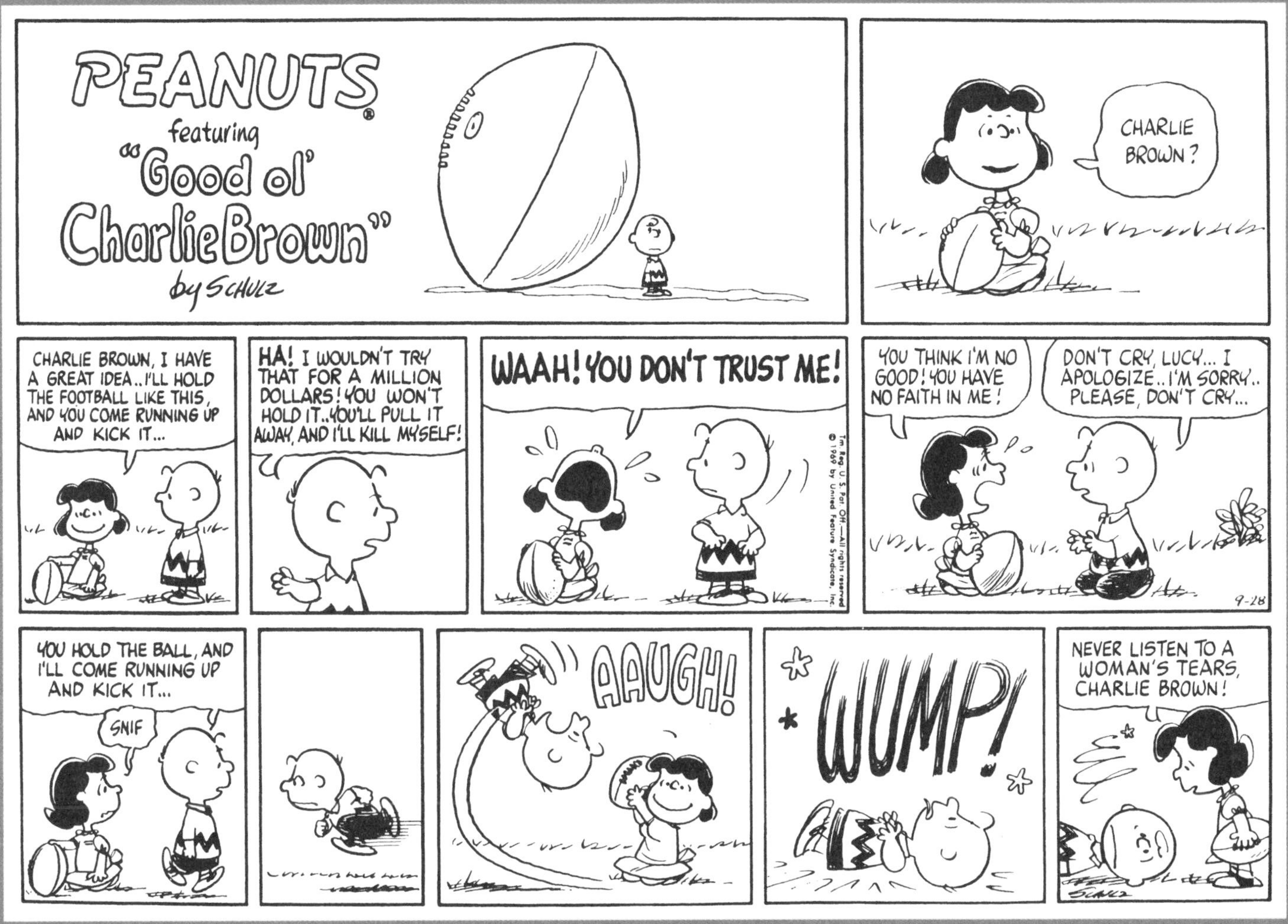
PEANUTS
featuring
"Good ol' Charlie Brown"
by SCHULZ
CHARLIE BROWN?
CHARLIE BROWN, I HAVE A GREAT IDEA..I'LL HOLD THE FOOTBALL LIKE THIS, AND YOU COME RUNNING UP AND KICK IT...
HA! I WOULDN'T TRY THAT FOR A MILLION DOLLARS! YOU WON'T HOLD IT..YOU'LL PULL IT AWAY, AND I'LL KILL MYSELF!
WAAH! YOU DON'T TRUST ME!
Tm Reg. U. S. Pat. Off.—All rights reserved
© 1969 by United Feature Syndicate, Inc.
YOU THINK I'M NO GOOD! YOU HAVE NO FAITH IN ME!
DON'T CRY, LUCY... I APOLOGIZE..I'M SORRY.. PLEASE, DON'T CRY...
9-28
YOU HOLD THE BALL, AND I'LL COME RUNNING UP AND KICK IT...
SNIF
AAUGH!
WUMP!
NEVER LISTEN TO A WOMAN'S TEARS, CHARLIE BROWN!
SCHULZ

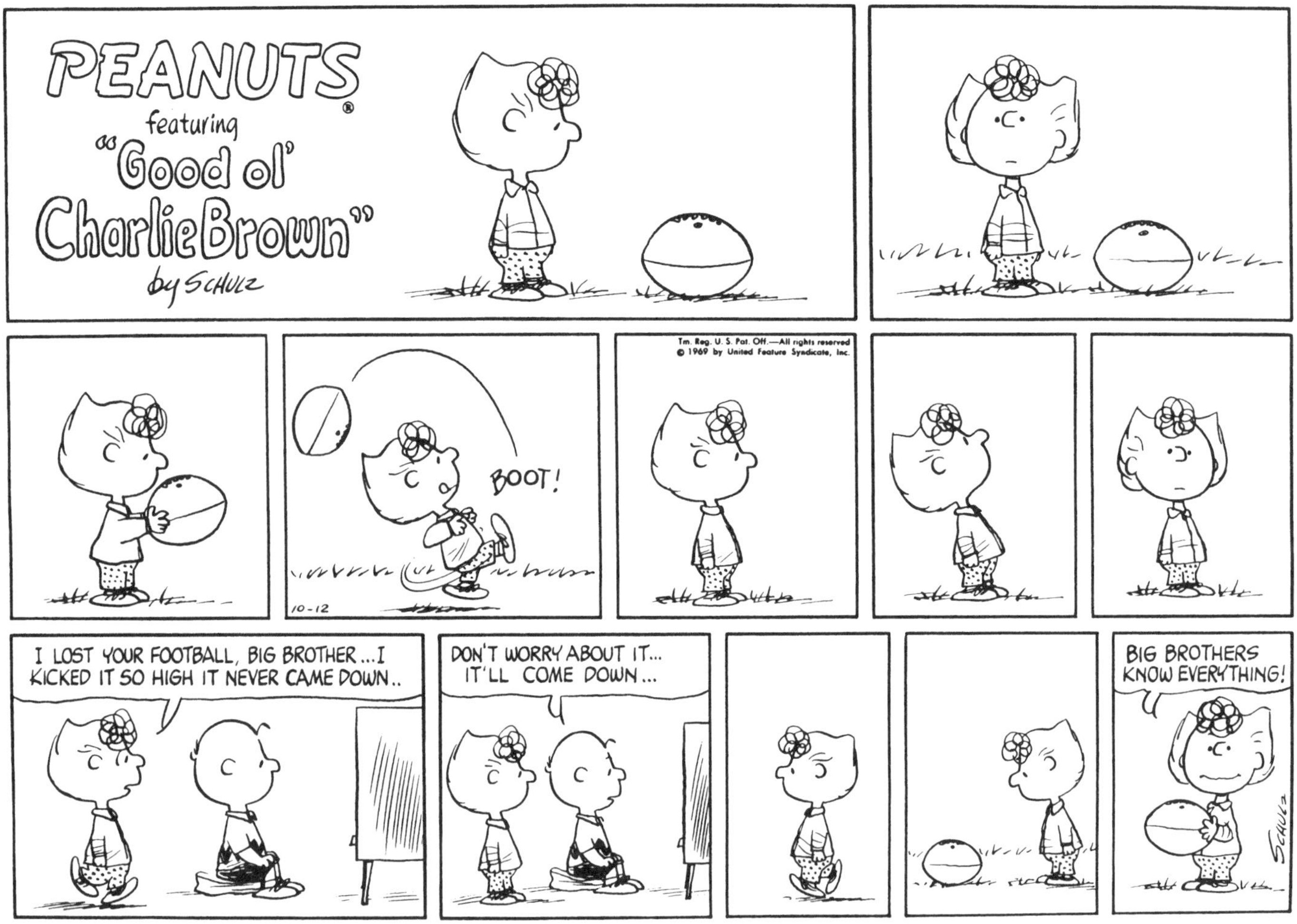
PEANUTS®
featuring
"Good ol' CharlieBrown"
by SCHULZ
Tm. Reg. U. S. Pat. Off.—All rights reserved
© 1969 by United Feature Syndicate, Inc.
BOOT!
10-12
I LOST YOUR FOOTBALL, BIG BROTHER...I KICKED IT SO HIGH IT NEVER CAME DOWN..
DON'T WORRY ABOUT IT... IT'LL COME DOWN...
BIG BROTHERS KNOW EVERYTHING!
SCHULZ

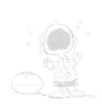

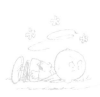

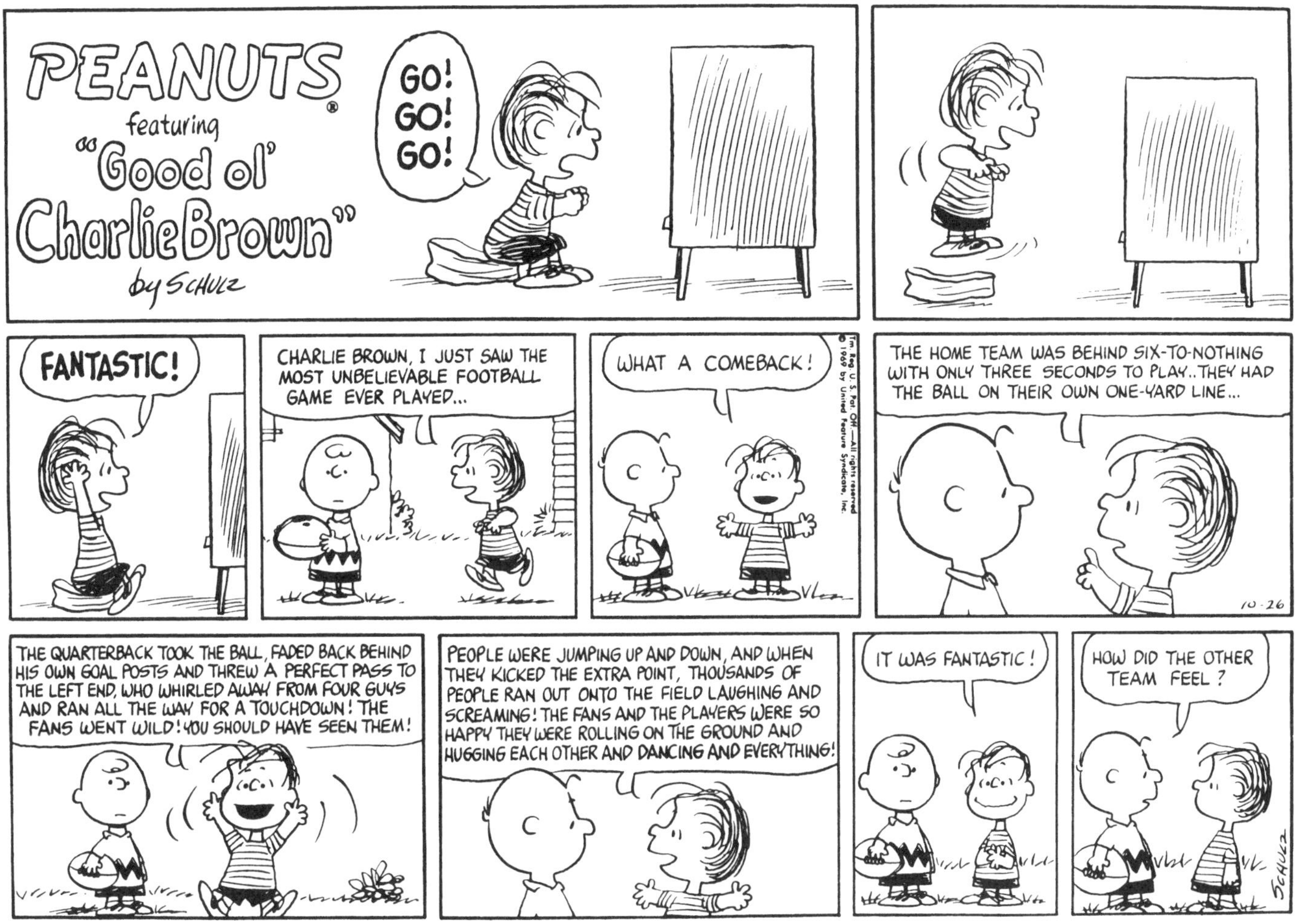
PEANUTS®
featuring "Good ol' Charlie Brown"
by SCHULZ
GO! GO! GO!
FANTASTIC!
CHARLIE BROWN, I JUST SAW THE MOST UNBELIEVABLE FOOTBALL GAME EVER PLAYED...
WHAT A COMEBACK!
Tm. Reg. U.S. Pat. Off.—All rights reserved © 1969 by United Feature Syndicate, Inc.
THE HOME TEAM WAS BEHIND SIX-TO-NOTHING WITH ONLY THREE SECONDS TO PLAY..THEY HAD THE BALL ON THEIR OWN ONE-YARD LINE...
10-26
THE QUARTERBACK TOOK THE BALL, FADED BACK BEHIND HIS OWN GOAL POSTS AND THREW A PERFECT PASS TO THE LEFT END, WHO WHIRLED AWAY FROM FOUR GUYS AND RAN ALL THE WAY FOR A TOUCHDOWN! THE FANS WENT WILD! YOU SHOULD HAVE SEEN THEM!
PEOPLE WERE JUMPING UP AND DOWN, AND WHEN THEY KICKED THE EXTRA POINT, THOUSANDS OF PEOPLE RAN OUT ONTO THE FIELD LAUGHING AND SCREAMING! THE FANS AND THE PLAYERS WERE SO HAPPY THEY WERE ROLLING ON THE GROUND AND HUGGING EACH OTHER AND DANCING AND EVERYTHING!
IT WAS FANTASTIC!
HOW DID THE OTHER TEAM FEEL?
SCHULZ

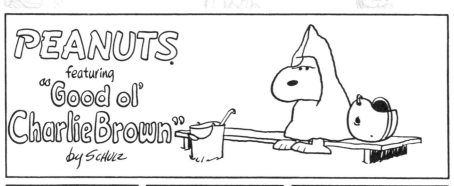

PEANUTS
featuring
"Good ol' Charlie Brown"
by SCHULZ
THREE MINUTES TO PLAY...
HERE'S THE WORLD FAMOUS QUARTERBACK COMING OFF THE BENCH TO WIN THE BIG GAME...
11-23
SIXTEEN! FORTY-TWO! SEVEN! HUT!!
HE FADES BACK, AND SPOTS AN OPEN RECEIVER...
HE HURLS THE BOMB!
Tm. Reg. U. S. Pat. Off.—All rights reserved © 1969 by United Feature Syndicate, Inc.
BONK!
BAD HANDS!
SCHULZ

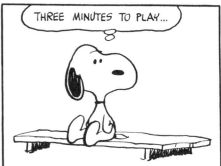

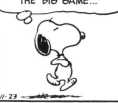

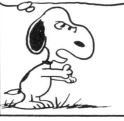

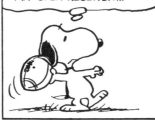

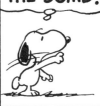

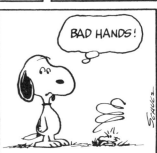

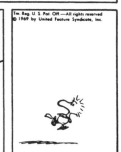

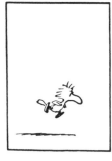

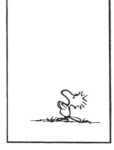

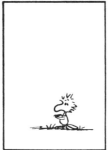

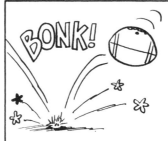

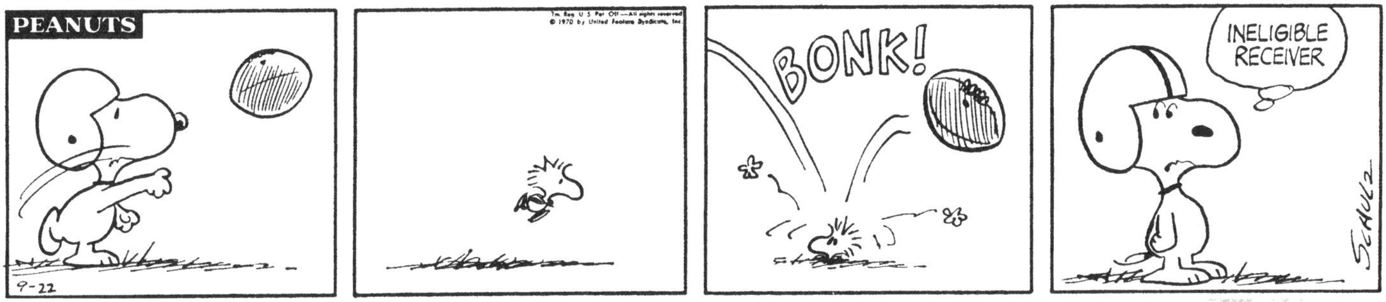
PEANUTS
9-22
Tm. Reg. U.S. Pat. Off.—All rights reserved © 1970 by United Feature Syndicate, Inc.
BONK!
INELIGIBLE RECEIVER
SCHULZ

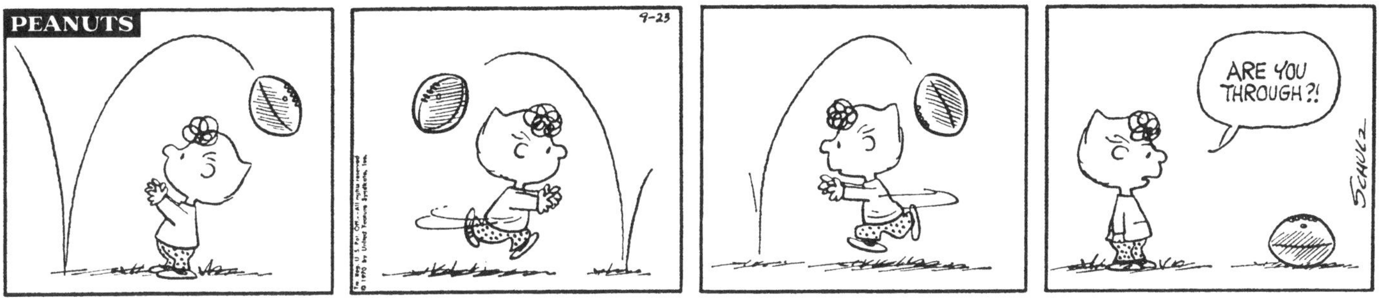
PEANUTS
9-23
Tm. Reg. U.S. Pat. Off.—All rights reserved © 1970 by United Feature Syndicate, Inc.
ARE YOU THROUGH?!
SCHULZ

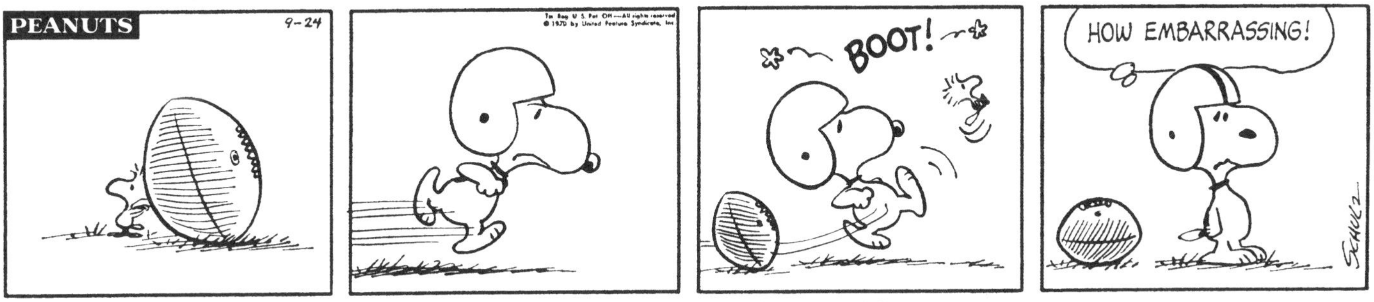
PEANUTS
9-24
Tm. Reg. U.S. Pat. Off.—All rights reserved © 1970 by United Feature Syndicate, Inc.
BOOT!
HOW EMBARRASSING!
SCHULZ

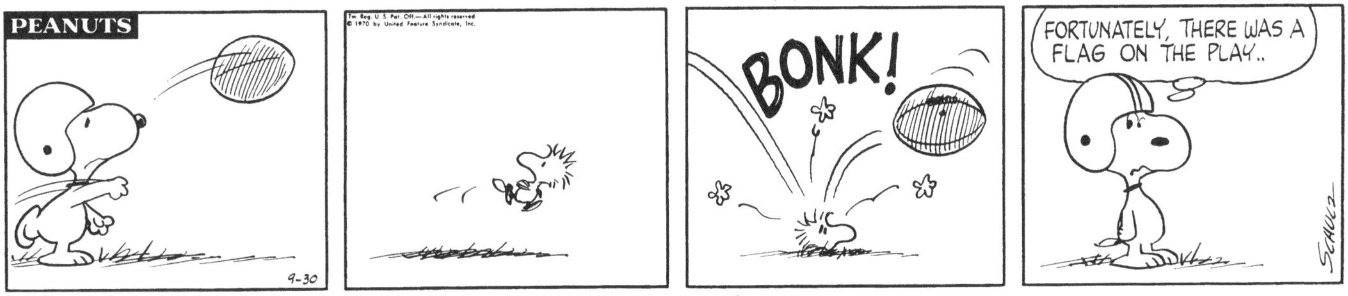
PEANUTS
9-30
Tm. Reg. U.S. Pat. Off.—All rights reserved © 1970 by United Feature Syndicate, Inc.
BONK!
FORTUNATELY, THERE WAS A FLAG ON THE PLAY..
SCHULZ

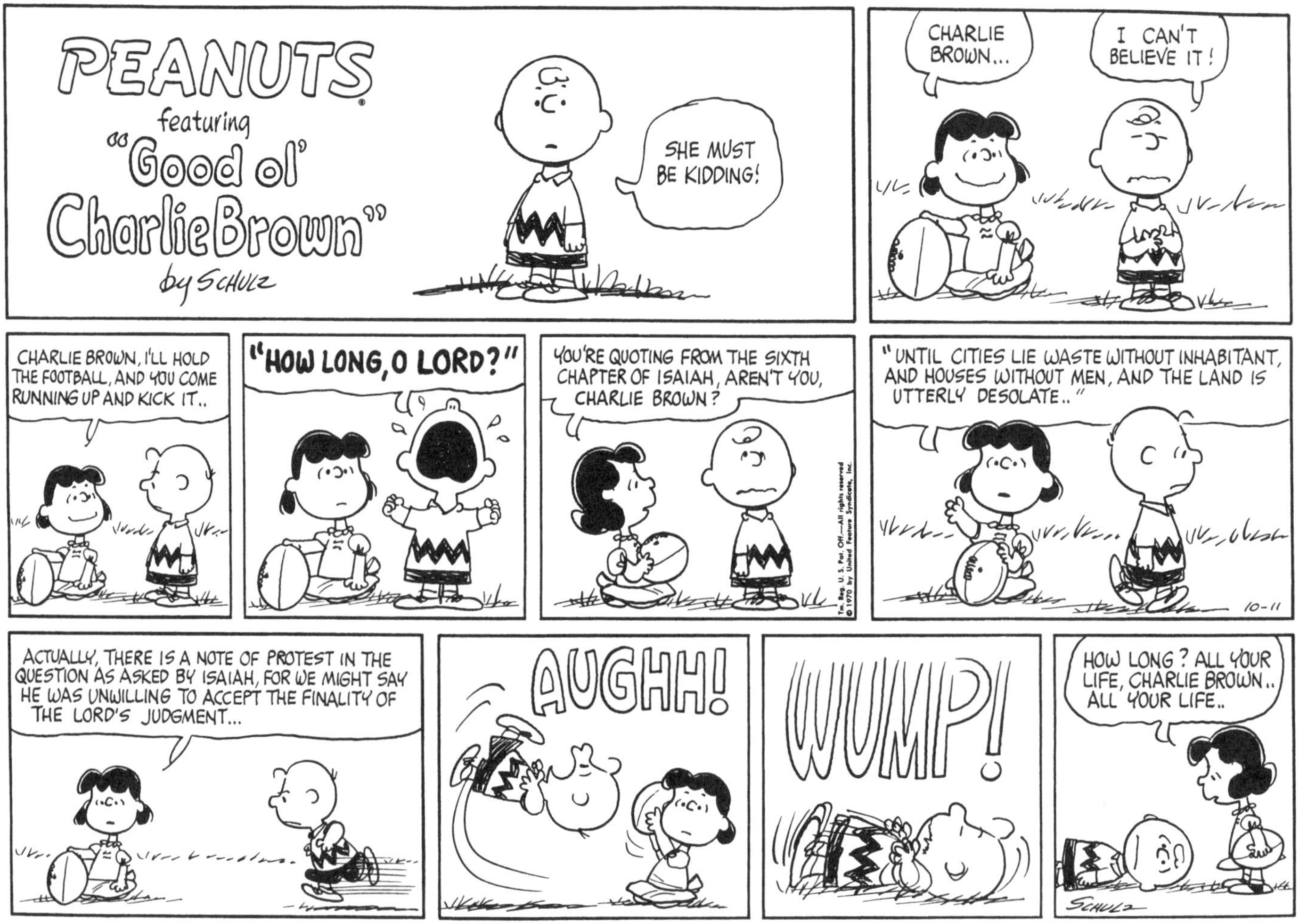
PEANUTS
featuring "Good ol' CharlieBrown"
by SCHULZ
SHE MUST BE KIDDING!
CHARLIE BROWN...
I CAN'T BELIEVE IT!
CHARLIE BROWN, I'LL HOLD THE FOOTBALL, AND YOU COME RUNNING UP AND KICK IT..
"HOW LONG, O LORD?"
YOU'RE QUOTING FROM THE SIXTH CHAPTER OF ISAIAH, AREN'T YOU, CHARLIE BROWN?
Tm. Reg. U.S. Pat. Off.—All rights reserved © 1970 by United Feature Syndicate, Inc.
"UNTIL CITIES LIE WASTE WITHOUT INHABITANT, AND HOUSES WITHOUT MEN, AND THE LAND IS UTTERLY DESOLATE.."
10-11
ACTUALLY, THERE IS A NOTE OF PROTEST IN THE QUESTION AS ASKED BY ISAIAH, FOR WE MIGHT SAY HE WAS UNWILLING TO ACCEPT THE FINALITY OF THE LORD'S JUDGMENT...
AUGHH!
WUMP!
HOW LONG? ALL YOUR LIFE, CHARLIE BROWN.. ALL YOUR LIFE..
SCHULZ

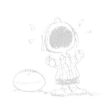

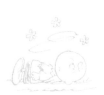

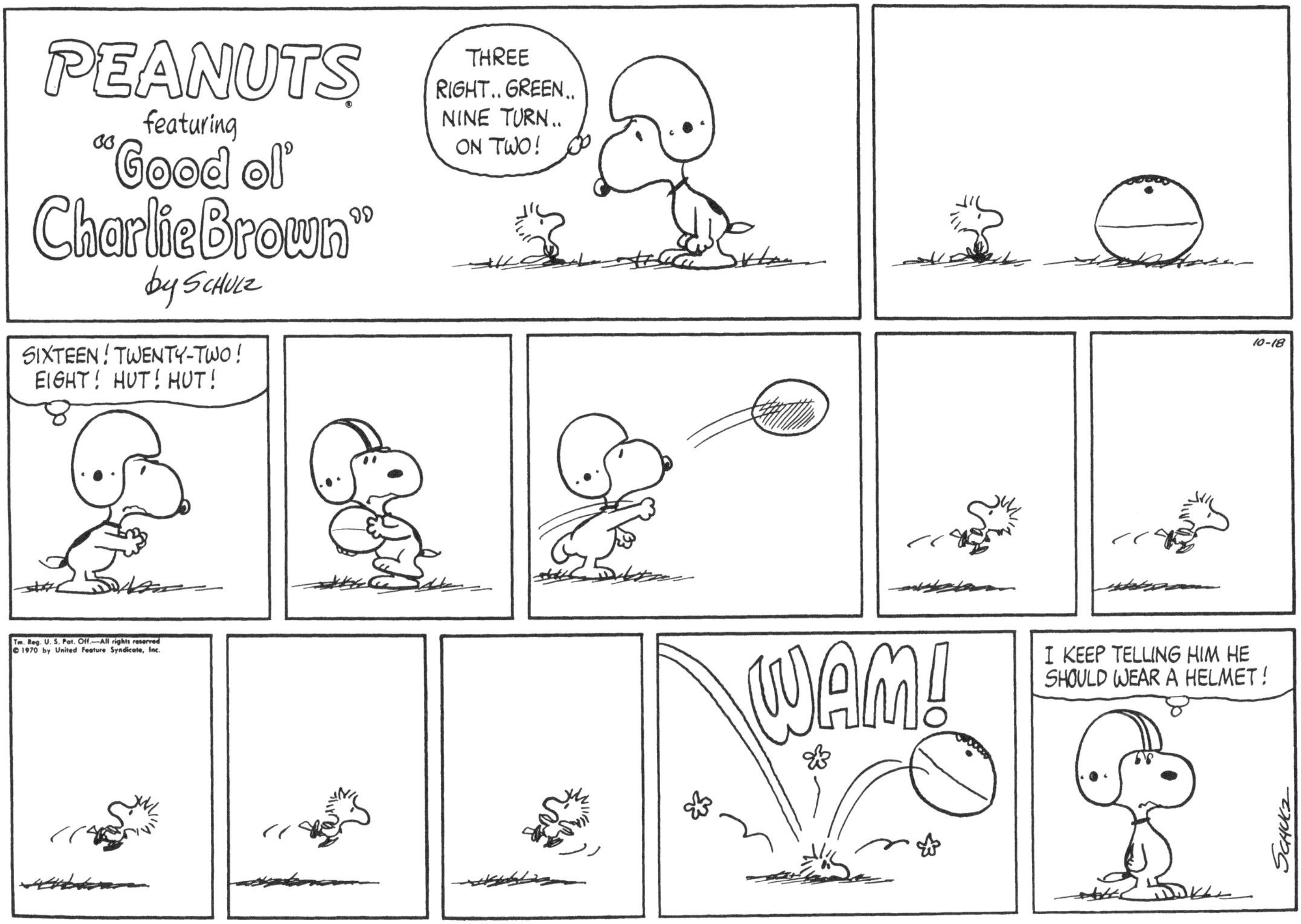
PEANUTS
featuring
"Good ol' CharlieBrown"
by SCHULZ
THREE RIGHT.. GREEN.. NINE TURN.. ON TWO!
SIXTEEN! TWENTY-TWO! EIGHT! HUT! HUT!
10-18
Tm. Reg. U. S. Pat. Off.—All rights reserved
© 1970 by United Feature Syndicate, Inc.
WAM!
I KEEP TELLING HIM HE SHOULD WEAR A HELMET!
SCHULZ

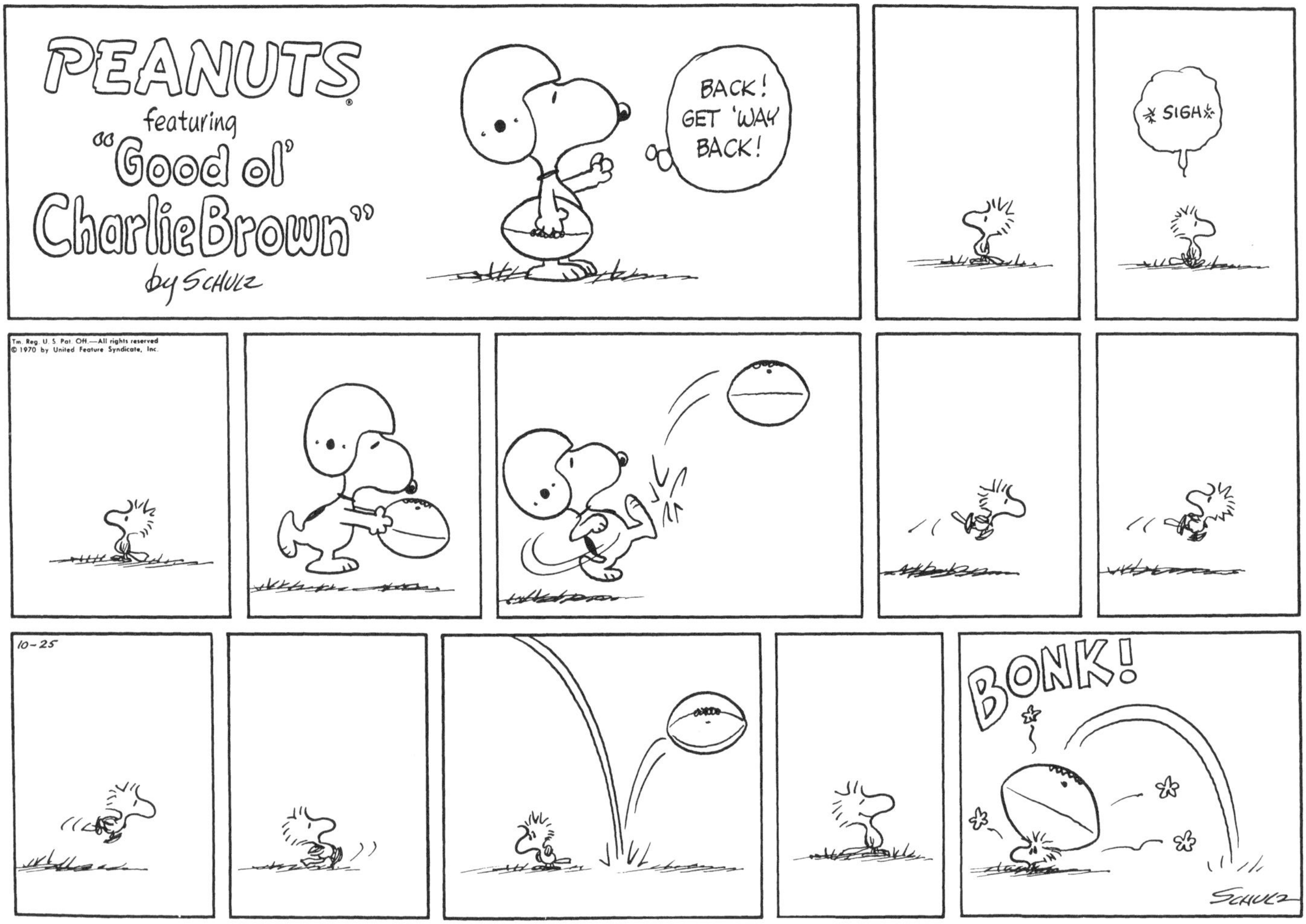
PEANUTS®
featuring
"Good ol' Charlie Brown"
by SCHULZ
BACK! GET 'WAY BACK!
SIGH
Tm. Reg. U. S. Pat. Off.—All rights reserved
© 1970 by United Feature Syndicate, Inc.
10-25
BONK!
SCHULZ

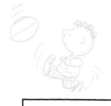

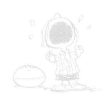

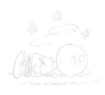

PEANUTS
Tm Reg U S Pat Off—All rights reserved © 1970 by United Feature Syndicate, Inc.
12-7
BONK!
THEN, AGAIN, THERE'S ALWAYS THE CHANCE THAT WE MIGHT NOT EVEN GET INVITED TO THE ROSE BOWL..
SCHULZ

PEANUTS
9-11
Tm. Reg. U. S. Pat. Off.—All rights reserved © 1971 by United Feature Syndicate, Inc.
SCHULZ

PEANUTS
9-18
Tm. Reg. U. S. Pat. Off.—All rights reserved © 1971 by United Feature Syndicate, Inc.
BONK!!
LAST ROUND DRAFT CHOICE!
SCHULZ

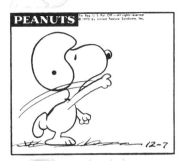

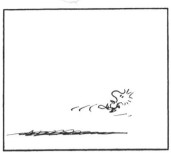

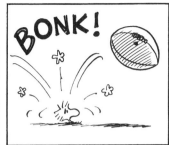

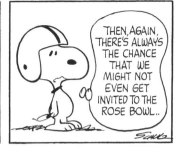

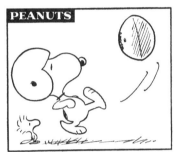

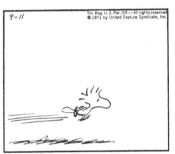

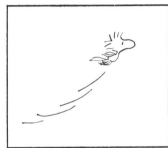

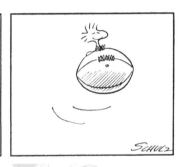

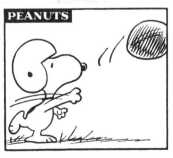

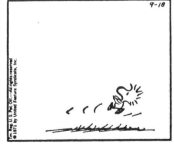

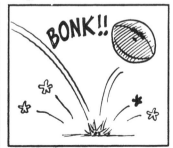

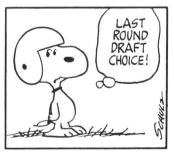

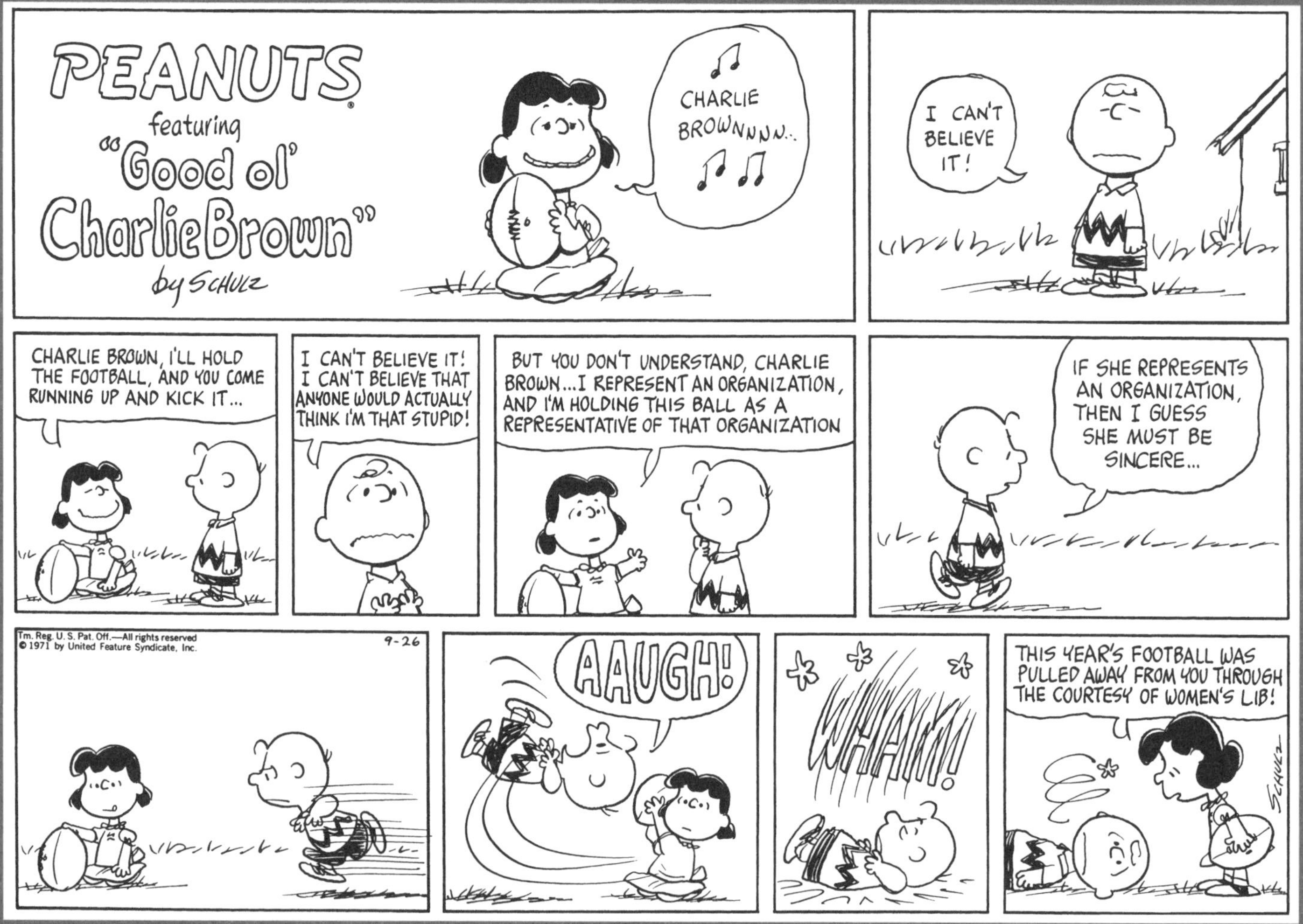
PEANUTS
featuring
"Good ol' CharlieBrown"
by SCHULZ
CHARLIE BROWNNNN...
I CAN'T BELIEVE IT!
CHARLIE BROWN, I'LL HOLD THE FOOTBALL, AND YOU COME RUNNING UP AND KICK IT...
I CAN'T BELIEVE IT! I CAN'T BELIEVE THAT ANYONE WOULD ACTUALLY THINK I'M THAT STUPID!
BUT YOU DON'T UNDERSTAND, CHARLIE BROWN...I REPRESENT AN ORGANIZATION, AND I'M HOLDING THIS BALL AS A REPRESENTATIVE OF THAT ORGANIZATION
IF SHE REPRESENTS AN ORGANIZATION, THEN I GUESS SHE MUST BE SINCERE...
Tm. Reg. U. S. Pat. Off.—All rights reserved
© 1971 by United Feature Syndicate, Inc.
9-26
AAUGH!
WHAM!
THIS YEAR'S FOOTBALL WAS PULLED AWAY FROM YOU THROUGH THE COURTESY OF WOMEN'S LIB!
SCHULZ

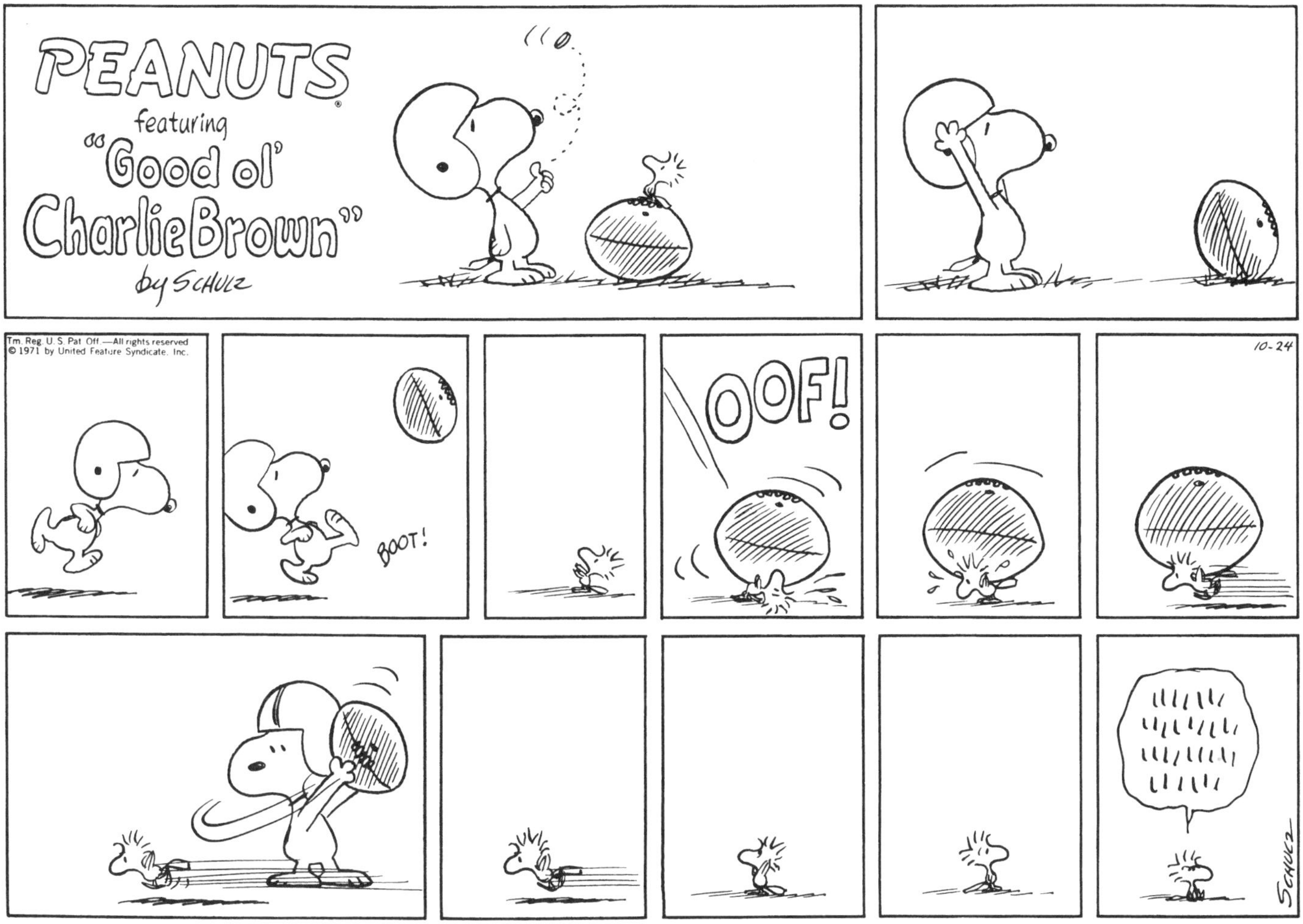
PEANUTS
featuring
"Good ol' Charlie Brown"
by SCHULZ
Tm. Reg. U.S. Pat. Off.—All rights reserved
© 1971 by United Feature Syndicate, Inc.
10-24
BOOT!
OOF!
SCHULZ

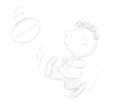

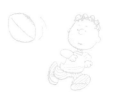

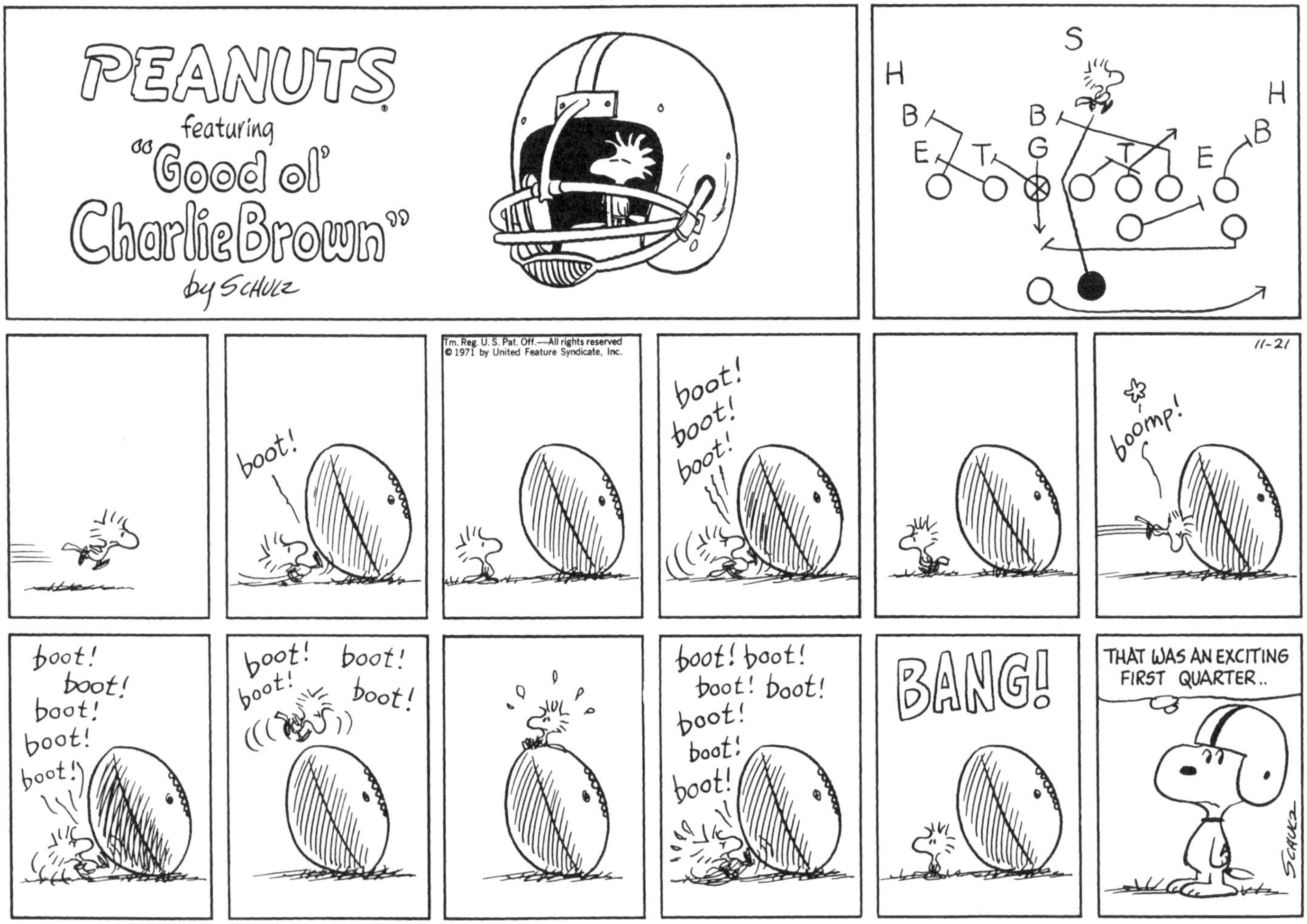
PEANUTS®
featuring
"Good ol' Charlie Brown"
by SCHULZ
S
H
H
B
B
B
E
T
G
T
E
Tm. Reg. U. S. Pat. Off.—All rights reserved
© 1971 by United Feature Syndicate, Inc.
11-21
boot!
boot! boot! boot!
boomp!
boot! boot! boot! boot! boot!
boot! boot! boot! boot!
boot! boot! boot! boot! boot! boot!
BANG!
THAT WAS AN EXCITING FIRST QUARTER..
SCHULZ

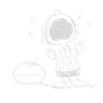

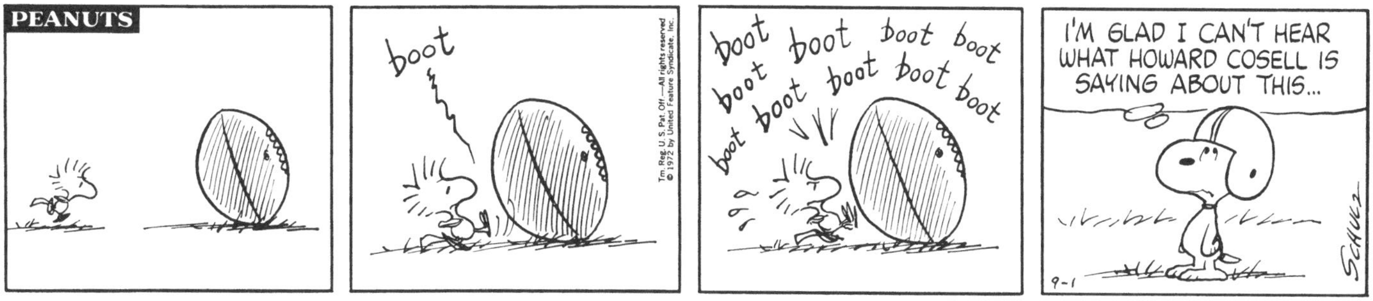
PEANUTS
boot
Tm. Reg. U.S. Pat. Off.—All rights reserved © 1972 by United Feature Syndicate, Inc.
boot boot boot boot
boot boot boot boot
boot boot
I'M GLAD I CAN'T HEAR WHAT HOWARD COSELL IS SAYING ABOUT THIS...
9-1
SCHULZ

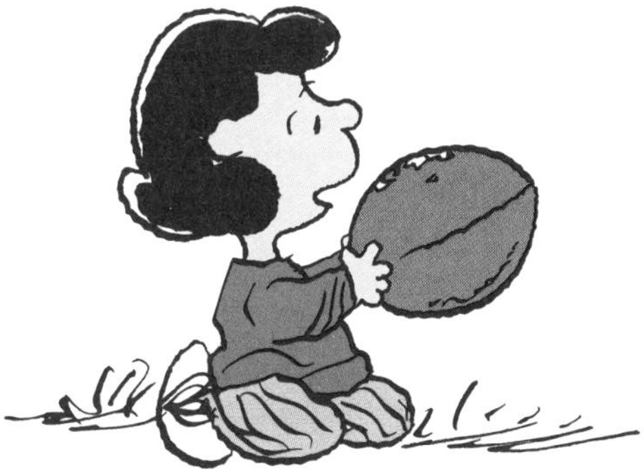

PEANUTS
9-2
KLUNK!
Tm. Reg. U.S. Pat. Off.—All rights reserved
© 1972 by United Feature Syndicate, Inc.
THAT'S WHAT IS CALLED "COMING IN OFF THE BENCH"
SCHULZ

PEANUTS
Tm. Reg. U.S. Pat. Off.—All rights reserved
© 1972 by United Feature Syndicate, Inc.
STOMP!
9-5
RAH?
SCHULZ

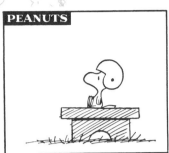

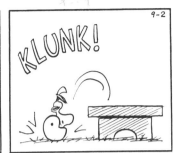

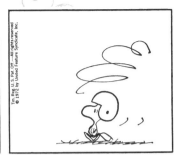

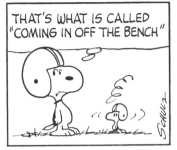

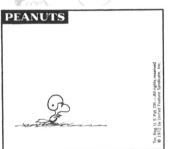

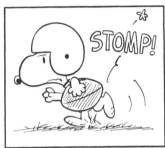

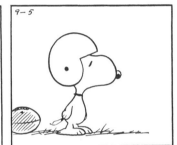

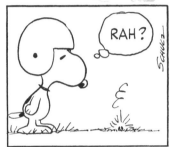

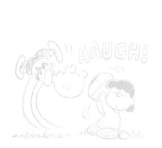

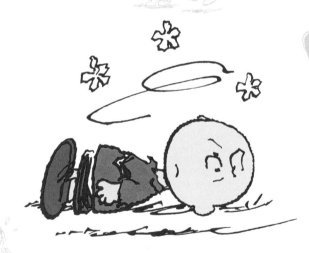

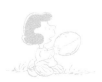

PEANUTS
Tm. Reg. U.S. Pat. Off.—All rights reserved © 1972 by United Feature Syndicate, Inc.
9-6
SCHULZ

PEANUTS
9-7
Tm. Reg. U.S. Pat. Off.—All rights reserved © 1972 by United Feature Syndicate, Inc.
BONK!
WOODSTOCK HAS DIFFICULTY RECOVERING FUMBLES...
SCHULZ

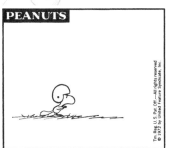

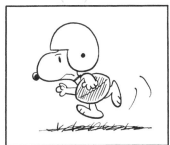

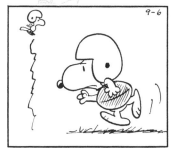

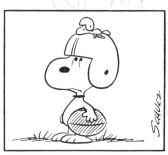

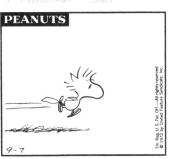

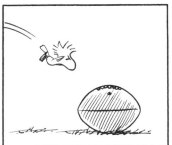

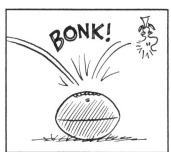

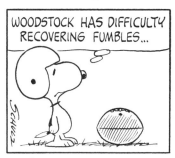

PEANUTS
9-8
THAT STUPID WOODSTOCK... HE LOST HIS BOOK WITH ALL OUR SECRET PLAYS!
Tm. Reg. U.S. Pat. Off.—All rights reserved © 1972 by United Feature Syndicate, Inc.
TWENTY THOUSAND LAPS AROUND THE FIELD!
SCHULZ

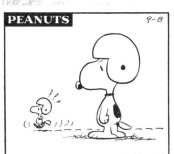

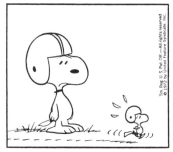

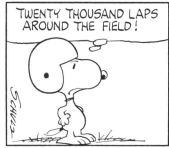

PEANUTS
WHAT A LOUSY BREAK!
Tm. Reg. U.S. Pat. Off.—All rights reserved © 1972 by United Feature Syndicate, Inc.
NO WONDER COACHES GO CRAZY...
FIRST GAME OF THE SEASON, AND WHAT HAPPENS?
MY MIDDLE LINEBACKER GETS HIS HEAD CAUGHT IN HIS LOCKER!

PEANUTS
PUNT!
Tm. Reg. U.S. Pat. Off.—All rights reserved © 1972 by United Feature Syndicate, Inc.
BONK!!
IF YOU DON'T PLAY EVERY DAY, YOU LOSE THAT FINE EDGE...

PEANUTS
boot!
Tm. Reg. U.S. Pat. Off.—All rights reserved © 1972 by United Feature Syndicate, Inc.
!

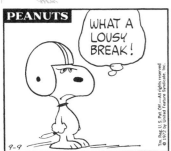

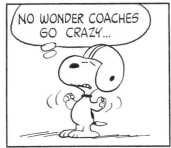

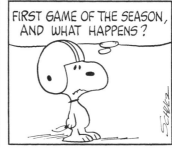

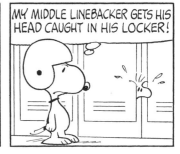

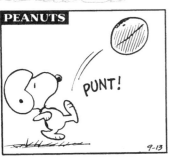

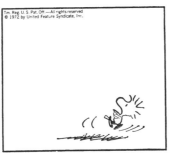

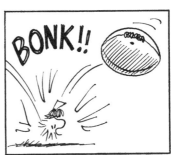

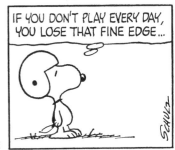

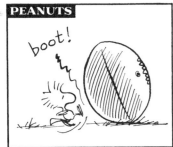

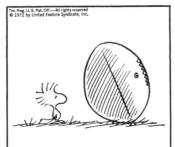

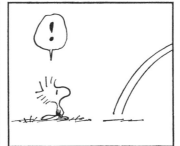

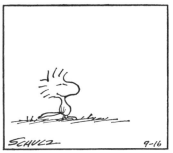

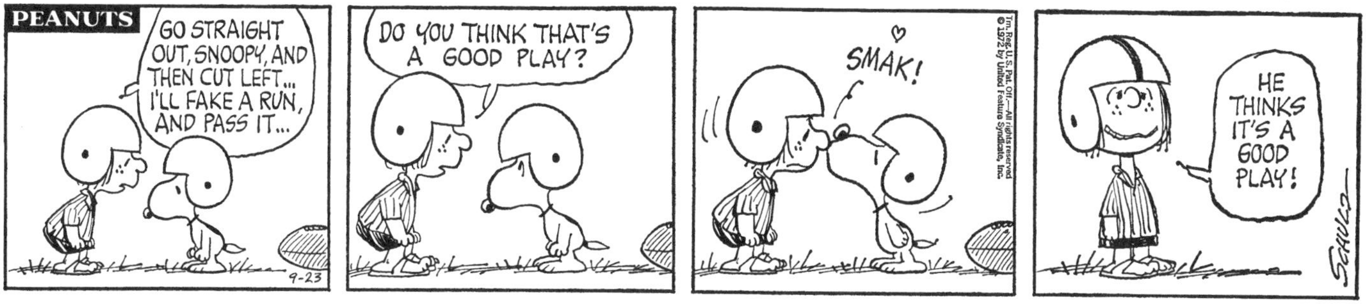
PEANUTS
GO STRAIGHT OUT, SNOOPY, AND THEN CUT LEFT... I'LL FAKE A RUN, AND PASS IT...
9-23
DO YOU THINK THAT'S A GOOD PLAY?
SMAK!
Tm. Reg. U.S. Pat. Off.—All rights reserved © 1972 by United Feature Syndicate, Inc.
HE THINKS IT'S A GOOD PLAY!
SCHULZ

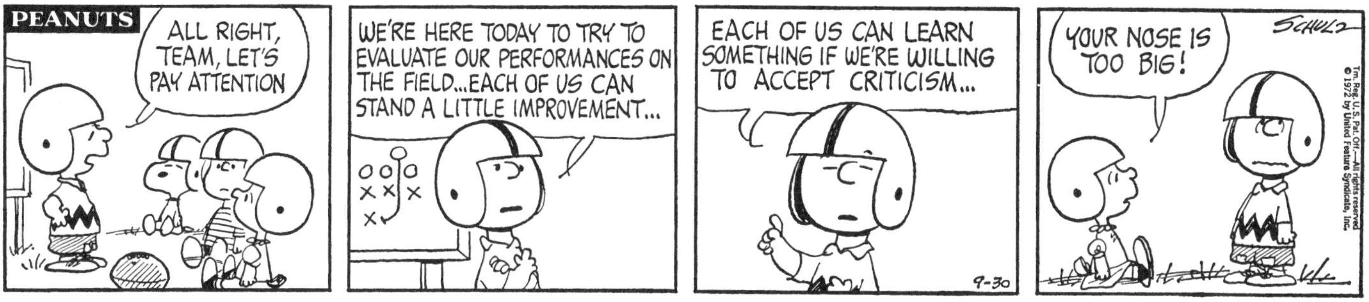
PEANUTS
ALL RIGHT, TEAM, LET'S PAY ATTENTION
WE'RE HERE TODAY TO TRY TO EVALUATE OUR PERFORMANCES ON THE FIELD...EACH OF US CAN STAND A LITTLE IMPROVEMENT...
EACH OF US CAN LEARN SOMETHING IF WE'RE WILLING TO ACCEPT CRITICISM...
9-30
SCHULZ
Tm. Reg. U.S. Pat. Off.—All rights reserved © 1972 by United Feature Syndicate, Inc.
YOUR NOSE IS TOO BIG!

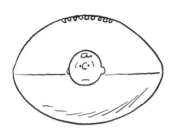

PEANUTS
featuring "Good ol' Charlie Brown"
by SCHULZ

♪ CHARLIE BROWNNNNN ♪

I'LL HOLD THE FOOTBALL, CHARLIE BROWN, AND YOU COME RUNNING UP, AND KICK IT..

I CAN'T

I NEVER DO ANYTHING WITHOUT CONSULTING MY PSYCHIATRIST...

WELL, YOU GO TALK WITH YOUR PSYCHIATRIST, AND SEE WHAT YOU WANT TO DO...OKAY?

PSYCHIATRIC HELP 5¢

THE DOCTOR IS IN

I HAVE A STRANGE PROBLEM

THERE'S THIS GIRL, SEE, AND SHE'S ALWAYS TRYING TO GET ME TO KICK THIS FOOTBALL, BUT SHE ALSO ALWAYS PULLS IT AWAY AND I LAND ON MY BACK AND KILL MYSELF...

SHE SOUNDS LIKE AN INTERESTING GIRL...SORT OF A FUN TYPE...

I GET THE IMPRESSION THAT YOU HAVE A REAL NEED TO KICK THIS FOOTBALL...I THINK YOU SHOULD TRY IT!

I THINK YOU SHOULD TRY IT BECAUSE IN MEDICAL TERMS, YOU HAVE WHAT WE CALL THE "NEED TO NEED TO TRY IT"

I'M GLAD I TALKED WITH MY PSYCHIATRIST BECAUSE THIS YEAR I'M GONNA KICK THAT BALL CLEAR TO THE MOON!

10-8

AUGH!

WHAM

UNFORTUNATELY, CHARLIE BROWN, YOUR AVERAGE PSYCHIATRIST KNOWS VERY LITTLE ABOUT KICKING FOOTBALLS

Tm. Reg. U.S. Pat. Off.—All rights reserved.
© 1972 by United Feature Syndicate, Inc.

PEANUTS
I'LL KICK THE BALL TO YOU, AND YOU COME RUNNING DOWN THE FIELD, AND I'LL TRY TO HUG YOU
1-20
TACKLE
HUG
TACKLE
HUG
Tm. Reg. U.S. Pat. Off.—All rights reserved
©1973 by United Feature Syndicate, Inc.
FORGET IT!
STUPID GAME!
SCHULZ

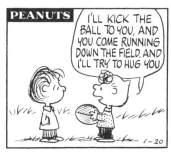

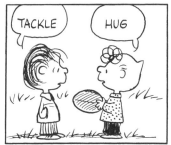

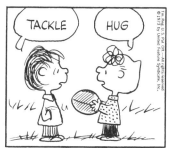

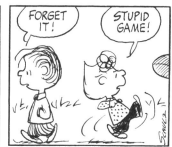

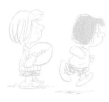

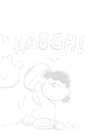

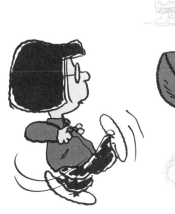

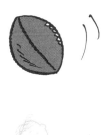

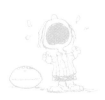

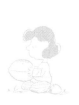

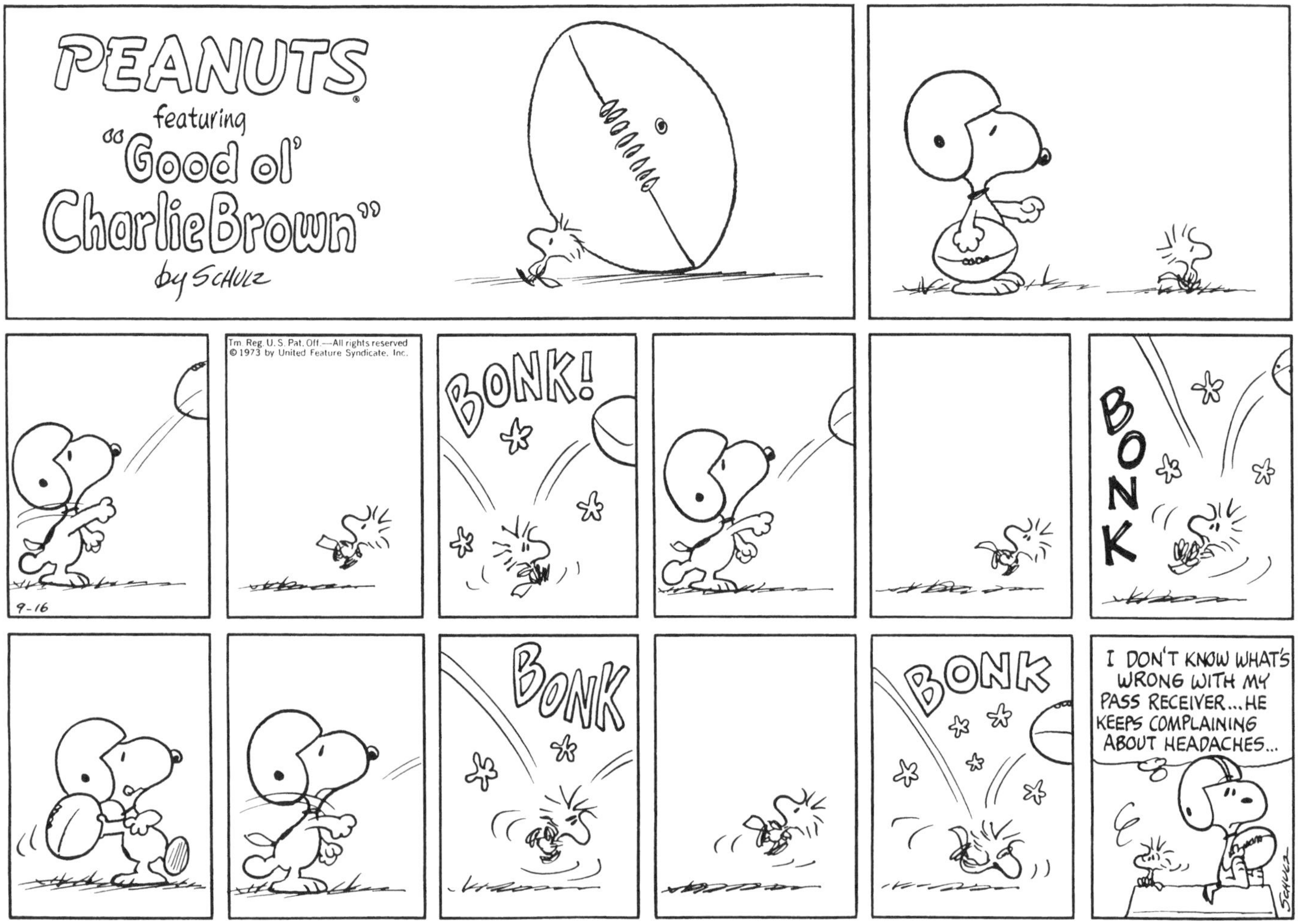
PEANUTS
featuring
"Good ol' CharlieBrown"
by SCHULZ
Tm. Reg. U.S. Pat. Off.—All rights reserved
© 1973 by United Feature Syndicate, Inc.
BONK!
BONK
BONK
BONK
I DON'T KNOW WHAT'S WRONG WITH MY PASS RECEIVER...HE KEEPS COMPLAINING ABOUT HEADACHES...

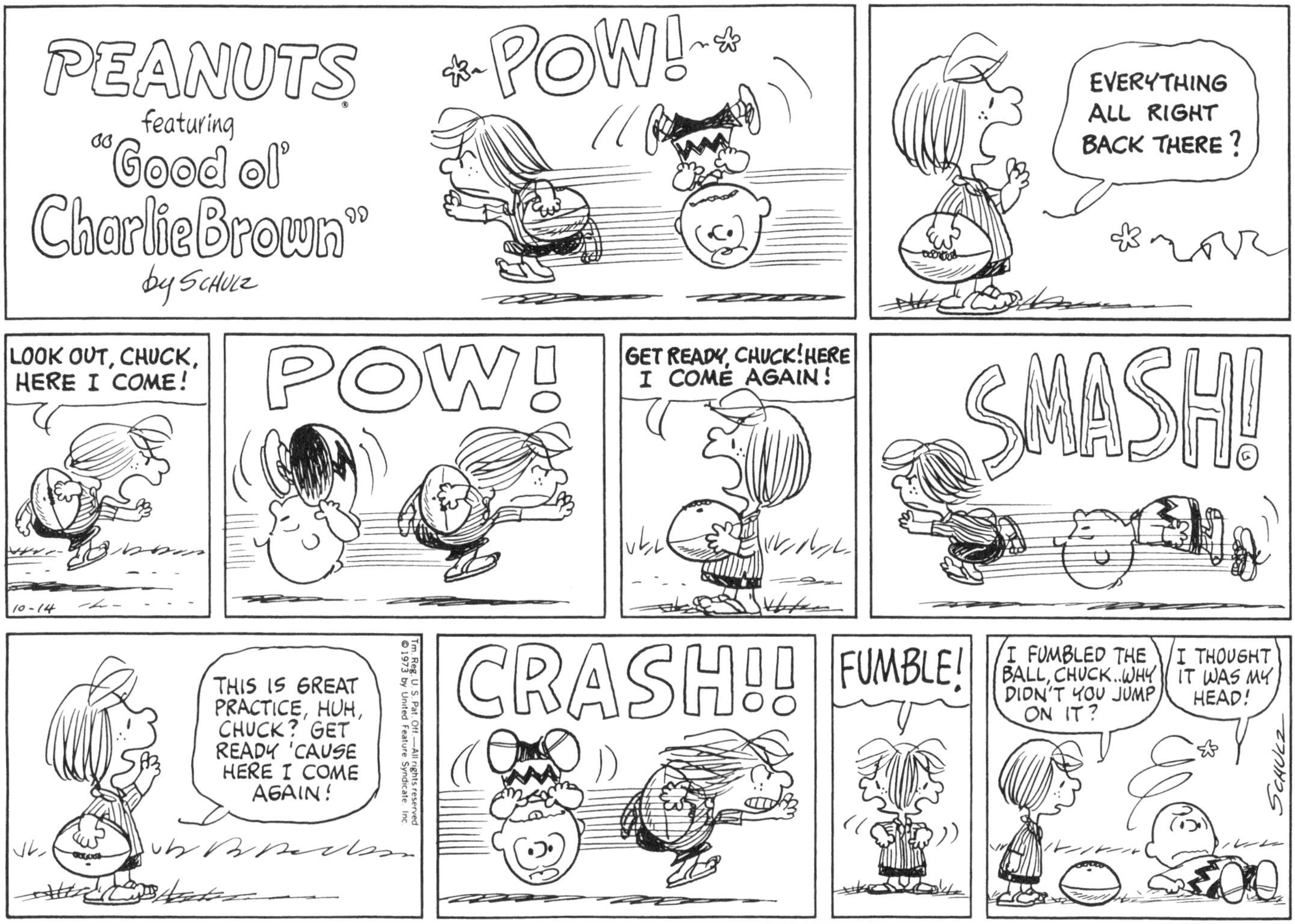
PEANUTS
featuring
"Good ol' Charlie Brown"
by SCHULZ
POW!
EVERYTHING ALL RIGHT BACK THERE?
LOOK OUT, CHUCK, HERE I COME!
10-14
POW!
GET READY, CHUCK! HERE I COME AGAIN!
SMASH!
THIS IS GREAT PRACTICE, HUH, CHUCK? GET READY 'CAUSE HERE I COME AGAIN!
Tm. Reg. U.S. Pat. Off.—All rights reserved © 1973 by United Feature Syndicate, Inc.
CRASH!!
FUMBLE!
I FUMBLED THE BALL, CHUCK..WHY DIDN'T YOU JUMP ON IT?
I THOUGHT IT WAS MY HEAD!
SCHULZ

Tm. Reg. U. S. Pat. Off.—All rights reserved
© 1973 by United Feature Syndicate, Inc.

10-27

SCHULZ

WOODSTOCK ALWAYS HAS TROUBLE WITH THAT HAND-OFF PLAY...

AAUGH!

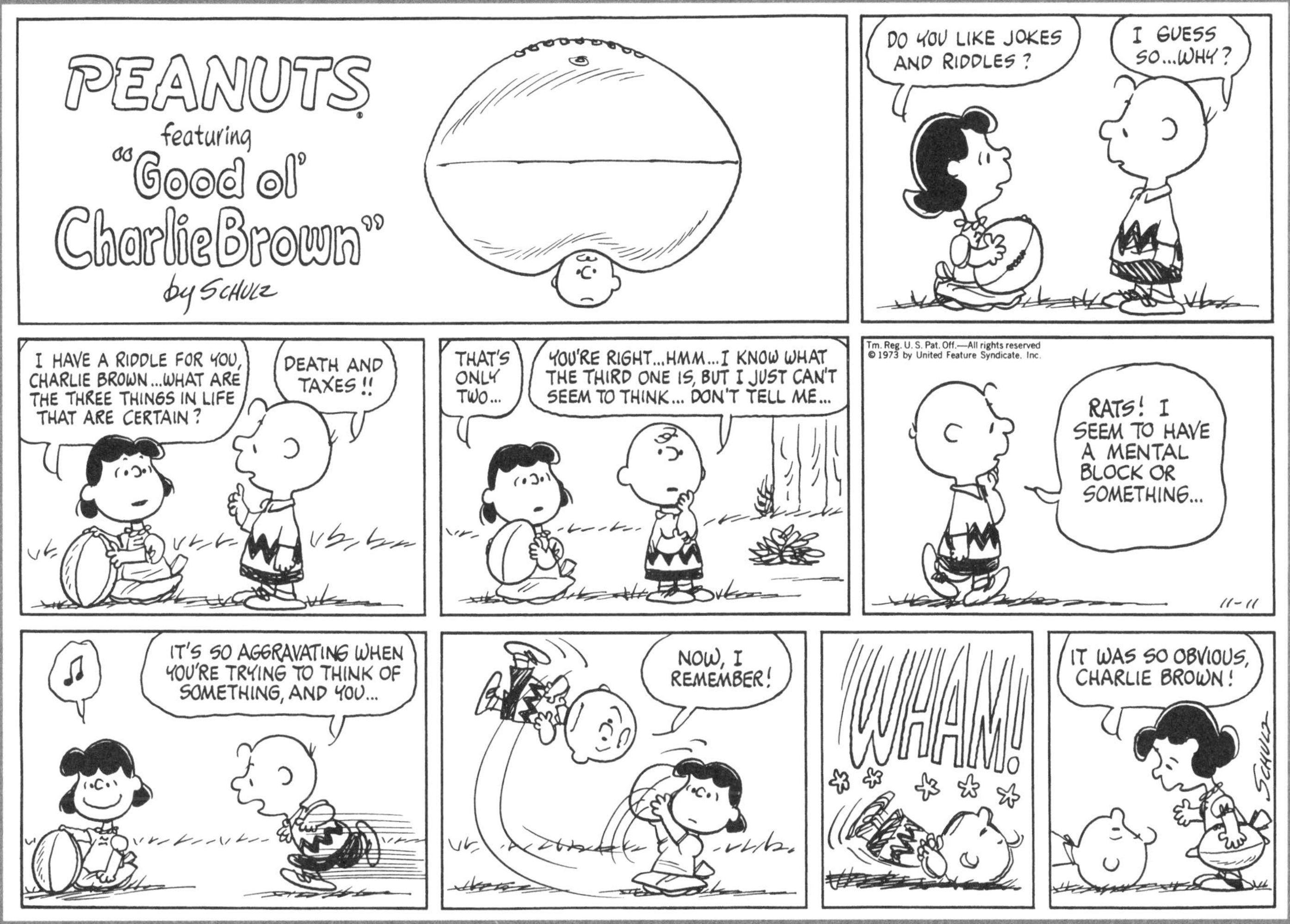
PEANUTS
featuring
"Good ol' Charlie Brown"
by SCHULZ
DO YOU LIKE JOKES AND RIDDLES ?
I GUESS SO...WHY ?
I HAVE A RIDDLE FOR YOU, CHARLIE BROWN...WHAT ARE THE THREE THINGS IN LIFE THAT ARE CERTAIN ?
DEATH AND TAXES !!
THAT'S ONLY TWO...
YOU'RE RIGHT...HMM...I KNOW WHAT THE THIRD ONE IS, BUT I JUST CAN'T SEEM TO THINK... DON'T TELL ME...
Tm. Reg. U. S. Pat. Off.—All rights reserved
© 1973 by United Feature Syndicate, Inc.
RATS! I SEEM TO HAVE A MENTAL BLOCK OR SOMETHING...
11-11
IT'S SO AGGRAVATING WHEN YOU'RE TRYING TO THINK OF SOMETHING, AND YOU...
NOW, I REMEMBER!
WHAM!
IT WAS SO OBVIOUS, CHARLIE BROWN!
SCHULZ

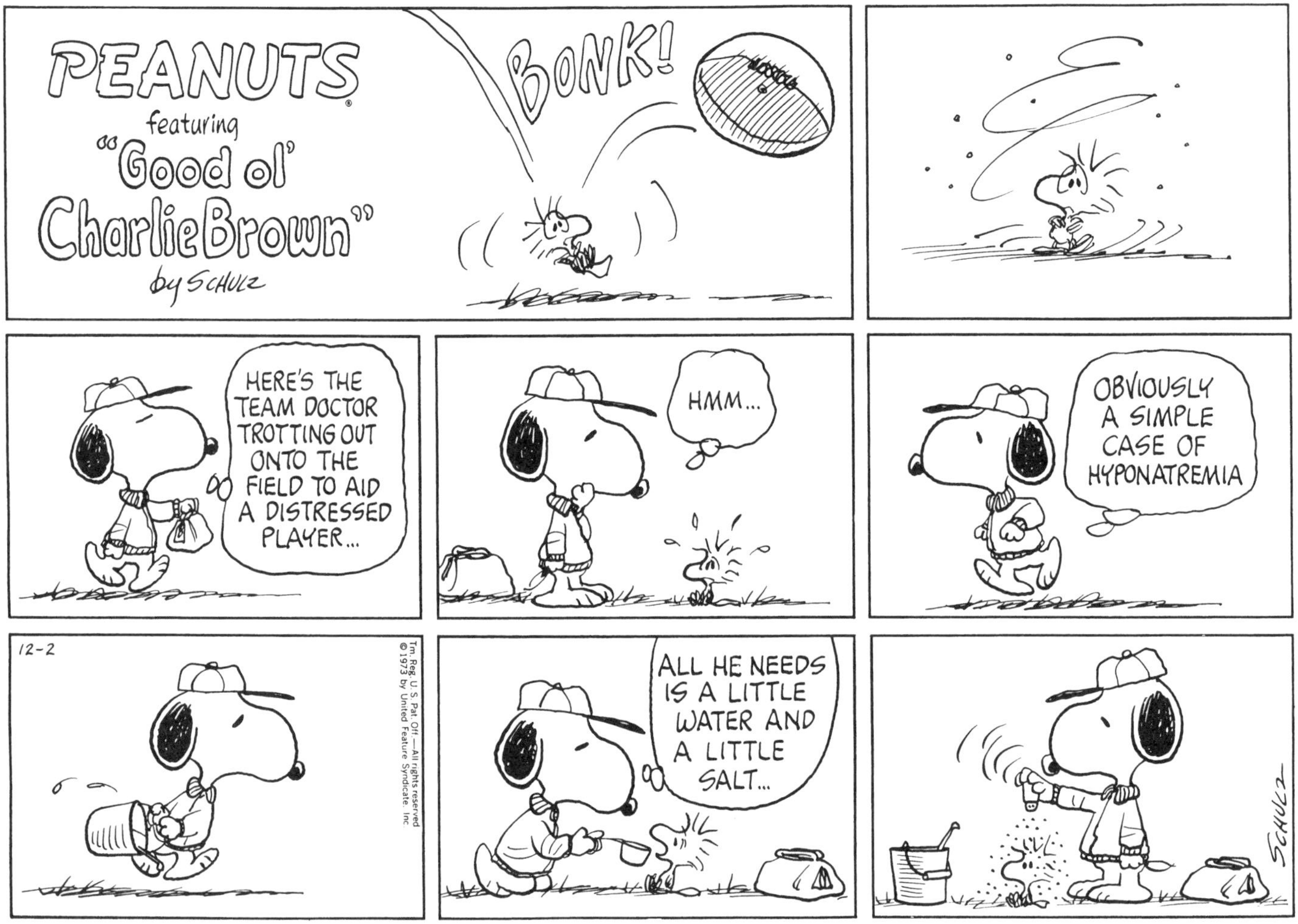
PEANUTS
featuring "Good ol' Charlie Brown"
by SCHULZ
BONK!
HERE'S THE TEAM DOCTOR TROTTING OUT ONTO THE FIELD TO AID A DISTRESSED PLAYER...
HMM...
OBVIOUSLY A SIMPLE CASE OF HYPONATREMIA
12-2
Tm. Reg. U.S. Pat. Off.—All rights reserved © 1973 by United Feature Syndicate, Inc.
ALL HE NEEDS IS A LITTLE WATER AND A LITTLE SALT...
SCHULZ

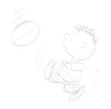

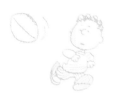

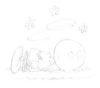

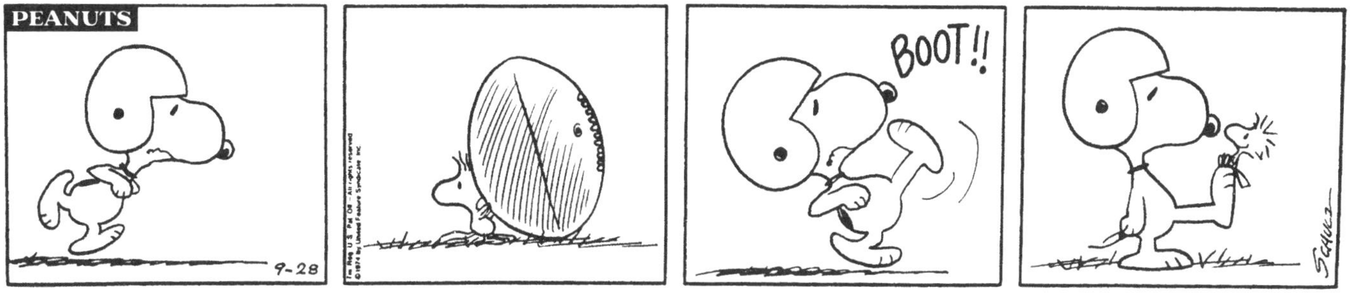
PEANUTS
9-28
BOOT!!
SCHULZ

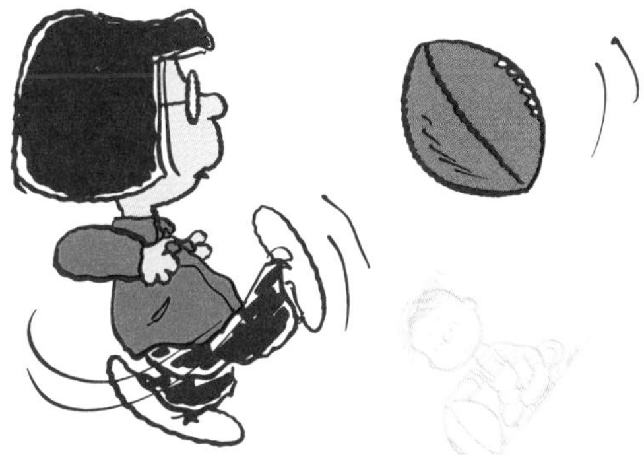

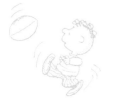

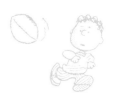

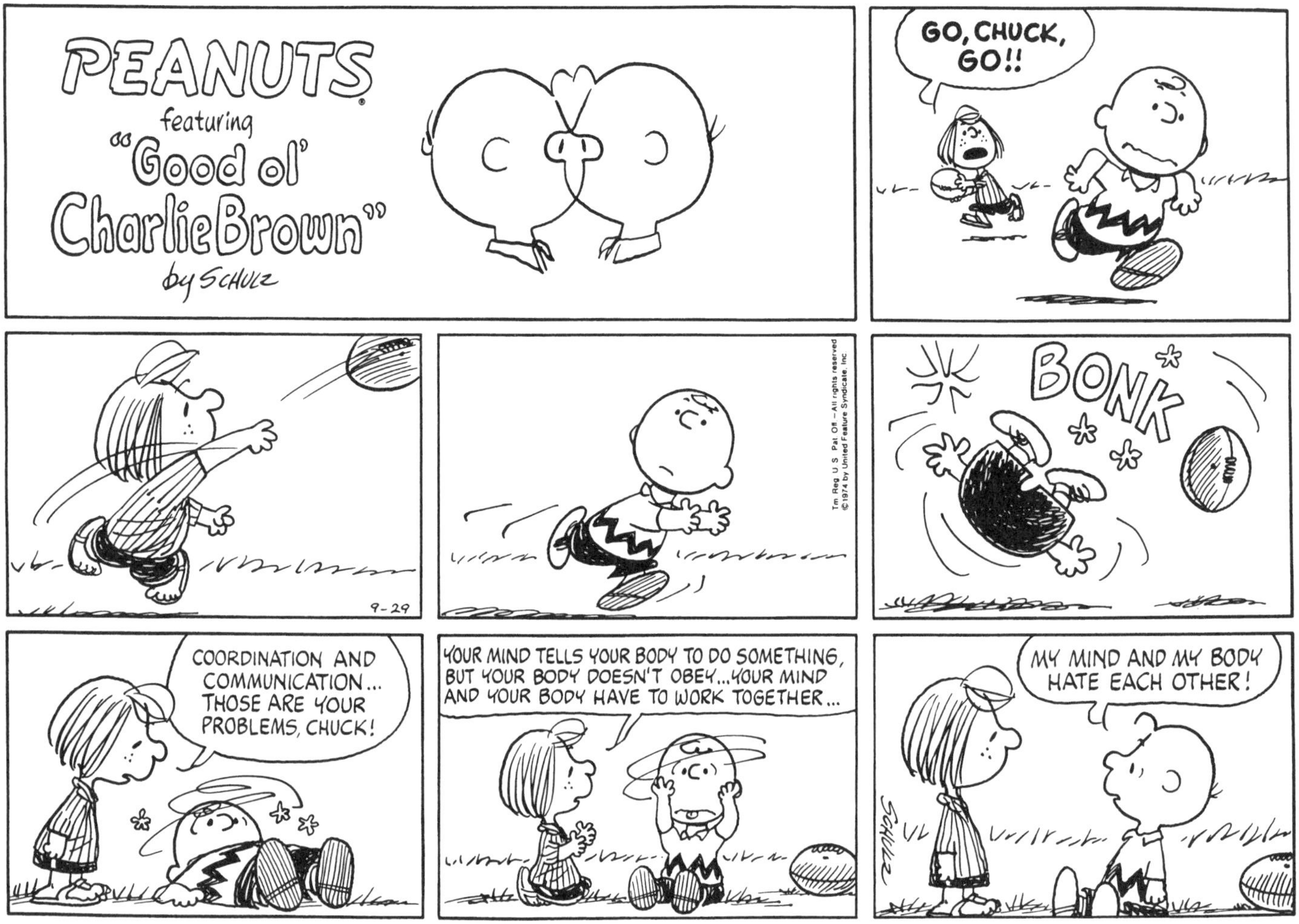
PEANUTS
featuring
"Good ol' Charlie Brown"
by SCHULZ
GO, CHUCK, GO!!
9-29
Tm Reg U S Pat Off — All rights reserved
©1974 by United Feature Syndicate, Inc
BONK
COORDINATION AND COMMUNICATION... THOSE ARE YOUR PROBLEMS, CHUCK!
YOUR MIND TELLS YOUR BODY TO DO SOMETHING, BUT YOUR BODY DOESN'T OBEY...YOUR MIND AND YOUR BODY HAVE TO WORK TOGETHER...
SCHULZ
MY MIND AND MY BODY HATE EACH OTHER!

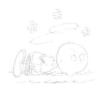

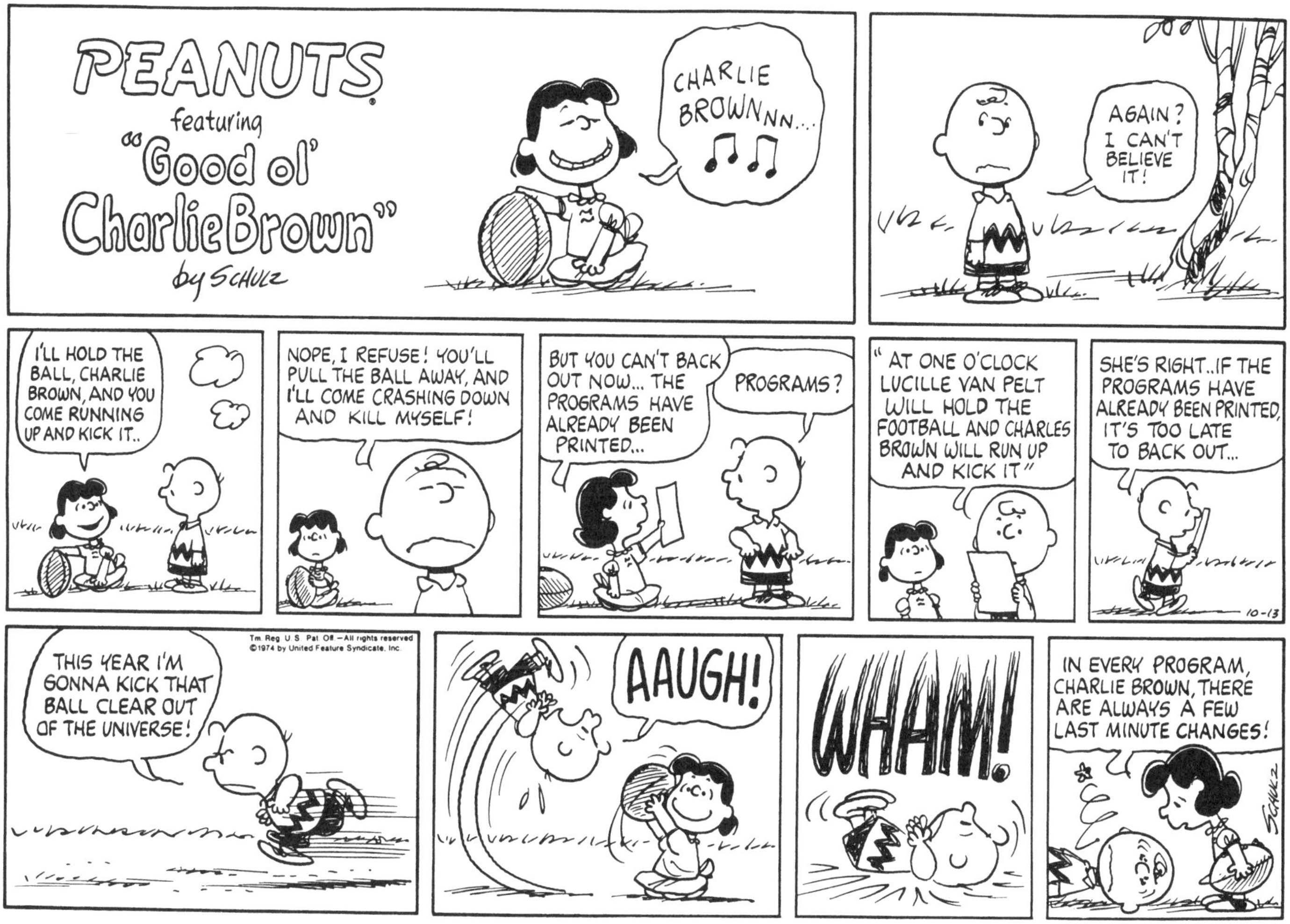
PEANUTS
featuring "Good ol' CharlieBrown"
by SCHULZ
CHARLIE BROWNNNN... ♫ ♫
AGAIN? I CAN'T BELIEVE IT!
I'LL HOLD THE BALL, CHARLIE BROWN, AND YOU COME RUNNING UP AND KICK IT..
NOPE, I REFUSE! YOU'LL PULL THE BALL AWAY, AND I'LL COME CRASHING DOWN AND KILL MYSELF!
BUT YOU CAN'T BACK OUT NOW... THE PROGRAMS HAVE ALREADY BEEN PRINTED...
PROGRAMS?
"AT ONE O'CLOCK LUCILLE VAN PELT WILL HOLD THE FOOTBALL AND CHARLES BROWN WILL RUN UP AND KICK IT"
SHE'S RIGHT..IF THE PROGRAMS HAVE ALREADY BEEN PRINTED, IT'S TOO LATE TO BACK OUT...
10-13
Tm Reg U.S. Pat. Off.—All rights reserved ©1974 by United Feature Syndicate, Inc.
THIS YEAR I'M GONNA KICK THAT BALL CLEAR OUT OF THE UNIVERSE!
AAUGH!
WHAM!
IN EVERY PROGRAM, CHARLIE BROWN, THERE ARE ALWAYS A FEW LAST MINUTE CHANGES!
SCHULZ

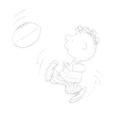

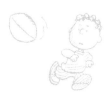

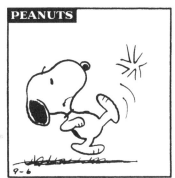

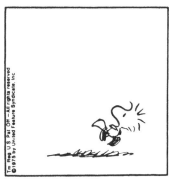

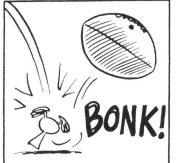

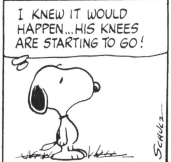

PEANUTS
9-6
Tm Reg U S Pat Off — All rights reserved
©1975 by United Feature Syndicate, Inc
BONK!
I KNEW IT WOULD HAPPEN...HIS KNEES ARE STARTING TO GO!
SCHULZ

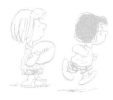

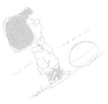

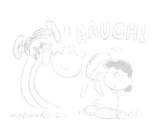

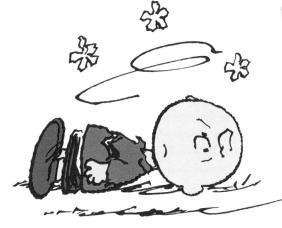

PEANUTS
featuring "Good ol' Charlie Brown"
by SCHULZ
CHARLIE BROWN-N-N
I CAN'T BELIEVE IT..
I'LL HOLD THE BALL, AND YOU RUN UP AND KICK IT
YOU NEVER HOLD IT! YOU ALWAYS PULL IT AWAY, AND I LAND FLAT ON MY BACK AND KILL MYSELF!
THAT'S MISTRUST! THAT'S MISTRUST OF ME AS AN ATHLETE, A PERSON AND A WOMAN! DO YOU MISTRUST ALL WOMEN? DO YOU MISTRUST EVEN YOUR MOTHER?
I DON'T MISTRUST MY MOTHER...GOOD GRIEF, NO!! IF THERE'S ANYONE IN THIS WORLD I DO TRUST, IT'S MY MOTHER!
10-19
Tm. Reg. U.S. Pat. Off.—All rights reserved
©1975 by United Feature Syndicate, Inc.
AUGH!
WAM!
I'M NOT YOUR MOTHER, CHARLIE BROWN!
SCHULZ

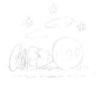

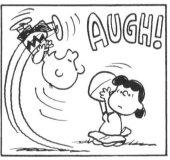

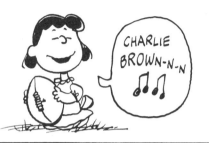

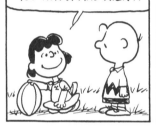

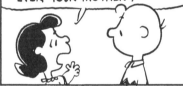

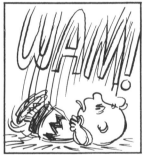

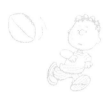

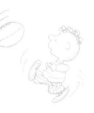

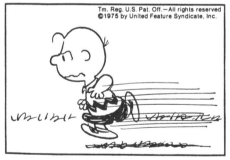

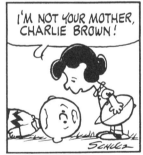

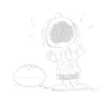

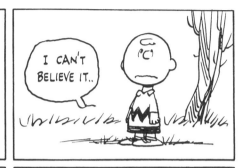

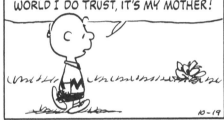

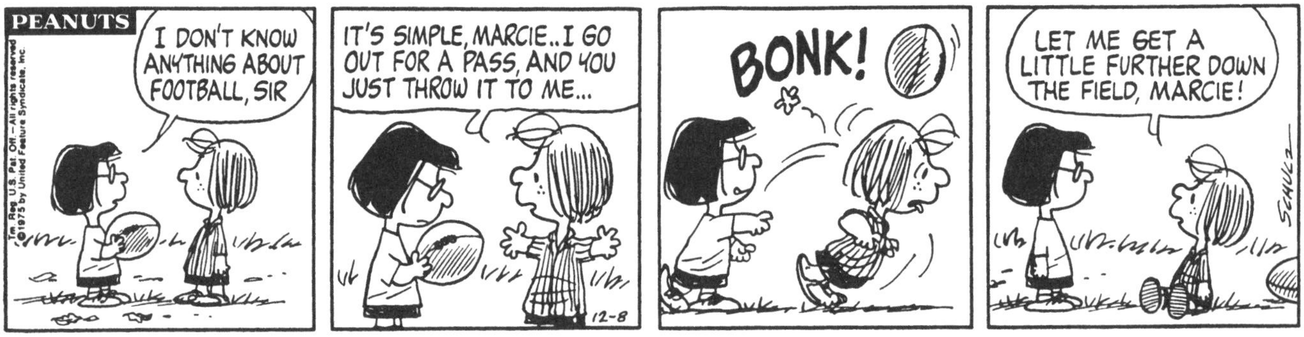
PEANUTS
I DON'T KNOW ANYTHING ABOUT FOOTBALL, SIR
IT'S SIMPLE, MARCIE..I GO OUT FOR A PASS, AND YOU JUST THROW IT TO ME...
BONK!
LET ME GET A LITTLE FURTHER DOWN THE FIELD, MARCIE!
Tm. Reg. U.S. Pat. Off.—All rights reserved ©1975 by United Feature Syndicate, Inc.
12-8
SCHULZ

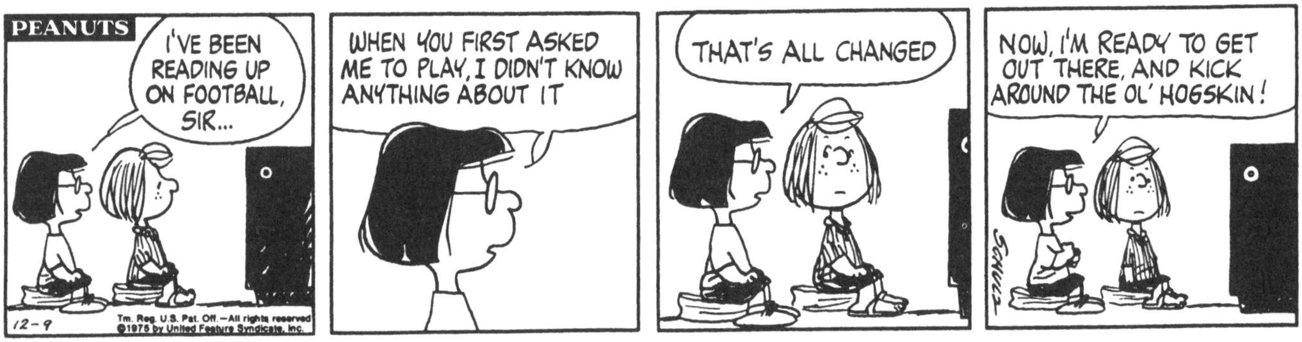
PEANUTS
I'VE BEEN READING UP ON FOOTBALL, SIR...
WHEN YOU FIRST ASKED ME TO PLAY, I DIDN'T KNOW ANYTHING ABOUT IT
THAT'S ALL CHANGED
NOW, I'M READY TO GET OUT THERE, AND KICK AROUND THE OL' HOGSKIN!
12-9
Tm. Reg. U.S. Pat. Off.—All rights reserved ©1975 by United Feature Syndicate, Inc.
SCHULZ

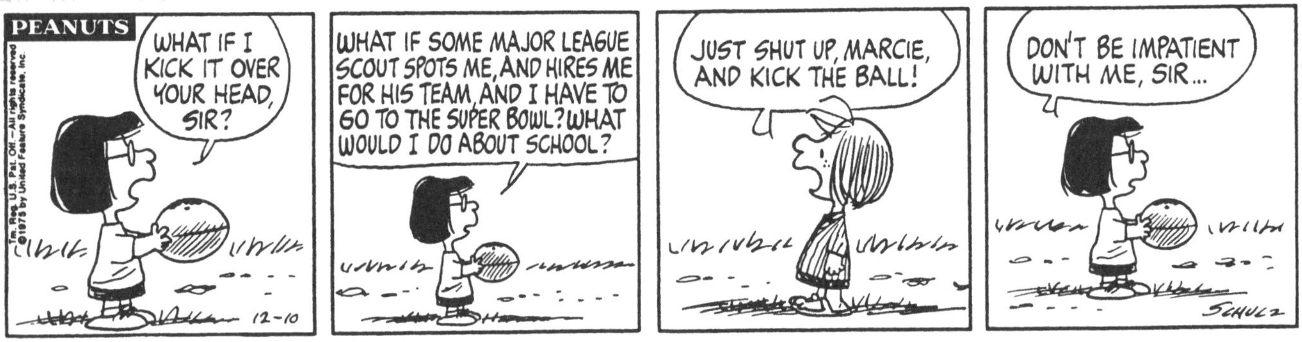
PEANUTS
WHAT IF I KICK IT OVER YOUR HEAD, SIR?
WHAT IF SOME MAJOR LEAGUE SCOUT SPOTS ME, AND HIRES ME FOR HIS TEAM, AND I HAVE TO GO TO THE SUPER BOWL? WHAT WOULD I DO ABOUT SCHOOL?
JUST SHUT UP, MARCIE, AND KICK THE BALL!
DON'T BE IMPATIENT WITH ME, SIR...
Tm. Reg. U.S. Pat. Off.—All rights reserved ©1975 by United Feature Syndicate, Inc.
12-10
SCHULZ

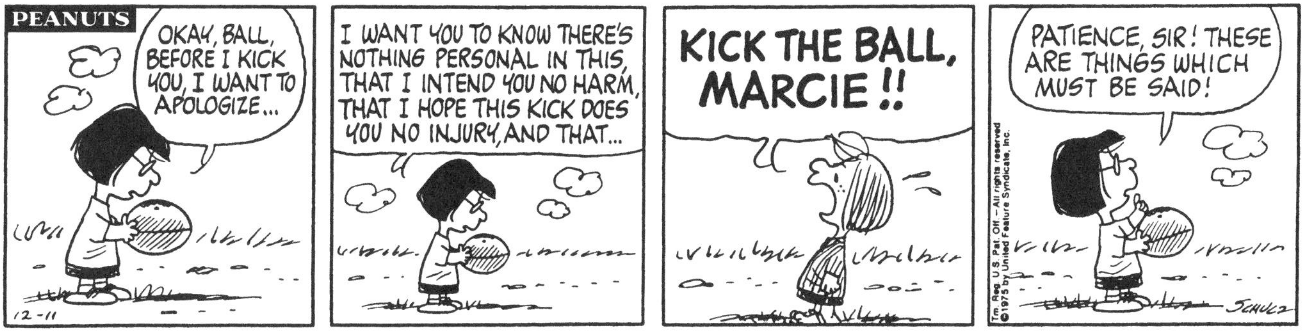
PEANUTS
OKAY, BALL, BEFORE I KICK YOU, I WANT TO APOLOGIZE...
12-11
I WANT YOU TO KNOW THERE'S NOTHING PERSONAL IN THIS, THAT I INTEND YOU NO HARM, THAT I HOPE THIS KICK DOES YOU NO INJURY, AND THAT...
KICK THE BALL, MARCIE !!
PATIENCE, SIR! THESE ARE THINGS WHICH MUST BE SAID!
Tm. Reg. U.S. Pat. Off.—All rights reserved
©1975 by United Feature Syndicate, Inc.
SCHULZ

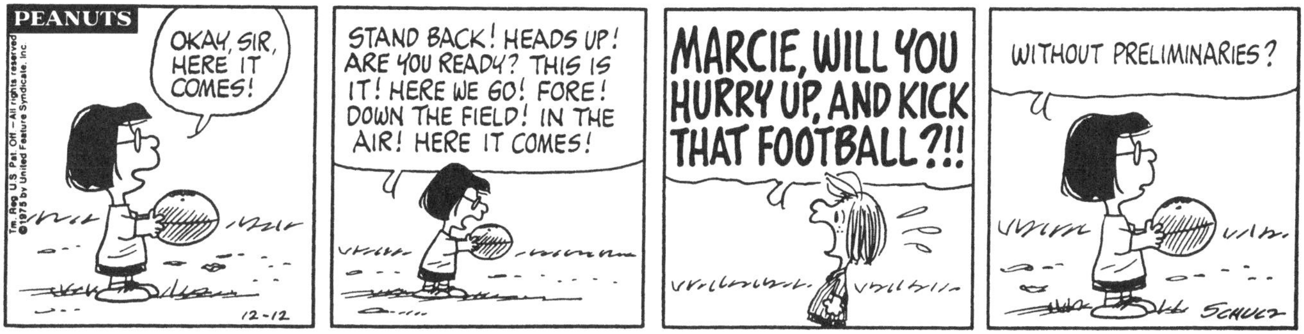
PEANUTS
Tm. Reg. U.S. Pat. Off.—All rights reserved
©1975 by United Feature Syndicate, Inc.
OKAY, SIR, HERE IT COMES!
12-12
STAND BACK! HEADS UP! ARE YOU READY? THIS IS IT! HERE WE GO! FORE! DOWN THE FIELD! IN THE AIR! HERE IT COMES!
MARCIE, WILL YOU HURRY UP, AND KICK THAT FOOTBALL?!!
WITHOUT PRELIMINARIES?
SCHULZ

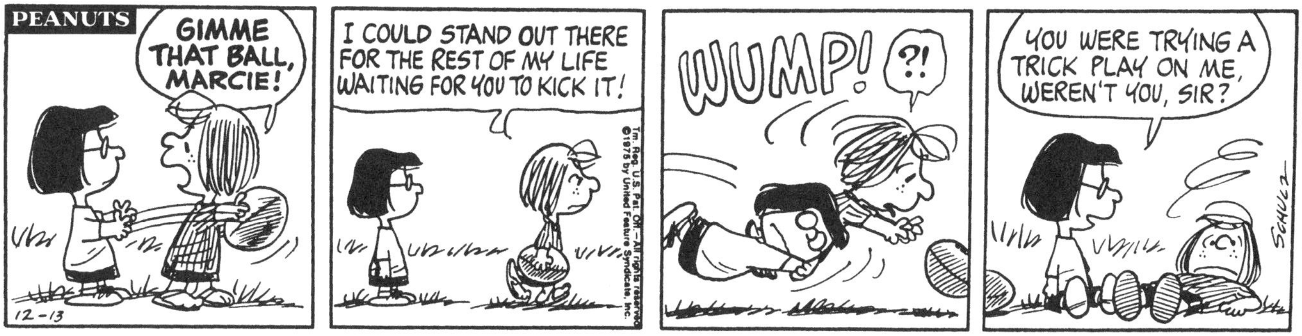
PEANUTS
GIMME THAT BALL, MARCIE!
12-13
I COULD STAND OUT THERE FOR THE REST OF MY LIFE WAITING FOR YOU TO KICK IT!
Tm. Reg. U.S. Pat. Off.—All rights reserved
©1975 by United Feature Syndicate, Inc.
WUMP!
?!
YOU WERE TRYING A TRICK PLAY ON ME, WEREN'T YOU, SIR?
SCHULZ

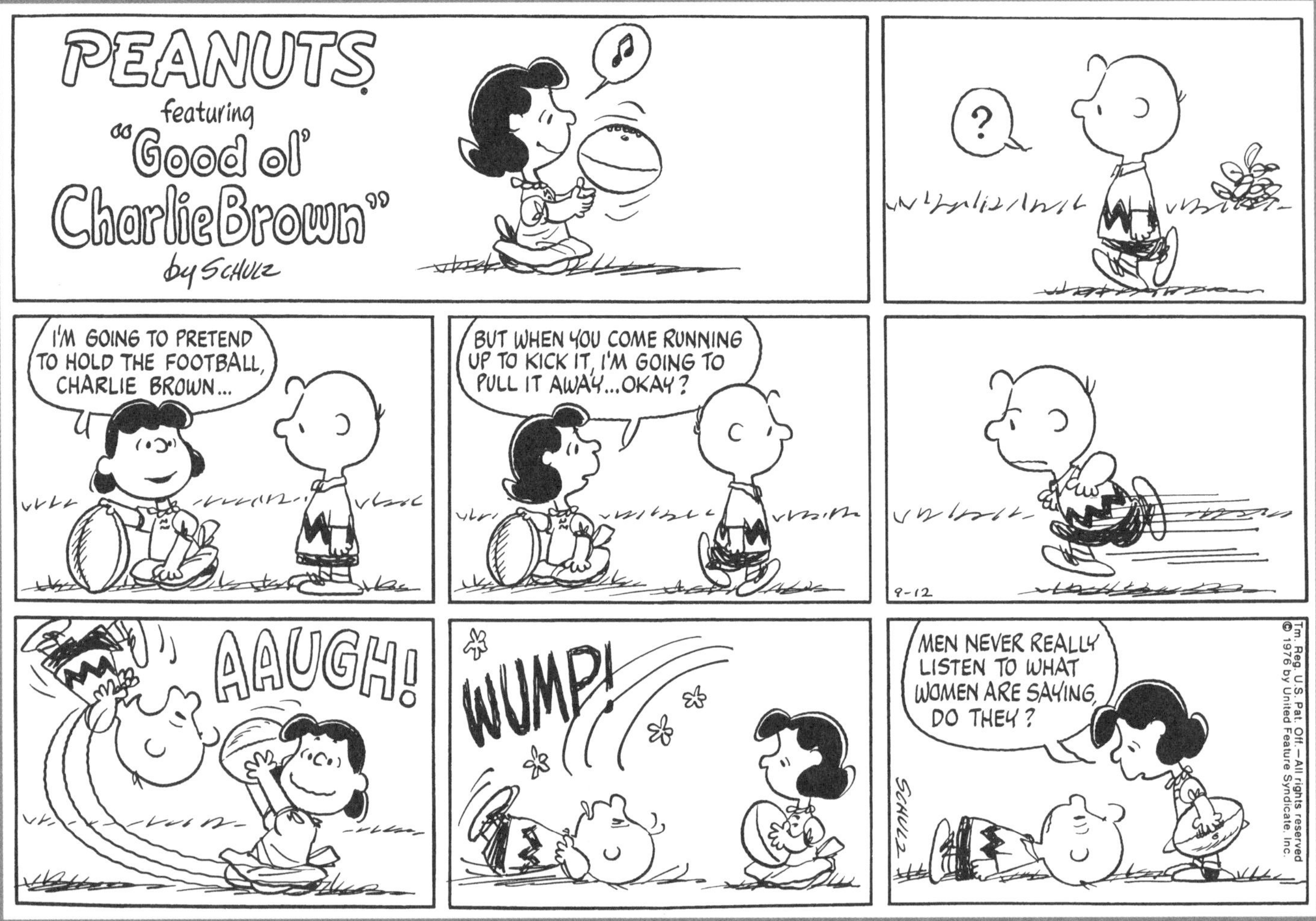
PEANUTS featuring "Good ol' Charlie Brown" by SCHULZ
?
I'M GOING TO PRETEND TO HOLD THE FOOTBALL, CHARLIE BROWN...
BUT WHEN YOU COME RUNNING UP TO KICK IT, I'M GOING TO PULL IT AWAY...OKAY?
9-12
AAUGH!
WUMP!
MEN NEVER REALLY LISTEN TO WHAT WOMEN ARE SAYING, DO THEY?
SCHULZ
Tm. Reg. U.S. Pat. Off.—All rights reserved © 1976 by United Feature Syndicate, Inc.

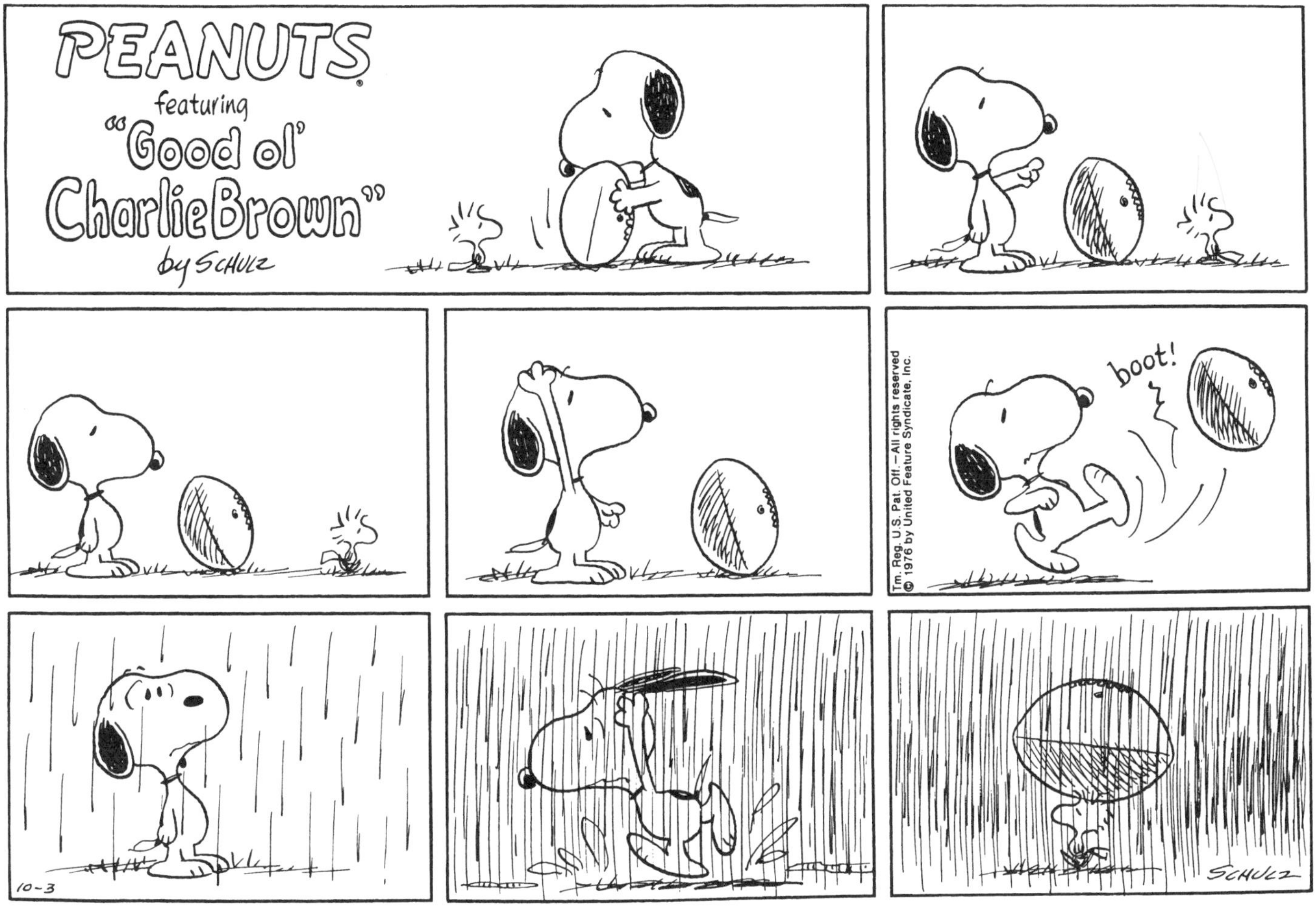
PEANUTS
featuring
"Good ol' CharlieBrown"
by SCHULZ
Tm. Reg. U.S. Pat. Off.—All rights reserved
© 1976 by United Feature Syndicate, Inc.
boot!
10-3
SCHULZ

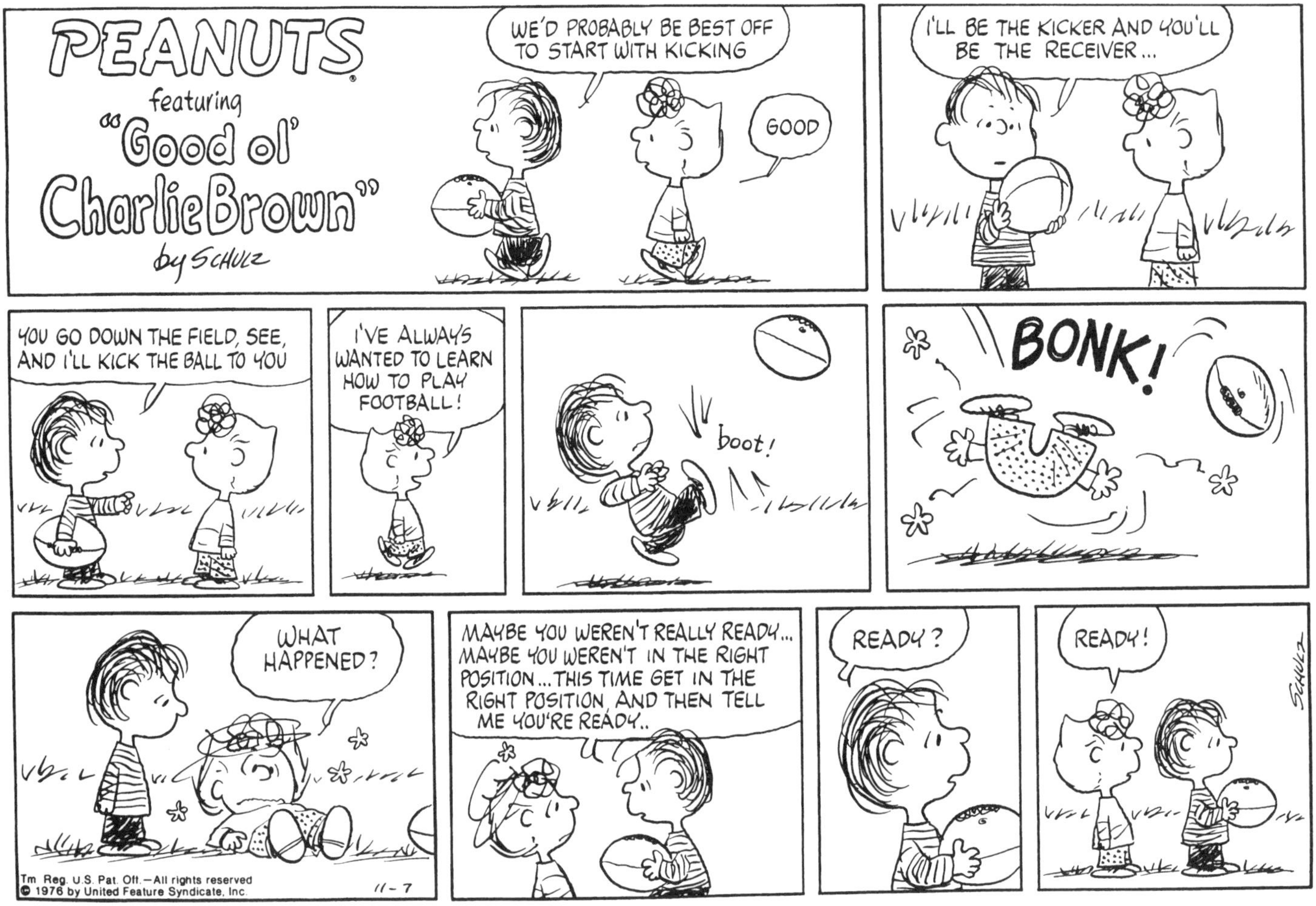
PEANUTS
featuring "Good ol' CharlieBrown"
by SCHULZ
WE'D PROBABLY BE BEST OFF TO START WITH KICKING
GOOD
I'LL BE THE KICKER AND YOU'LL BE THE RECEIVER...
YOU GO DOWN THE FIELD, SEE, AND I'LL KICK THE BALL TO YOU
I'VE ALWAYS WANTED TO LEARN HOW TO PLAY FOOTBALL!
boot!
BONK!
WHAT HAPPENED?
MAYBE YOU WEREN'T REALLY READY... MAYBE YOU WEREN'T IN THE RIGHT POSITION... THIS TIME GET IN THE RIGHT POSITION, AND THEN TELL ME YOU'RE READY..
READY?
READY!
SCHULZ
11-7

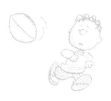

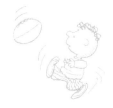

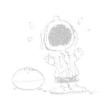

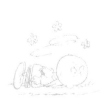

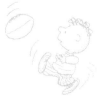

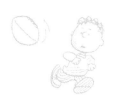

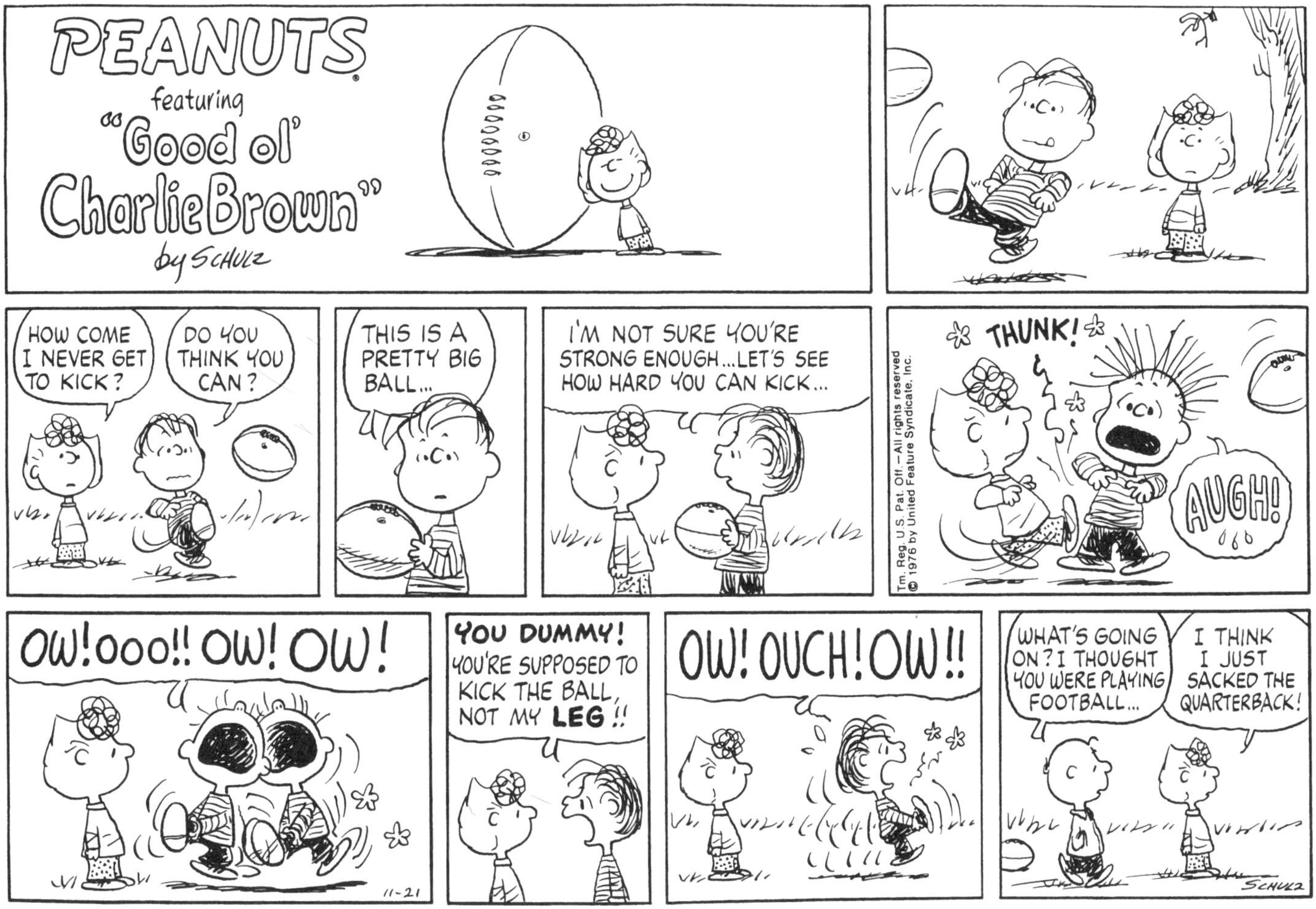
PEANUTS
featuring
"Good ol' Charlie Brown"
by SCHULZ
HOW COME I NEVER GET TO KICK?
DO YOU THINK YOU CAN?
THIS IS A PRETTY BIG BALL...
I'M NOT SURE YOU'RE STRONG ENOUGH...LET'S SEE HOW HARD YOU CAN KICK...
Tm. Reg. U.S. Pat. Off.—All rights reserved
© 1976 by United Feature Syndicate, Inc.
THUNK!
AUGH!
OW! OOO!! OW! OW!
11-21
YOU DUMMY! YOU'RE SUPPOSED TO KICK THE BALL, NOT MY LEG!!
OW! OUCH! OW!!
WHAT'S GOING ON? I THOUGHT YOU WERE PLAYING FOOTBALL...
I THINK I JUST SACKED THE QUARTERBACK!
SCHULZ

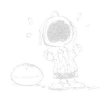

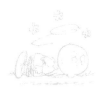

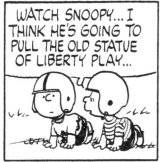

WATCH SNOOPY... I THINK HE'S GOING TO PULL THE OLD STATUE OF LIBERTY PLAY...
HOW DO YOU KNOW?
9-12
SOMEHOW I JUST SENSE IT...
SCHULZ
© 1977 United Feature Syndicate, Inc

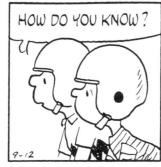

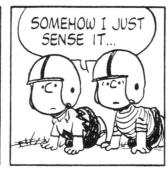

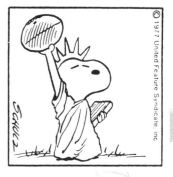

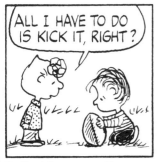

ALL I HAVE TO DO IS KICK IT, RIGHT?
RIGHT
9-21
WHAT IF IT KICKS ME BACK?
SCHULZ
© 1977 United Feature Syndicate, Inc

9-22
I'VE DECIDED I DON'T WANT TO KICK IT
WHY NOT?
© 1977 United Feature Syndicate, Inc
WHAT DID IT EVER DO TO ME?
SCHULZ

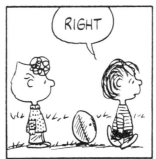

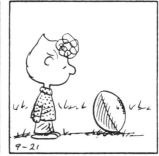

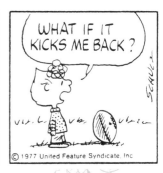

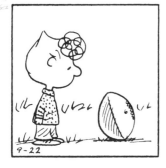

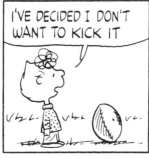

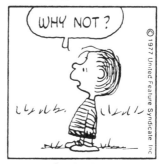

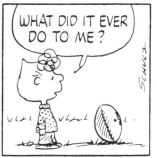

THIS BALL IS HISSING AT ME
S S S S
© 1977 United Feature Syndicate, Inc.
9-23
MAYBE SOME OF THE AIR IS LEAKING OUT
NO, I THINK IT'S HISSING AT ME
S S S S S S
THIS BALL HATES ME!
S S S S S S
SCHULZ

I'M NOT GOING TO STAND HERE WHILE SOME STUPID BALL HISSES AT ME!
S S S S S
WELL, THEN, KICK IT!
I THINK I SCARED IT...
© 1977 United Feature Syndicate, Inc.
9-24
IT JUST PASSED OUT!
SCHULZ

10-3
SCHULZ
© 1977 United Feature Syndicate, Inc.

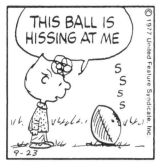

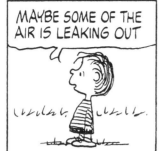

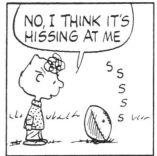

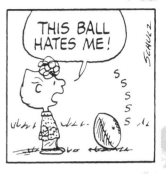

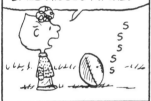

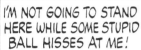

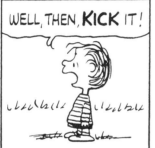

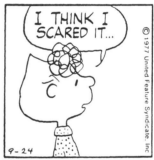

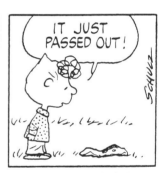

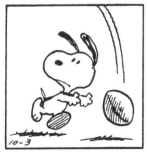

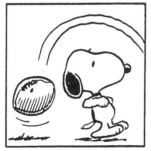

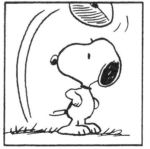

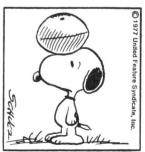

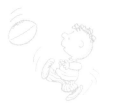

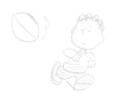

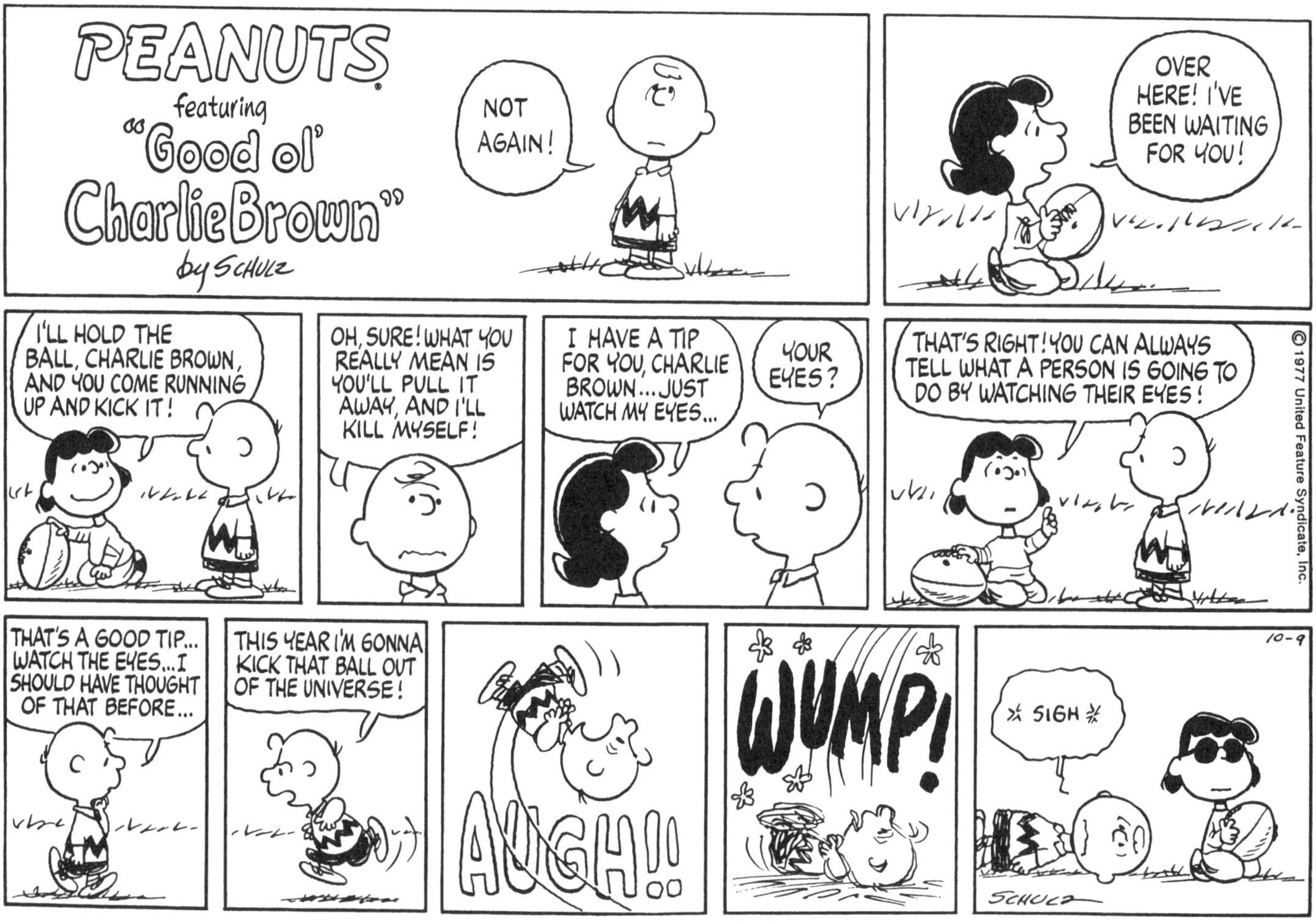
PEANUTS
featuring "Good ol' Charlie Brown"
by SCHULZ
NOT AGAIN!
OVER HERE! I'VE BEEN WAITING FOR YOU!
I'LL HOLD THE BALL, CHARLIE BROWN, AND YOU COME RUNNING UP AND KICK IT!
OH, SURE! WHAT YOU REALLY MEAN IS YOU'LL PULL IT AWAY, AND I'LL KILL MYSELF!
I HAVE A TIP FOR YOU, CHARLIE BROWN... JUST WATCH MY EYES...
YOUR EYES?
THAT'S RIGHT! YOU CAN ALWAYS TELL WHAT A PERSON IS GOING TO DO BY WATCHING THEIR EYES!
© 1977 United Feature Syndicate, Inc.
THAT'S A GOOD TIP... WATCH THE EYES... I SHOULD HAVE THOUGHT OF THAT BEFORE...
THIS YEAR I'M GONNA KICK THAT BALL OUT OF THE UNIVERSE!
AUGH!!
WUMP!
10-9
SIGH
SCHULZ

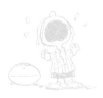

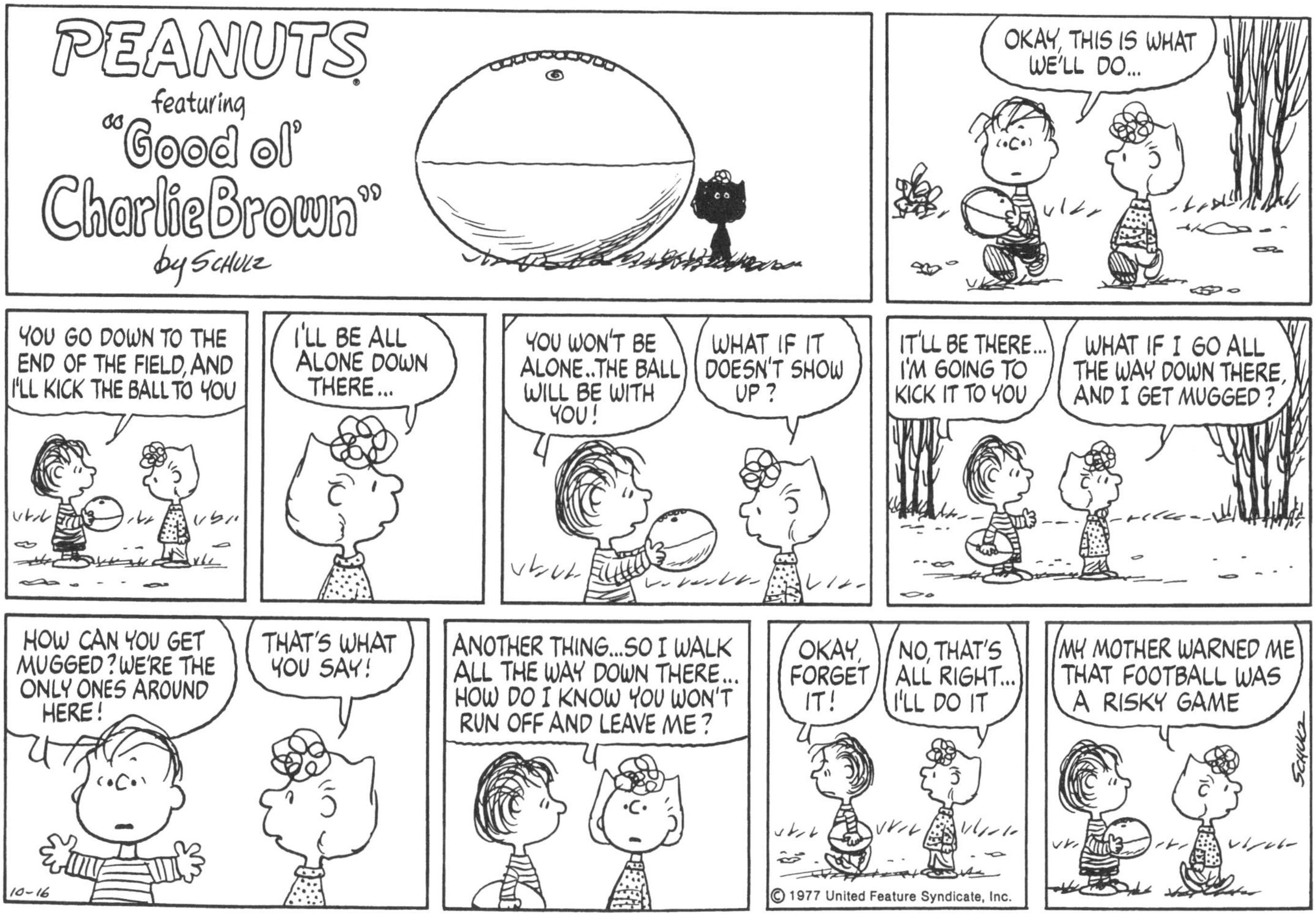
PEANUTS
featuring "Good ol' CharlieBrown"
by SCHULZ
OKAY, THIS IS WHAT WE'LL DO...
YOU GO DOWN TO THE END OF THE FIELD, AND I'LL KICK THE BALL TO YOU
I'LL BE ALL ALONE DOWN THERE...
YOU WON'T BE ALONE..THE BALL WILL BE WITH YOU!
WHAT IF IT DOESN'T SHOW UP?
IT'LL BE THERE... I'M GOING TO KICK IT TO YOU
WHAT IF I GO ALL THE WAY DOWN THERE, AND I GET MUGGED?
HOW CAN YOU GET MUGGED? WE'RE THE ONLY ONES AROUND HERE!
THAT'S WHAT YOU SAY!
10-16
ANOTHER THING...SO I WALK ALL THE WAY DOWN THERE... HOW DO I KNOW YOU WON'T RUN OFF AND LEAVE ME?
OKAY, FORGET IT!
NO, THAT'S ALL RIGHT... I'LL DO IT
© 1977 United Feature Syndicate, Inc.
MY MOTHER WARNED ME THAT FOOTBALL WAS A RISKY GAME
SCHULZ

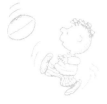

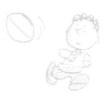

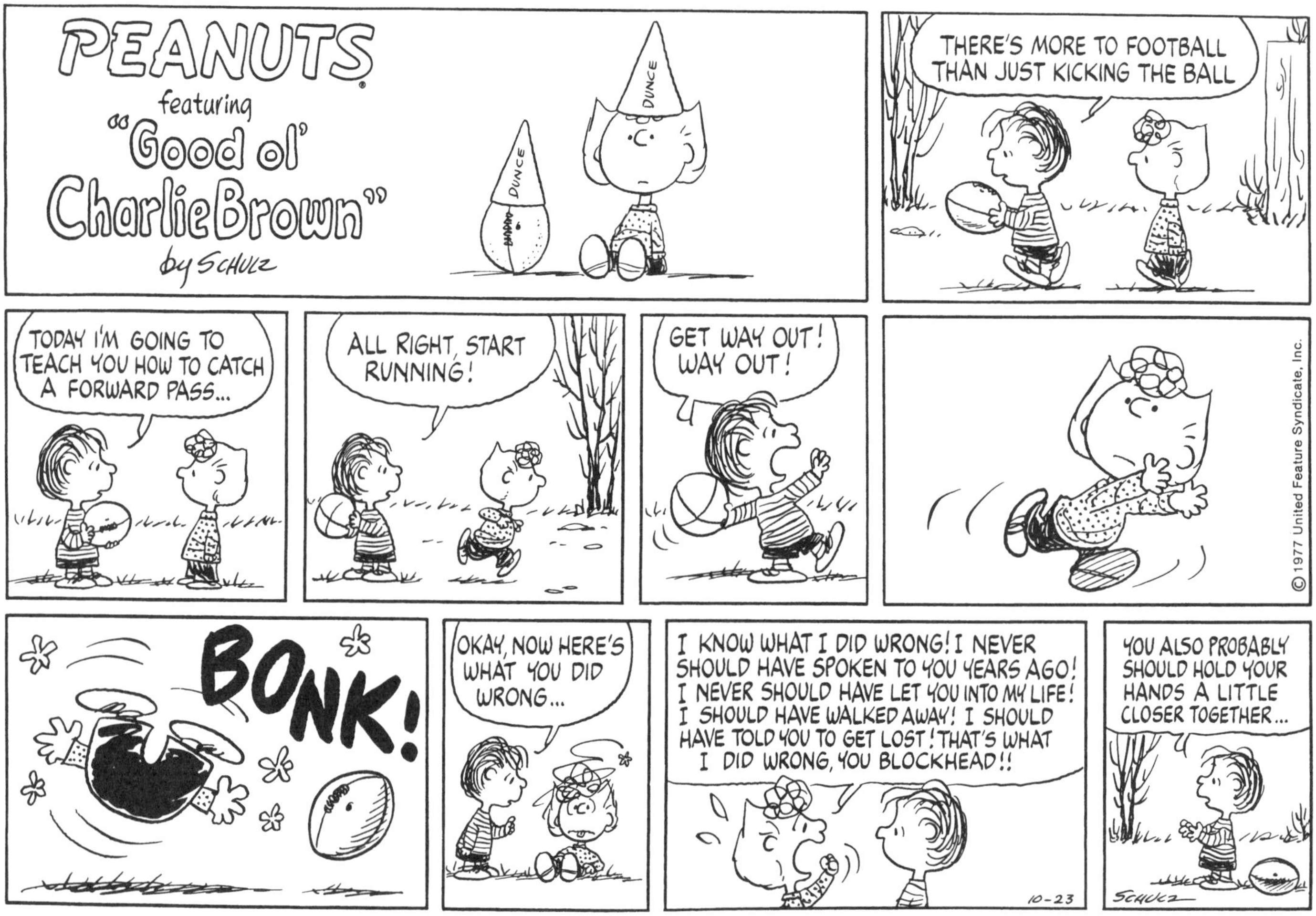
PEANUTS
featuring "Good ol' Charlie Brown"
by SCHULZ
DUNCE
DUNCE
THERE'S MORE TO FOOTBALL THAN JUST KICKING THE BALL
TODAY I'M GOING TO TEACH YOU HOW TO CATCH A FORWARD PASS...
ALL RIGHT, START RUNNING!
GET WAY OUT! WAY OUT!
© 1977 United Feature Syndicate, Inc.
BONK!
OKAY, NOW HERE'S WHAT YOU DID WRONG...
I KNOW WHAT I DID WRONG! I NEVER SHOULD HAVE SPOKEN TO YOU YEARS AGO! I NEVER SHOULD HAVE LET YOU INTO MY LIFE! I SHOULD HAVE WALKED AWAY! I SHOULD HAVE TOLD YOU TO GET LOST! THAT'S WHAT I DID WRONG, YOU BLOCKHEAD!!
10-23
YOU ALSO PROBABLY SHOULD HOLD YOUR HANDS A LITTLE CLOSER TOGETHER...
SCHULZ

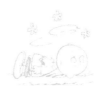

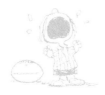

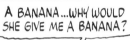

PEANUTS featuring "Good ol' Charlie Brown" by SCHULZ

OVER HERE!

I DON'T BELIEVE IT...

I HAVE A BONUS FOR YOU, CHARLIE BROWN...

A BONUS?

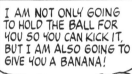

I AM **NOT** ONLY GOING TO HOLD THE BALL FOR YOU SO YOU CAN KICK IT, BUT I AM ALSO GOING TO GIVE YOU A BANANA!

A BANANA...WHY WOULD SHE GIVE ME A BANANA?

OH, WELL, IF SOMEONE GIVES YOU A BANANA, I GUESS YOU HAVE TO TRUST HER

GET READY, BALL! YOU'RE GOING TO THE MOON!

10-1

AAUGH!

WHAM!

BANANAS ARE HIGH IN POTASSIUM, CHARLIE BROWN, WHICH PROMOTES HEALING OF MUSCLES!

SCHULZ

© 1978 United Feature Syndicate, Inc.

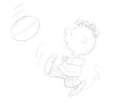

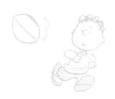

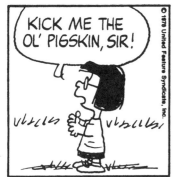

KICK ME THE OL' PIGSKIN, SIR!
© 1978 United Feature Syndicate, Inc.
I HATE TO DISILLUSION YOU, MARCIE...
11-7
THIS BALL ISN'T MADE OUT OF PIGSKIN... IT'S PLASTIC..
KICK ME THE OL' PLASTIC, SIR!
SCHULZ

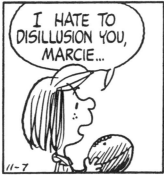

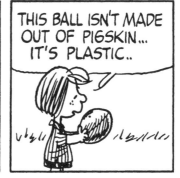

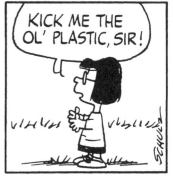

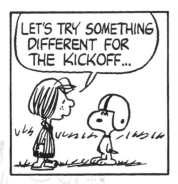

LET'S TRY SOMETHING DIFFERENT FOR THE KICKOFF...
INSTEAD OF HAVING SOMEONE HOLD THE BALL WITH HIS FINGER, LET'S USE A KICKING TEE...
11-8
A KICKING TEE...RIGHT!
© 1978 United Feature Syndicate, Inc.
SCHULZ

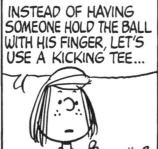

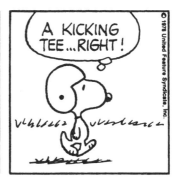

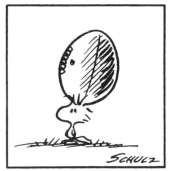

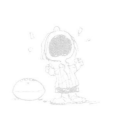

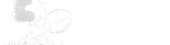

GO ALL THE WAY DOWN THE FIELD, MARCIE...

I'LL HIT YOU WITH A PASS

© 1978 United Feature Syndicate, Inc.

11-9

WE'VE ALWAYS BEEN FRIENDS, SIR...WHY WOULD YOU WANT TO HIT ME?

BOOT!

11-11

© 1978 United Feature Syndicate, Inc.

BONK!

THAT'S GONNA CUT DOWN ON THE ENDORSEMENTS

CHARLIE BROWN, I KNOW YOU CAN'T HEAR ME, BUT I WANT TO MAKE YOU A PROMISE...
7-27
IF YOU GET WELL, I PROMISE I'LL NEVER PULL THE FOOTBALL AWAY AGAIN!
THAT'S QUITE A PROMISE
I'LL BET HE FEELS BETTER ALREADY!
© 1979 United Feature Syndicate, Inc.

LET ME GET THIS STRAIGHT
IF CHARLIE BROWN GETS WELL, YOU PROMISE NEVER TO PULL THE FOOTBALL AWAY AGAIN?
7-28
THAT IS MY SOLEMN PROMISE!
HE'S SURE TO GET WELL NOW.. HE HAS SOMETHING TO LIVE FOR!
© 1979 United Feature Syndicate, Inc.

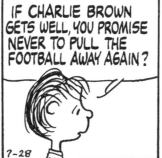

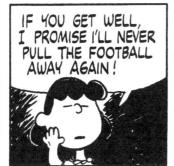

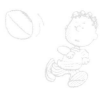

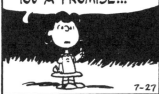

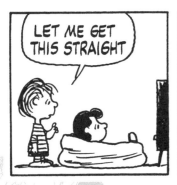

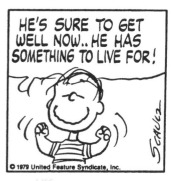

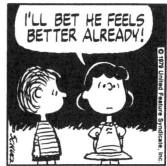

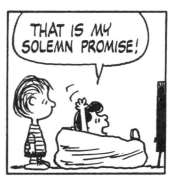

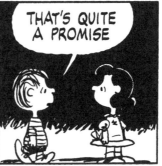

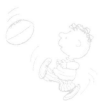

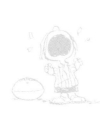

Panel 1:
KNOCK KNOCK KNOCK

Panel 2:
7-30
© 1979 United Feature Syndicate, Inc.

Panel 3:
CHARLIE BROWN! YOU'RE BACK!! YOU'RE WELL!

Panel 4:
I HEARD SOMETHING ABOUT A PROMISE..

OH, GOOD GRIEF!

Panel 5:
YOU HOLD THE BALL, AND I'LL COME RUNNING UP AND KICK IT

© 1979 United Feature Syndicate, Inc.

Panel 6:
REMEMBER, YOU PROMISED THAT IF I GOT WELL, YOU'D NEVER PULL THE FOOTBALL AWAY AGAIN

7-31

Panel 7:
CAN'T I CHANGE MY MIND?

NO, YOU CAN'T BREAK A PROMISE TO A SICK FRIEND

Panel 8:
HA! NOW, WHAT ARE YOU GONNA DO?

QUIET! I'M THINKING!

Panel 1: THIS TIME I'M REALLY GONNA KICK THAT FOOTBALL!

Panel 2: YOU'RE CRAZY, CHARLIE BROWN! SHE'LL PULL IT AWAY LIKE SHE ALWAYS DOES! DON'T TRUST HER!

Panel 3: BUT SHE PROMISED SHE'D NEVER PULL IT AWAY AGAIN IF I GOT WELL..

© 1979 United Feature Syndicate, Inc.

8-1

Panel 4: I FEEL GREAT! HERE I GO!! — I CAN'T LOOK..

SCHULZ

Panel 5: © 1979 United Feature Syndicate, Inc.

8-2

Panel 6: AAUGH!

Panel 7: MY FINGER! MY HAND! MY ARM!

Panel 8: YOU MISSED THE BALL, YOU BLOCKHEAD! YOU KICKED MY FINGER! YOU KICKED MY HAND!! — OW! OW! OW!

SCHULZ

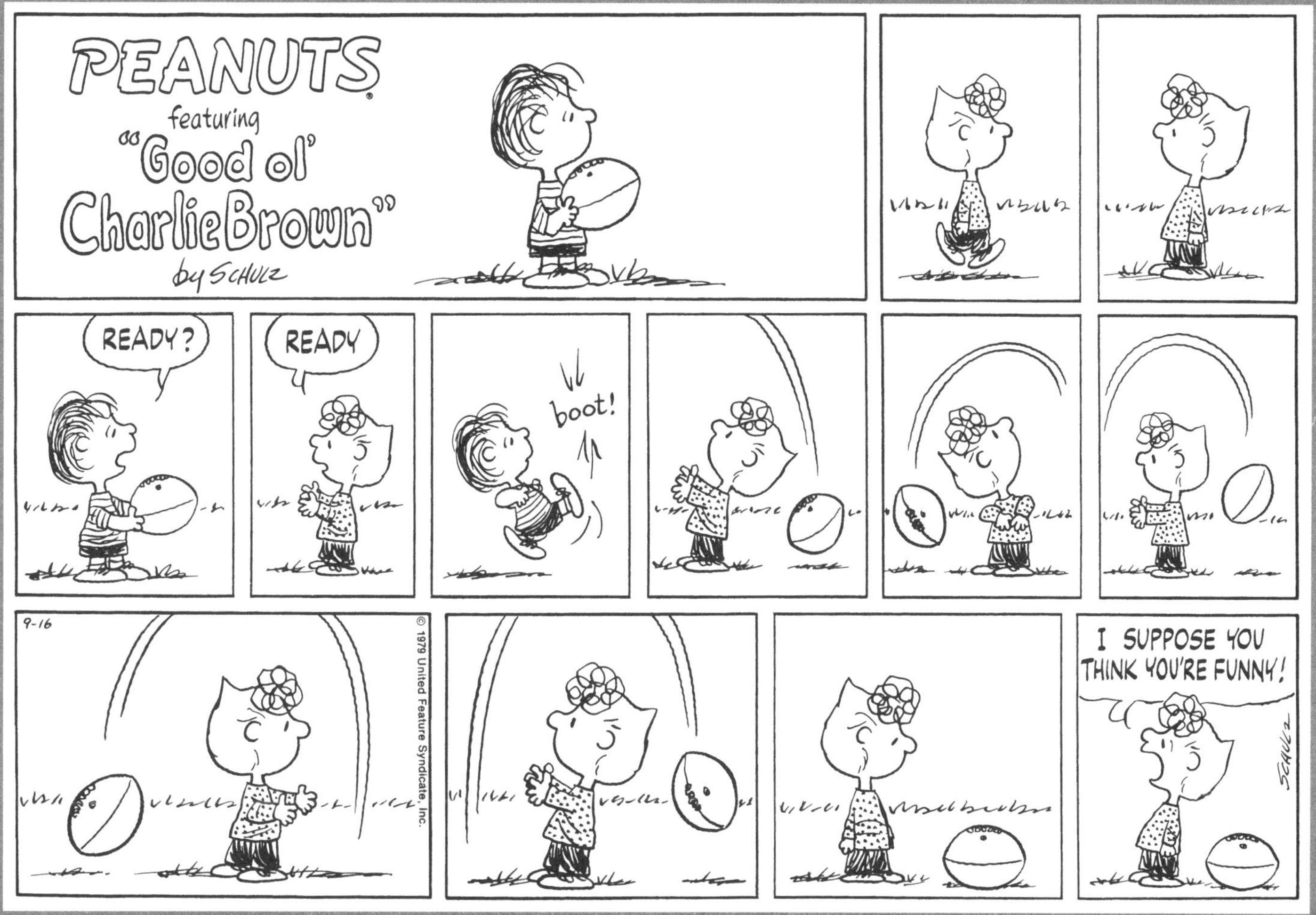
PEANUTS
featuring
"Good ol' CharlieBrown"
by SCHULZ
READY?
READY
boot!
9-16
© 1979 United Feature Syndicate, Inc.
I SUPPOSE YOU THINK YOU'RE FUNNY!
SCHULZ

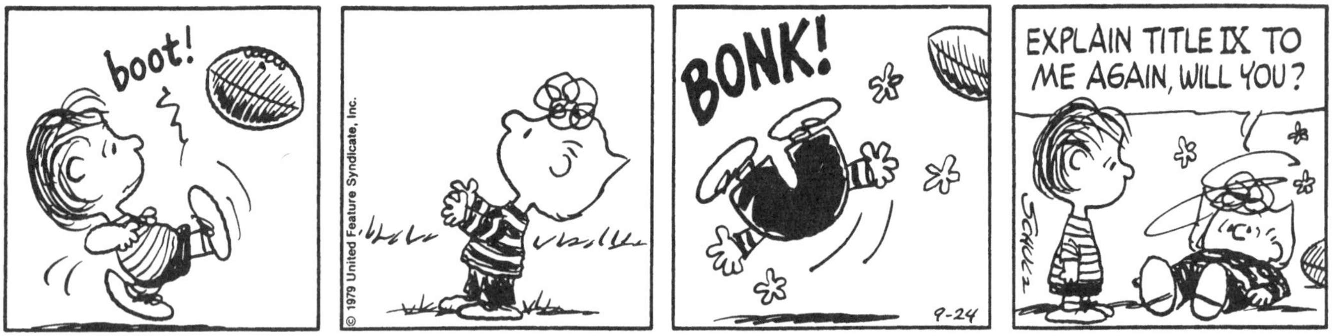
boot!
© 1979 United Feature Syndicate, Inc.
BONK!
9-24
EXPLAIN TITLE IX TO ME AGAIN, WILL YOU?
SCHULZ

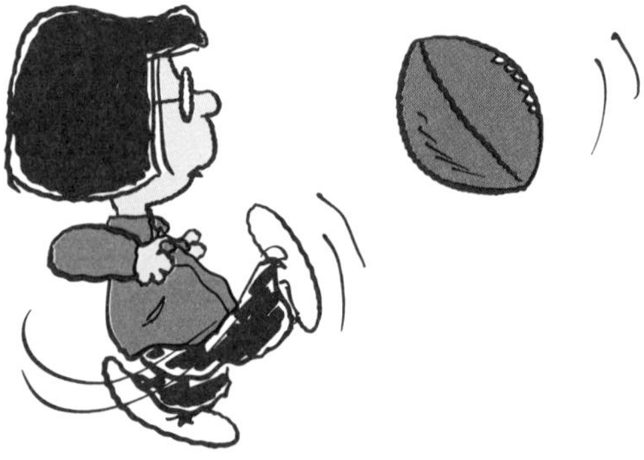

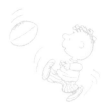

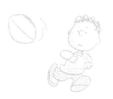

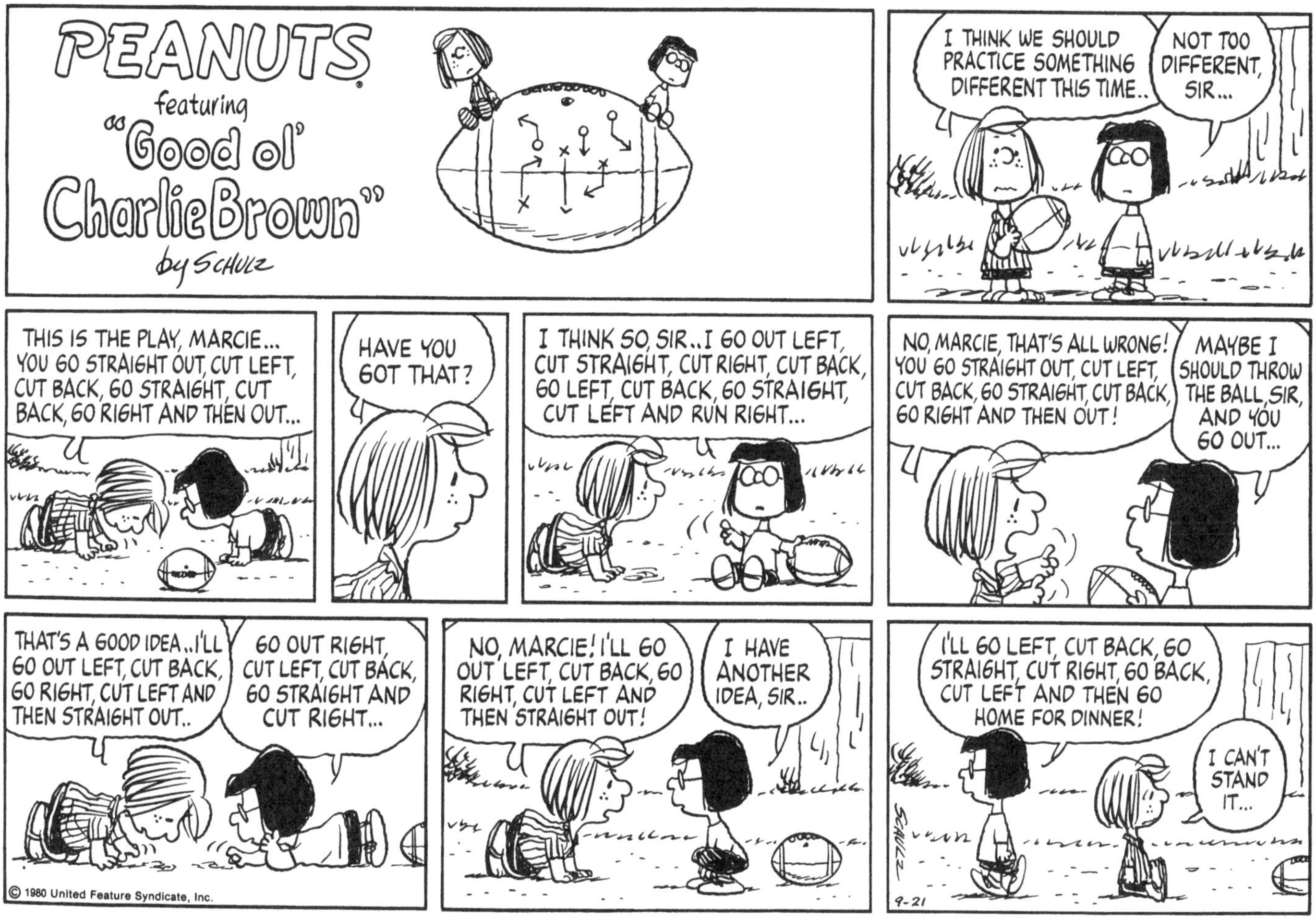
PEANUTS
featuring "Good ol' CharlieBrown"
by SCHULZ
I THINK WE SHOULD PRACTICE SOMETHING DIFFERENT THIS TIME..
NOT TOO DIFFERENT, SIR...
THIS IS THE PLAY, MARCIE... YOU GO STRAIGHT OUT, CUT LEFT, CUT BACK, GO STRAIGHT, CUT BACK, GO RIGHT AND THEN OUT...
HAVE YOU GOT THAT?
I THINK SO, SIR..I GO OUT LEFT, CUT STRAIGHT, CUT RIGHT, CUT BACK, GO LEFT, CUT BACK, GO STRAIGHT, CUT LEFT AND RUN RIGHT...
NO, MARCIE, THAT'S ALL WRONG! YOU GO STRAIGHT OUT, CUT LEFT, CUT BACK, GO STRAIGHT, CUT BACK, GO RIGHT AND THEN OUT!
MAYBE I SHOULD THROW THE BALL, SIR, AND YOU GO OUT...
THAT'S A GOOD IDEA..I'LL GO OUT LEFT, CUT BACK, GO RIGHT, CUT LEFT AND THEN STRAIGHT OUT..
GO OUT RIGHT, CUT LEFT, CUT BACK, GO STRAIGHT AND CUT RIGHT...
NO, MARCIE! I'LL GO OUT LEFT, CUT BACK, GO RIGHT, CUT LEFT AND THEN STRAIGHT OUT!
I HAVE ANOTHER IDEA, SIR..
I'LL GO LEFT, CUT BACK, GO STRAIGHT, CUT RIGHT, GO BACK, CUT LEFT AND THEN GO HOME FOR DINNER!
I CAN'T STAND IT...
SCHULZ
9-21
© 1980 United Feature Syndicate, Inc.

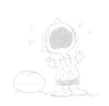

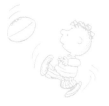

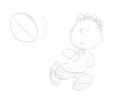

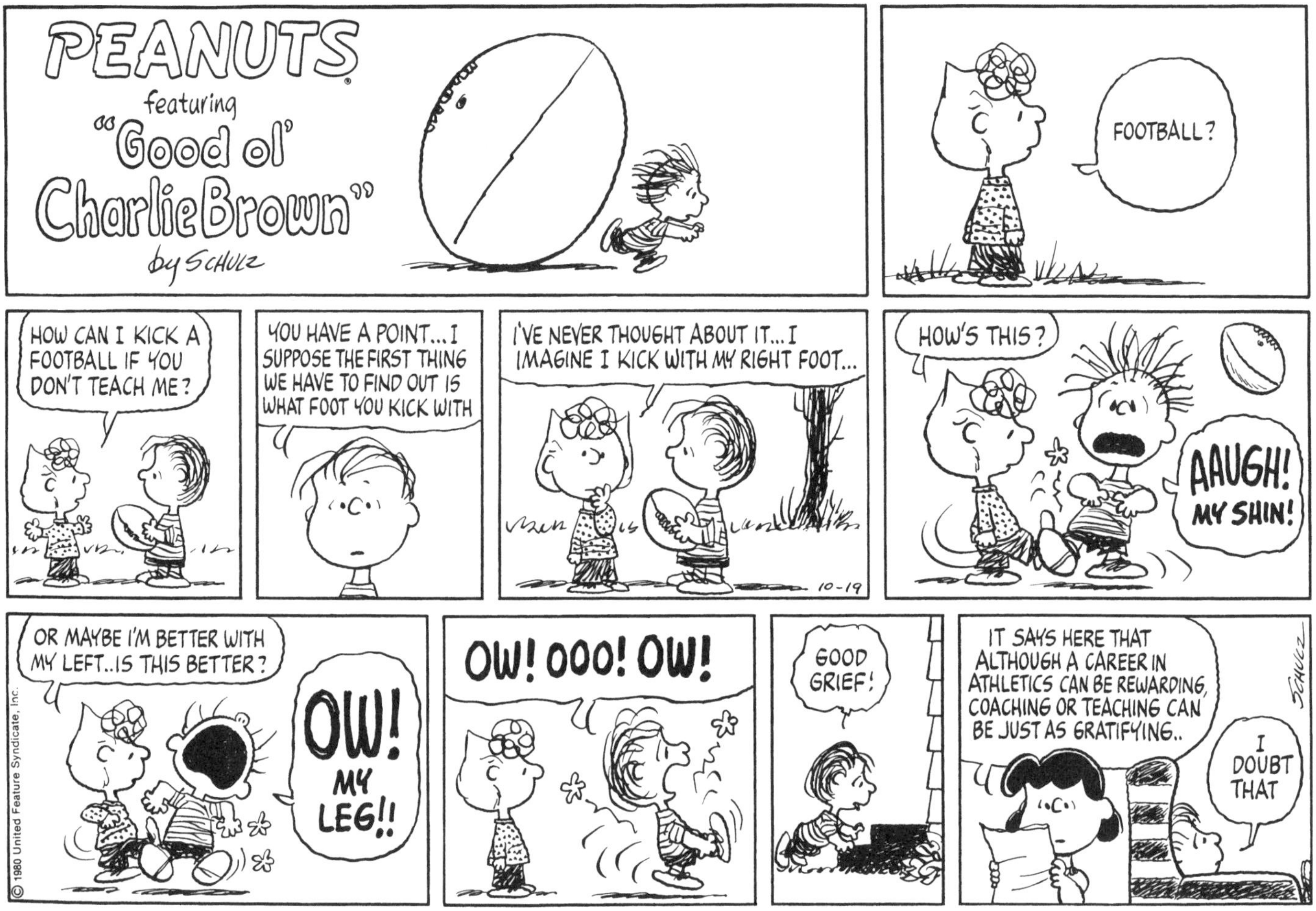
PEANUTS
featuring "Good ol' CharlieBrown"
by SCHULZ
FOOTBALL?
HOW CAN I KICK A FOOTBALL IF YOU DON'T TEACH ME?
YOU HAVE A POINT... I SUPPOSE THE FIRST THING WE HAVE TO FIND OUT IS WHAT FOOT YOU KICK WITH
I'VE NEVER THOUGHT ABOUT IT... I IMAGINE I KICK WITH MY RIGHT FOOT...
10-19
HOW'S THIS?
AAUGH! MY SHIN!
OR MAYBE I'M BETTER WITH MY LEFT..IS THIS BETTER?
OW! MY LEG!!
© 1980 United Feature Syndicate, Inc.
OW! OOO! OW!
GOOD GRIEF!
IT SAYS HERE THAT ALTHOUGH A CAREER IN ATHLETICS CAN BE REWARDING, COACHING OR TEACHING CAN BE JUST AS GRATIFYING..
I DOUBT THAT
SCHULZ

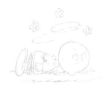

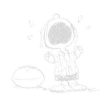

PEANUTS featuring "Good ol' CharlieBrown" by SCHULZ

ECCLESIASTES.. THIRD CHAPTER..

AH! JUST THE PERSON I WANTED TO SEE...

"TO EVERY THING THERE IS A SEASON," CHARLIE BROWN...

"A TIME TO BE BORN, AND A TIME TO DIE"

"A TIME TO PLANT, AND A TIME TO PLUCK UP THAT WHICH IS PLANTED"

"A TIME TO WEEP, AND A TIME TO LAUGH.. A TIME TO MOURN, AND A TIME TO DANCE.."

11-16

"A TIME TO LOVE, AND A TIME TO HATE.. A TIME OF WAR, AND A TIME OF PEACE"

© 1980 United Feature Syndicate, Inc.

AAUGH!

WHAM!

AND A TIME TO PULL AWAY THE FOOTBALL

SCHULZ

Panel 1: MY GRANDFATHER SAYS LIFE IS A LOT LIKE A FOOTBALL GAME...

3-7

Panel 2: DOES HE FEEL LIKE HE'S IN THE FOURTH QUARTER?

Panel 3: WORSE THAN THAT..

© 1981 United Feature Syndicate, Inc.

Panel 4: HE'S AFRAID HE DOESN'T HAVE ANY MORE "TIME OUTS"

120

PEANUTS
featuring
"Good ol' CharlieBrown"
by SCHULZ

WELL, SURE.. TRY IT IF YOU THINK IT'LL HELP...

BOOT!

9-27

© 1981 United Feature Syndicate, Inc.

BONK!

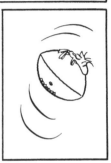

BUMP!

BONK!

THEN AGAIN, MAYBE YOU SHOULDN'T USE QUITE SO MUCH "STICKUM"

BOOT!

BONK!

BUT THAT'S THE NAME OF THE GAME... "BOOTBONK"!

I DON'T THINK HE BELIEVED ME

11-5

© 1981 United Feature Syndicate, Inc.

OKAY, MARCIE, WE'RE GONNA PRACTICE THE OL' STATUE OF LIBERTY PLAY...

YOU FADE BACK TO PASS, AND I COME RUNNING AROUND AND GRAB THE BALL

11-6 © 1981 United Feature Syndicate, Inc.

MARCIE! YOU'RE SUPPOSED TO LET GO OF THE BALL!

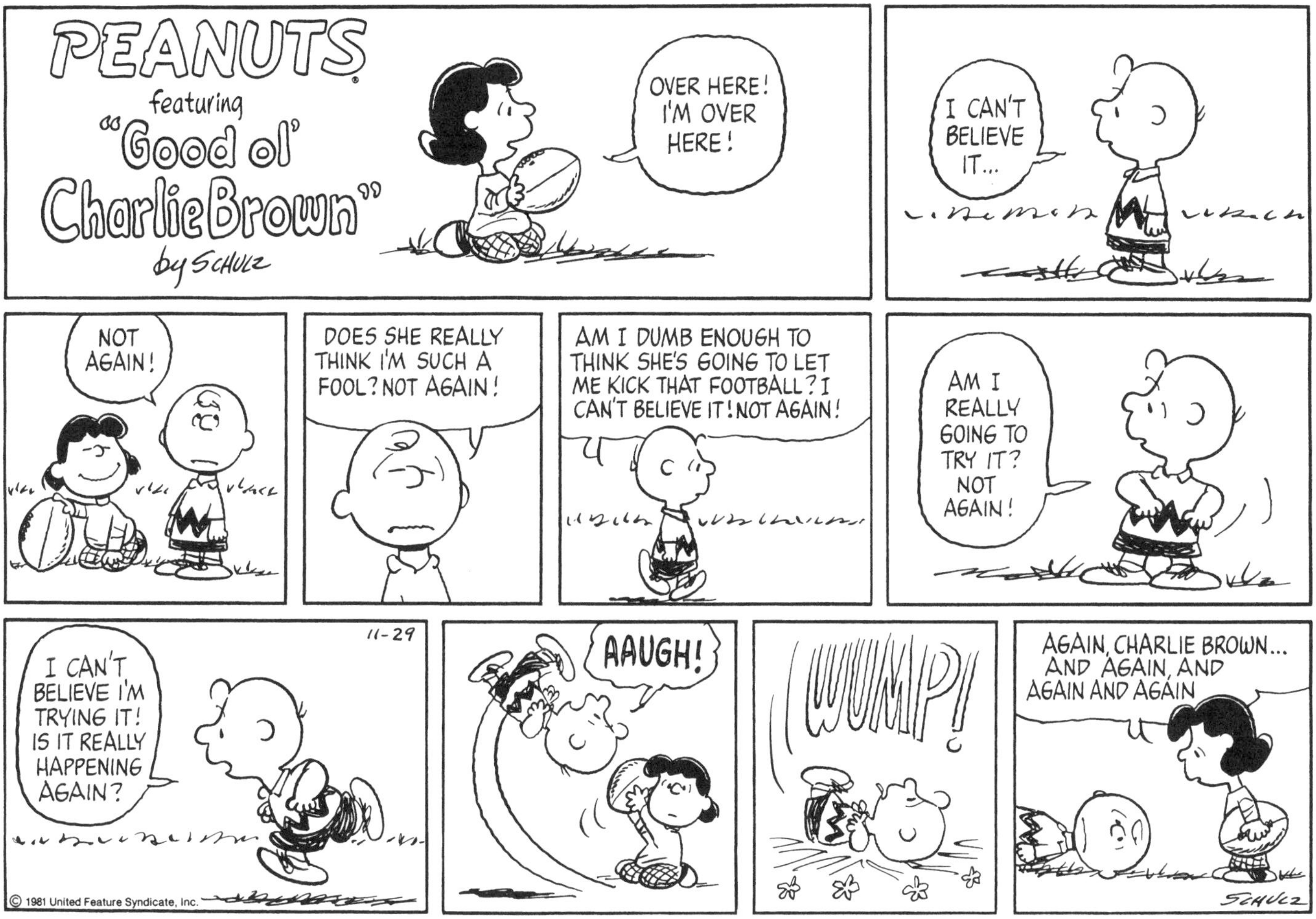
PEANUTS
featuring "Good ol' CharlieBrown"
by SCHULZ
OVER HERE! I'M OVER HERE!
I CAN'T BELIEVE IT...
NOT AGAIN!
DOES SHE REALLY THINK I'M SUCH A FOOL? NOT AGAIN!
AM I DUMB ENOUGH TO THINK SHE'S GOING TO LET ME KICK THAT FOOTBALL? I CAN'T BELIEVE IT! NOT AGAIN!
AM I REALLY GOING TO TRY IT? NOT AGAIN!
11-29
I CAN'T BELIEVE I'M TRYING IT! IS IT REALLY HAPPENING AGAIN?
© 1981 United Feature Syndicate, Inc.
AAUGH!
WUMP!
AGAIN, CHARLIE BROWN... AND AGAIN, AND AGAIN AND AGAIN
SCHULZ

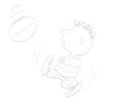

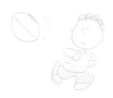

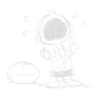

PEANUTS
featuring "Good ol' CharlieBrown"
by SCHULZ
I'M READY.. THE BALL'S READY.. ARE YOU READY?
YES, MARCIE, I'M READY! I'VE BEEN READY FOR TWENTY MINUTES!
DO FOOTBALLS MIND BEING KICKED, SIR? DO YOU THINK IT CAUSES THEM TO BE TRAUMATIZED?
PLEASE, MARCIE.. JUST KICK THE BALL!
LOOK WHAT HAPPENED, SIR.. I KICKED THE BALL, AND MY SHOE CAME OFF!
© 1982 United Feature Syndicate, Inc.
AND NOW LOOK WHAT HAPPENED, SIR! HEE HEE! I ACCIDENTALLY TIED MY SHOE WITH THE LACES ON THE FOOTBALL!
9-12
IS THAT MY MOTHER CALLING ME? IT MUST BE SUPPERTIME
I GUESS I'LL JUST HAVE TO HOP ALL THE WAY HOME
I HATE PLAYING WITH YOU, MARCIE!!
SCHULZ

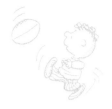

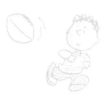

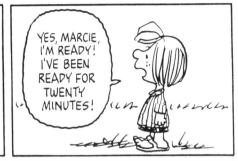

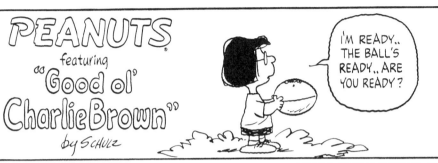

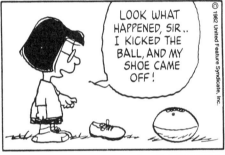

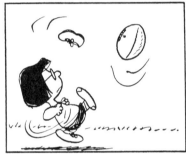

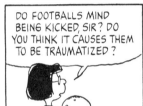

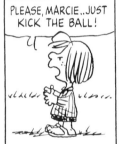

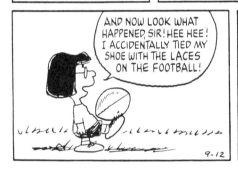

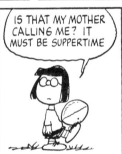

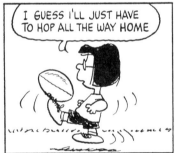

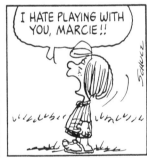

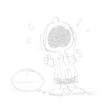

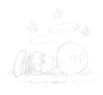

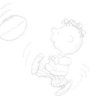

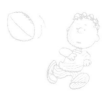

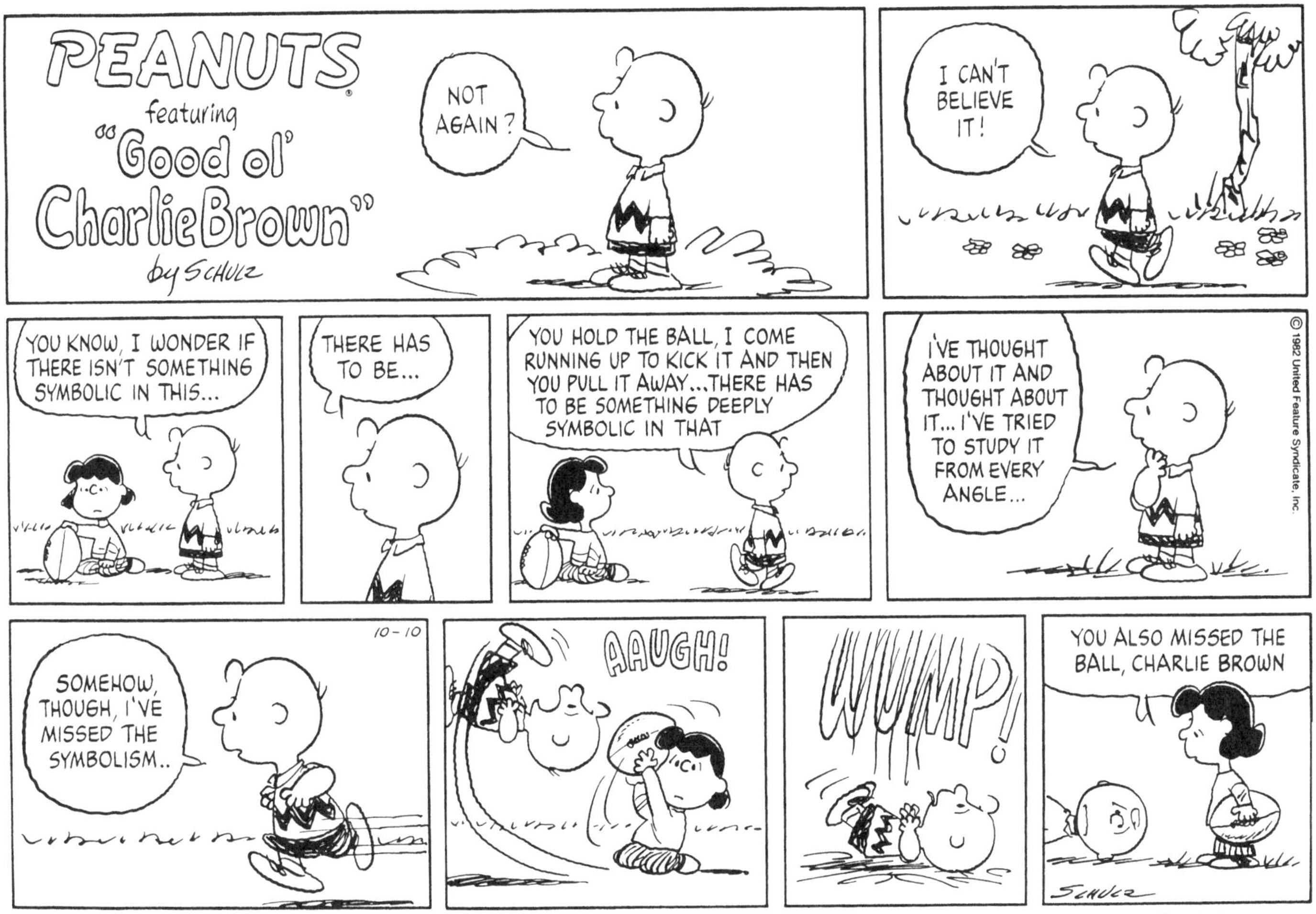
PEANUTS
featuring
"Good ol' CharlieBrown"
by SCHULZ
NOT AGAIN?
I CAN'T BELIEVE IT!
YOU KNOW, I WONDER IF THERE ISN'T SOMETHING SYMBOLIC IN THIS...
THERE HAS TO BE...
YOU HOLD THE BALL, I COME RUNNING UP TO KICK IT AND THEN YOU PULL IT AWAY...THERE HAS TO BE SOMETHING DEEPLY SYMBOLIC IN THAT
I'VE THOUGHT ABOUT IT AND THOUGHT ABOUT IT... I'VE TRIED TO STUDY IT FROM EVERY ANGLE...
© 1962 United Feature Syndicate, Inc.
10-10
SOMEHOW, THOUGH, I'VE MISSED THE SYMBOLISM..
AAUGH!
WUMP!
YOU ALSO MISSED THE BALL, CHARLIE BROWN
SCHULZ

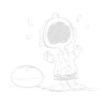

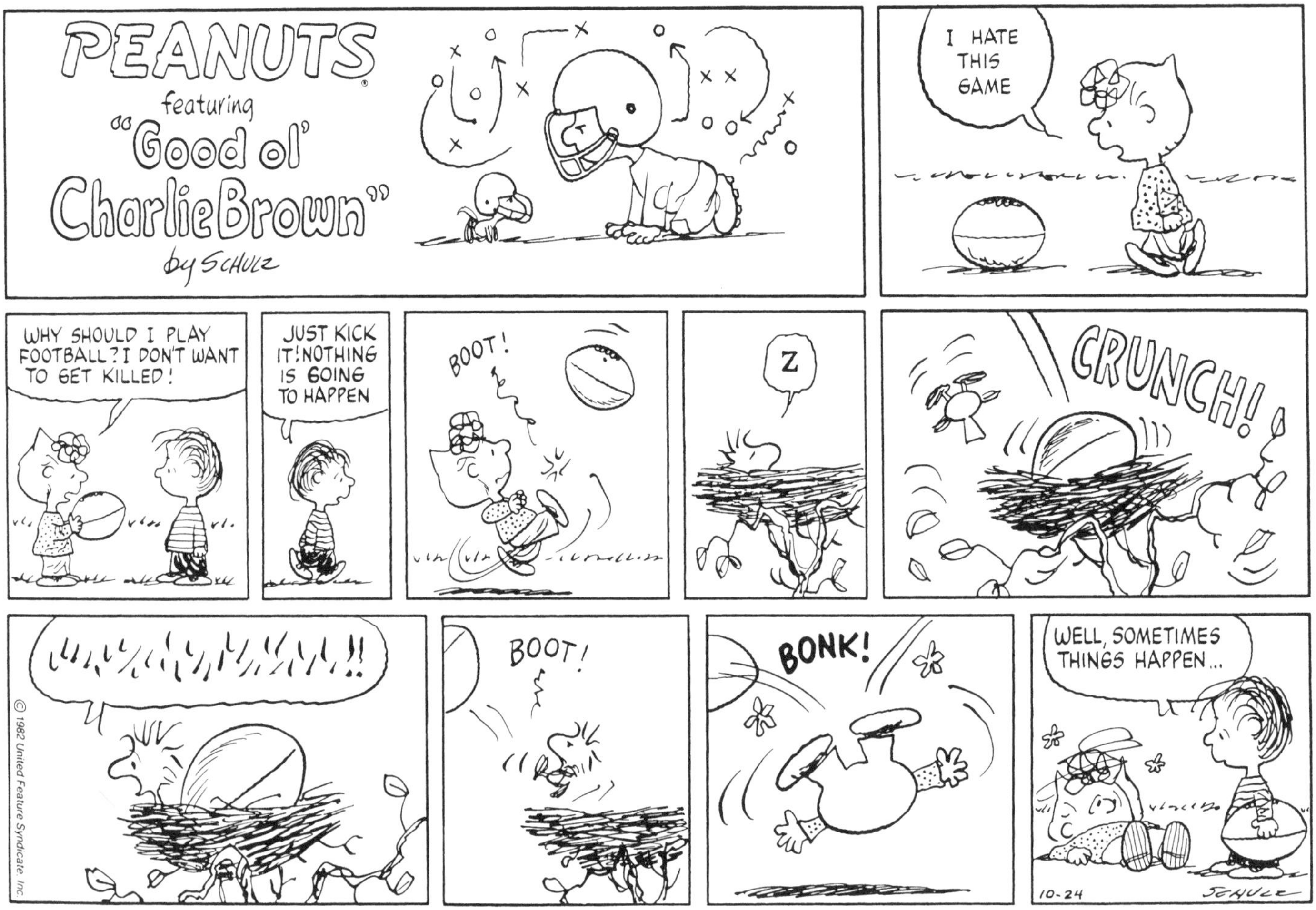
PEANUTS
featuring
"Good ol' CharlieBrown"
by SCHULZ
I HATE THIS GAME
WHY SHOULD I PLAY FOOTBALL? I DON'T WANT TO GET KILLED!
JUST KICK IT! NOTHING IS GOING TO HAPPEN
BOOT!
Z
CRUNCH!
BOOT!
BONK!
WELL, SOMETIMES THINGS HAPPEN...
© 1982 United Feature Syndicate, Inc.
10-24
SCHULZ

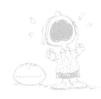

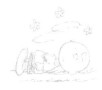

PEANUTS featuring "Good ol' Charlie Brown" by SCHULZ

WHAT AM I SUPPOSED TO DO WITH THIS?

WHY DO I HAVE TO EXPLAIN EVERYTHING?

I HATE FOOTBALL, SIR...

JUST THROW THE BALL TO ME, MARCIE, WHEN I GET DOWN THE FIELD...

BONK!

DID YOU SEE THAT, SIR? I THREW THE BALL, AND IT CAME RIGHT BACK TO ME!

MARCIE! I TOLD YOU TO WAIT 'TIL I GOT DOWN THE FIELD!!

10-2

BONK!

© 1983 United Feature Syndicate, Inc.

IT DID IT AGAIN, SIR! DID YOU SEE THAT? I THREW THE BALL, AND IT CAME RIGHT BACK TO ME!

I CHANGED MY MIND, SIR...THIS GAME IS A LOT OF FUN...

I CAN'T STAND IT...

SCHULZ

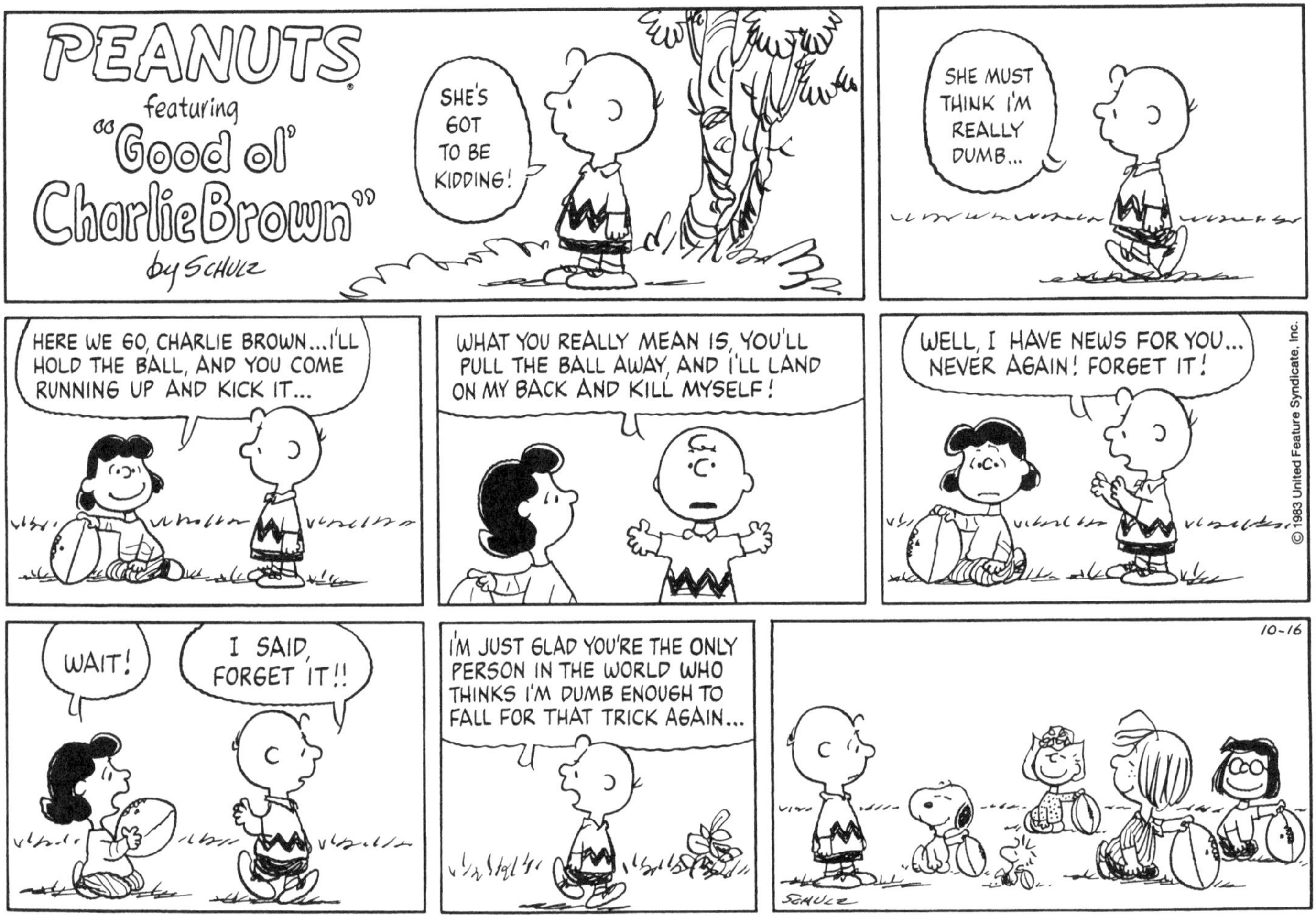
PEANUTS®
featuring "Good ol' CharlieBrown"
by SCHULZ
SHE'S GOT TO BE KIDDING!
SHE MUST THINK I'M REALLY DUMB...
HERE WE GO, CHARLIE BROWN...I'LL HOLD THE BALL, AND YOU COME RUNNING UP AND KICK IT...
WHAT YOU REALLY MEAN IS, YOU'LL PULL THE BALL AWAY, AND I'LL LAND ON MY BACK AND KILL MYSELF!
WELL, I HAVE NEWS FOR YOU... NEVER AGAIN! FORGET IT!
© 1983 United Feature Syndicate, Inc.
WAIT!
I SAID, FORGET IT!!
I'M JUST GLAD YOU'RE THE ONLY PERSON IN THE WORLD WHO THINKS I'M DUMB ENOUGH TO FALL FOR THAT TRICK AGAIN...
10-16
SCHULZ

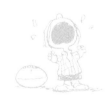

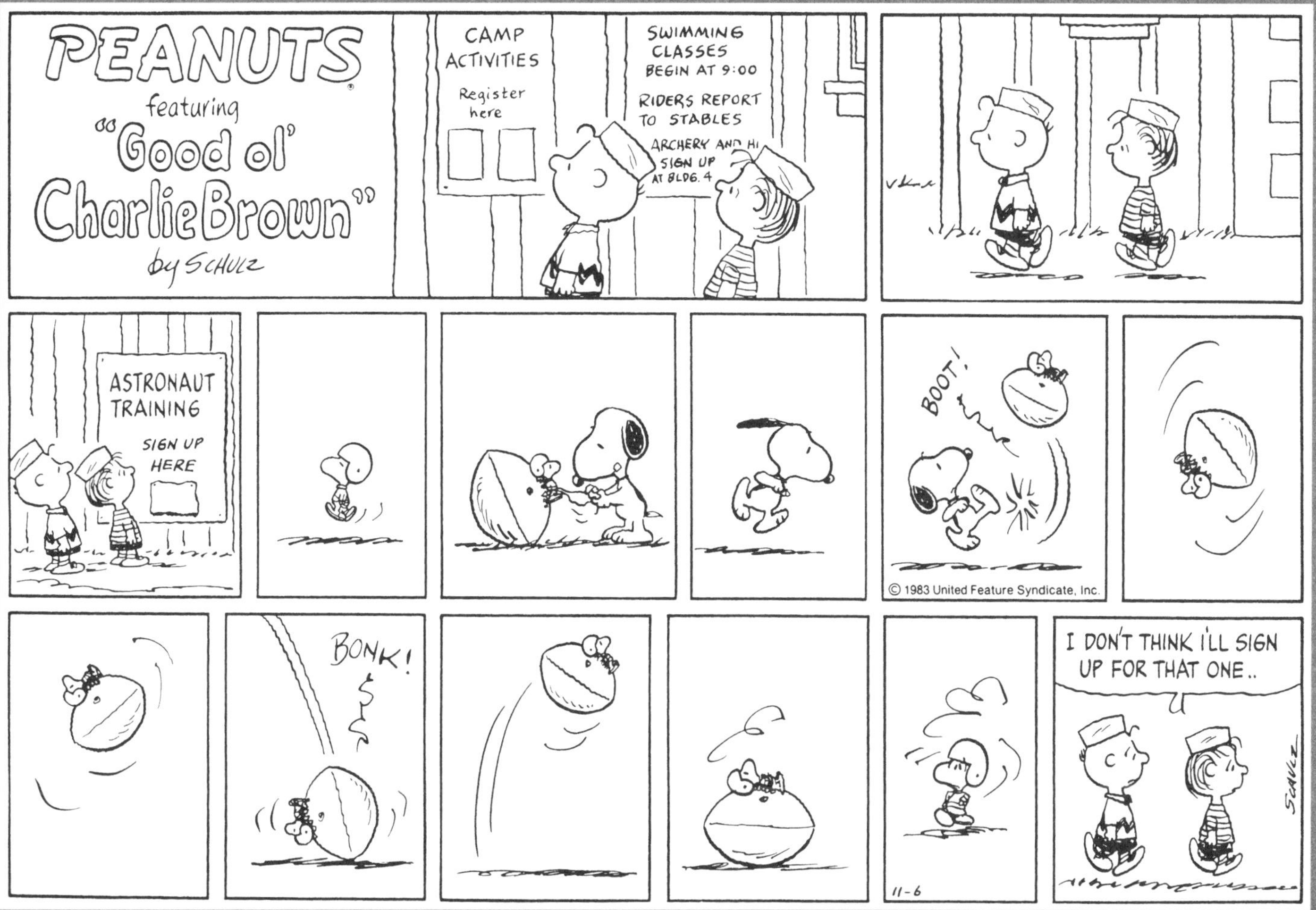
PEANUTS
featuring
"Good ol' CharlieBrown"
by SCHULZ
CAMP ACTIVITIES
Register here
SWIMMING CLASSES BEGIN AT 9:00
RIDERS REPORT TO STABLES
ARCHERY AND HI
SIGN UP AT BLDG. 4
ASTRONAUT TRAINING
SIGN UP HERE
BOOT!
© 1983 United Feature Syndicate, Inc.
BONK!
11-6
I DON'T THINK I'LL SIGN UP FOR THAT ONE..
SCHULZ

Panel 1: I'VE BEEN WATCHING AN EXCITING FOOTBALL GAME..THE CONGREGATION IS GOING WILD...

Panel 2: FOOTBALL GAMES HAVE FANS.. CHURCHES HAVE CONGREGATIONS..CONCERTS HAVE AUDIENCES...

Panel 3: COURTROOMS HAVE SPECTATORS..RIOTS HAVE MOBS AND ACCIDENTS HAVE ONLOOKERS...

Panel 4: THE CONGREGATION JUST TORE DOWN THE GOAL POSTS!

11-17 © 1983 United Feature Syndicate, Inc.

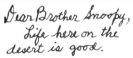

Panel 1: Dear Brother Snoopy, Life here on the desert is good.

3-20

Panel 2: I read a lot and go on long walks.

Panel 3: When there is nothing else to do, I practice a few field goals.

© 1984 United Feature Syndicate, Inc.

Panel 4: SCHULZ

I USED TO WONDER WHY I HATED THE KICKOFF..NOW I KNOW

© 1984 United Feature Syndicate, Inc.   9-26

boot! boot!
boot!
boot!
boot!

MY ARMS GET TIRED!

YOU NEED TO PRACTICE YOUR TACKLING, MARCIE

I'LL COME RUNNING BY YOU, AND YOU TRY TO GRAB ME BEFORE I GET TO THE GOAL LINE...

10-10   © 1984 United Feature Syndicate, Inc.

I HATE PLAYING WITH YOU, MARCIE!

© 1984 United Feature Syndicate, Inc.

Panel 1: MARCIE, YOU DON'T TACKLE ANOTHER PLAYER BY GRABBING HER HAIR!

Panel 2: WHAT DO I GRAB, SIR? / JUST DON'T GRAB MY HAIR!

Panel 3: OKAY, TRY IT AGAIN... HERE I COME!

10-11

Panel 4: SCHULZ

Panel 5: MARCIE, YOU CAN'T PLAY FOOTBALL WHILE YOU'RE WEARING GLASSES..

Panel 6: I'LL TAKE THEM OFF AND PUT THEM RIGHT HERE...HOW'S THAT?

Panel 7: OKAY, HERE I COME AGAIN... SEE IF YOU CAN TACKLE ME...

10-12

© 1984 United Feature Syndicate, Inc.

Panel 8: GOTCHA, SIR!

SCHULZ

HI, CHUCK..HOW'VE YOU BEEN? MARCIE'S DRIVING ME CRAZY..SHE'LL NEVER BE A FOOTBALL PLAYER..
SOME PEOPLE JUST NEVER LEARN, DO THEY, CHUCK?
© 1984 United Feature Syndicate, Inc.
CHARLIE BROWN...♫♫ C'MON OUTSIDE...I'LL HOLD THE BALL, AND YOU KICK IT...
10-13
NO, WE DON'T
SCHULZ

WHERE'S THE FOOTBALL GAME?
I THOUGHT THERE WAS FOOTBALL ON THURSDAY NIGHTS
© 1984 United Feature Syndicate, Inc.
THIS IS WEDNESDAY
1-2-85
THAT'S NO EXCUSE!
SCHULZ

PEANUTS
featuring
"Good ol' Charlie Brown"
by SCHULZ
WE'LL PRETEND IT'S THE KICKOFF, OKAY?
I'LL COME RUNNING DOWN THE FIELD, AND YOU TRY TO TACKLE ME...
SIGH
9-22
TOUCHDOWN!
I GUESS I WAS WRONG.. YOU'RE TOO SMALL TO PLAY FOOTBALL
MAYBE WE CAN FIND A PLACE FOR YOU IN THE BAND...
© 1985 United Feature Syndicate, Inc.
SCHULZ

boot!
9-30
© 1985 United Feature Syndicate, Inc.
BONK!
WHAT ARE **YOU** LOOKING AT ?!
SCHULZ

WATCHING A FOOTBALL GAME, I SEE...
WHY DOES SOMEONE ALWAYS HANG A SIGN OVER THE RAILING THAT SAYS, "JOHN 3:16"?
11-23
© 1985 United Feature Syndicate, Inc.
IT'S A SCRIPTURAL REFERENCE
REALLY? THEN I WAS WRONG...
I ALWAYS THOUGHT IT HAD SOMETHING TO DO WITH JOHN MADDEN..
SCHULZ

TODAY, MARCIE, I'M GONNA TEACH YOU HOW TO BLOCK A PUNT...
OKAY, YOU PUNT IT, AND I'LL COME RUNNING IN TO BLOCK IT!
© 1985 United Feature Syndicate, Inc.
OOF!
11-27
SOMEHOW, SIR, LEARNING THAT DOESN'T REALLY INTEREST ME..
SCHULZ

THIS TIME, MARCIE, I'LL PUNT, AND YOU BE THE ONE WHO TRIES TO BLOCK IT...

READY, SIR? HERE I COME!

THUMP!

© 1985 United Feature Syndicate, Inc.

YOUR STYLE, MARCIE, LEAVES A LOT TO BE DESIRED!

11-29

KICK THE BALL, MARCIE!

© 1985 United Feature Syndicate, Inc.

IT'LL HATE ME, SIR..

11-30

FOOTBALLS DON'T HATE, MARCIE!

HOW NICE OF YOU..

WHAT HAPPENED? DID I MISS ANYTHING?

HE MADE A TOUCHDOWN, AND THE GREAT CROWD GAVE HIM A BIG HAND...

© 1985 United Feature Syndicate, Inc.

OR MAYBE THE BIG CROWD GAVE HIM A GREAT HAND...I DON'T KNOW..

12-2

WHATEVER.. WHO CARES?

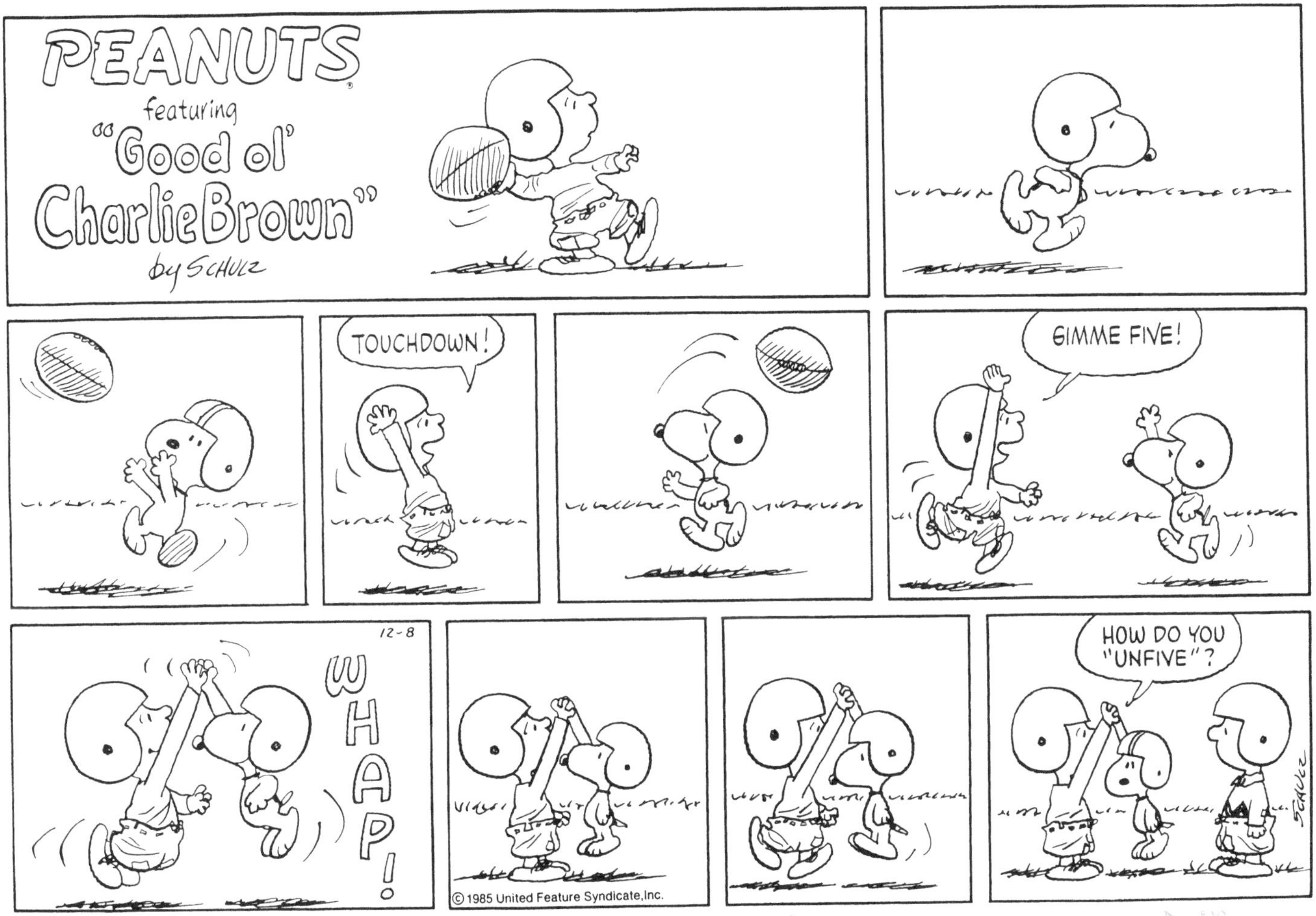
PEANUTS
featuring "Good ol' Charlie Brown"
by SCHULZ
TOUCHDOWN!
GIMME FIVE!
12-8
WHAP!
© 1985 United Feature Syndicate, Inc.
HOW DO YOU "UNFIVE"?
SCHULZ

10-1
NO!
© 1986 United Feature Syndicate, Inc.
I SAID WE'RE GOING OUT TO KICK AROUND THE OL' PIGSKIN..
I DIDN'T SAY "BEAGLESKIN"!
SCHULZ

WE SHOULD ORGANIZE A FOOTBALL TEAM, MARCIE
10-14
WE CAN'T, SIR..WE DON'T HAVE COSTUMES
UNIFORMS
© 1986 United Feature Syndicate, Inc.
WHATEVER
SCHULZ

I DON'T WANT TO PLAY FOOTBALL, SIR..IT'S NOT FEMININE ENOUGH!
NOT FEMININE ENOUGH?!!
© 1986 United Feature Syndicate, Inc.
WHAT DO YOU WANT TO DO, TIE A RIBBON AROUND THE BALL OR SOMETHING?
10-15
LOOKS CUTE, DOESN'T IT?
SCHULZ

Panel 1: I'LL HOLD THE BALL, SIR, AND YOU KICK IT... 10-16

Panel 2: MARCIE, I'M NOT GONNA KICK A BALL THAT HAS A CUTE RIBBON TIED AROUND IT!

Panel 3: I'LL BET THE ICEBOX WOULD

Panel 4: "REFRIGERATOR" WHATEVER

Panel 5: AND MARCIE SAYS FOOTBALL ISN'T FEMININE, CHUCK..ISN'T SHE SOMETHING?

Panel 6: IF I LIKE TO PLAY FOOTBALL, DOES THAT MEAN I'M NOT FEMININE, CHUCK?

Panel 7: WHAT DO YOU THINK, CHUCK? HUH? WHAT DO YOU THINK? 10/17

Panel 8: WE'RE SORRY..THE NUMBER YOU HAVE REACHED IS NO LONGER IN SERVICE..

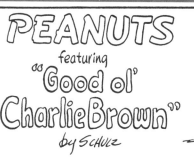

PEANUTS
featuring
"Good ol' CharlieBrown"
by Schulz

ONCE A YEAR...JUST ONCE A YEAR..

CHARLIE BROWNNN.. ♪

CHARLIE BROWN, I'LL HOLD THE BALL, AND YOU COME RUNNING UP AND KICK IT!

SURE! SURE I WILL! YOU MUST THINK I'M REALLY STUPID!

© 1986 United Feature Syndicate, Inc.

PLEASE, CHARLIE BROWN..I LOOK FORWARD TO THIS SPECIAL MOMENT ALL YEAR...

10-19

I SUPPOSE IF SOMEONE LOOKS FORWARD TO SOMETHING, IT'S WRONG TO SPOIL IT..

THIS YEAR I'M GONNA KICK THAT BALL CLEAR TO BULLHEAD CITY!

AAUGH!

WHAM!

HOW DEPRESSING...YOU LOOK FORWARD ALL YEAR TO A SPECIAL MOMENT, AND BEFORE YOU KNOW IT, IT'S OVER!

IT'S SO DEPRESSING

I CAN'T STAND IT!

Schulz

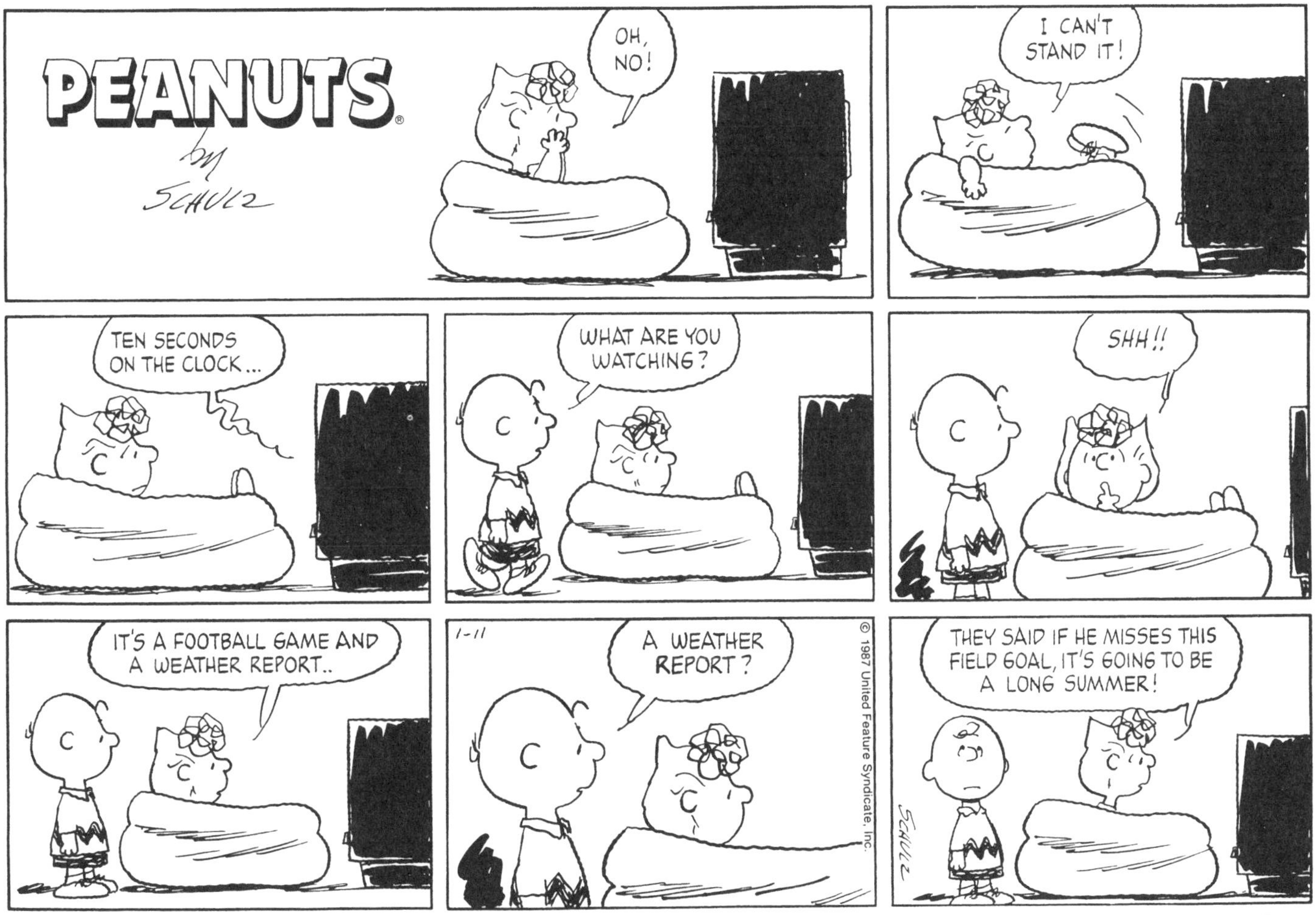
PEANUTS
by SCHULZ
OH, NO!
I CAN'T STAND IT!
TEN SECONDS ON THE CLOCK...
WHAT ARE YOU WATCHING?
SHH!!
IT'S A FOOTBALL GAME AND A WEATHER REPORT..
1-11
A WEATHER REPORT?
© 1987 United Feature Syndicate, Inc.
THEY SAID IF HE MISSES THIS FIELD GOAL, IT'S GOING TO BE A LONG SUMMER!
SCHULZ

PEANUTS by Schulz

CHARLIE BROWNNN...

BASEBALL SEASON ISN'T EVEN OVER YET..

I'LL HOLD THE BALL, CHARLIE BROWN, AND YOU COME RUNNING UP AND KICK IT..

AREN'T YOU STARTING IN KIND OF EARLY?

WELL, I HAVE A LOT OF THINGS TO DO..MY APPOINTMENT BOOK IS JUST ABOUT FILLED...

THIS IS THE ONLY TIME I CAN REALLY FIT YOU IN..

I GUESS EVERYBODY IS BUSY THESE DAYS...

THIS YEAR I'M GONNA KICK THAT BALL ALL THE WAY TO MOUNT RUSHMORE!

10-4

AAUGH!

© 1987 United Feature Syndicate, Inc.

UUHLAM!

I THINK I MADE A MISTAKE..I HAVE AN OPEN SPOT DURING THE FIRST PART OF NOVEMBER..SHALL WE TRY IT AGAIN THEN?

NOVEMBER WILL BE FINE.. IN THE YEAR 2000!

Schulz

WAIT 'TIL I GET DOWN NEAR THAT TREE, MARCIE..
THEN YOU KICK THE OL' PIGSKIN TO ME...
© 1987 United Feature Syndicate, Inc.
WHY WOULD I WANT TO DO THAT?
10-5
POOR PIGGY..
SCHULZ

MR. BROWN, MY NAME IS LELAND..WE'D LIKE TO PLAY FOR YOUR FOOTBALL TEAM
I DON'T HAVE A FOOTBALL TEAM, LELAND
10/8
IF YOU DID, WE'D SURE LIKE TO PLAY FOR YOU..
WHY DO YOU KEEP SAYING "WE"?
THERE'S MORE THAN ONE OF US UNDER HERE!
SCHULZ
© 1987 United Feature Syndicate, Inc.

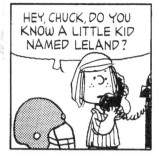

HEY, CHUCK, DO YOU KNOW A LITTLE KID NAMED LELAND?
HE SAYS THEY WANT TO PLAY ON MY FOOTBALL TEAM..
THEY'RE SO LITTLE, CHUCK, THERE'S TWO OF 'EM UNDER ONE HELMET...
THREE!
SCHULZ 10-9
© 1987 United Feature Syndicate, Inc.

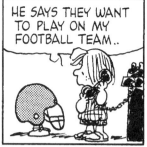

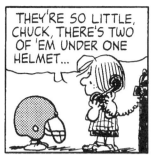

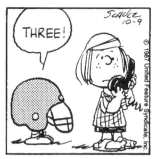

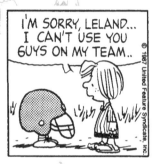

I'M SORRY, LELAND... I CAN'T USE YOU GUYS ON MY TEAM..
© 1987 United Feature Syndicate, Inc.
LET'S FACE IT.. YOU'RE RIDICULOUS!
WHOEVER HEARD OF THREE PLAYERS UNDER ONE HELMET?
10-10
YOU SHOULD SEE US WITH THE SHOULDER PADS!
SCHULZ

AAUGH!

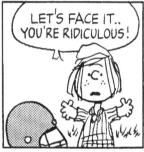

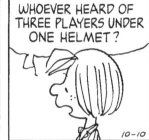

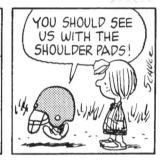

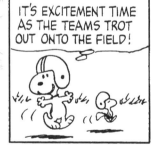

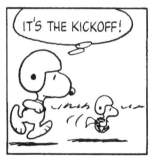

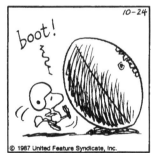

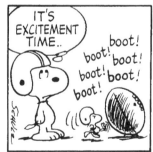

IT'S EXCITEMENT TIME AS THE TEAMS TROT OUT ONTO THE FIELD!
IT'S THE KICKOFF!
10-24
boot!
© 1987 United Feature Syndicate, Inc.
IT'S EXCITEMENT TIME..
boot! boot! boot! boot! boot! boot!
SCHULZ

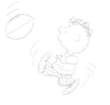

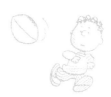

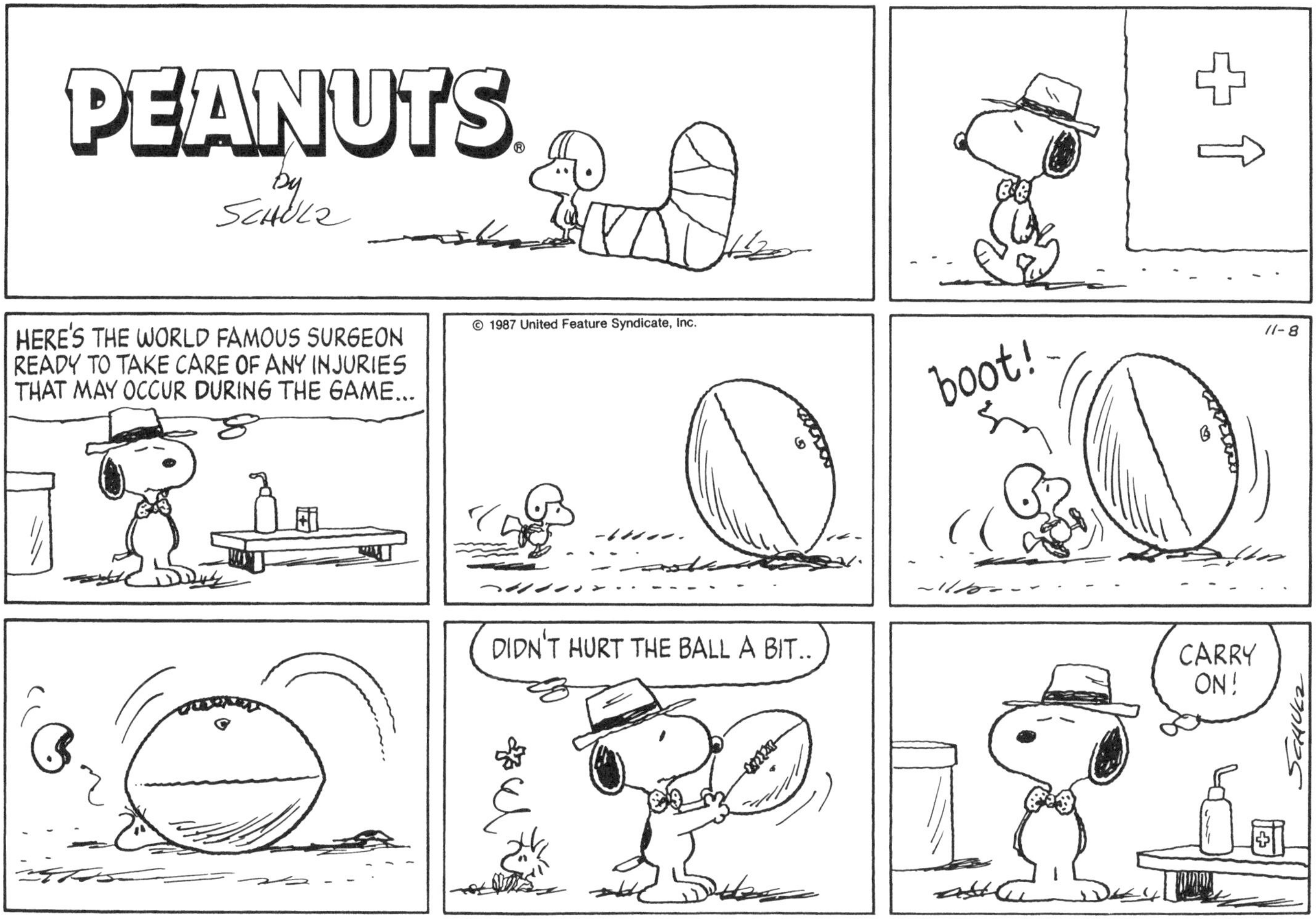
PEANUTS
by SCHULZ
HERE'S THE WORLD FAMOUS SURGEON READY TO TAKE CARE OF ANY INJURIES THAT MAY OCCUR DURING THE GAME...
© 1987 United Feature Syndicate, Inc.
11-8
boot!
DIDN'T HURT THE BALL A BIT..
CARRY ON!
SCHULZ

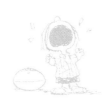

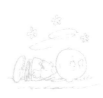

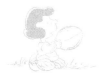

PEANUTS

by SCHULZ

© 1988 United Feature Syndicate, Inc.

10-23

WUMP

IT'S SO SAD..EVENTUALLY EVERYTHING IN LIFE JUST BECOMES ROUTINE..

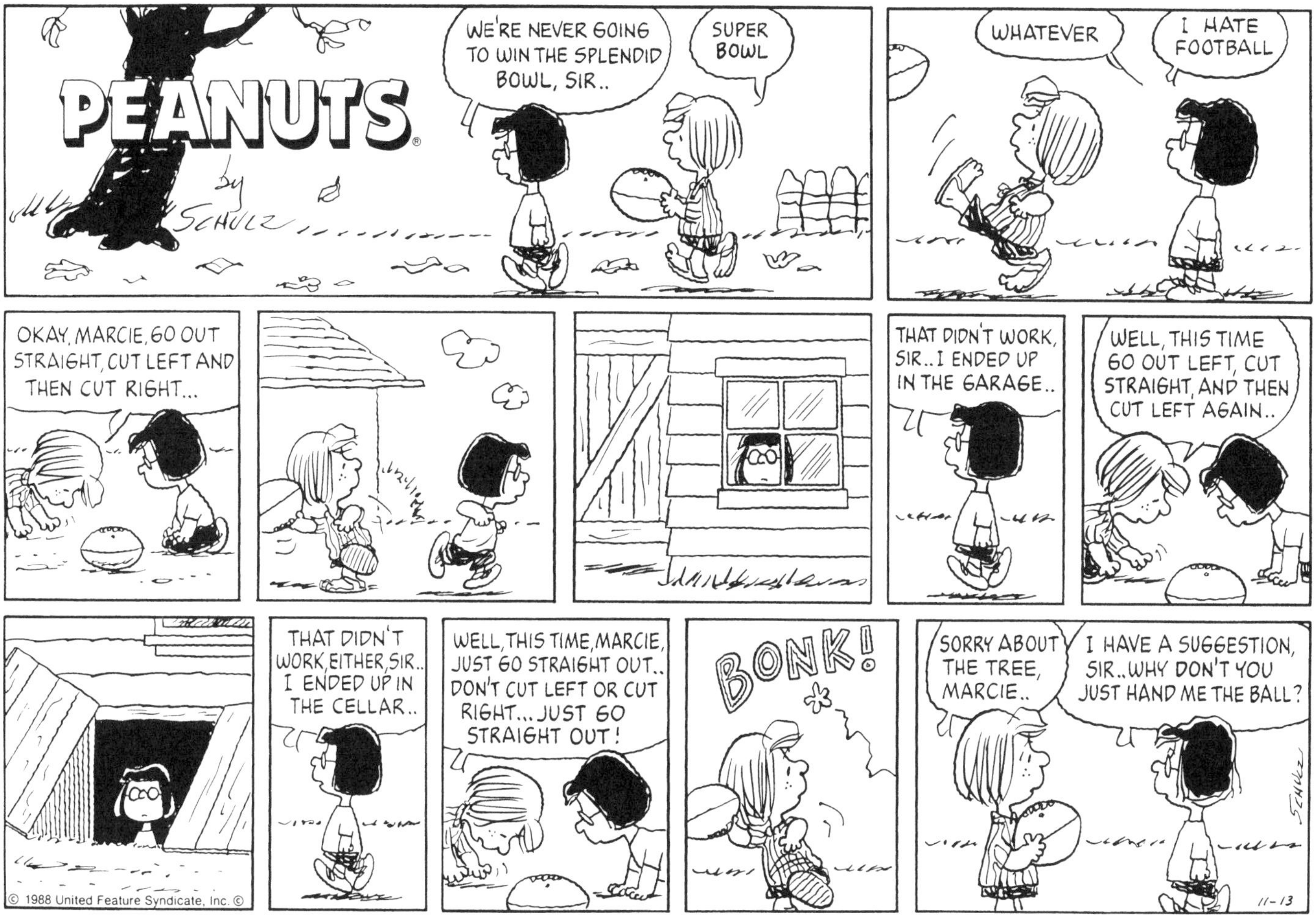
PEANUTS
by SCHULZ
WE'RE NEVER GOING TO WIN THE SPLENDID BOWL, SIR..
SUPER BOWL
WHATEVER
I HATE FOOTBALL
OKAY, MARCIE, GO OUT STRAIGHT, CUT LEFT AND THEN CUT RIGHT...
THAT DIDN'T WORK, SIR.. I ENDED UP IN THE GARAGE..
WELL, THIS TIME GO OUT LEFT, CUT STRAIGHT, AND THEN CUT LEFT AGAIN..
THAT DIDN'T WORK, EITHER, SIR.. I ENDED UP IN THE CELLAR..
WELL, THIS TIME, MARCIE, JUST GO STRAIGHT OUT.. DON'T CUT LEFT OR CUT RIGHT... JUST GO STRAIGHT OUT!
BONK!
SORRY ABOUT THE TREE, MARCIE..
I HAVE A SUGGESTION, SIR.. WHY DON'T YOU JUST HAND ME THE BALL?
SCHULZ
11-13

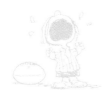

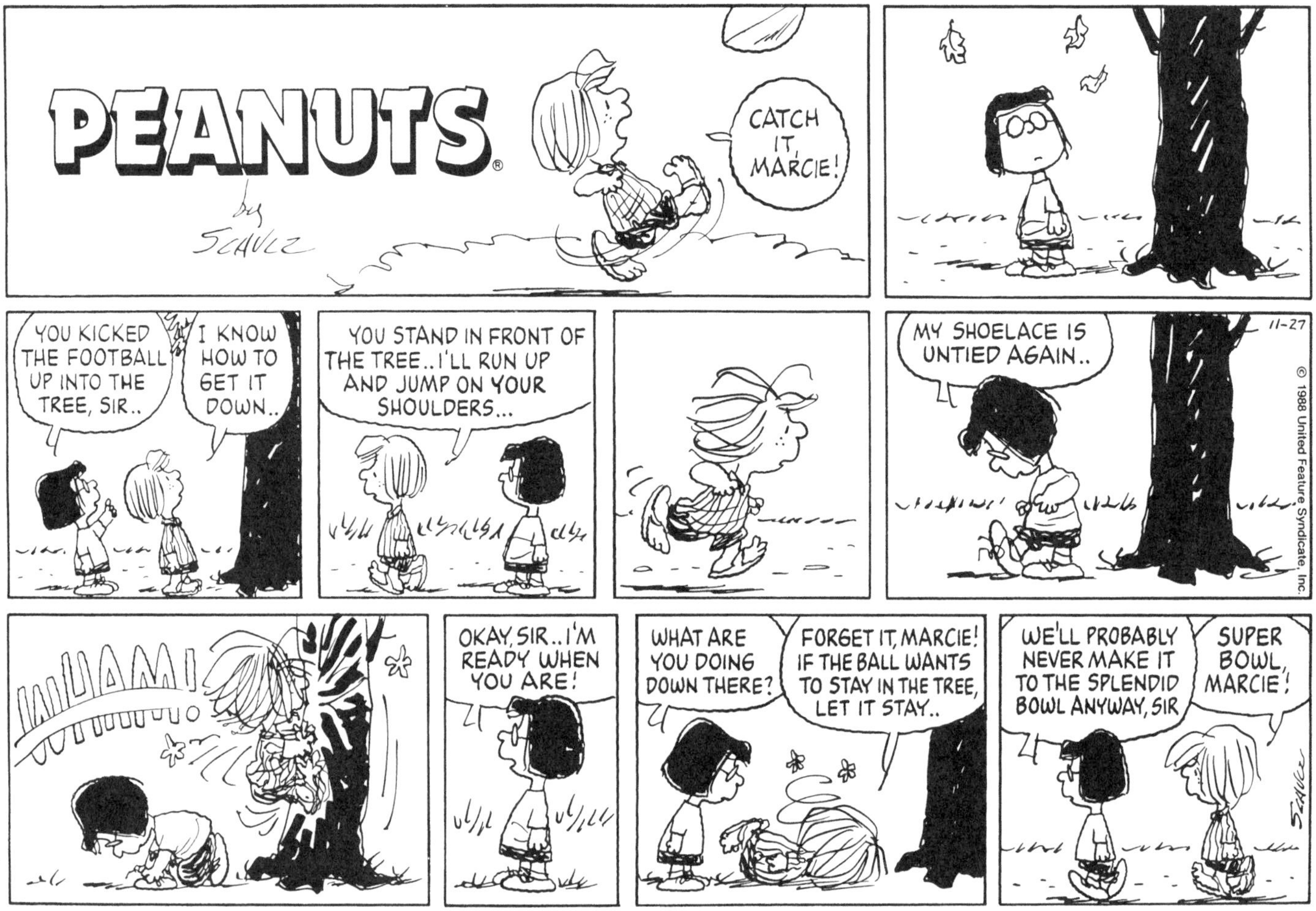
PEANUTS
by SCHULZ
CATCH IT, MARCIE!
YOU KICKED THE FOOTBALL UP INTO THE TREE, SIR..
I KNOW HOW TO GET IT DOWN..
YOU STAND IN FRONT OF THE TREE.. I'LL RUN UP AND JUMP ON YOUR SHOULDERS...
MY SHOELACE IS UNTIED AGAIN..
11-27
© 1988 United Feature Syndicate, Inc.
WHAM!
OKAY, SIR.. I'M READY WHEN YOU ARE!
WHAT ARE YOU DOING DOWN THERE?
FORGET IT, MARCIE! IF THE BALL WANTS TO STAY IN THE TREE, LET IT STAY..
WE'LL PROBABLY NEVER MAKE IT TO THE SPLENDID BOWL ANYWAY, SIR
SUPER BOWL, MARCIE!
SCHULZ

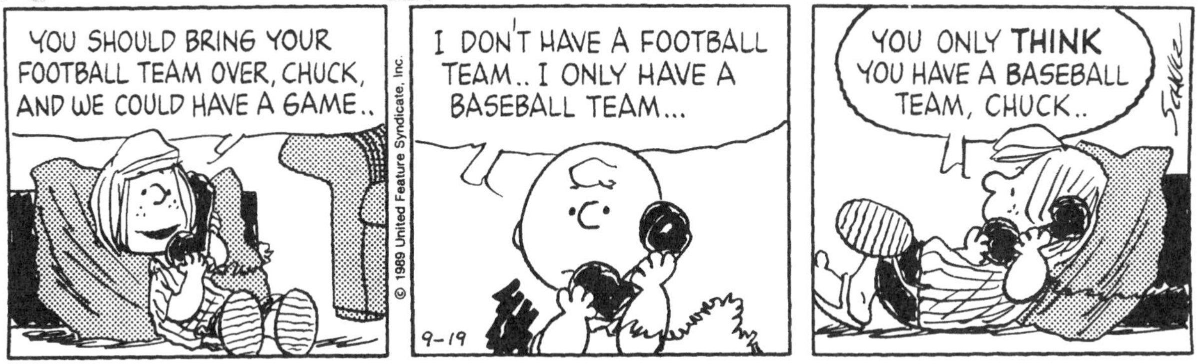
YOU SHOULD BRING YOUR FOOTBALL TEAM OVER, CHUCK, AND WE COULD HAVE A GAME..
© 1989 United Feature Syndicate, Inc.
I DON'T HAVE A FOOTBALL TEAM.. I ONLY HAVE A BASEBALL TEAM...
9-19
YOU ONLY **THINK** YOU HAVE A BASEBALL TEAM, CHUCK..
SCHULZ

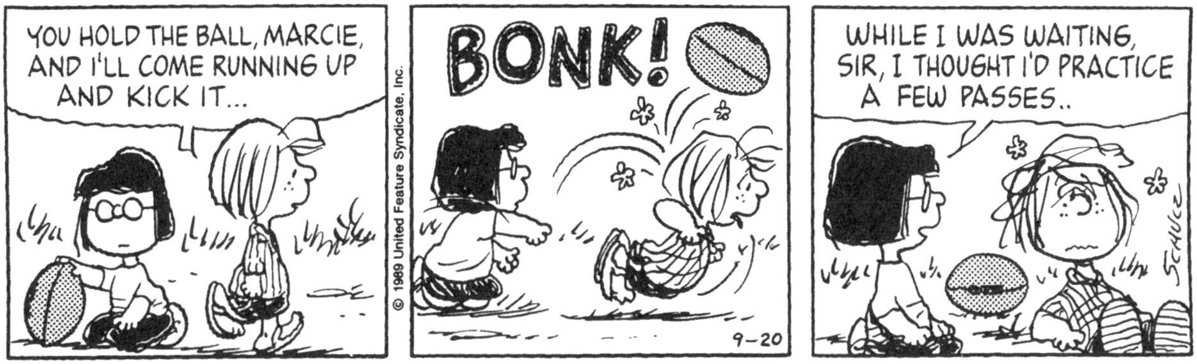
YOU HOLD THE BALL, MARCIE, AND I'LL COME RUNNING UP AND KICK IT...
© 1989 United Feature Syndicate, Inc.
BONK!
9-20
WHILE I WAS WAITING, SIR, I THOUGHT I'D PRACTICE A FEW PASSES..
SCHULZ

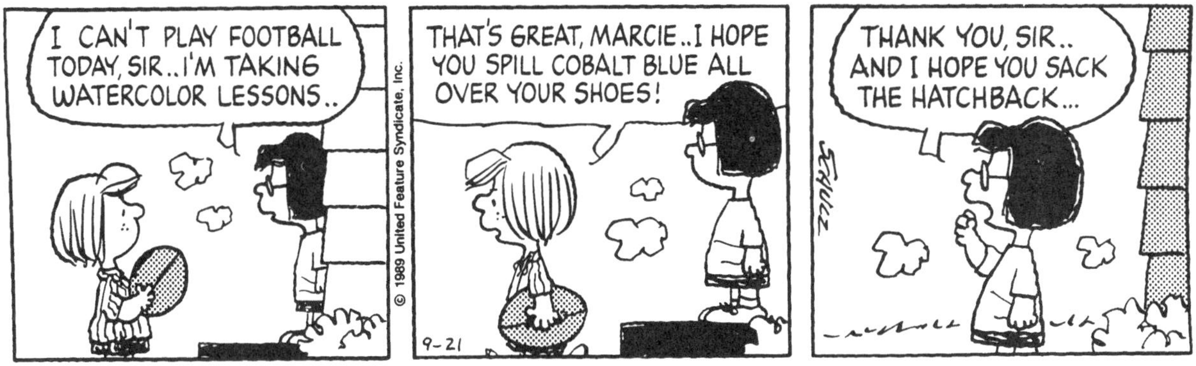
I CAN'T PLAY FOOTBALL TODAY, SIR..I'M TAKING WATERCOLOR LESSONS..
© 1989 United Feature Syndicate, Inc.
THAT'S GREAT, MARCIE..I HOPE YOU SPILL COBALT BLUE ALL OVER YOUR SHOES!
9-21
SCHULZ
THANK YOU, SIR.. AND I HOPE YOU SACK THE HATCHBACK...

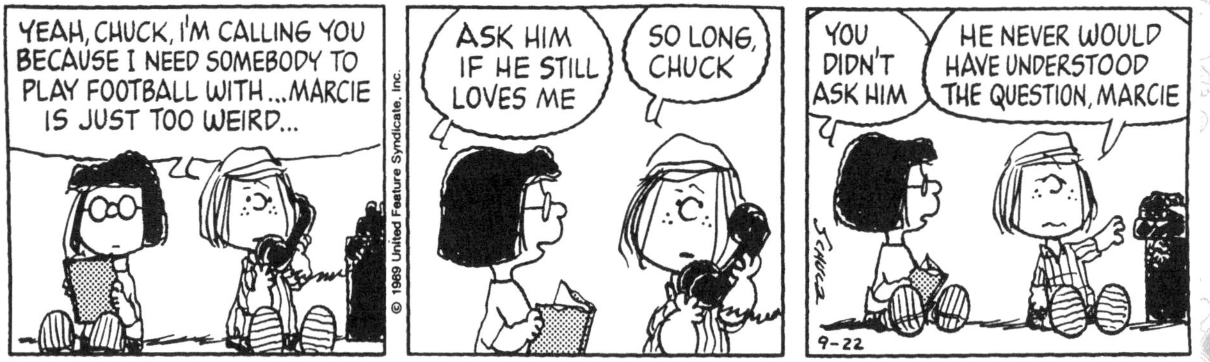
YEAH, CHUCK, I'M CALLING YOU BECAUSE I NEED SOMEBODY TO PLAY FOOTBALL WITH ... MARCIE IS JUST TOO WEIRD...
© 1989 United Feature Syndicate, Inc.
ASK HIM IF HE STILL LOVES ME
SO LONG, CHUCK
YOU DIDN'T ASK HIM
HE NEVER WOULD HAVE UNDERSTOOD THE QUESTION, MARCIE
SCHULZ
9-22

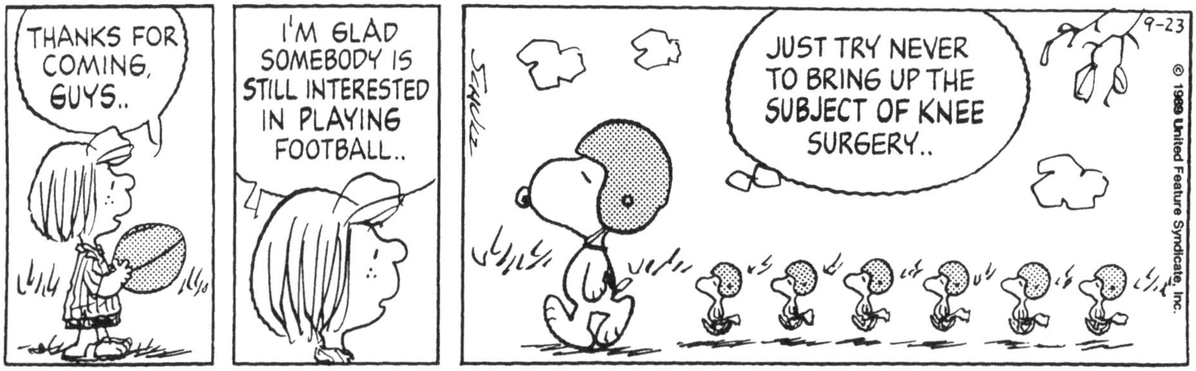
THANKS FOR COMING, GUYS..
I'M GLAD SOMEBODY IS STILL INTERESTED IN PLAYING FOOTBALL..
SCHULZ
9-23
JUST TRY NEVER TO BRING UP THE SUBJECT OF KNEE SURGERY..
© 1989 United Feature Syndicate, Inc.

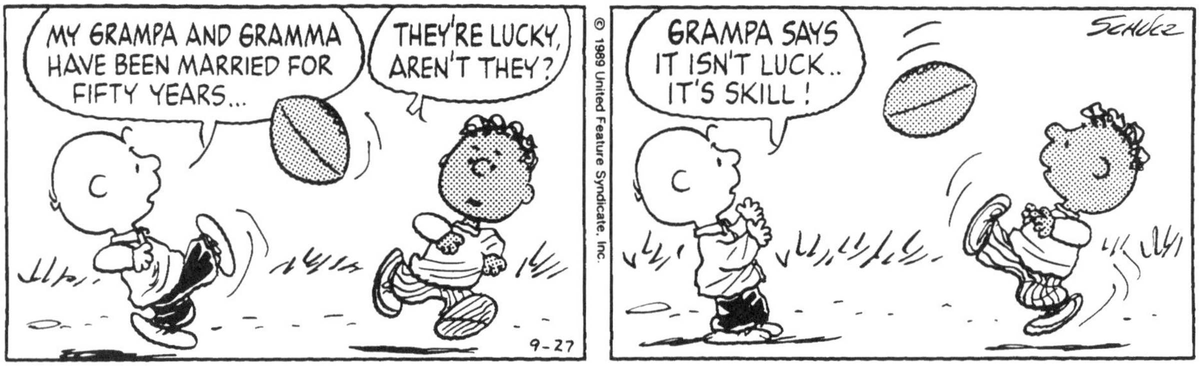
MY GRAMPA AND GRAMMA HAVE BEEN MARRIED FOR FIFTY YEARS...
THEY'RE LUCKY, AREN'T THEY?
9-27
© 1989 United Feature Syndicate, Inc.
GRAMPA SAYS IT ISN'T LUCK.. IT'S SKILL!
SCHULZ

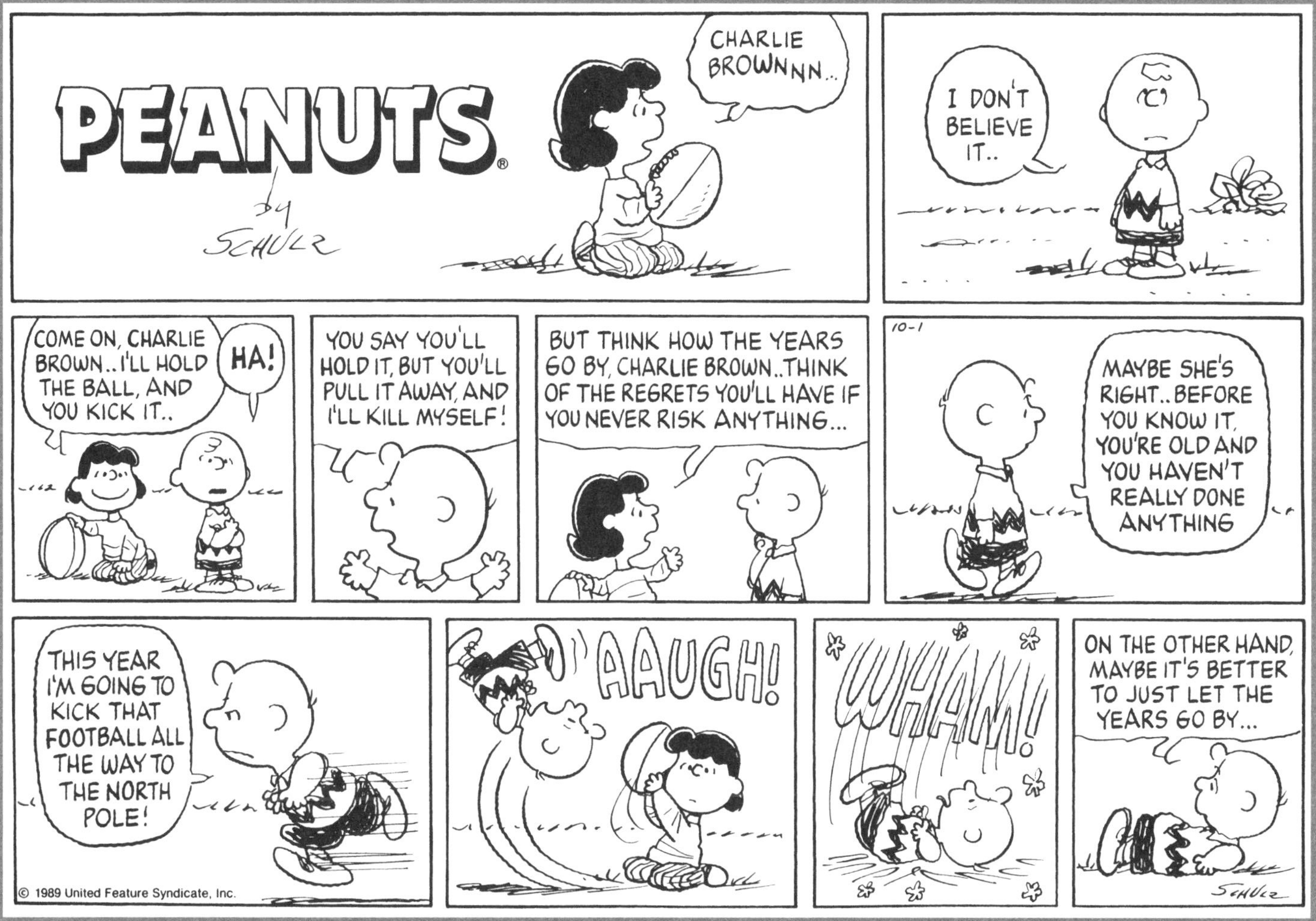
PEANUTS®
by Schulz
CHARLIE BROWNNNN...
I DON'T BELIEVE IT..
COME ON, CHARLIE BROWN..I'LL HOLD THE BALL, AND YOU KICK IT..
HA!
YOU SAY YOU'LL HOLD IT, BUT YOU'LL PULL IT AWAY, AND I'LL KILL MYSELF!
BUT THINK HOW THE YEARS GO BY, CHARLIE BROWN..THINK OF THE REGRETS YOU'LL HAVE IF YOU NEVER RISK ANYTHING...
10-1
MAYBE SHE'S RIGHT..BEFORE YOU KNOW IT, YOU'RE OLD AND YOU HAVEN'T REALLY DONE ANYTHING
THIS YEAR I'M GOING TO KICK THAT FOOTBALL ALL THE WAY TO THE NORTH POLE!
AAUGH!
WHAM!
ON THE OTHER HAND, MAYBE IT'S BETTER TO JUST LET THE YEARS GO BY...
SCHULZ

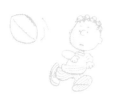

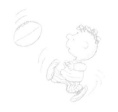

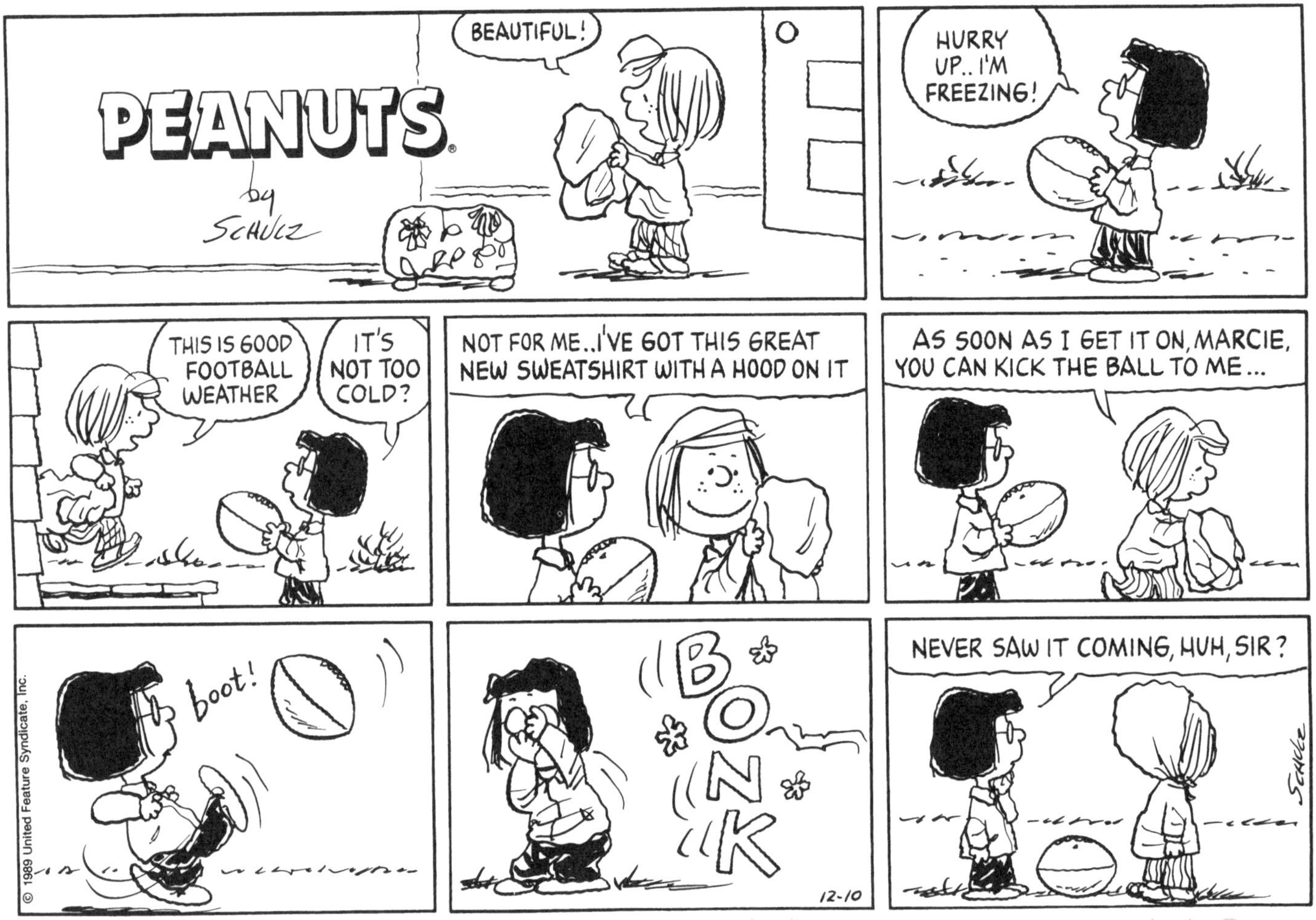
PEANUTS
by SCHULZ
BEAUTIFUL!
HURRY UP.. I'M FREEZING!
THIS IS GOOD FOOTBALL WEATHER
IT'S NOT TOO COLD?
NOT FOR ME..I'VE GOT THIS GREAT NEW SWEATSHIRT WITH A HOOD ON IT
AS SOON AS I GET IT ON, MARCIE, YOU CAN KICK THE BALL TO ME...
© 1989 United Feature Syndicate, Inc.
boot!
BONK
12-10
NEVER SAW IT COMING, HUH, SIR?
SCHULZ

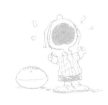

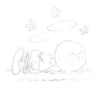

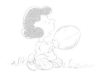

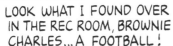

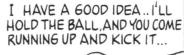

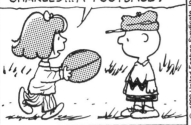

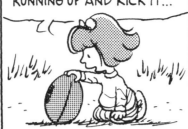

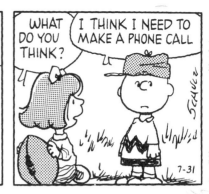

LOOK WHAT I FOUND OVER IN THE REC ROOM, BROWNIE CHARLES... A FOOTBALL!
© 1990 United Feature Syndicate, Inc.
I HAVE A GOOD IDEA.. I'LL HOLD THE BALL, AND YOU COME RUNNING UP AND KICK IT...
WHAT DO YOU THINK?
I THINK I NEED TO MAKE A PHONE CALL
SCHULZ
7-31

LINUS, WHAT AM I GOING TO DO?
SHE'S WAITING OUT THERE WITH A FOOTBALL, AND EXPECTS ME TO GO RUNNING UP AND KICK IT...
© 1990 United Feature Syndicate, Inc.
DO YOU THINK SHE'LL PULL IT AWAY LIKE YOUR STUPID SISTER ALWAYS DOES?
8-1
WHO'S STUPID?
SORRY, WRONG NUMBER..
SCHULZ

I'M WAITING, BROWNIE CHARLES! I'M HOLDING THE BALL! ALL YOU HAVE TO DO IS KICK IT!
IF YOU CAN'T TRUST THE PRETTIEST LITTLE GIRL YOU'VE EVER SEEN, WHO CAN YOU TRUST?
© 1990 United Feature Syndicate, Inc.
8-2
SCREECH!!
THAT WAS JUST A PRACTICE RUN, OKAY?
SCHULZ

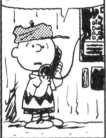

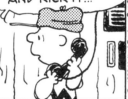

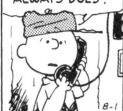

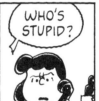

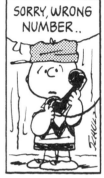

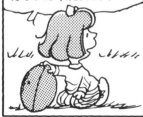

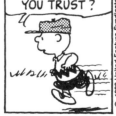

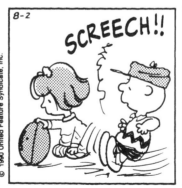

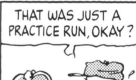

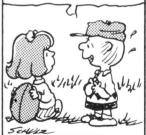

LINUS, WHAT AM I GOING TO DO?
SHE'S SUCH A PRETTY LITTLE GIRL..DO YOU THINK SHE'LL PULL THE BALL AWAY? TELL ME I CAN TRUST HER, LINUS..
8-3
© 1990 United Feature Syndicate, Inc.
YOU CAN TRUST HER, CHARLIE BROWN! YOU'RE IN LOVE, AREN'T YOU? GO FOR IT! KICK THAT FOOTBALL, CHARLIE BROWN!
WHAT HAVE I DONE?
SCHULZ

BROWNIE CHARLES! I'M WAITING! I'M HOLDING THE BALL!
AND I'M WONDERING IF I SHOULD TRUST HER.. I HATE MYSELF!
© 1990 United Feature Syndicate, Inc.
I NEED SOMEBODY WHO WILL MAKE UP MY MIND FOR ME..
8-4
boot!
SCHULZ

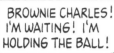

WHERE DID SHE GO? PEGGY JEAN? WHERE ARE YOU?!
8-6
HEY, IS YOUR NAME BROWNIE CHARLES? WHAT A WEIRD NAME...ANYWAY, A GIRL ASKED ME IF I'D GIVE YOU THIS NOTE...
© 1990 United Feature Syndicate, Inc.
"DEAR BROWNIE CHARLES, YOU NEVER TRUSTED ME, DID YOU? I THOUGHT YOU LIKED ME...I'M GOING HOME.."
THAT HAPPENED TO ME ONCE WITH A GOLDEN RETRIEVER..
SCHULZ

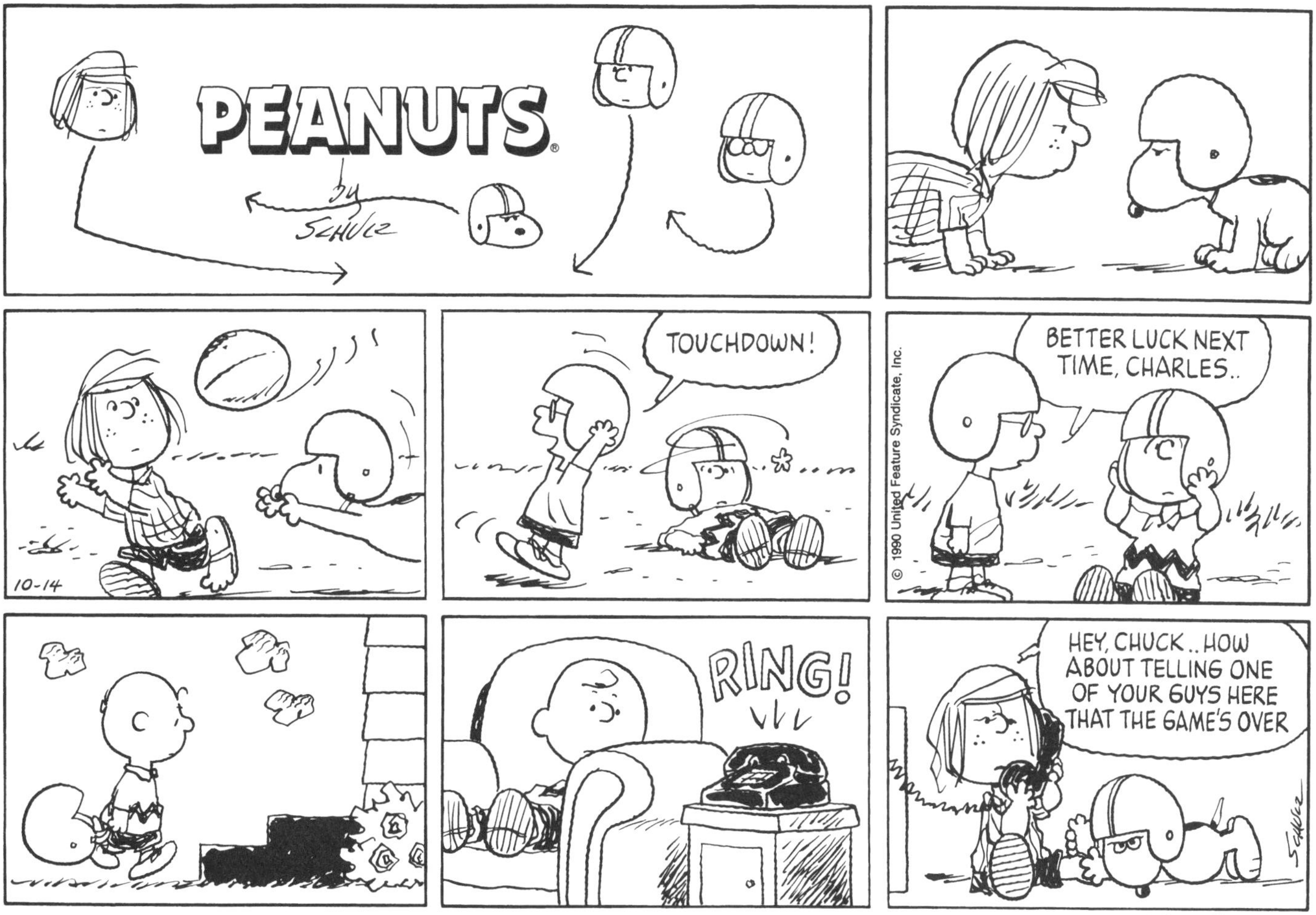
PEANUTS
by SCHULZ
10-14
TOUCHDOWN!
© 1990 United Feature Syndicate, Inc.
BETTER LUCK NEXT TIME, CHARLES..
RING!
HEY, CHUCK..HOW ABOUT TELLING ONE OF YOUR GUYS HERE THAT THE GAME'S OVER
SCHULZ

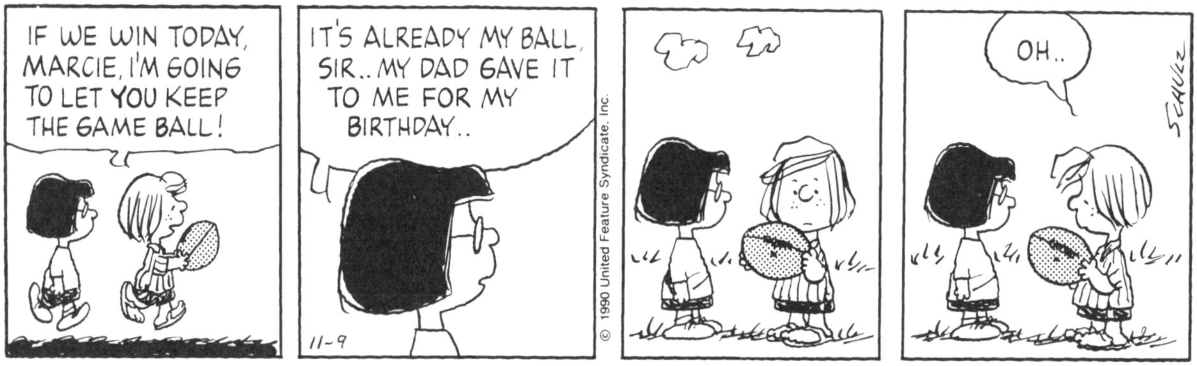
IF WE WIN TODAY, MARCIE, I'M GOING TO LET YOU KEEP THE GAME BALL!
IT'S ALREADY MY BALL, SIR.. MY DAD GAVE IT TO ME FOR MY BIRTHDAY..
11-9
© 1990 United Feature Syndicate, Inc.
OH..
SCHULZ

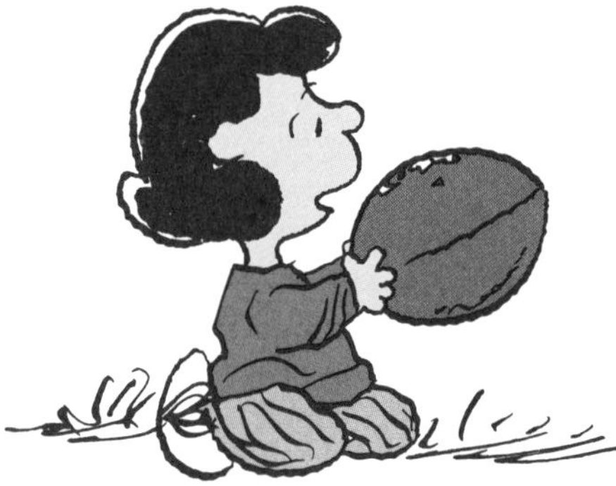

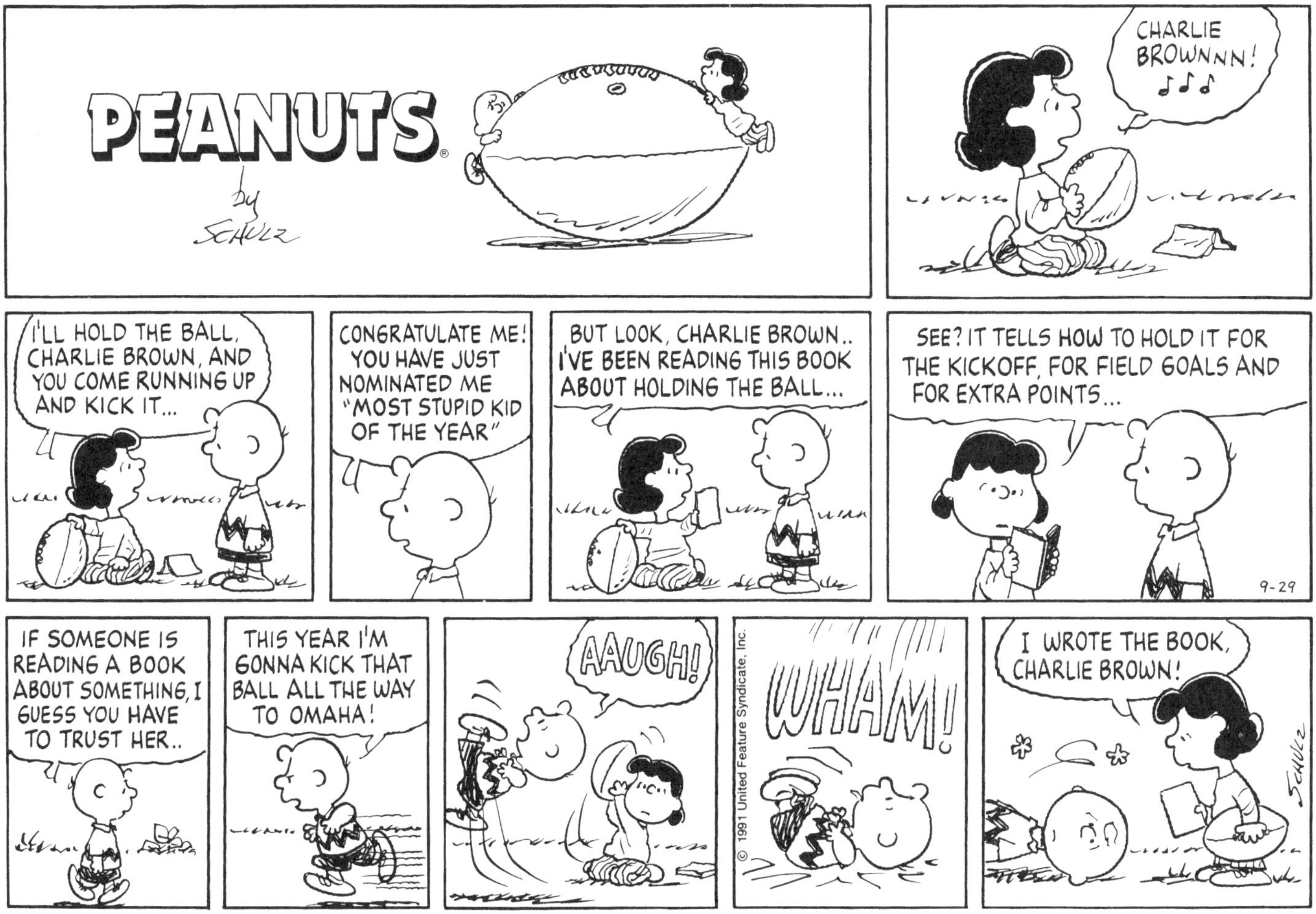
PEANUTS
by SCHULZ
CHARLIE BROWNNN! ♪♪♪
I'LL HOLD THE BALL, CHARLIE BROWN, AND YOU COME RUNNING UP AND KICK IT...
CONGRATULATE ME! YOU HAVE JUST NOMINATED ME "MOST STUPID KID OF THE YEAR"
BUT LOOK, CHARLIE BROWN.. I'VE BEEN READING THIS BOOK ABOUT HOLDING THE BALL...
SEE? IT TELLS HOW TO HOLD IT FOR THE KICKOFF, FOR FIELD GOALS AND FOR EXTRA POINTS...
9-29
IF SOMEONE IS READING A BOOK ABOUT SOMETHING, I GUESS YOU HAVE TO TRUST HER..
THIS YEAR I'M GONNA KICK THAT BALL ALL THE WAY TO OMAHA!
AAUGH!
© 1991 United Feature Syndicate, Inc.
WHAM!
I WROTE THE BOOK, CHARLIE BROWN!
SCHULZ

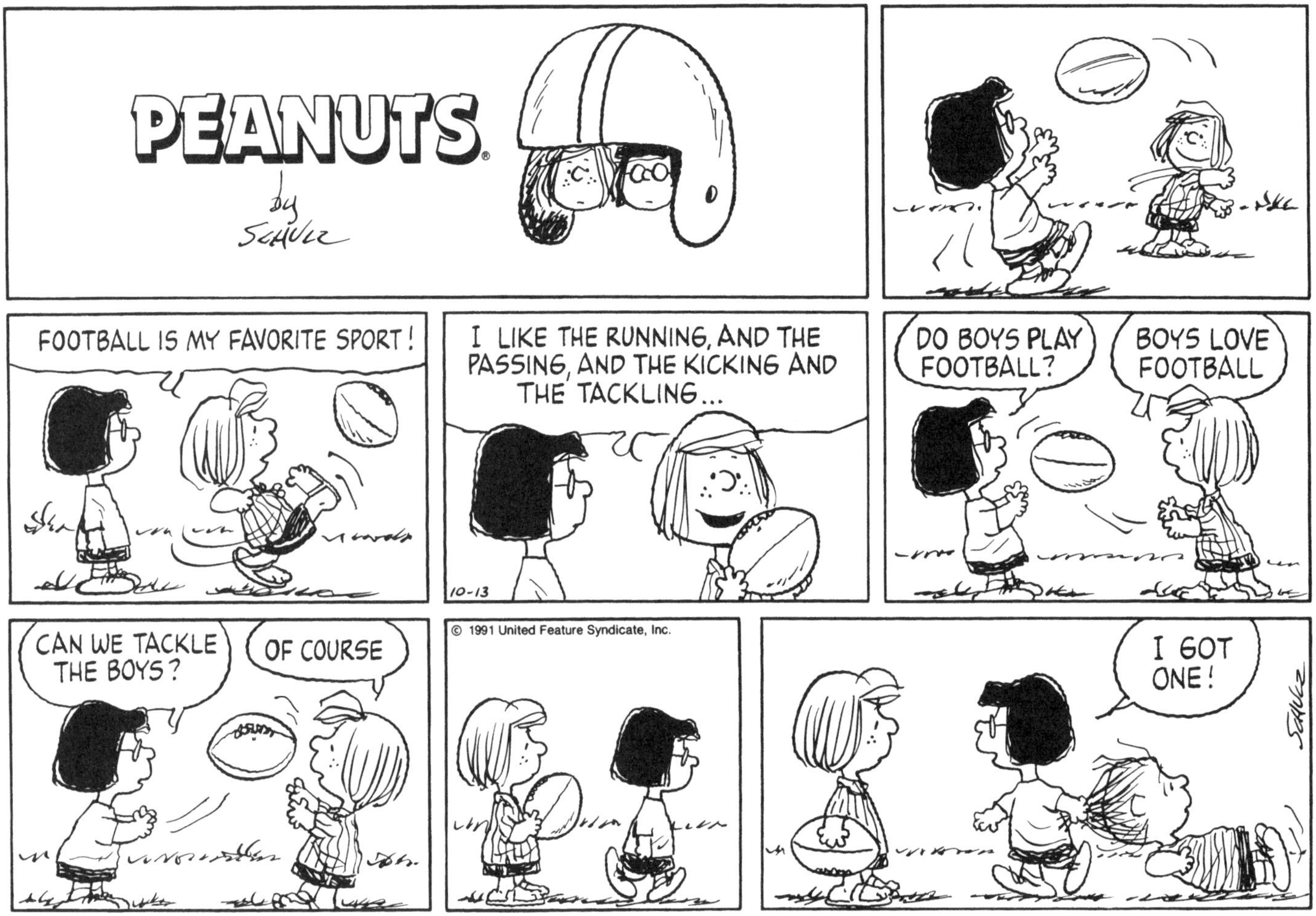
PEANUTS
by SCHULZ
FOOTBALL IS MY FAVORITE SPORT!
I LIKE THE RUNNING, AND THE PASSING, AND THE KICKING AND THE TACKLING...
10-13
DO BOYS PLAY FOOTBALL?
BOYS LOVE FOOTBALL
CAN WE TACKLE THE BOYS?
OF COURSE
© 1991 United Feature Syndicate, Inc.
I GOT ONE!
SCHULZ

YOU KICK THE BALL, MARCIE, AND I'LL CATCH IT..
© 1991 United Feature Syndicate, Inc.
11-13
SCHULZ
WHERE WERE YOU?

OKAY, MARCIE..I'LL KICK THE BALL, AND YOU CATCH IT!
WHAT IF IT HITS ME IN THE STOMACH?
© 1991 United Feature Syndicate, Inc.
IT WON'T HIT YOU IN THE STOMACH IF YOU'RE CAREFUL...
11-14
SCHULZ

MARCIE, HOW CAN YOU CATCH THE BALL IF YOU'RE STANDING BEHIND A TREE?
I DON'T WANT TO GET HIT IN THE STOMACH WITH THE BALL...
© 1991 United Feature Syndicate, Inc.
11-15
PRETTY GOOD CATCH, HUH, SIR?
SCHULZ

MARCIE, I DON'T THINK YOU HAVE WHAT IT TAKES TO BE A FOOTBALL PLAYER..
DON'T BE TOO SURE... I COULD STILL TURN OUT TO BE ANOTHER JOE IOWA!
MONTANA!
© 1991 United Feature Syndicate, Inc.
WHATEVER
bonk!
SCHULZ
11-16

WHAT HAPPENED TO MONDAY NOON FOOTBALL?
12-23
© 1991 United Feature Syndicate, Inc.
YOU MEAN MONDAY NIGHT FOOTBALL..
SCHULZ
NO WONDER I NEVER SEE ANY GAMES..

Hockey

PEANUTS
Tm. Reg. U. S. Pat. Off.—All rights reserved
© 1968 by United Feature Syndicate, Inc.
1-31
OKAY, I'M READY... THROW ME THE HOCKEY BALL!
YOU INVITED HER.. I DIDN'T
SCHULZ

PEANUTS
Tm. Reg. U. S. Pat. Off.—All rights reserved
© 1968 by United Feature Syndicate, Inc.
2-1
I LOVE PLAYING HOCKEY BALL!
SCHULZ

PEANUTS
NOW HERE'S THE WAY WE START THE GAME..
WE HAVE A "FACE-OFF," SEE... WE LEAN OVER AND TAP OUR STICKS TOGETHER THREE TIMES.... OKAY, LET'S GO...
SMAK!
Tm. Reg. U. S. Pat. Off.—All rights reserved © 1968 by United Feature Syndicate, Inc.
PENALTY BOX
SCHULZ
2-2

PEANUTS
HERE'S THE WORLD-FAMOUS HOCKEY PLAYER SKATING OUT ONTO THE ICE..
Tm. Reg. U. S. Pat. Off.—All rights reserved © 1968 by United Feature Syndicate, Inc.
10-8
I PICK UP THE PUCK NEAR THE BLUE LINE...
I SHOOT! THE GOALIE NEVER EVEN SEES THE PUCK!
THEY'RE NOT SLEEPING WELL IN MONTREAL TONIGHT...
SCHULZ

PEANUTS
I DON'T THINK YOU'RE A REAL HOCKEY PLAYER AT ALL..
Tm. Reg. U. S. Pat. Off.—All rights reserved © 1968 by United Feature Syndicate, Inc.
10-9
PROVE TO ME THAT YOU'RE A REAL HOCKEY PLAYER..
YOU'RE A REAL HOCKEY PLAYER!
SCHULZ

PEANUTS
IT'S THE THIRD PERIOD OF THE BIG HOCKEY GAME...
10-10
TEMPERS ARE RUNNING SHORT... A FAN AT RINKSIDE SHOUTS A DEROGATORY REMARK...
WHOP!
Tm. Reg. U. S. Pat. Off.—All rights reserved © 1968 by United Feature Syndicate, Inc.
WE HOCKEY PLAYERS HATE DEROGATORY REMARKS!
SCHULZ

PEANUTS
Tm. Reg. U. S. Pat. Off.—All rights reserved © 1968 by United Feature Syndicate, Inc.
10-11
HERE'S THE WORLD-FAMOUS HOCKEY PLAYER WINDING UP FOR ONE OF HIS SPECTACULAR SLAP SHOTS...
POW!
SOME PEOPLE HAVE DOGS WHO BARK TOO MUCH... SOME PEOPLE HAVE DOGS WHO CHASE CHICKENS... SOME PEOPLE HAVE DOGS WHO DIG UP FLOWERS...
"GREAT SHOT!" THANK YOU, STAN.. THANK YOU, BOBBY.. THANK YOU, MAURICE...
SCHULZ

PEANUTS
HERE'S THE WORLD FAMOUS HOCKEY PLAYER STANDING AT ATTENTION WHILE THEY PLAY THE NATIONAL ANTHEM
12-12
WHAT AN INSPIRING MOMENT!
Tm. Reg. U. S. Pat. Off.—All rights reserved © 1968 by United Feature Syndicate, Inc.
BEAUTIFUL!
TEN MORE SECONDS, AND I CAN CLOBBER SOMEBODY!
SCHULZ

PEANUTS
HERE'S THE WORLD FAMOUS HOCKEY PLAYER SITTING IN THE PENALTY BOX..
12-13
I HATE EVERYBODY!
Tm. Reg. U. S. Pat. Off.—All rights reserved © 1968 by United Feature Syndicate, Inc.
I'M MEAN! I'M TOUGH!
I EAT GOALIES!
SCHULZ

PEANUTS
GO, TEAM, GO!
THE FANS ARE NOISY TONIGHT..WE HOCKEY PLAYERS LIKE NOISY FANS
WHAT'S THE MATTER WITH YOU GUYS, CAN'T YOU SKATE?
12-14
Tm. Reg. U. S. Pat. Off.—All rights reserved © 1968 by United Feature Syndicate, Inc
BONK!
BUT NOT TOO NOISY!
SCHULZ

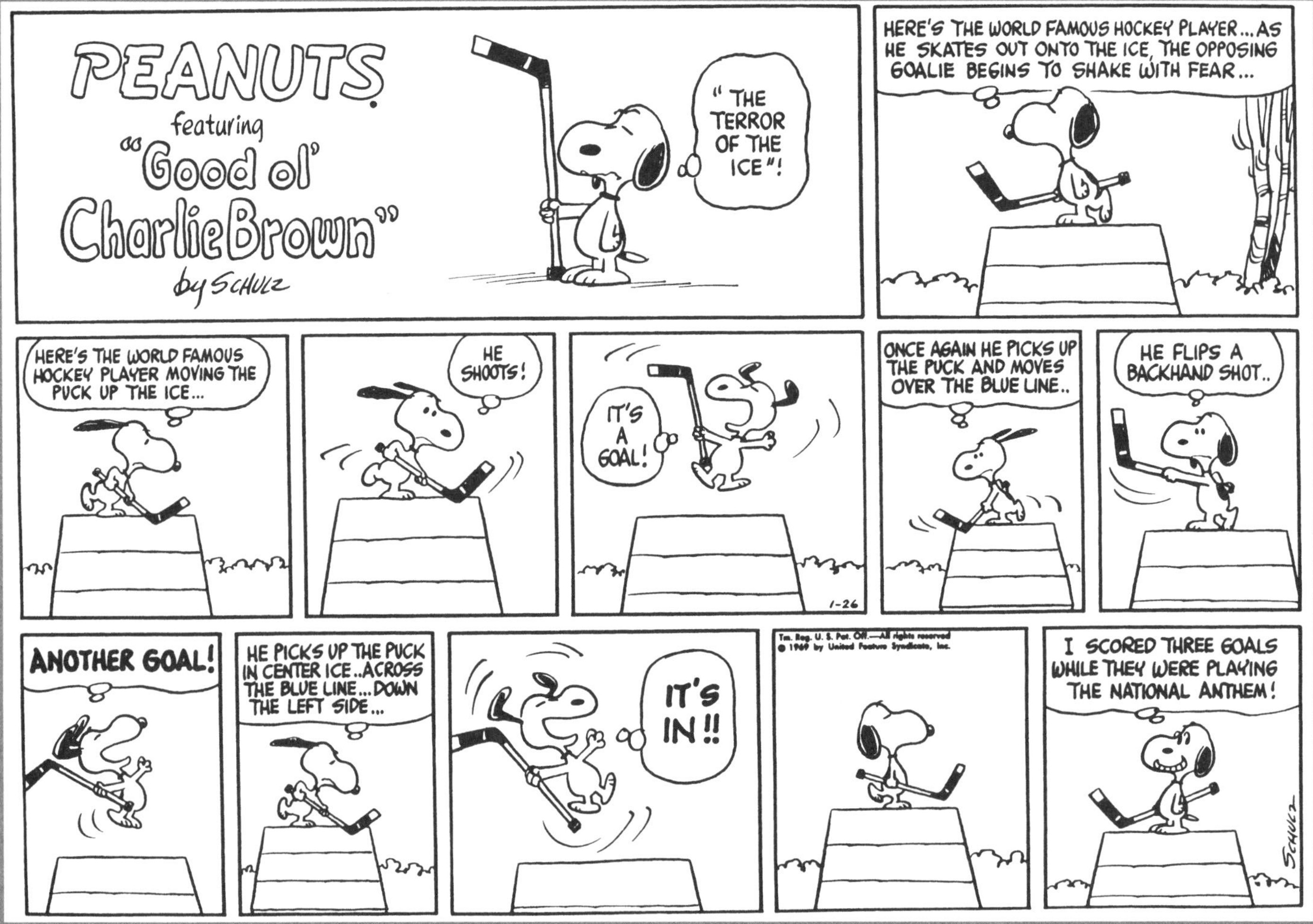
PEANUTS
featuring "Good ol' Charlie Brown"
by SCHULZ
"THE TERROR OF THE ICE"!
HERE'S THE WORLD FAMOUS HOCKEY PLAYER... AS HE SKATES OUT ONTO THE ICE, THE OPPOSING GOALIE BEGINS TO SHAKE WITH FEAR...
HERE'S THE WORLD FAMOUS HOCKEY PLAYER MOVING THE PUCK UP THE ICE...
HE SHOOTS!
IT'S A GOAL!
1-26
ONCE AGAIN HE PICKS UP THE PUCK AND MOVES OVER THE BLUE LINE..
HE FLIPS A BACKHAND SHOT..
ANOTHER GOAL!
HE PICKS UP THE PUCK IN CENTER ICE..ACROSS THE BLUE LINE...DOWN THE LEFT SIDE...
IT'S IN!!
Tm. Reg. U. S. Pat. Off.—All rights reserved © 1969 by United Feature Syndicate, Inc.
I SCORED THREE GOALS WHILE THEY WERE PLAYING THE NATIONAL ANTHEM!
SCHULZ

PEANUTS
HERE'S THE WORLD-FAMOUS HOCKEY GOALIE GUARDING THE NET..
2-10
Tm. Reg. U. S. Pat. Off.—All rights reserved © 1969 by United Feature Syndicate, Inc.
AAUGH!
NOBODY SCORES!
SCHULZ

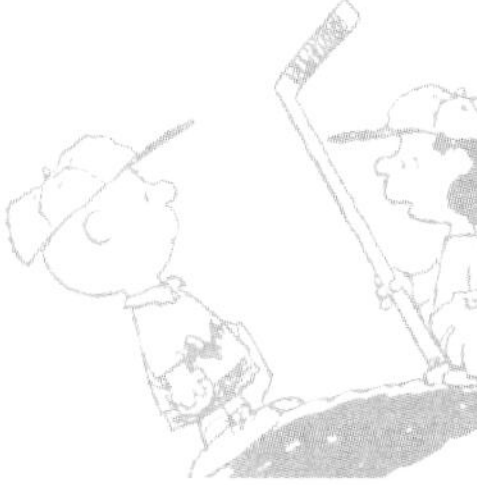
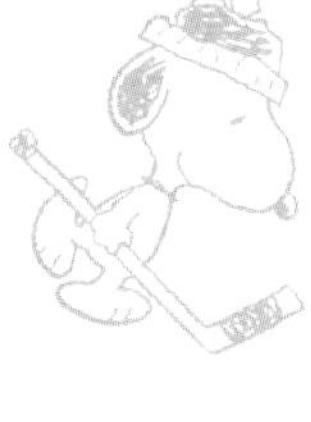
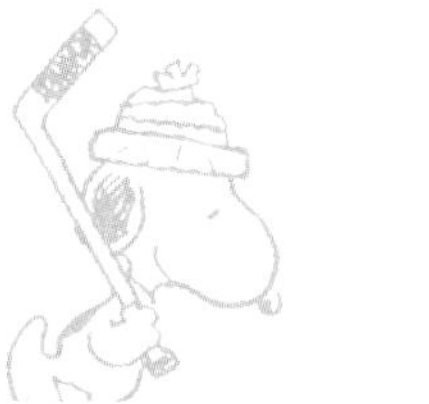

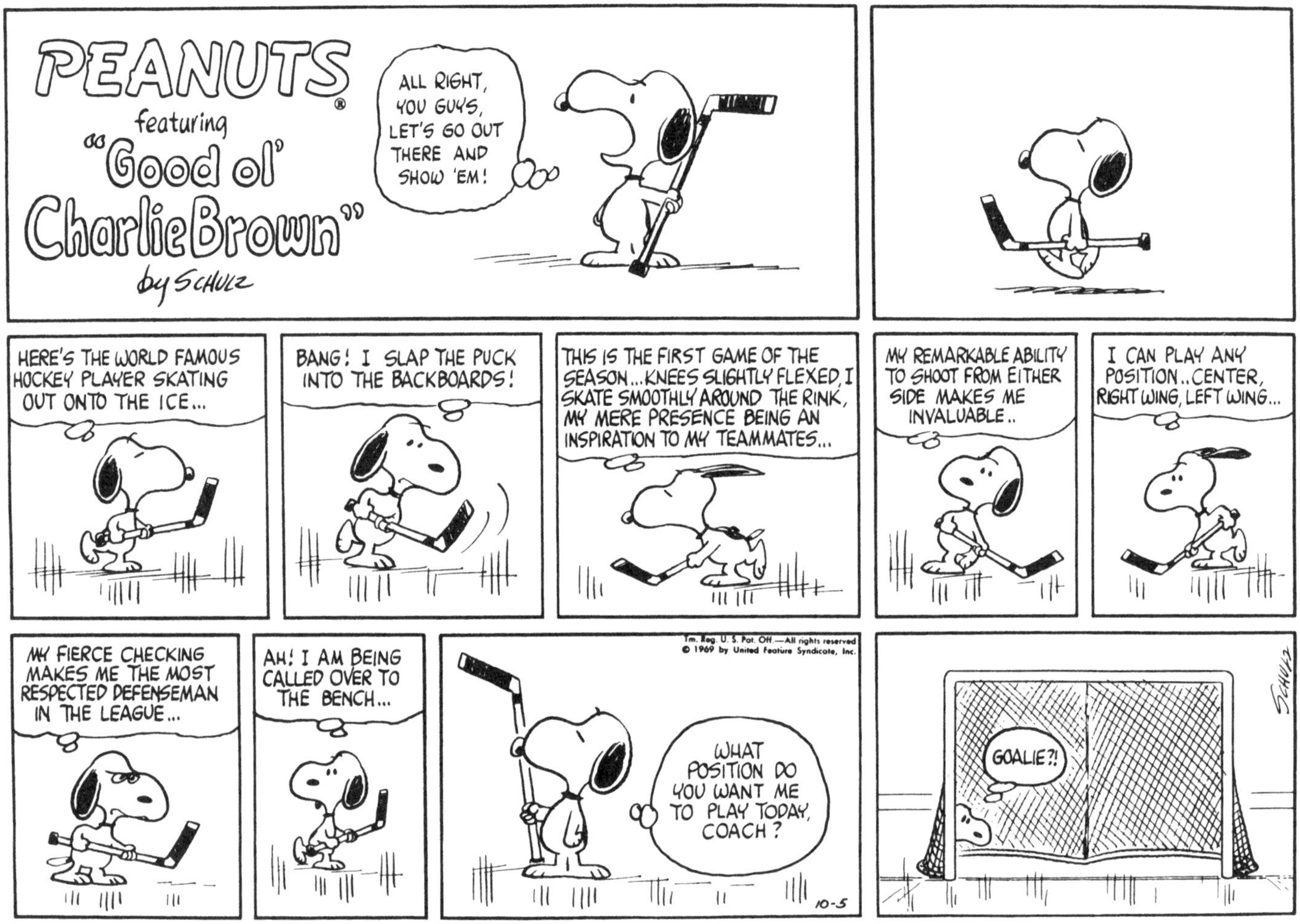

PEANUTS®
featuring "Good ol' CharlieBrown"
by SCHULZ
ALL RIGHT, YOU GUYS, LET'S GO OUT THERE AND SHOW 'EM!
HERE'S THE WORLD FAMOUS HOCKEY PLAYER SKATING OUT ONTO THE ICE...
BANG! I SLAP THE PUCK INTO THE BACKBOARDS!
THIS IS THE FIRST GAME OF THE SEASON...KNEES SLIGHTLY FLEXED, I SKATE SMOOTHLY AROUND THE RINK, MY MERE PRESENCE BEING AN INSPIRATION TO MY TEAMMATES...
MY REMARKABLE ABILITY TO SHOOT FROM EITHER SIDE MAKES ME INVALUABLE..
I CAN PLAY ANY POSITION..CENTER, RIGHT WING, LEFT WING...
MY FIERCE CHECKING MAKES ME THE MOST RESPECTED DEFENSEMAN IN THE LEAGUE...
AH! I AM BEING CALLED OVER TO THE BENCH...
Tm. Reg. U. S. Pat. Off.—All rights reserved © 1969 by United Feature Syndicate, Inc.
WHAT POSITION DO YOU WANT ME TO PLAY TODAY, COACH?
10-5
SCHULZ
GOALIE?!

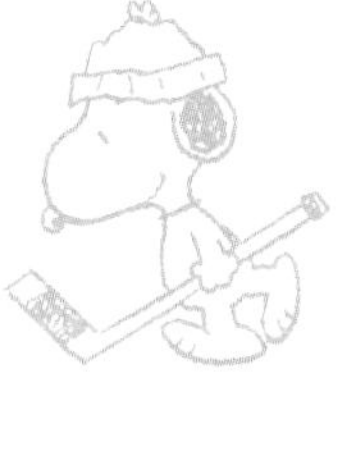
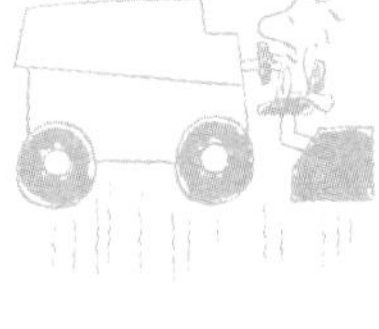
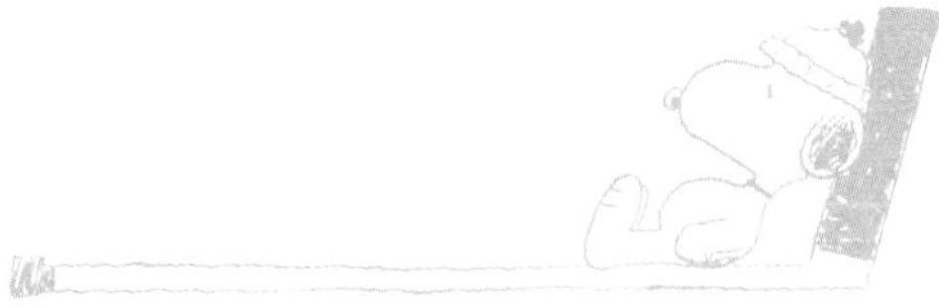

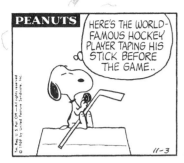

PEANUTS
HERE'S THE WORLD-FAMOUS HOCKEY PLAYER TAPING HIS STICK BEFORE THE GAME..
WE HOCKEY PLAYERS ARE VERY FUSSY ABOUT THE WAY WE TAPE OUR STICKS
SOMETIMES, OF COURSE, WE HAVE A LITTLE TROUBLE WITH THE TAPE...
11-3
Tm. Reg. U.S. Pat. Off.—All rights reserved
© 1969 by United Feature Syndicate, Inc.
SCHULZ

PEANUTS
HERE'S THE WORLD-FAMOUS HOCKEY PLAYER SITTING IN THE PENALTY BOX
TWO MINUTES FOR SLASHING... FIVE MINUTES FOR FIGHTING.... TEN MINUTES MISCONDUCT...
I DON'T UNDERSTAND IT..
I'M SO INNOCENT!
11-5
Tm. Reg. U.S. Pat. Off.—All rights reserved
© 1969 by United Feature Syndicate, Inc.
SCHULZ

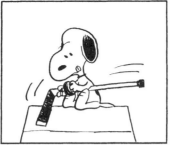

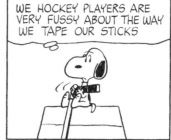

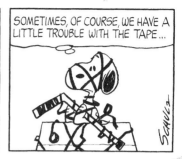

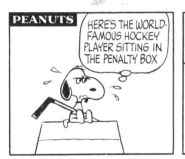

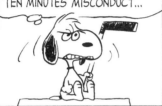

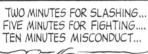

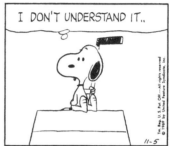

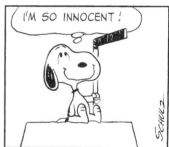

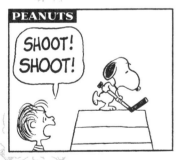

PEANUTS
SHOOT! SHOOT!
BOOOOO! OFFSIDE! MAN IN THE CREASE!
BOOOOOOO!! HEY, REF, CAN'T YOU SEE?!! HOW ABOUT ICING?!?
SEASON-TICKET HOLDER!
11-7
Tm. Reg. U.S. Pat. Off.—All rights reserved
© 1969 by United Feature Syndicate, Inc.
SCHULZ

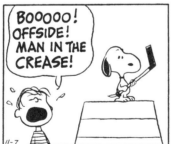

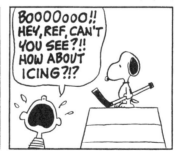

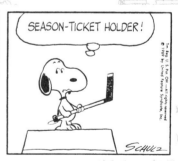

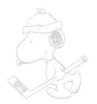

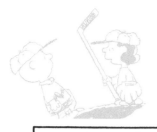

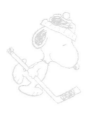

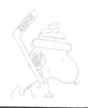

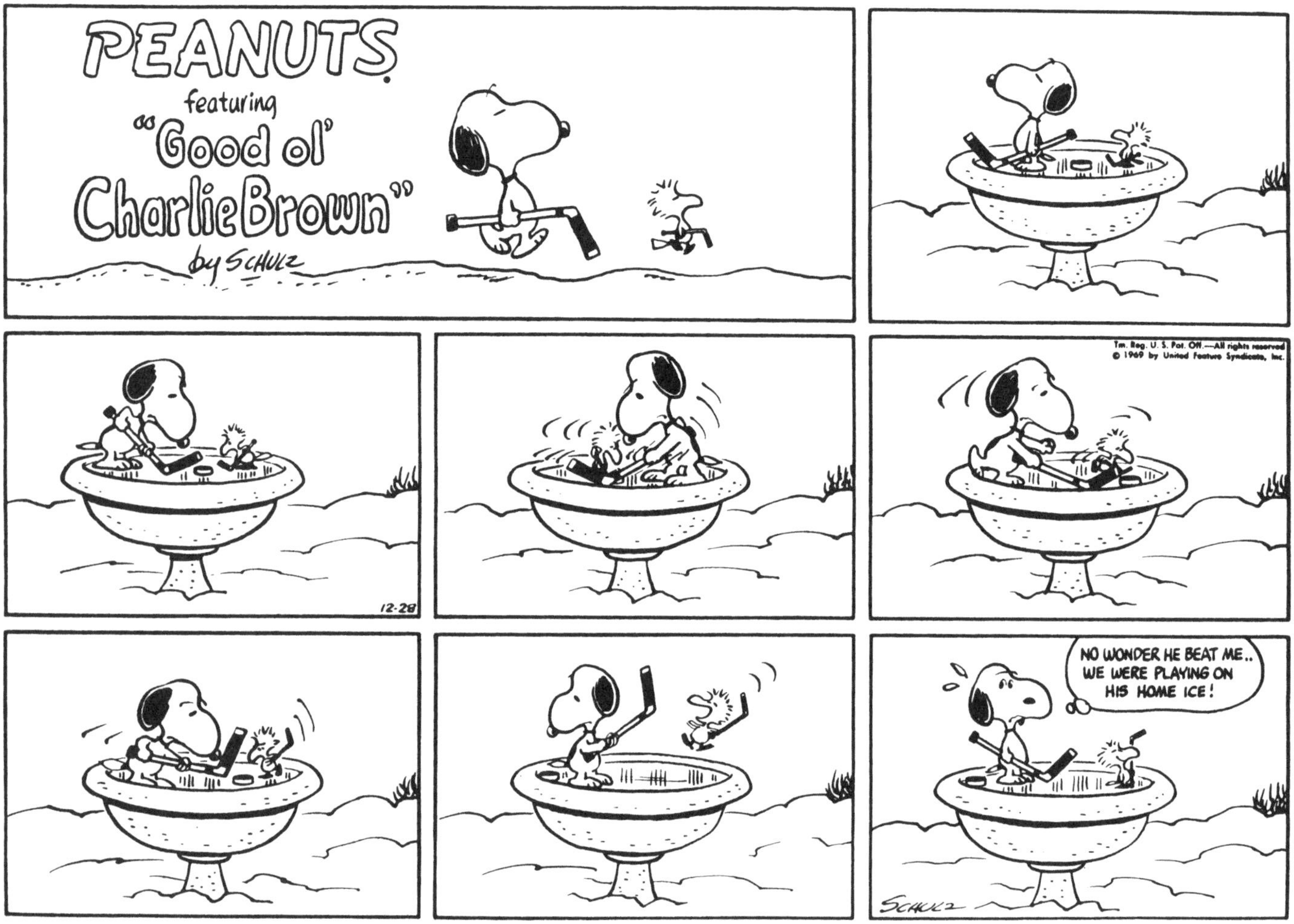
PEANUTS
featuring
"Good ol' CharlieBrown"
by SCHULZ
Tm. Reg. U. S. Pat. Off.—All rights reserved © 1969 by United Feature Syndicate, Inc.
12-28
NO WONDER HE BEAT ME.. WE WERE PLAYING ON HIS HOME ICE!
SCHULZ

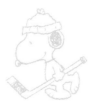

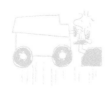

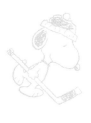

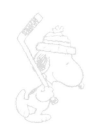

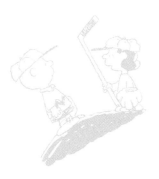

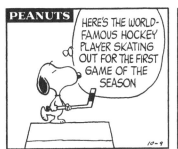

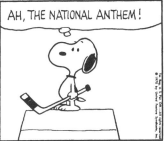

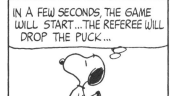

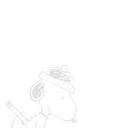

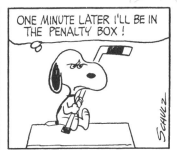

PEANUTS
HERE'S THE WORLD-FAMOUS HOCKEY PLAYER SKATING OUT FOR THE FIRST GAME OF THE SEASON
10-9
AH, THE NATIONAL ANTHEM!
Tm. Reg. U. S. Pat. Off.—All rights reserved
© 1970 by United Feature Syndicate, Inc.
IN A FEW SECONDS, THE GAME WILL START...THE REFEREE WILL DROP THE PUCK...
ONE MINUTE LATER I'LL BE IN THE PENALTY BOX!
SCHULZ

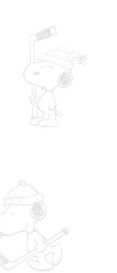

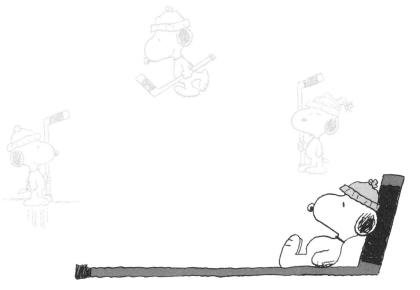

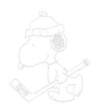

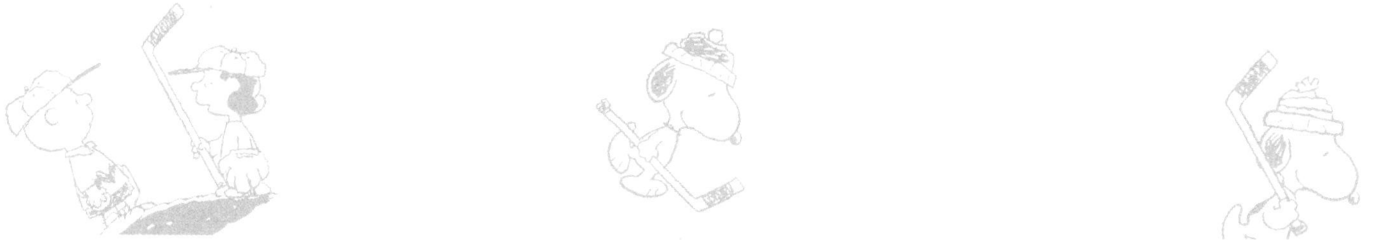

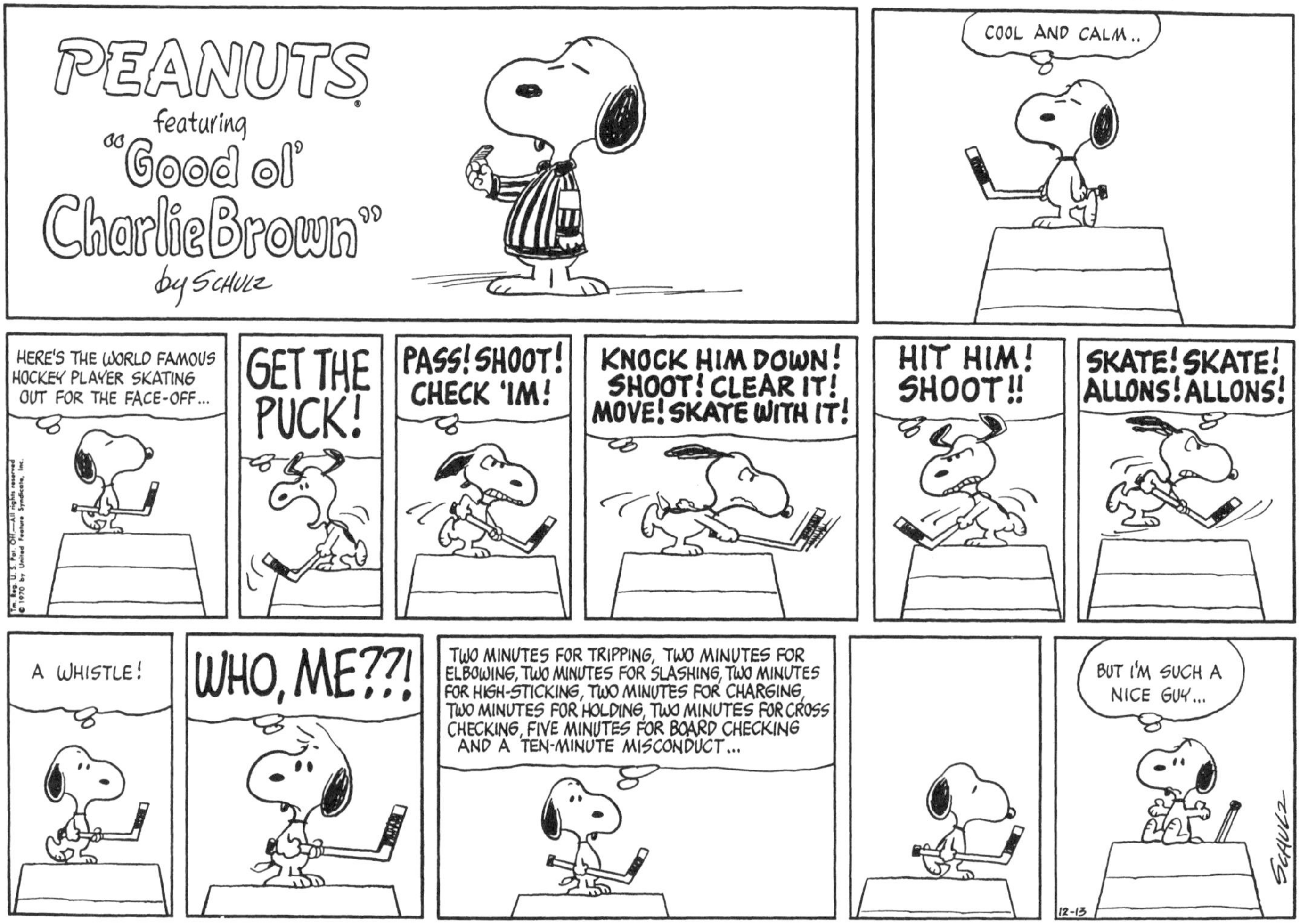

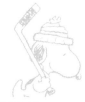

PEANUTS
featuring "Good ol' Charlie Brown"
by SCHULZ
COOL AND CALM..
HERE'S THE WORLD FAMOUS HOCKEY PLAYER SKATING OUT FOR THE FACE-OFF...
Tm. Reg. U.S. Pat. Off.—All rights reserved © 1970 by United Feature Syndicate, Inc.
GET THE PUCK!
PASS! SHOOT! CHECK 'IM!
KNOCK HIM DOWN! SHOOT! CLEAR IT! MOVE! SKATE WITH IT!
HIT HIM! SHOOT!!
SKATE! SKATE! ALLONS! ALLONS!
A WHISTLE!
WHO, ME??!
TWO MINUTES FOR TRIPPING, TWO MINUTES FOR ELBOWING, TWO MINUTES FOR SLASHING, TWO MINUTES FOR HIGH-STICKING, TWO MINUTES FOR CHARGING, TWO MINUTES FOR HOLDING, TWO MINUTES FOR CROSS CHECKING, FIVE MINUTES FOR BOARD CHECKING AND A TEN-MINUTE MISCONDUCT...
BUT I'M SUCH A NICE GUY...
12-13
SCHULZ

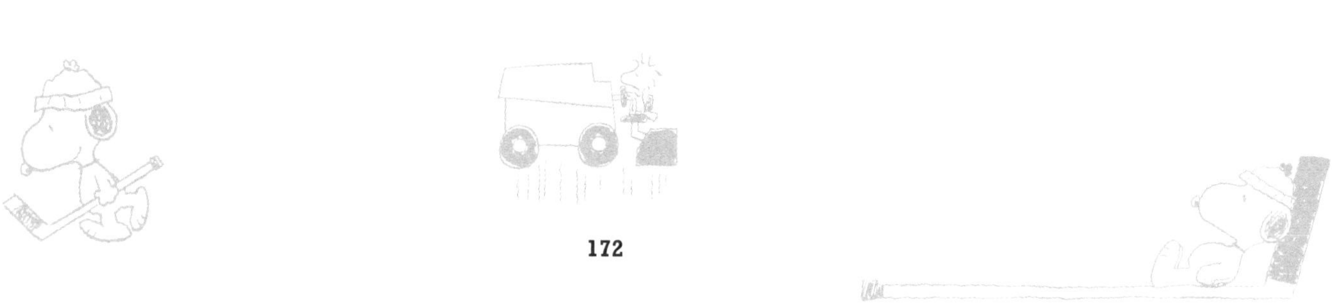

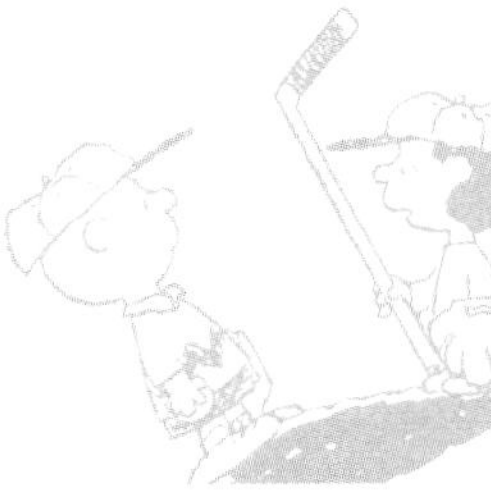

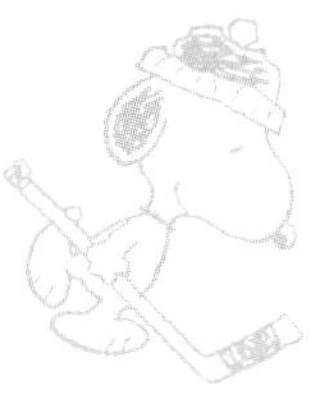

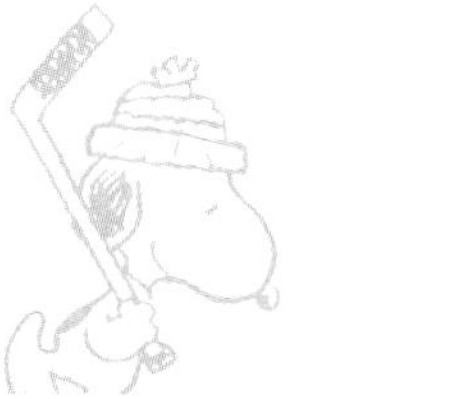

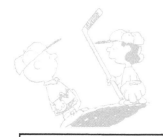

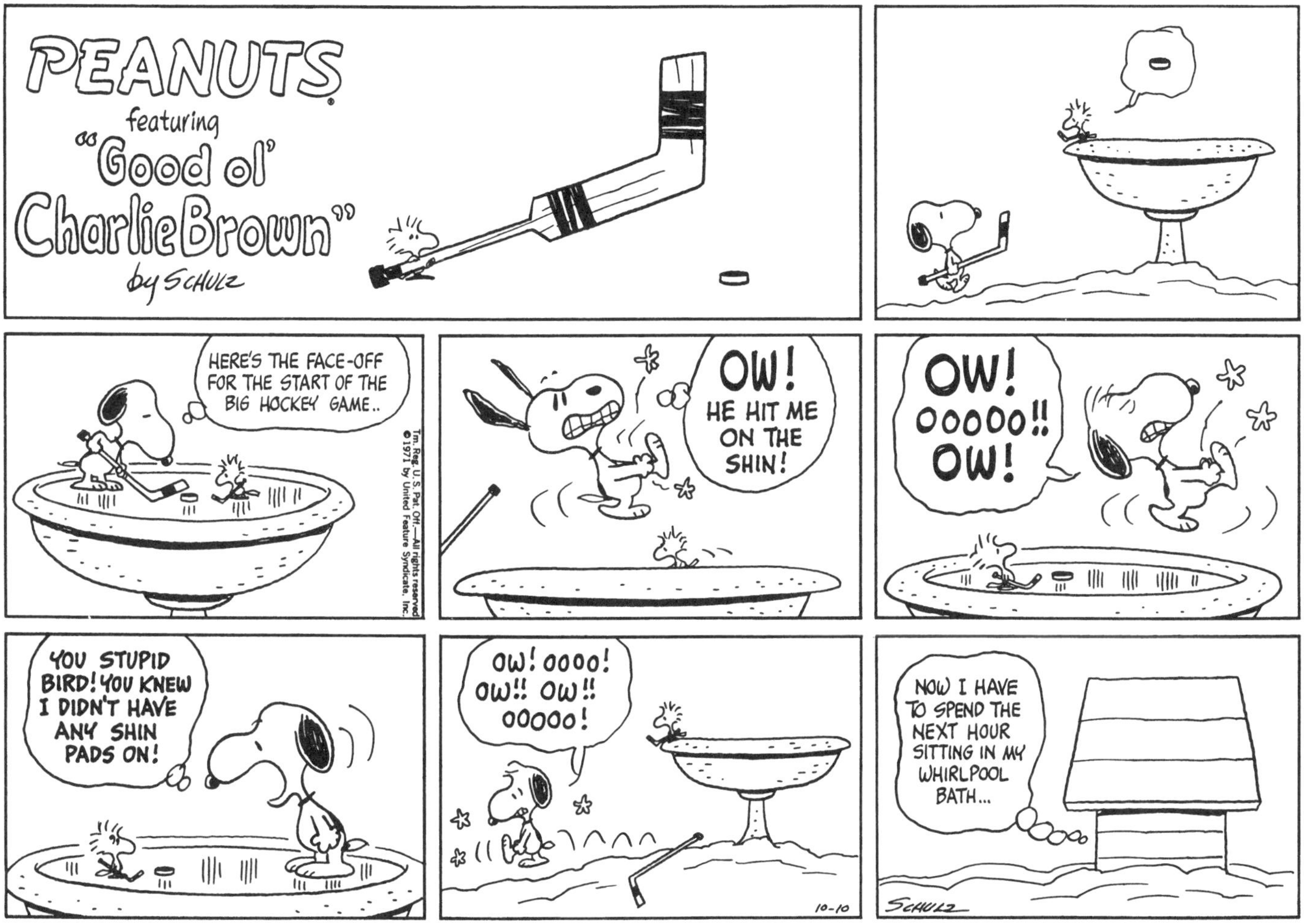
PEANUTS
featuring
"Good ol' CharlieBrown"
by SCHULZ
HERE'S THE FACE-OFF FOR THE START OF THE BIG HOCKEY GAME..
Tm. Reg. U.S. Pat. Off.—All rights reserved © 1971 by United Feature Syndicate, Inc.
OW! HE HIT ME ON THE SHIN!
OW! OOOOO!! OW!
YOU STUPID BIRD! YOU KNEW I DIDN'T HAVE ANY SHIN PADS ON!
OW! OOOO! OW!! OW!! OOOOO!
10-10
NOW I HAVE TO SPEND THE NEXT HOUR SITTING IN MY WHIRLPOOL BATH...
SCHULZ

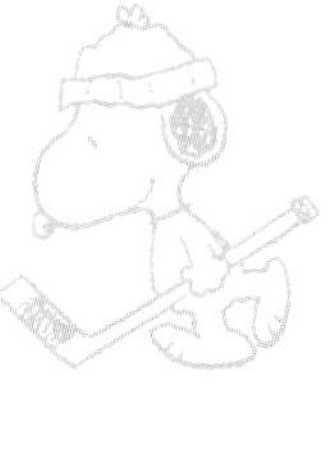

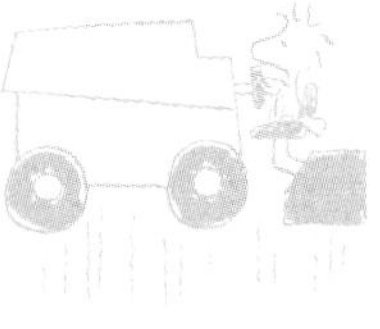

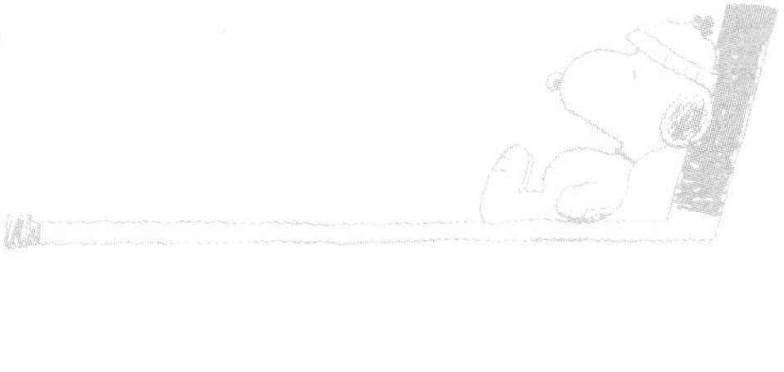

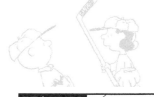

PEANUTS
HERE'S THE WORLD-FAMOUS HOCKEY PLAYER SKATING OUT FOR THE BIG GAME..
10-19
THIS IS GOING TO BE A ROUGH, TOUGH, KNOCK-'EM-DOWN GAME! SHOW NO MERCY..
..BUT REMEMBER NOW...
Tm. Reg. U.S. Pat. Off.—All rights reserved © 1971 by United Feature Syndicate, Inc.
NO RAISING!
SCHULZ

PEANUTS
HERE'S THE WORLD FAMOUS HOCKEY PLAYER SKATING OUT ONTO THE ICE
TONIGHT'S GAME IS AGAINST DETROIT... WHERE'S GORDIE HOWE?
11-20
GORDIE HOWE ISN'T PLAYING?! GORDIE HOWE HAS RETIRED?!?
Tm. Reg. U.S. Pat. Off.—All rights reserved © 1971 by United Feature Syndicate, Inc.
RATS! I WAS GOING TO GIVE HIM AN ELBOW!
SCHULZ

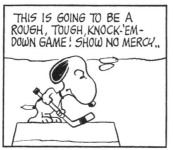

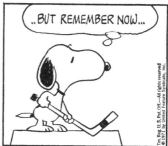

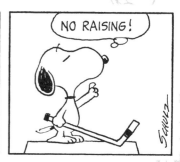

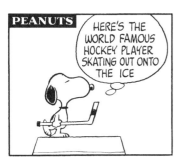

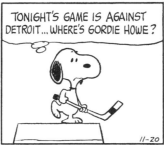

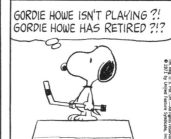

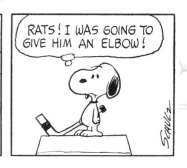

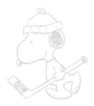

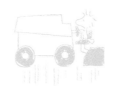

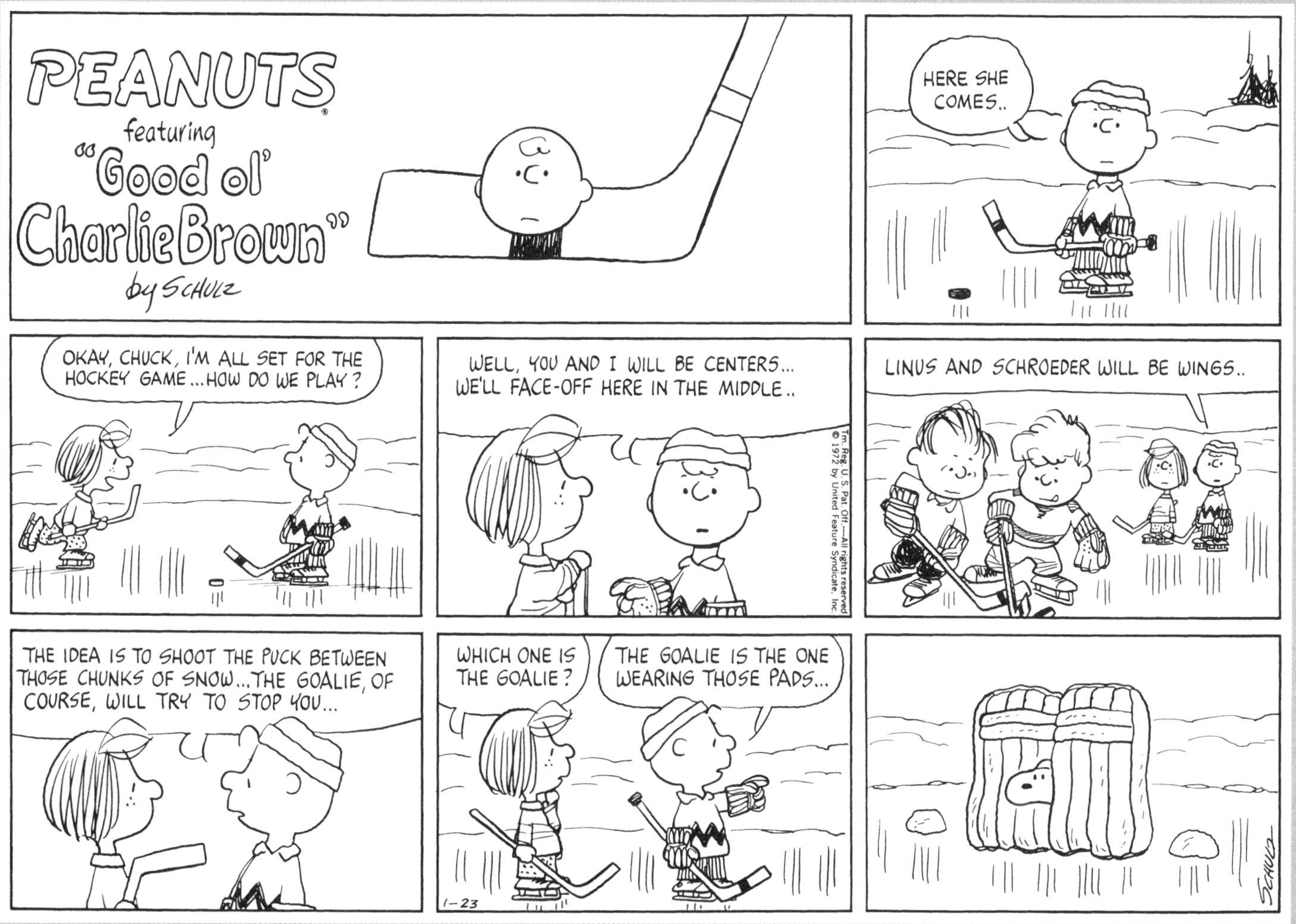
PEANUTS
featuring
"Good ol' Charlie Brown"
by SCHULZ
HERE SHE COMES..
OKAY, CHUCK, I'M ALL SET FOR THE HOCKEY GAME...HOW DO WE PLAY?
WELL, YOU AND I WILL BE CENTERS... WE'LL FACE-OFF HERE IN THE MIDDLE..
Tm. Reg. U.S. Pat. Off.—All rights reserved
© 1972 by United Feature Syndicate, Inc.
LINUS AND SCHROEDER WILL BE WINGS..
THE IDEA IS TO SHOOT THE PUCK BETWEEN THOSE CHUNKS OF SNOW...THE GOALIE, OF COURSE, WILL TRY TO STOP YOU...
WHICH ONE IS THE GOALIE?
THE GOALIE IS THE ONE WEARING THOSE PADS...
1-23
SCHULZ

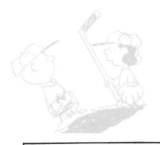

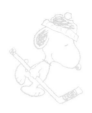

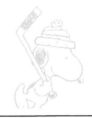

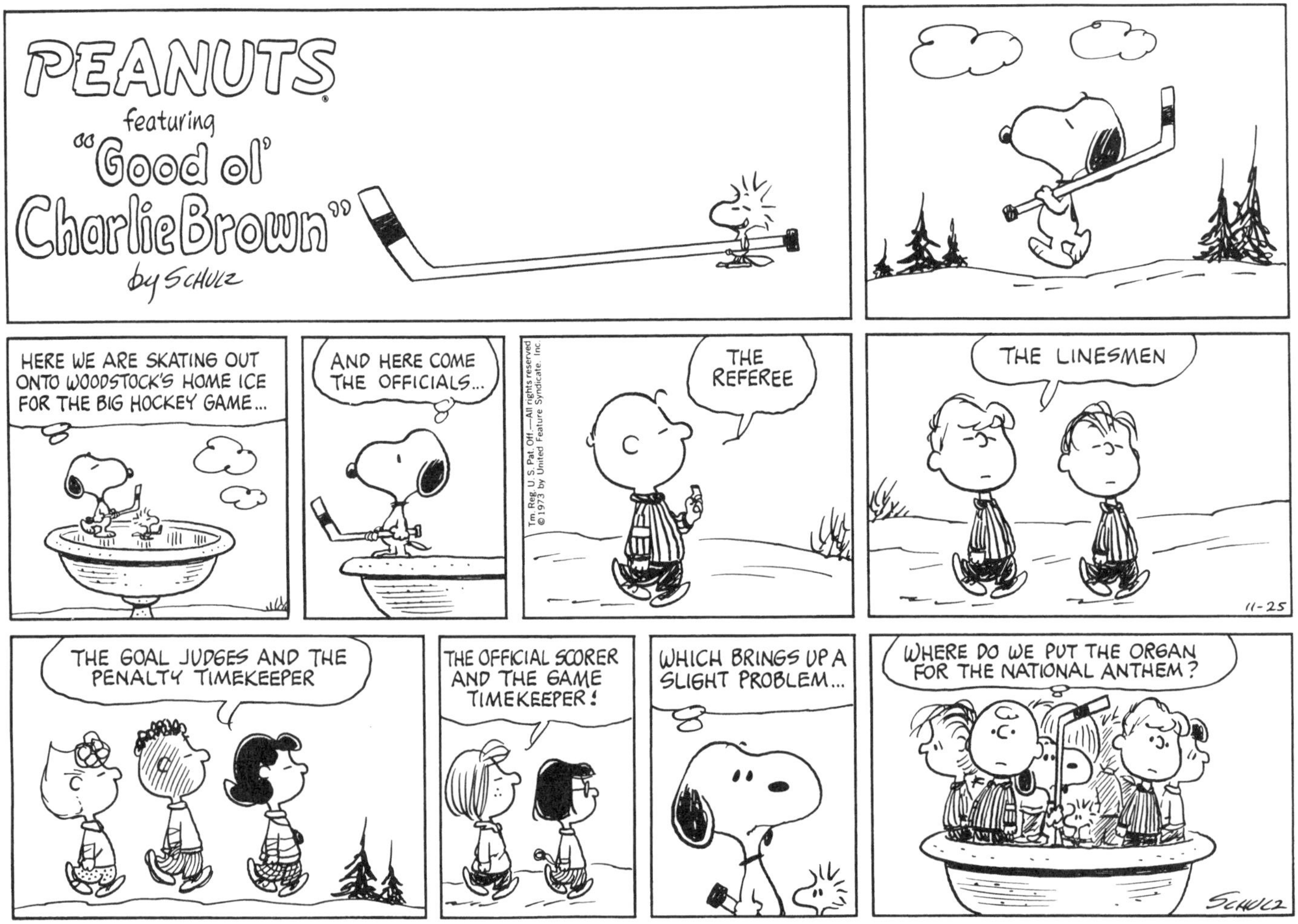
PEANUTS®
featuring "Good ol' CharlieBrown"
by SCHULZ
HERE WE ARE SKATING OUT ONTO WOODSTOCK'S HOME ICE FOR THE BIG HOCKEY GAME...
AND HERE COME THE OFFICIALS...
Tm Reg. U.S. Pat. Off.—All rights reserved © 1973 by United Feature Syndicate, Inc.
THE REFEREE
THE LINESMEN
11-25
THE GOAL JUDGES AND THE PENALTY TIMEKEEPER
THE OFFICIAL SCORER AND THE GAME TIMEKEEPER!
WHICH BRINGS UP A SLIGHT PROBLEM...
WHERE DO WE PUT THE ORGAN FOR THE NATIONAL ANTHEM?
SCHULZ

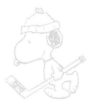

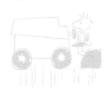

PEANUTS
featuring
"Good ol' Charlie Brown"
by SCHULZ
Tm. Reg. U.S. Pat. Off.—All rights reserved
©1974 by United Feature Syndicate, Inc.
11-10
bump!
CHEAP SHOT! CHEAP SHOT!
!
ACTUALLY, IT WAS A GOOD LEGAL CHECK, BUT YOU NEVER WANT TO ADMIT IT!
SCHULZ

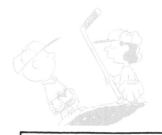

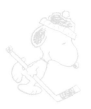

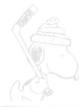

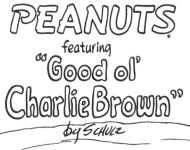

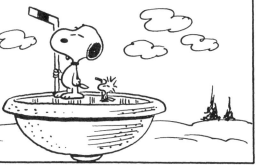

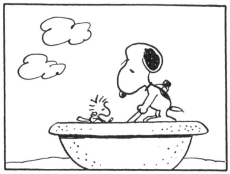

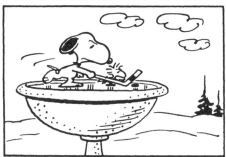

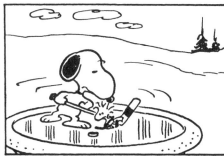

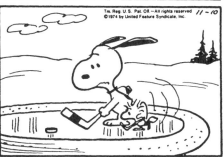

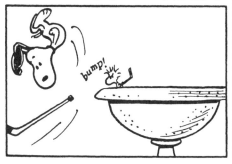

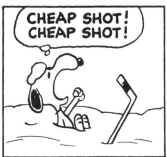

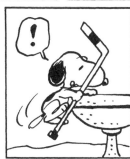

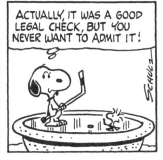

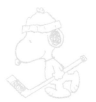

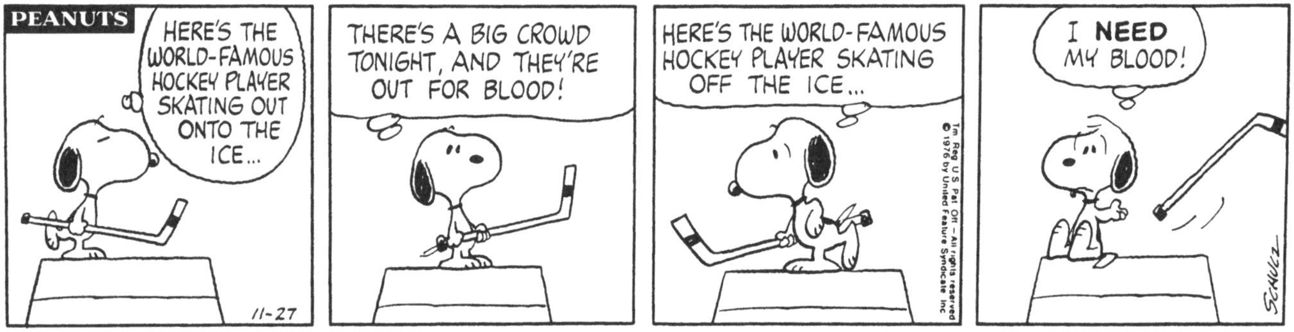
PEANUTS
HERE'S THE WORLD-FAMOUS HOCKEY PLAYER SKATING OUT ONTO THE ICE...
11-27
THERE'S A BIG CROWD TONIGHT, AND THEY'RE OUT FOR BLOOD!
HERE'S THE WORLD-FAMOUS HOCKEY PLAYER SKATING OFF THE ICE...
Tm Reg U S Pat Off – All rights reserved © 1976 by United Feature Syndicate Inc
I **NEED** MY BLOOD!
SCHULZ

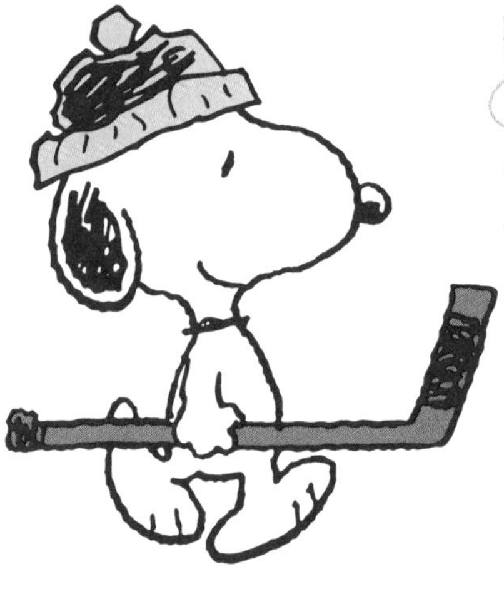

PEANUTS
featuring
"Good ol' Charlie Brown"
by SCHULZ
HOCKEY TODAY! (IF BIRDBATH FREEZES)
Tm Reg U.S. Pat. Off.—All rights reserved © 1977 by United Feature Syndicate, Inc.
!
?
2-27
THEY'RE RIGHT...HOCKEY IS GETTING TOO VIOLENT!
SCHULZ

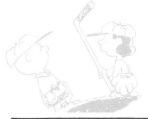

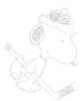

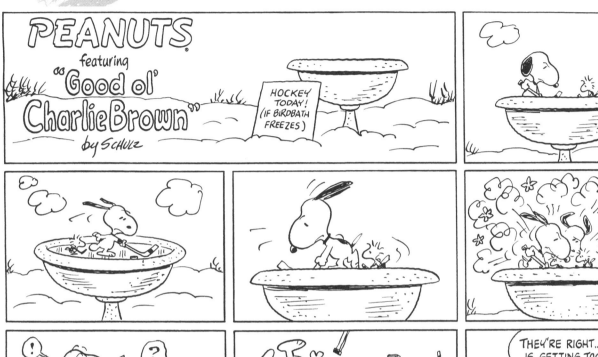

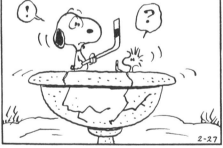

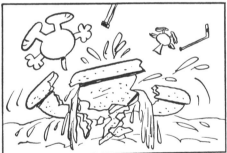

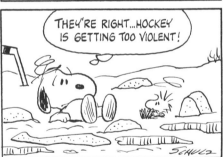

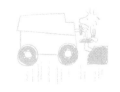

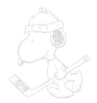

 OKAY, BEAUTIFUL, GET OFF THE ICE!! WE'RE GONNA PLAY HOCKEY!

 HOCKEY?! GET LOST, NECKHEAD! I WAS HERE FIRST!!

© 1978 United Feature Syndicate, Inc.

1-5

 YOU WOULDN'T LIKE TO GET HIT WITH A HOCKEY STICK WOULD YOU, BEAUTIFUL?

HOW WOULD YOU LIKE TO BE FORCE-FED A PAIR OF GOALIE PADS?!

LISTEN, BEAUTIFUL, GET YOUR STUPID FIGURE SKATES OFF THE ICE! WE WANNA PLAY HOCKEY, SEE?

WE HAVE TEN HOCKEY STICKS HERE TELLING YOU TO "GET OFF THE ICE!"

OH, YEAH? COME ON AND TRY SOMETHING! ME AND MY COACH'LL TAKE YOU ALL ON!!

© 1978 United Feature Syndicate, Inc.

I THINK I'LL GO HOME.. I HAVE SOME CHAIN LETTERS TO WRITE...

1-6

180

Panel 1: HOW CAN WE PLAY HOCKEY WITH THAT STUPID GIRL LYING ON THE ICE?

Panel 2: DO YOU GUYS HAVE A PUCK? SURE! WHAT DO YOU THINK THIS IS?

1-10

Panel 3: GIVE IT TO ME... I WANT TO SHOW YOU A LITTLE TRICK...

Panel 4: © 1978 United Feature Syndicate, Inc.

Panel 5: I WAS THE HERO! I SCORED THE WINNING GOAL!

11-1

Panel 6: LUCKY SHOT?!

© 1979 United Feature Syndicate, Inc.

Panel 7: I WOULDN'T SAY THAT

Panel 8: JUST BECAUSE IT BOUNCED OFF A WAITRESS IN THE COFFEE SHOP!

YOU DON'T HAVE ANY SHIN PADS?

YOU CAN'T PLAY HOCKEY WITHOUT SHIN PADS...

12-27

I WONDER IF A COUPLE OF MAGAZINES WOULD WORK...

NO, I GUESS NOT

© 1979 United Feature Syndicate, Inc.

THAT STUPID WOODSTOCK!

HE COST US THE HOCKEY GAME...

HE TRIED TO USE MAGAZINES FOR SHIN PADS...SO WHAT HAPPENED?

12-28

THE OTHER TEAM SCORED WHILE HE WAS READING HIS SHIN PADS!

© 1979 United Feature Syndicate, Inc.

SNOOPY? WHERE ARE YOU?
3-2
I THINK HE WENT OFF TO PLAY HOCKEY...
A HOCKEY GAME SHOULDN'T LAST THIS LONG...
© 1981 United Feature Syndicate, Inc.
I HATE THESE ALL-NIGHT PENALTIES!
SCHULZ

HERE WE GO FOR THE FIRST HOCKEY GAME OF THE SEASON...
© 1981 United Feature Syndicate, Inc.
I CAN SEE MYSELF NOW OUT ON THE OL' POND RACING DOWN THE ICE WITH THE PUCK!
11-2
AFTER IT GETS A LITTLE COLDER
SCHULZ

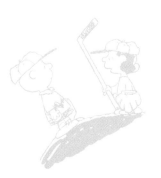

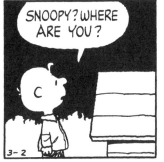

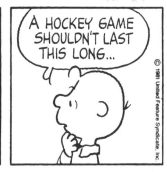

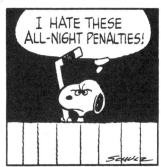

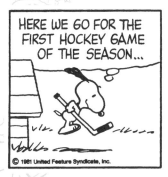

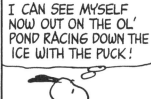

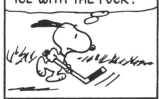

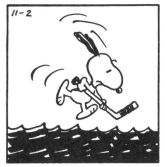

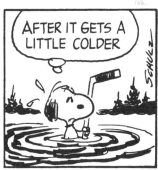

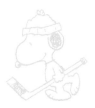

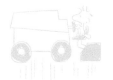

Panel 1: HERE'S THE WORLD FAMOUS HOCKEY PLAYER STANDING FOR THE NATIONAL ANTHEM

Panel 2: © 1982 United Feature Syndicate, Inc.

Panel 3: 2-3

Panel 4: THAT'S THE LONGEST I'VE EVER GONE WITHOUT A PENALTY!

Panel 5: WELL, HOW WAS HOCKEY PRACTICE?

Panel 6: I DON'T THINK THE COACH LIKES ME   11-6

Panel 7: I ASKED HIM WHAT POSITION HE WANTED ME TO PLAY...

Panel 8: HE TOLD ME TO STAND IN FRONT OF THE ZAMBONI

Panel 9:

Panel 10: AS LONG AS WE'RE JUST PRACTICING, I HAVE A SUGGESTION

Panel 11: MAYBE YOU SHOULD SHOOT AT THE OTHER GOAL FOR A WHILE...   12-27

Panel 12: SCHULZ   © 1982 United Feature Syndicate, Inc.

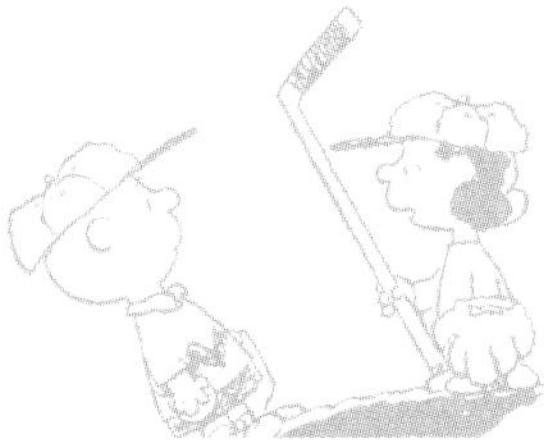
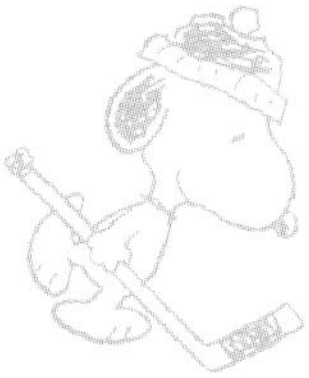
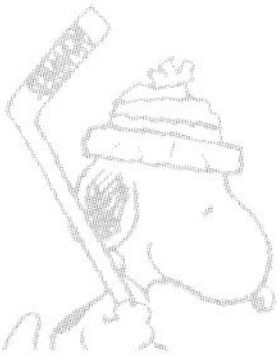

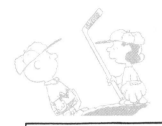

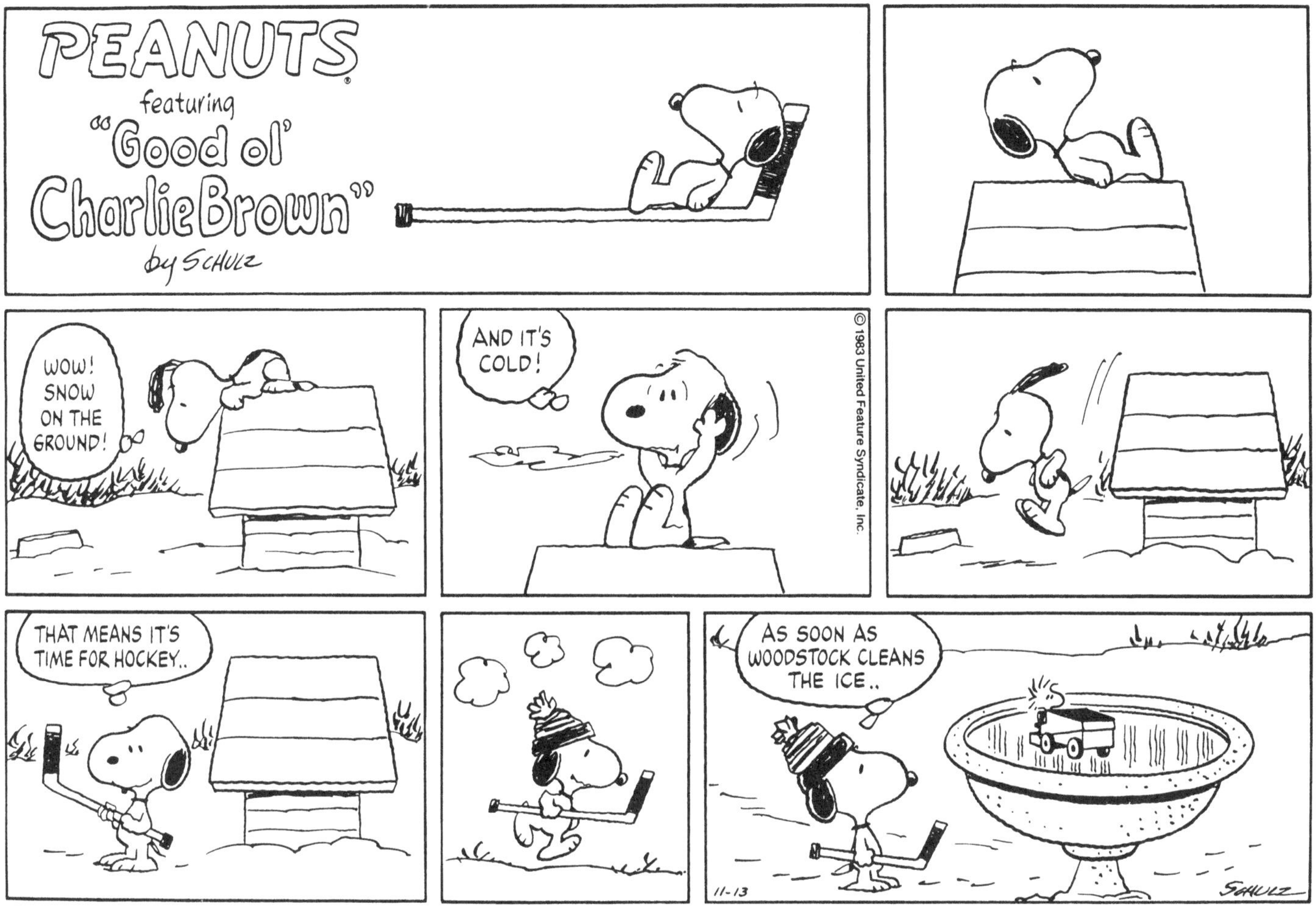
PEANUTS
featuring
"Good ol' CharlieBrown"
by SCHULZ
WOW! SNOW ON THE GROUND!
AND IT'S COLD!
© 1983 United Feature Syndicate, Inc.
THAT MEANS IT'S TIME FOR HOCKEY..
AS SOON AS WOODSTOCK CLEANS THE ICE..
11-13
SCHULZ

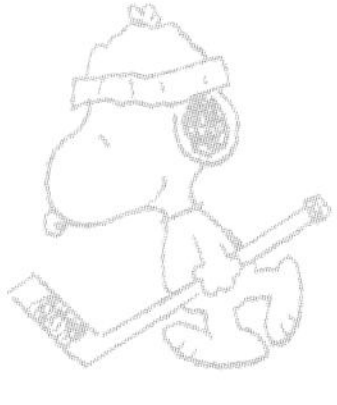
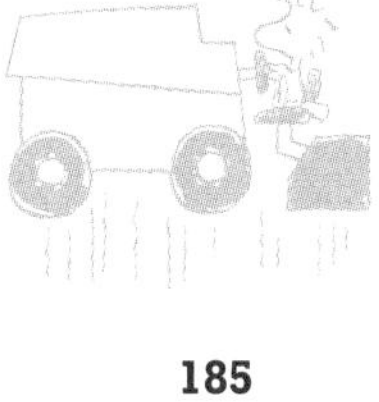
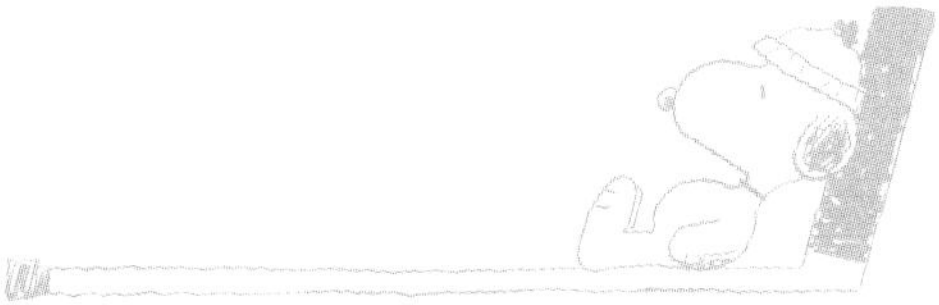

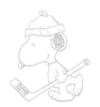

© 1984 United Feature Syndicate, Inc.

DESERT HOCKEY IS A GREAT GAME..

JUST DON'T GET NEAR THE GOALIE

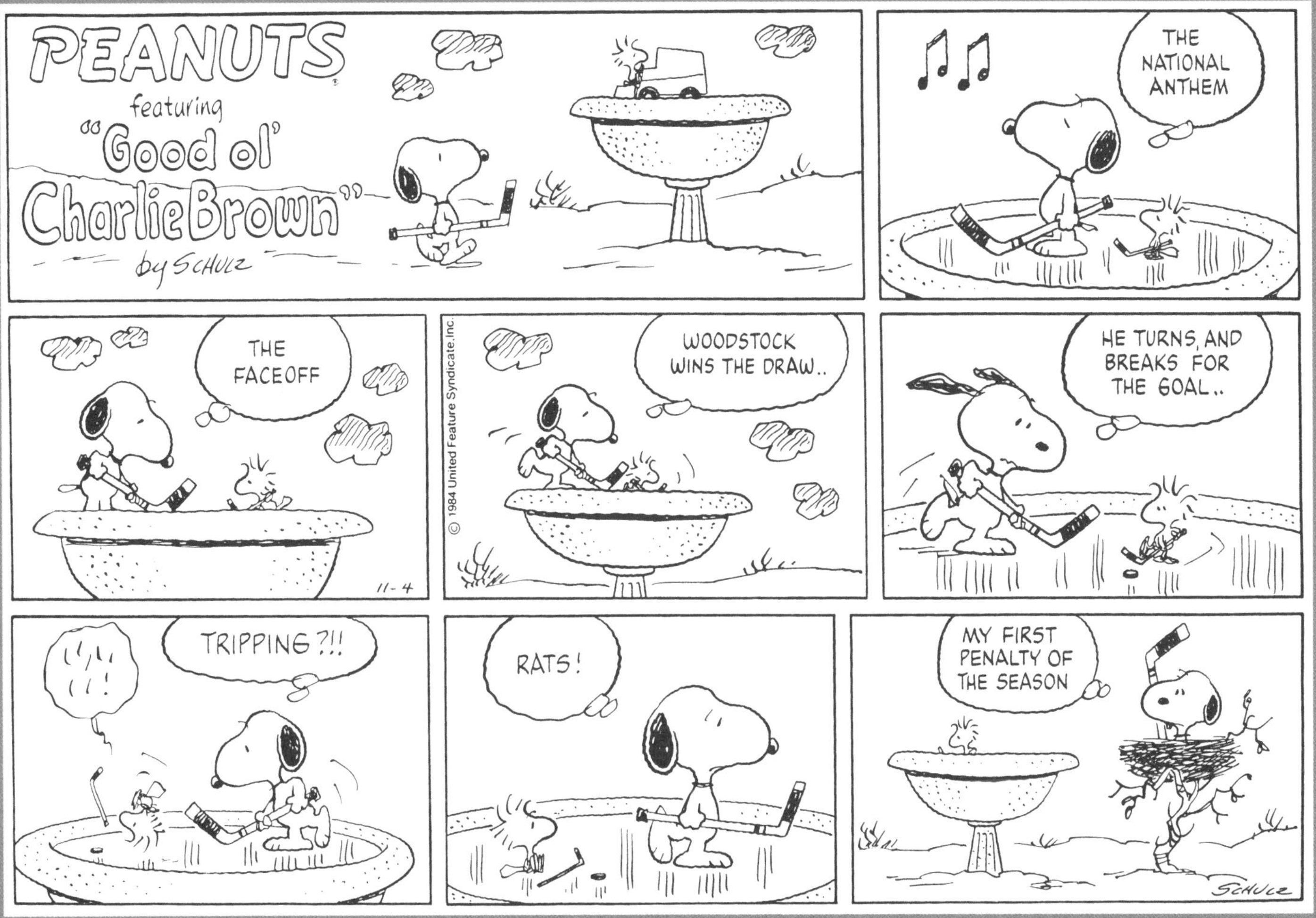
PEANUTS
featuring
"Good ol' Charlie Brown"
by SCHULZ
THE NATIONAL ANTHEM
THE FACEOFF
11-4
© 1984 United Feature Syndicate, Inc.
WOODSTOCK WINS THE DRAW..
HE TURNS, AND BREAKS FOR THE GOAL..
TRIPPING?!!
RATS!
MY FIRST PENALTY OF THE SEASON
SCHULZ

I HATE PLAYING HOCKEY WITH WOODSTOCK AND HIS FRIENDS...

© 1984 United Feature Syndicate, Inc.

TINY LITTLE PLAYERS WITH TINY LITTLE STICKS...

..ON A TINY LITTLE RINK..

12-11

..BUT BIG BODY CHECKS!

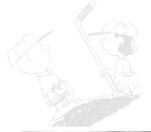

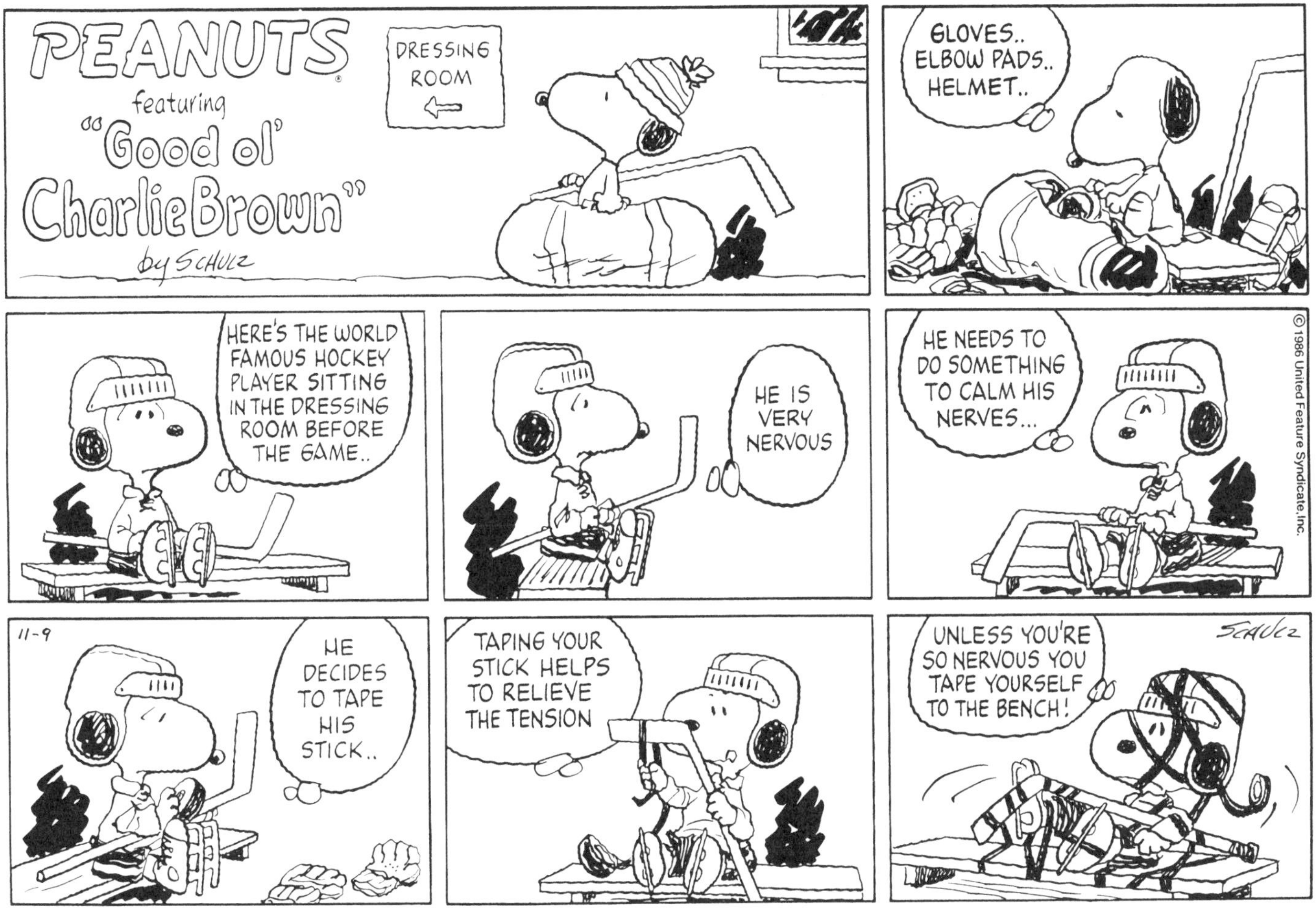
PEANUTS
featuring
"Good ol' Charlie Brown"
by SCHULZ
DRESSING ROOM
GLOVES.. ELBOW PADS.. HELMET..
HERE'S THE WORLD FAMOUS HOCKEY PLAYER SITTING IN THE DRESSING ROOM BEFORE THE GAME..
HE IS VERY NERVOUS
HE NEEDS TO DO SOMETHING TO CALM HIS NERVES...
© 1986 United Feature Syndicate, Inc.
11-9
HE DECIDES TO TAPE HIS STICK..
TAPING YOUR STICK HELPS TO RELIEVE THE TENSION
SCHULZ
UNLESS YOU'RE SO NERVOUS YOU TAPE YOURSELF TO THE BENCH!

HERE'S THE WORLD FAMOUS HOCKEY PLAYER RACING DOWN THE ICE!
© 1986 United Feature Syndicate, Inc.
11-29
HE FAKES A SLAPSHOT..
BUT IT DOESN'T FAZE THE GOALIE..
HE KNOWS I DON'T HAVE A SLAPSHOT..
SCHULZ

ANOTHER BIG HOCKEY GAME TODAY..
© 1986 United Feature Syndicate, Inc.
12-17
SOMEHOW, WE ALWAYS END UP PLAYING ON WOODSTOCK'S HOME ICE
IT WOULDN'T BE SO BAD EXCEPT FOR ONE THING..
HE NEVER LETS ME DRIVE THE ZAMBONI!
SCHULZ

SOMEONE ON YOUR HOCKEY TEAM SAID YOU AREN'T AS FAST AS YOU USED TO BE..
BUT DON'T WORRY ABOUT IT...
ONE OF THE OTHER PLAYERS STUCK UP FOR YOU..
11-14
© 1987 United Feature Syndicate, Inc.
HE SAID YOU NEVER WERE VERY FAST!
SCHULZ

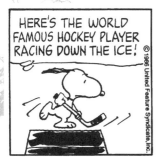

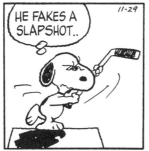

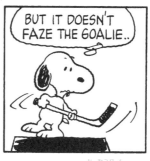

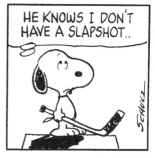

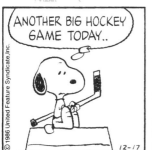

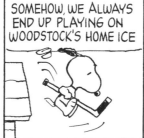

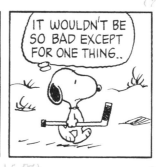

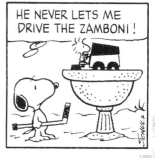

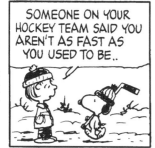

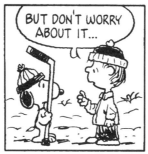

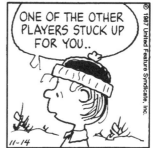

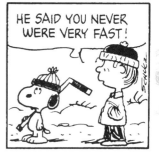

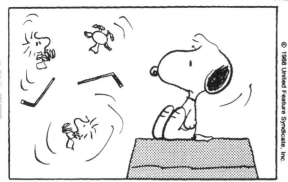

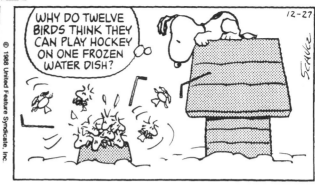

© 1988 United Feature Syndicate, Inc.
12-27
WHY DO TWELVE BIRDS THINK THEY CAN PLAY HOCKEY ON ONE FROZEN WATER DISH?
SCHULZ

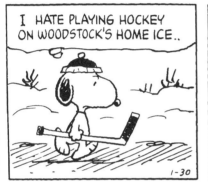

I HATE PLAYING HOCKEY ON WOODSTOCK'S HOME ICE..
1-30
AT OTHER RINKS THEY PLAY THE NATIONAL ANTHEM BEFORE THE GAME...
© 1989 United Feature Syndicate, Inc.
HERE WE HAVE TO DO THE "HOKEYPOKEY"!
SCHULZ

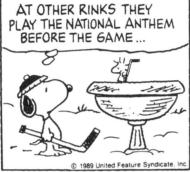

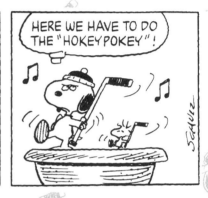

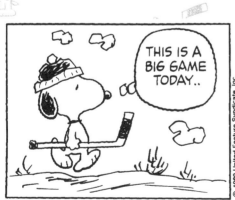

THIS IS A BIG GAME TODAY..
© 1989 United Feature Syndicate, Inc.
EVERY SEAT IN THE ARENA IS TAKEN..
12-1
SCHULZ

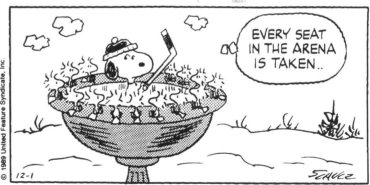

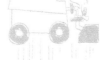

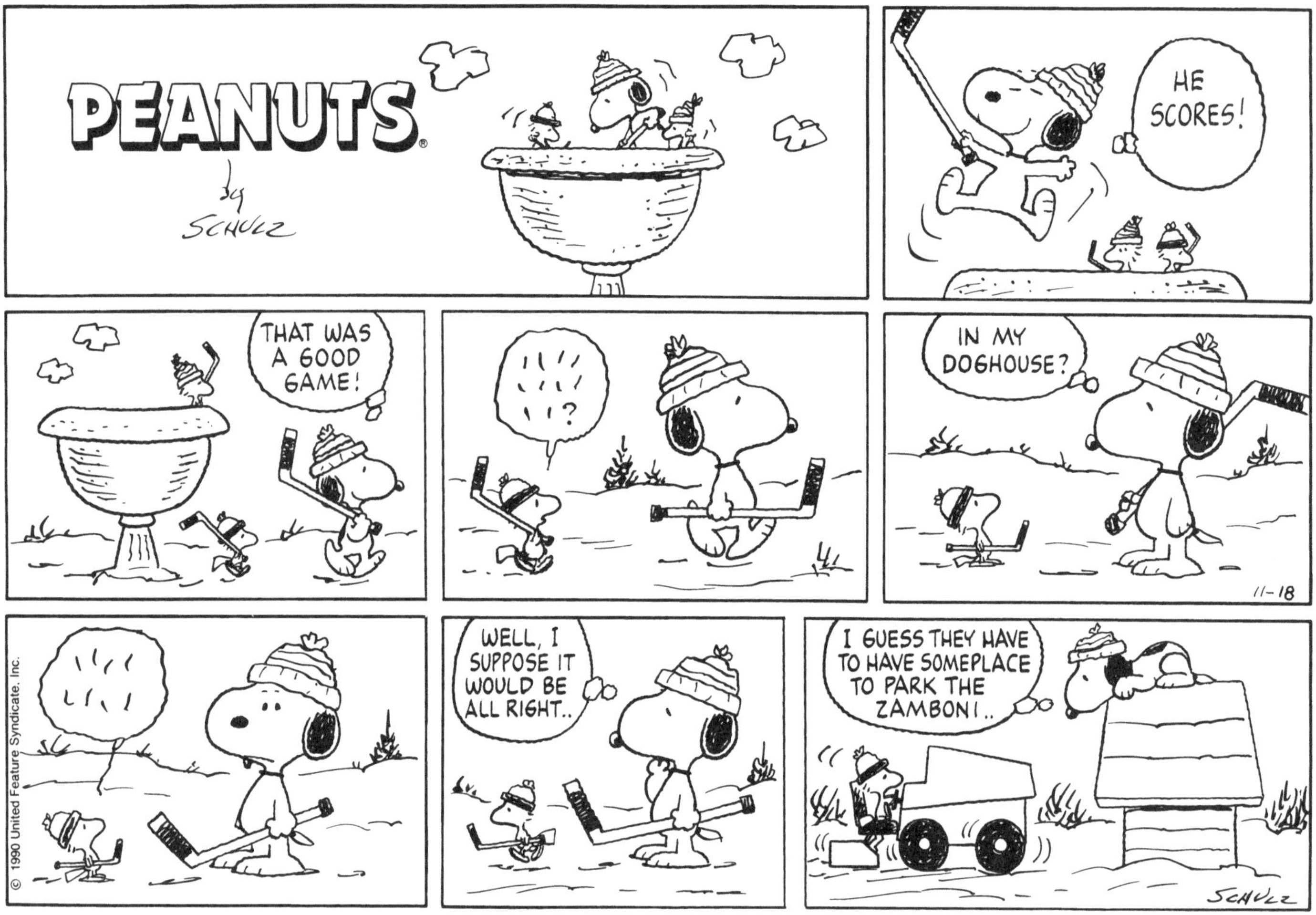
PEANUTS
by SCHULZ
HE SCORES!
THAT WAS A GOOD GAME!
?
IN MY DOGHOUSE?
11-18
© 1990 United Feature Syndicate, Inc.
WELL, I SUPPOSE IT WOULD BE ALL RIGHT..
I GUESS THEY HAVE TO HAVE SOMEPLACE TO PARK THE ZAMBONI..
SCHULZ

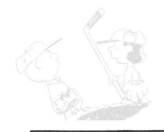

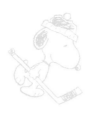

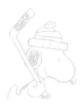

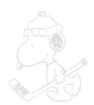

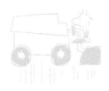

I THOUGHT WOODSTOCK AND HIS FRIENDS HAD INVITED ME TO PLAY ON THEIR HOCKEY TEAM
2-8
© 1991 United Feature Syndicate, Inc.
BUT WHAT A DISAPPOINTMENT
ALL THEY WANTED ME FOR WAS TO DRIVE THE ZAMBONI!
SCHULZ

HERE'S THE WORLD FAMOUS HOCKEY PLAYER ON HIS WAY TO THE ARENA..
© 1991 United Feature Syndicate, Inc.
11-9
I THINK WOODSTOCK HAS THE HOME CROWD ADVANTAGE..
SCHULZ

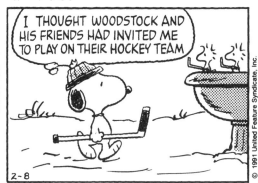

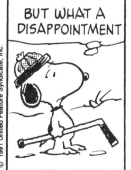

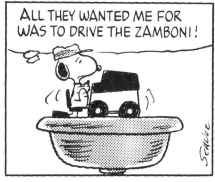

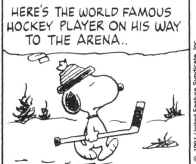

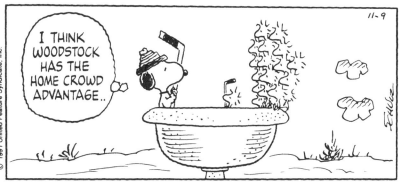

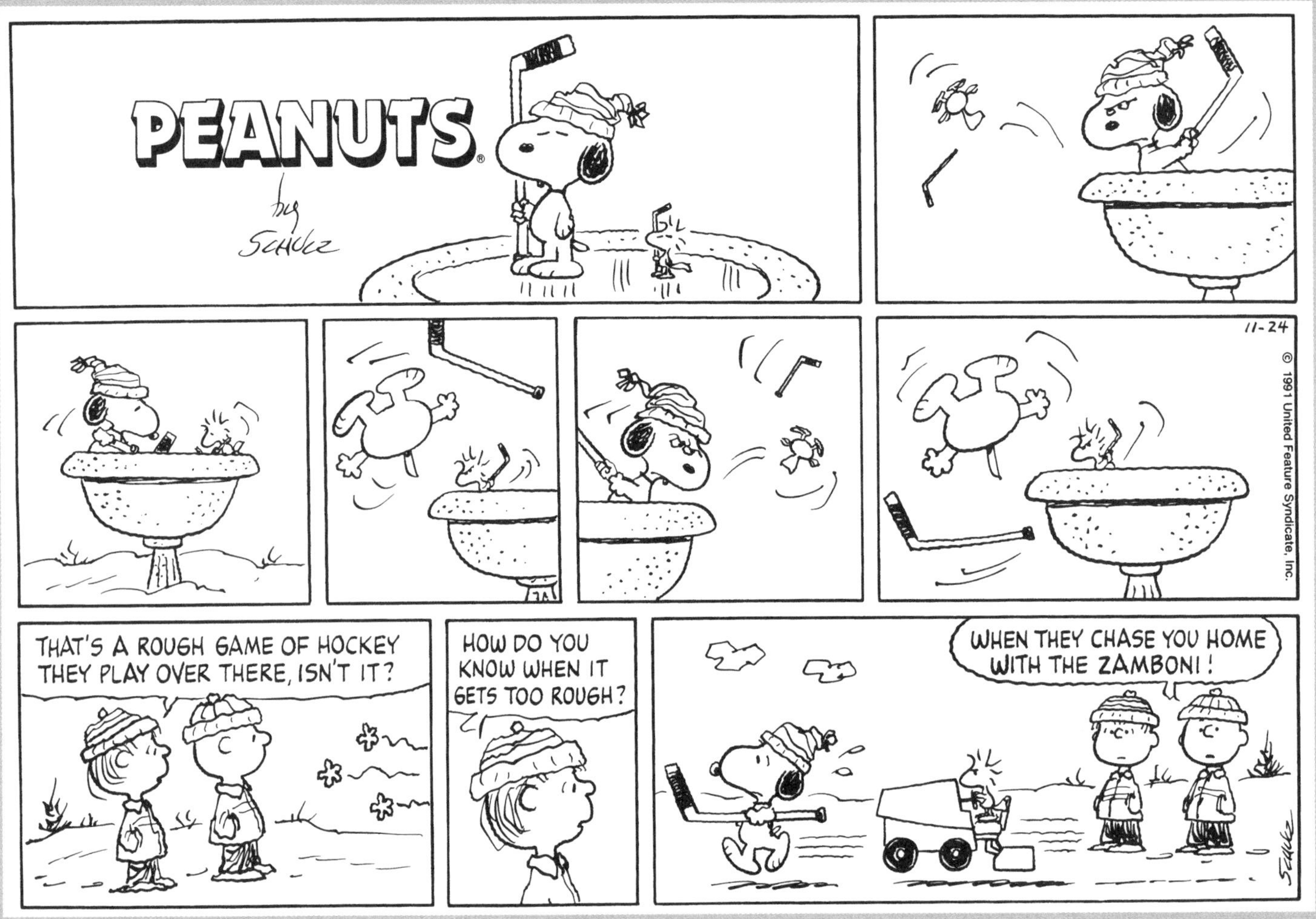
PEANUTS®
by SCHULZ
11-24
© 1991 United Feature Syndicate, Inc.
THAT'S A ROUGH GAME OF HOCKEY THEY PLAY OVER THERE, ISN'T IT?
HOW DO YOU KNOW WHEN IT GETS TOO ROUGH?
WHEN THEY CHASE YOU HOME WITH THE ZAMBONI!
SCHULZ

HERE'S THE WORLD FAMOUS HOCKEY PLAYER ON HIS WAY TO THE GAME..

1-27

UNDER THE NEW RULES IF YOU START A FIGHT, YOU ARE AUTOMATICALLY EJECTED FROM THE GAME...

SO I MIGHT AS WELL GO HOME NOW..

© 1993 United Feature Syndicate, Inc.

MY DAD TOOK ME TO MY FIRST HOCKEY GAME LAST NIGHT..

IT WAS REALLY GREAT..

© 1993 United Feature Syndicate, Inc.

9-21

I LOVED WATCHING THE ZAMBONI GO AROUND..

YOU'RE VERY WEIRD, MARCIE..

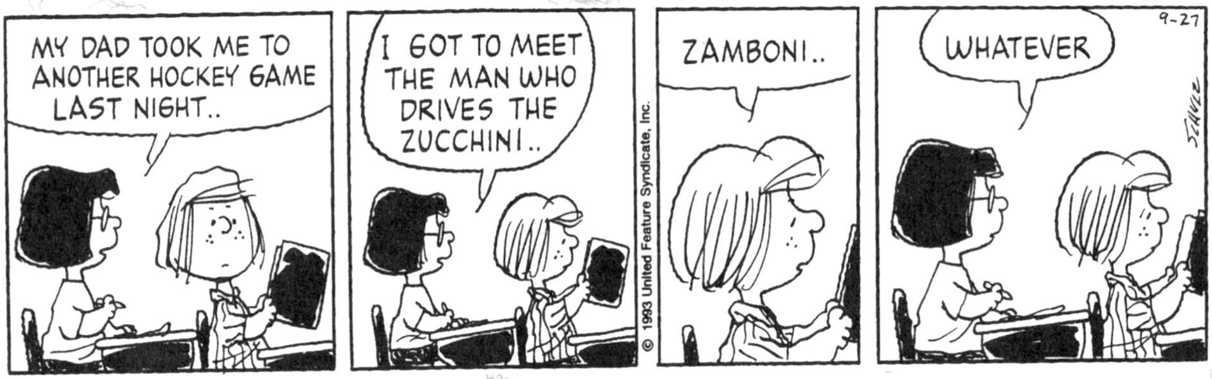
MY DAD TOOK ME TO ANOTHER HOCKEY GAME LAST NIGHT..
I GOT TO MEET THE MAN WHO DRIVES THE ZUCCHINI..
© 1993 United Feature Syndicate, Inc.
ZAMBONI..
9-27
WHATEVER
SCHULZ

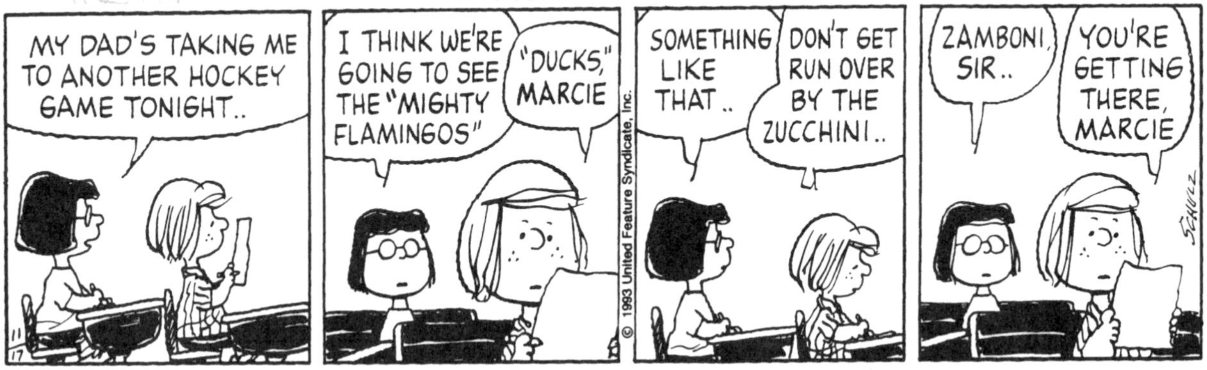
MY DAD'S TAKING ME TO ANOTHER HOCKEY GAME TONIGHT..
11/17
I THINK WE'RE GOING TO SEE THE "MIGHTY FLAMINGOS"
"DUCKS," MARCIE
© 1993 United Feature Syndicate, Inc.
SOMETHING LIKE THAT..
DON'T GET RUN OVER BY THE ZUCCHINI..
ZAMBONI, SIR..
YOU'RE GETTING THERE, MARCIE
SCHULZ

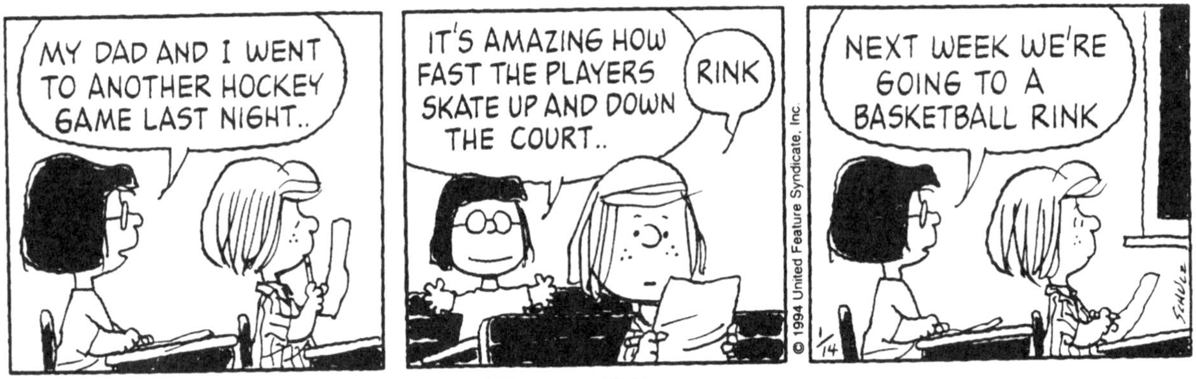
MY DAD AND I WENT TO ANOTHER HOCKEY GAME LAST NIGHT..
IT'S AMAZING HOW FAST THE PLAYERS SKATE UP AND DOWN THE COURT..
RINK
© 1994 United Feature Syndicate, Inc.
1/14
NEXT WEEK WE'RE GOING TO A BASKETBALL RINK
SCHULZ

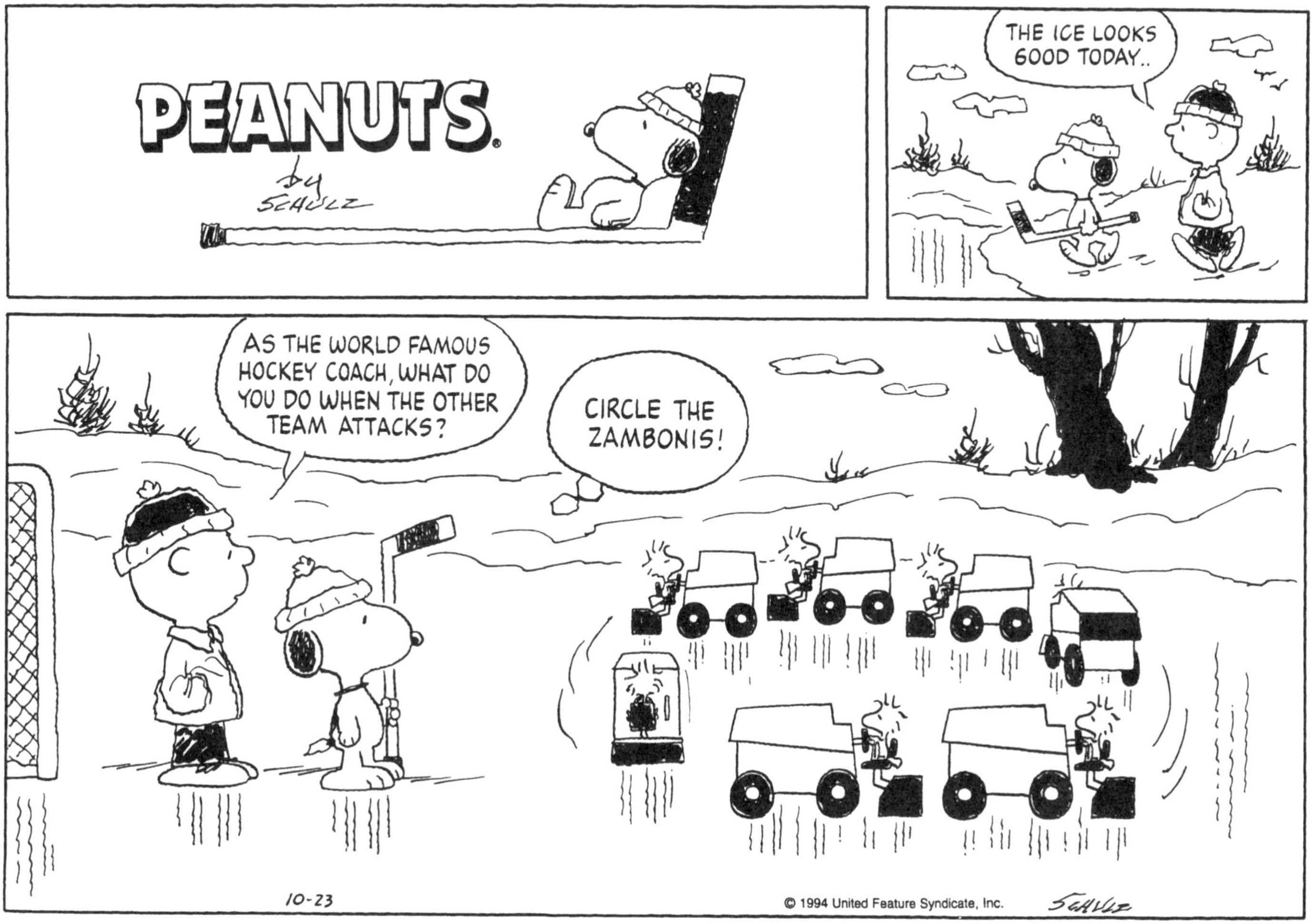
PEANUTS®
by SCHULZ
THE ICE LOOKS GOOD TODAY..
AS THE WORLD FAMOUS HOCKEY COACH, WHAT DO YOU DO WHEN THE OTHER TEAM ATTACKS?
CIRCLE THE ZAMBONIS!
10-23
© 1994 United Feature Syndicate, Inc.
SCHULZ

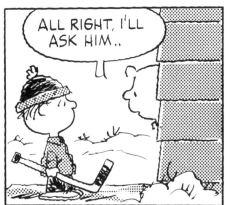

ALL RIGHT, I'LL ASK HIM..
THAT LITTLE KID WANTS YOU TO COME OUT AND PLAY HOCKEY..
© 1995 United Feature Syndicate, Inc.
OKAY, WE'LL PLAY THREE TWENTY-MINUTE PERIODS, AND I GET TO DRIVE THE ZAMBONI!
SCHULZ
1-13

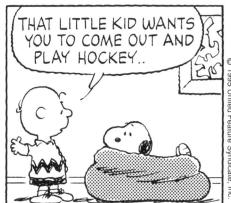

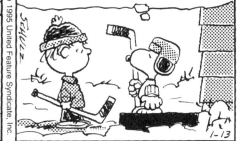

Panel 1: SO WE'RE IN THIS COFFEE SHOP, SEE, TRYING TO DECIDE ABOUT DESSERT..

Panel 2: "HOW ABOUT ICE CREAM?" SAYS MY DAD.. "GREAT," I SAID.."I'LL HAVE ZAMBONI"

Panel 3: THEN MY DAD SAYS, "AT THE HOCKEY GAME TONIGHT, DID YOU ENJOY WATCHING THE SPUMONI CLEAN THE ICE?"

© 1995 United Feature Syndicate, Inc.

Panel 4: HA HA HA HA! YOU AND YOUR DAD ARE VERY WEIRD, MARCIE..

199

PEANUTS
by SCHULZ
I'M READY..
© 1996 United Feature Syndicate, Inc.
NO NATIONAL ANTHEM?
NO HOKEY-POKEY?
12-1
YOU'RE KIDDING! BEFORE EVERY GAME?
THE "MACARENA"!
SCHULZ

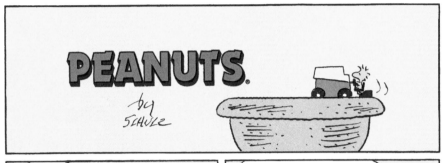

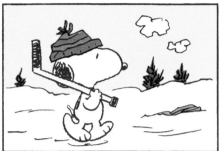

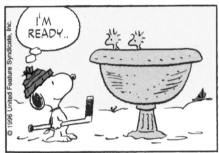

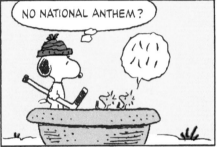

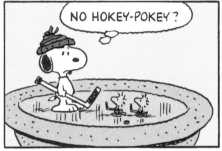

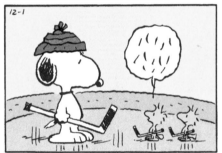

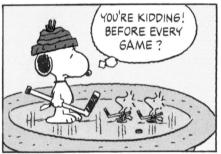

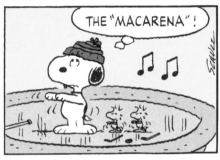

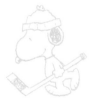

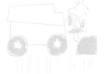

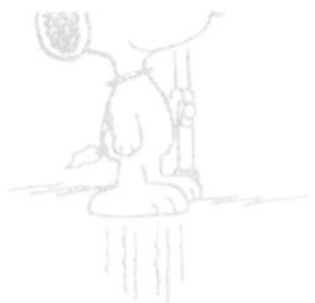

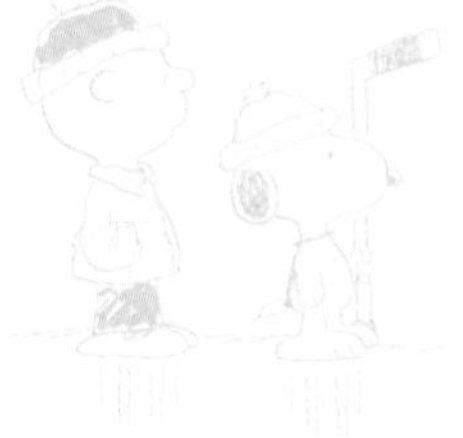

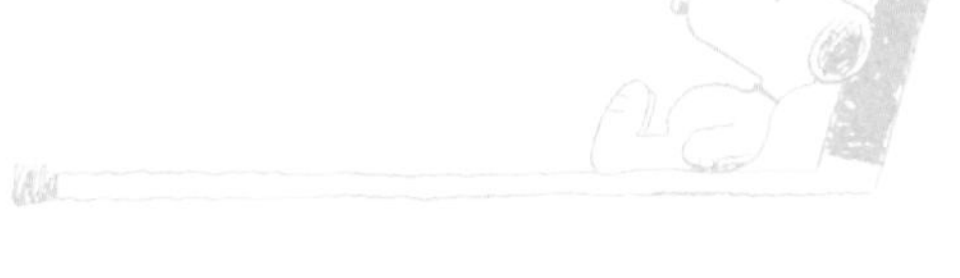

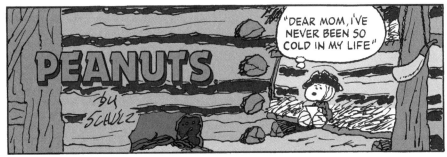

PEANUTS
by SCHULZ
"DEAR MOM, I'VE NEVER BEEN SO COLD IN MY LIFE"
AT LEAST IT'S STOPPED SNOWING..
HERE'S THE WORLD FAMOUS REVOLUTIONARY WAR PATRIOT STANDING GUARD AT VALLEY FORGE..
TELL GENERAL WASHINGTON ONE OF HIS MEN WANTS TO SEE HIM..
YES, SIR..I HAVE A LITTLE SUGGESTION..
YOU MAY OR MAY NOT HAVE NOTICED THAT THERE'S A LOT OF SNOW HERE..
© 1997 United Feature Syndicate, Inc.
1-12
MY IDEA IS WE BUILD A SKATING RINK OUT THERE..WE COULD ORGANIZE A HOCKEY TEAM..
www.unitedmedia.com
MAYBE EVEN START SOME KIND OF A FIGURE SKATING CLUB..
WE COULD EVEN INVITE SOME OF THE CHICKS FROM TOWN FOR A SKATING PARTY..
I DIDN'T GET A CHANCE TO TELL HIM HE COULD DRIVE THE ZAMBONI..
SCHULZ

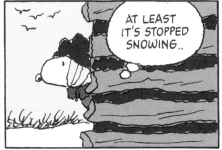

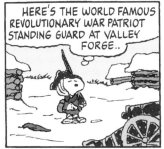

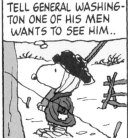

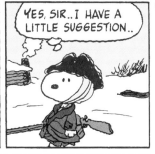

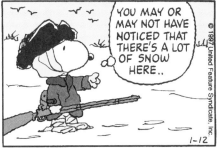

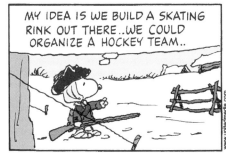

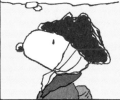

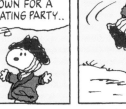

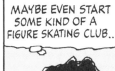

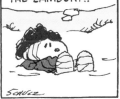

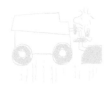

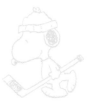

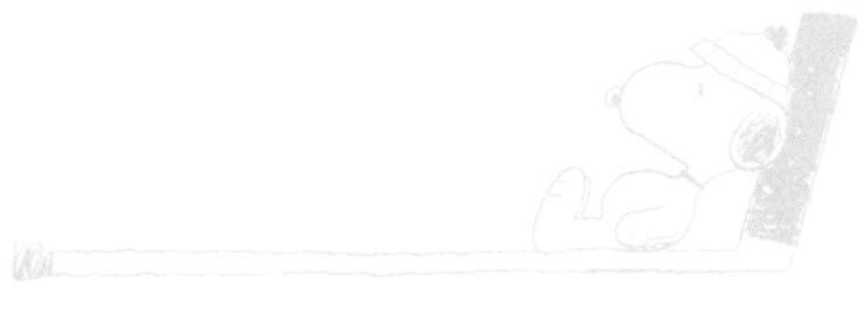

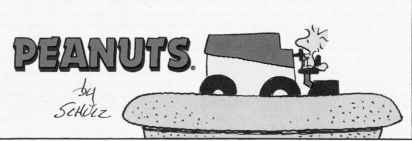

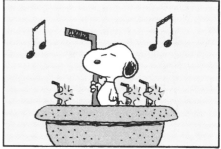

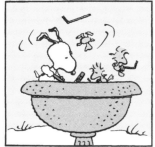

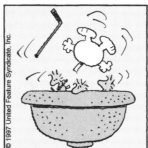

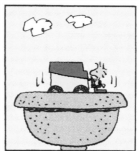

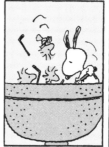

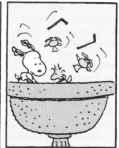

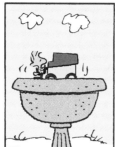

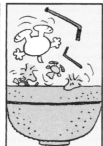

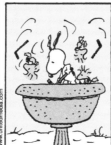

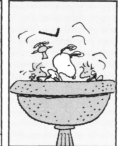

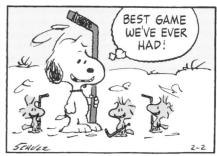

PEANUTS
by SCHULZ
© 1997 United Feature Syndicate, Inc.
www.unitedmedia.com
BEST GAME WE'VE EVER HAD!
SCHULZ
2-2

Tennis

"PEANUTS"
RATS!
SWISH!
THIS IS GETTING ME DOWN.... LET'S CHANGE THE RULES, SHERMY...
5/29
SCHULZ
ONE POINT IF YOU HIT THE BALL, TWO POINTS IF YOU GET IT OVER THE NET!
Copr. 1951 by United Feature Syndicate, Inc.

"PEANUTS"
HIT IT, LUCY! HIT IT!
Tm Reg U S Pat Off—All rights reserved Copr 1952 by United Feature Syndicate, Inc
WELL, GOOD GRIEF! WHY DIDN'T YOU HIT IT?! YOU DIDN'T EVEN TRY!
I DID, TOO!
BUT I COULDN'T LIFT THE RACKET!
7/15
SCHULZ

PEANUTS
AW, C'MON...YOU CAN'T BLAME EVERYTHING ON THE RACQUET!
Tm. Reg. U. S. Pat. Off.—All rights reserved Copr. 1959 by United Feature Syndicate, Inc.
5-4
DID YOU EVER CONSIDER THAT IT MIGHT BE THE MAN **BEHIND** THE RACQUET?
STOP THINKING OF SO MANY EXCUSES!
I STILL THINK IT'S THE RACQUET!
SCHULZ

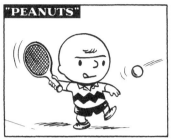

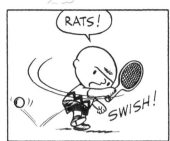

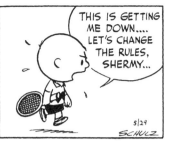

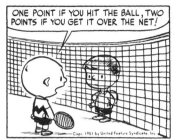

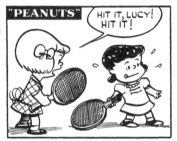

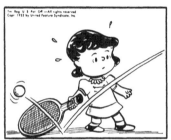

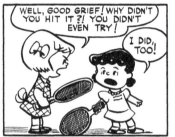

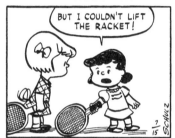

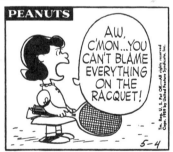

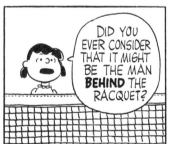

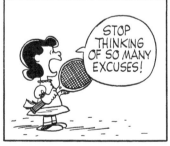

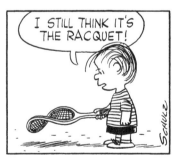

PEANUTS
HERE'S THE WORLD-FAMOUS TENNIS PLAYER WALKING OUT ONTO THE COURT
Tm. Reg. U.S. Pat. Off.—All rights reserved © 1970 by United Feature Syndicate, Inc.
I HATE IT WHEN THEY SERVE HARD!
SCHULZ
6-11

PEANUTS
GOOD MORNING, PAL!
GOOD MORNING, FUZZY-FACE!
Tm. Reg. U.S. Pat. Off.—All rights reserved © 1973 by United Feature Syndicate, Inc.
RATS!
5-30
NO ONE EVER CALLS ME "PANCHO"!
SCHULZ

PEANUTS
ANYONE NEED AN OPPONENT FOR SINGLES?
A FOURTH FOR DOUBLES?
5-31
Tm. Reg. U.S. Pat. Off.—All rights reserved © 1973 by United Feature Syndicate, Inc.
A GUEST FOR LUNCH?
SCHULZ

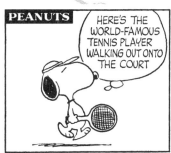

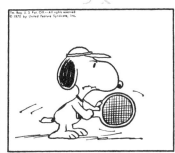

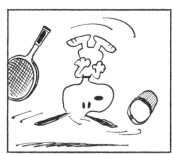

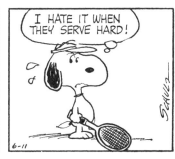

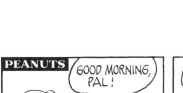

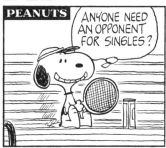

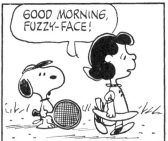

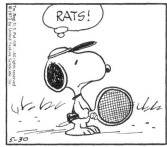

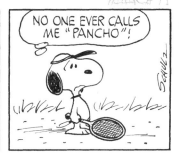

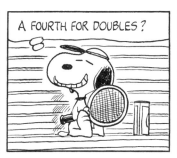

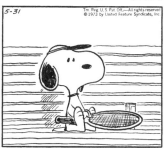

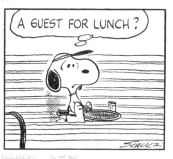

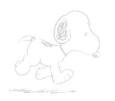

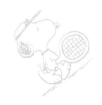

PEANUTS
Tm. Reg. U.S. Pat. Off.—All rights reserved © 1973 by United Feature Syndicate, Inc.
I HATE IT WHEN THEY RETURN MY SERVE!
6-1
SCHULZ

PEANUTS
GAME! SET!! MATCH!
RATS!
6-2
Tm. Reg. U.S. Pat. Off.—All rights reserved © 1973 by United Feature Syndicate, Inc.
I DON'T UNDERSTAND IT...
I CALLED SIXTY-TWO FOOT-FAULTS, BUT I STILL LOST!
SCHULZ

PEANUTS
Tm. Reg. U.S. Pat. Off.—All rights reserved © 1973 by United Feature Syndicate, Inc.
WHAP!
6-5
NYAHH! NYAHH! NYAHH!!!
ACTUALLY, AFTER YOU ACE SOMEONE, YOU REALLY SHOULDN'T SAY, "NYAHH, NYAHH, NYAHH!"
SCHULZ

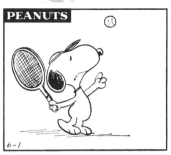

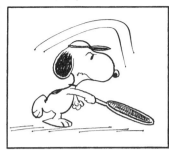

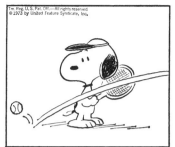

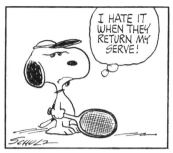

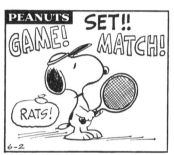

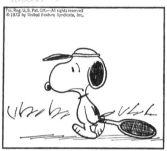

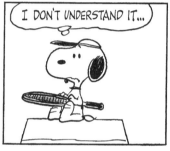

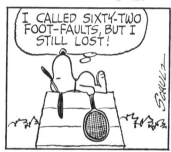

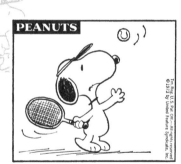

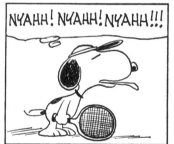

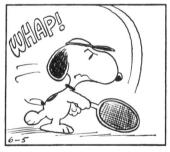

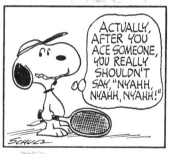

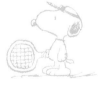

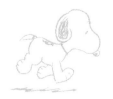

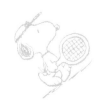

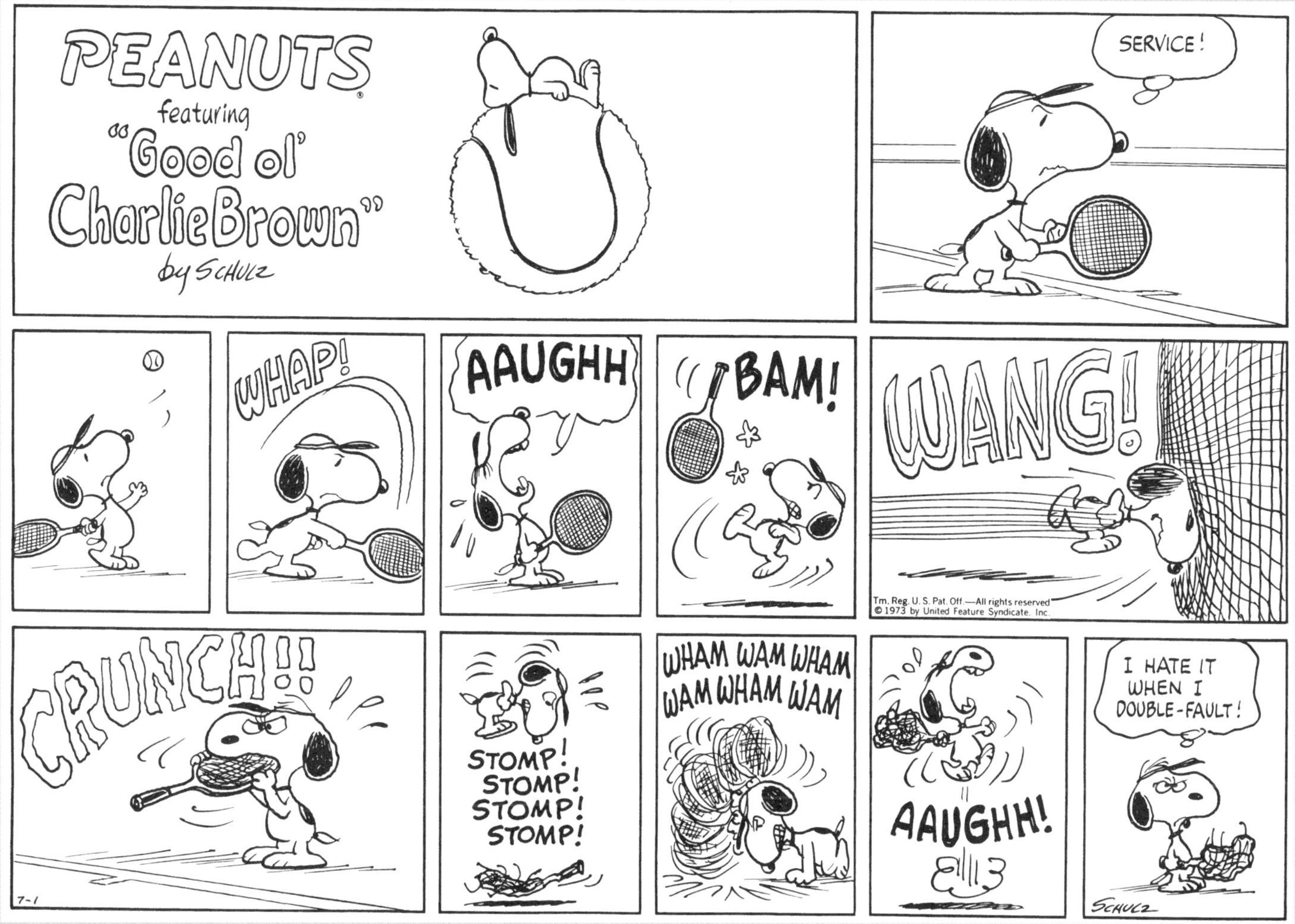
PEANUTS
featuring
"Good ol' Charlie Brown"
by SCHULZ
SERVICE!
WHAP!
AAUGHH
BAM!
WANG!
Tm. Reg. U. S. Pat. Off.—All rights reserved
© 1973 by United Feature Syndicate, Inc.
CRUNCH!!
7-1
STOMP! STOMP! STOMP! STOMP!
WHAM WAM WHAM WAM WHAM WAM
AAUGHH!
I HATE IT WHEN I DOUBLE-FAULT!
SCHULZ

PEANUTS Tm. Reg. U.S. Pat. Off. — All rights reserved
© 1973 by United Feature Syndicate, Inc.

BOUNCE
BOUNCE
BOUNCE

BOUNCE BOUNCE BOUNCE
BOUNCE BOUNCE
BOUNCE
BOUNCE
BOUNCE

7-7

IT UNNERVES YOUR OPPONENT IF YOU BOUNCE THE BALL A LOT BEFORE YOU SERVE!

SCHULZ

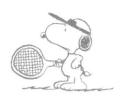

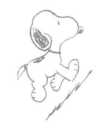

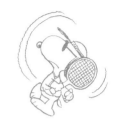

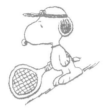

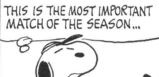

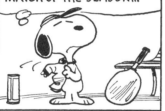

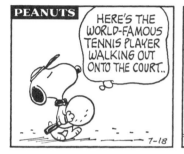

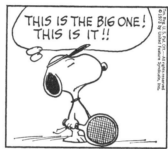

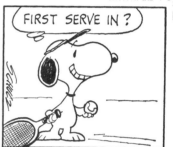

PEANUTS
HERE'S THE WORLD-FAMOUS TENNIS PLAYER WALKING OUT ONTO THE COURT..
7-18
THIS IS THE MOST IMPORTANT MATCH OF THE SEASON...
THIS IS THE BIG ONE! THIS IS IT!!
Tm. Reg. U.S. Pat. Off.—All rights reserved
© 1973 by United Feature Syndicate, Inc.
FIRST SERVE IN?
SCHULZ

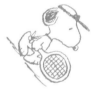

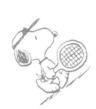

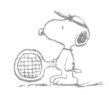

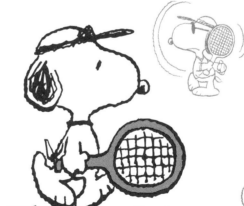

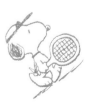

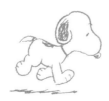

PEANUTS I'VE BEEN ANXIOUS TO HAVE WOODSTOCK SEE MY NEW RACKET...

Tm. Reg. U.S. Pat. Off.—All rights reserved
© 1973 by United Feature Syndicate, Inc.

HOW DISAPPOINTING...HE HATES MY GUT!

SCHULZ

7-24

PEANUTS Tm. Reg. U.S. Pat. Off.—All rights reserved
© 1973 by United Feature Syndicate, Inc.

OVERHEAD SMASH!

SCHULZ

8-7

PEANUTS

I HOPE HE DOUBLE-FAULTS...

9-3

PLEASE DOUBLE-FAULT! DOUBLE-FAULT! DOUBLE-FAULT! DOUBLE-FAULT!

THAT WAS TOO BAD!

PEANUTS

RATS!

4-6

HE WHO LIVES BY THE LOB DIES BY THE LOB!

SCHULZ

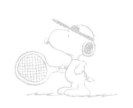

PEANUTS
OUT ?!!
4-13
Tm Reg U S Pat Off — All rights reserved
© 1974 by United Feature Syndicate Inc
BAD CALL!
IT HIT THE EXACT MIDDLE OF THE OUTER PART OF THE EDGE OF THE FRONT PART OF THE BACK PART OF THE LINE!
SCHULZ

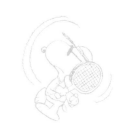

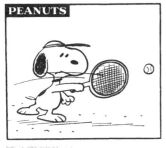

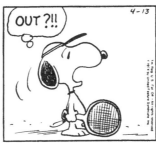

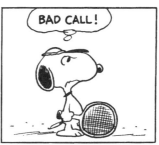

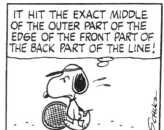

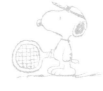

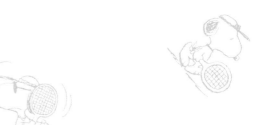

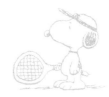

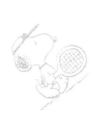

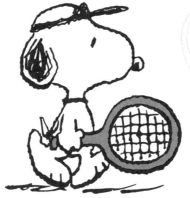

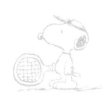

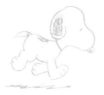

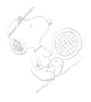

PEANUTS

6-20

Tm Reg U S Pat Off — All rights reserved
© 1974 by United Feature Syndicate Inc

RATS!

I WOULD HAVE WON, BUT I GOT OFF TO A BAD FINISH!

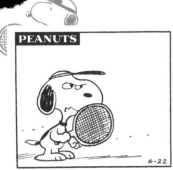

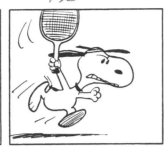

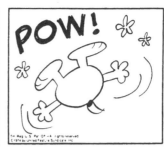

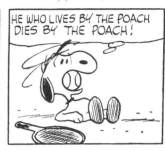

PEANUTS
6-22
POW!
HE WHO LIVES BY THE POACH DIES BY THE POACH!

PEANUTS
WHAM!
RATS!
7-15
Tm Reg U.S. Pat Off—All rights reserved ©1974 by United Feature Syndicate, Inc.
I SHOULD'VE HAD THAT POINT, AND I SHOULD'VE HAD THAT GAME AND I SHOULD'VE HAD THAT SET...
UNFORTUNATELY, WE'RE NOT PLAYING "SHOULD'VES"!
SCHULZ

PEANUTS
7-18
Tm Reg U.S. Pat Off—All rights reserved ©1974 by United Feature Syndicate, Inc.
PAW FAULT ?!!
SCHULZ

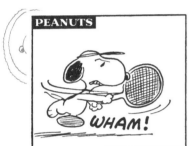

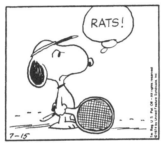

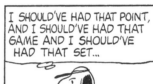

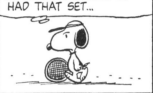

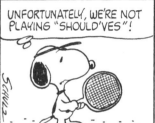

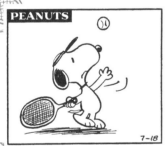

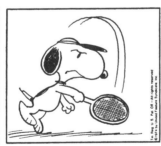

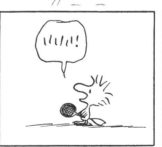

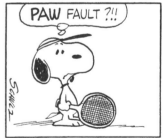

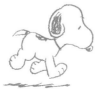

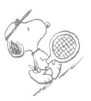

PEANUTS

Panel 1: !

Panel 2: oo!!

Panel 3: !! &cool

Panel 4: I HAVE A SUGGESTION...LET'S NOT PLAY "FIRST SERVE IN"

7-20

SCHULZ

PEANUTS

Panel 1: OKAY, HERE COMES THE BIGGIE!

Panel 4: THE BIGGIE WAS A SMALLIE!

8-2

SCHULZ

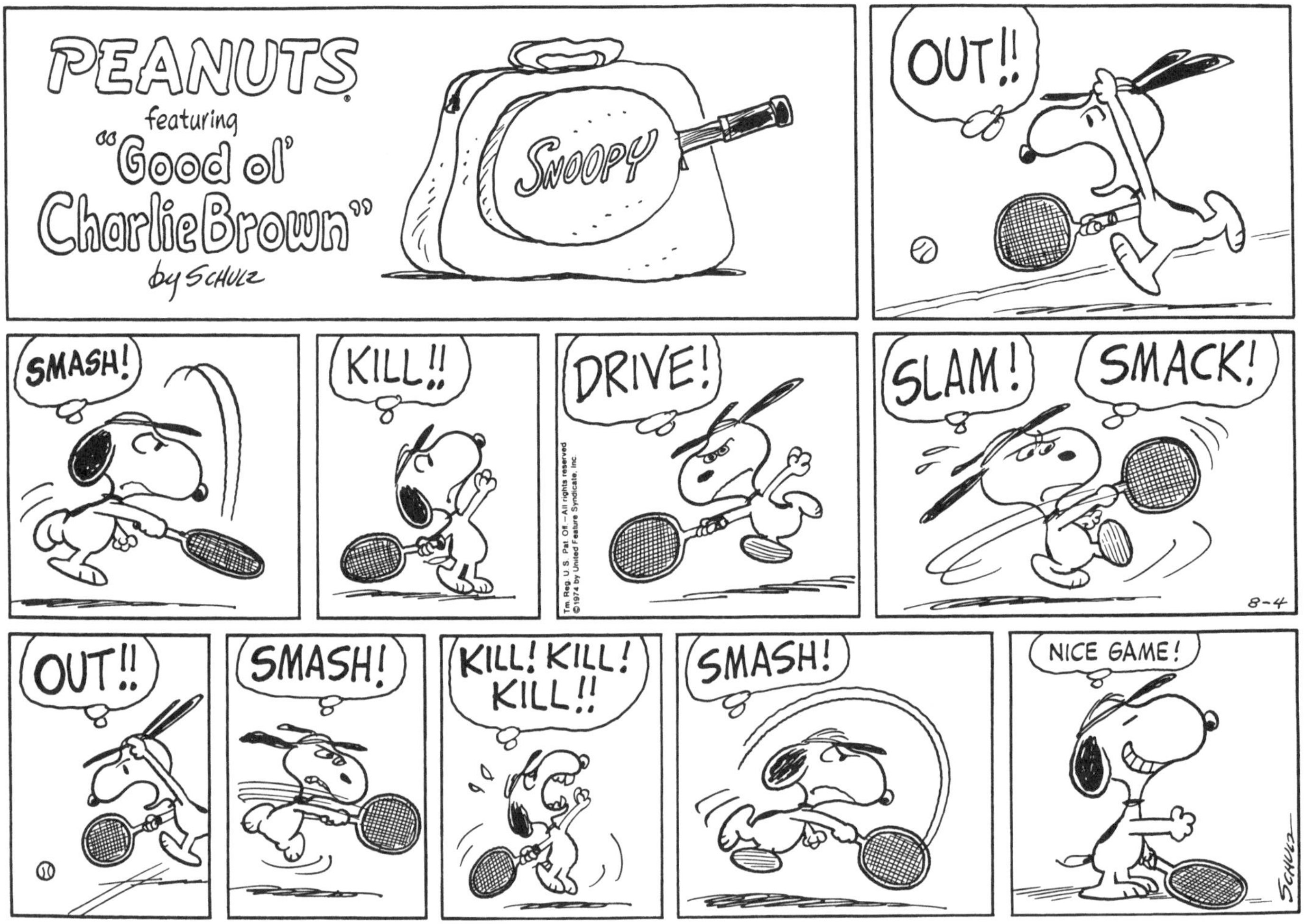
PEANUTS
featuring
"Good ol' Charlie Brown"
by SCHULZ
SNOOPY
OUT!!
SMASH!
KILL!!
DRIVE!
Tm. Reg. U.S. Pat. Off.—All rights reserved
©1974 by United Feature Syndicate, Inc
SLAM!
SMACK!
8-4
OUT!!
SMASH!
KILL! KILL! KILL!!
SMASH!
NICE GAME!
SCHULZ

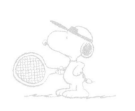

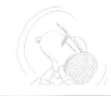

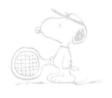

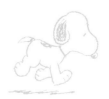

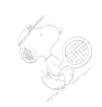

PEANUTS

AH!

THIS IS GOING TO BE A GOOD DAY...

I GOT THE NEW CAN OF BALLS OPEN WITHOUT CUTTING MYSELF!

9-19

PEANUTS

HA!

I GOT 'IM NOW!

TWO GOOD SERVES AND A COUPLE OF BAD CALLS, AND I'M IN!

10-26

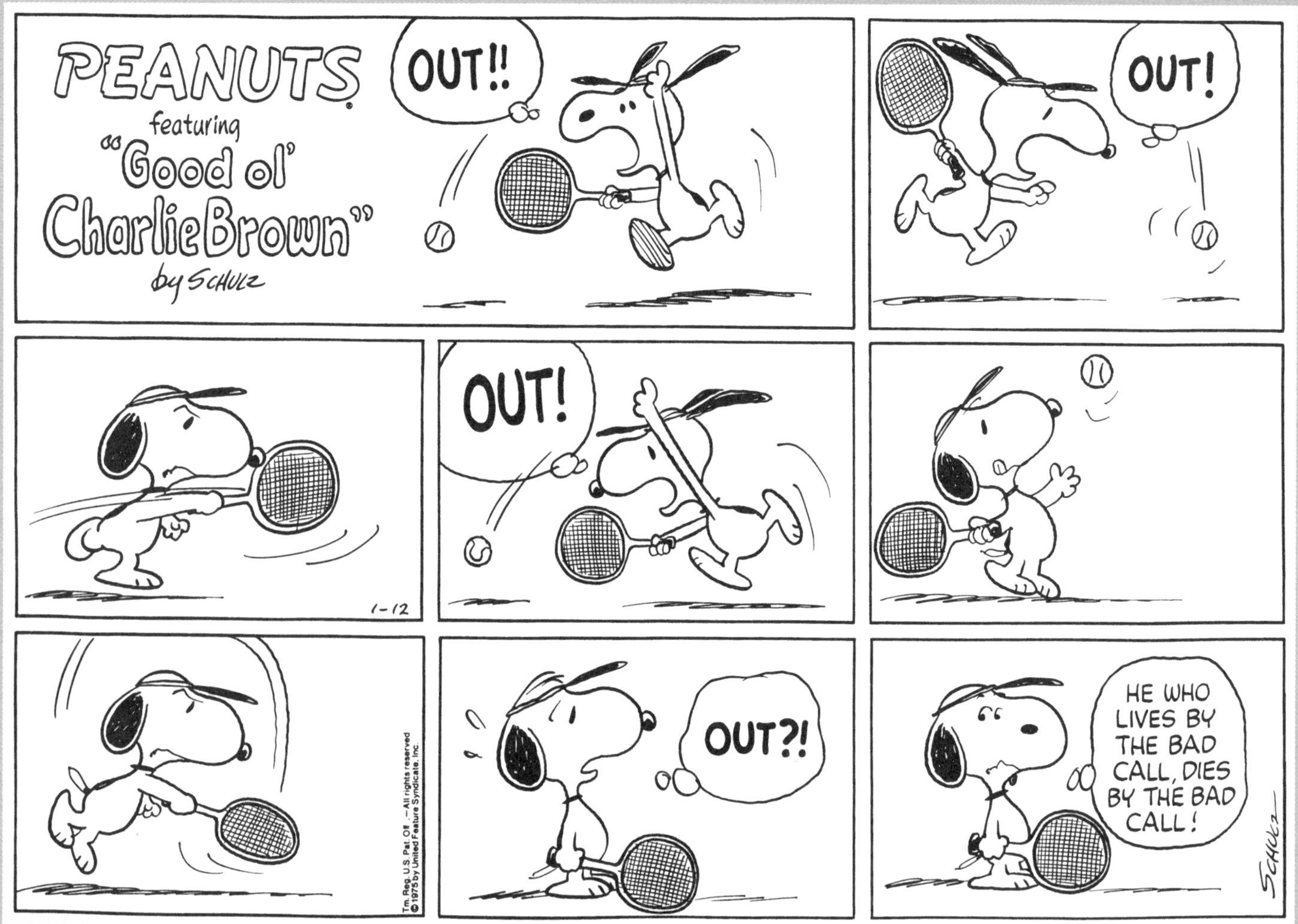
PEANUTS
featuring
"Good ol' Charlie Brown"
by SCHULZ
OUT!!
OUT!
1-12
OUT!
Tm. Reg. U.S. Pat. Off.—All rights reserved
© 1975 by United Feature Syndicate, Inc.
OUT?!
HE WHO LIVES BY THE BAD CALL, DIES BY THE BAD CALL!
SCHULZ

1-13

Tm. Reg. U.S. Pat. Off. — All rights reserved
© 1975 by United Feature Syndicate, Inc.

CLANK

THE NEXT TIME YOU SERVE, TAKE THE BALLS OUT OF THE CAN!

SCHULZ

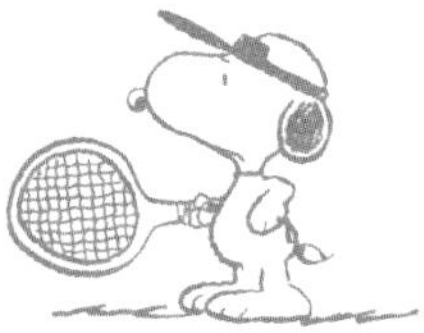

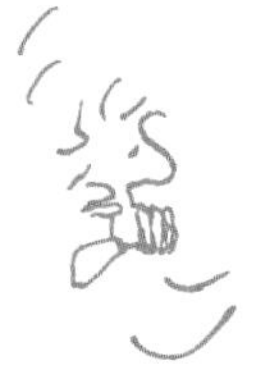

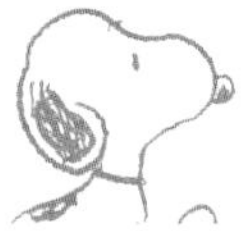

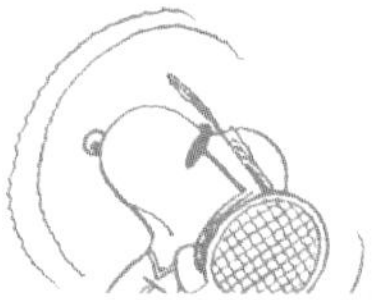

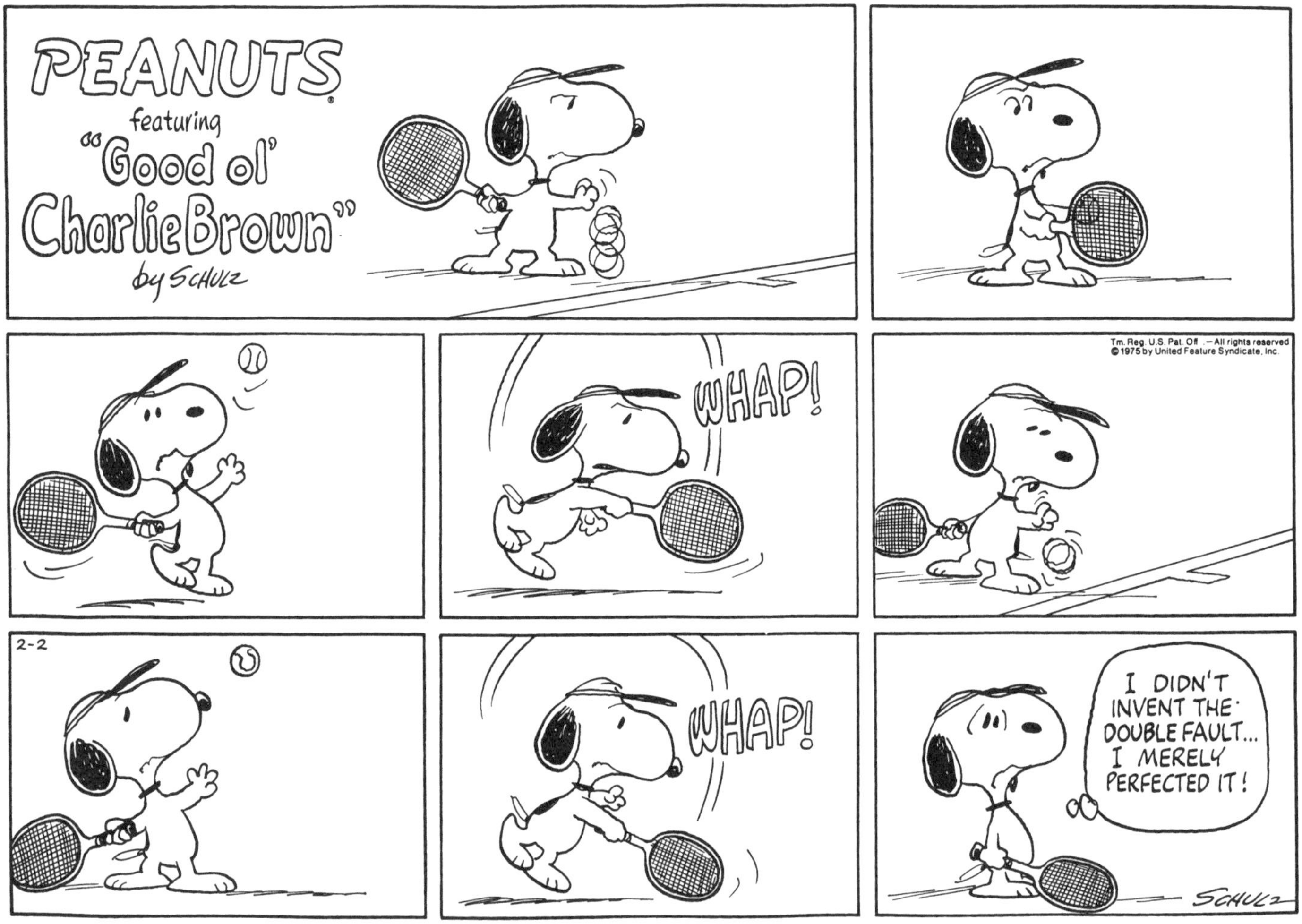
PEANUTS
featuring
"Good ol' CharlieBrown"
by SCHULZ
Tm. Reg. U.S. Pat. Off. —All rights reserved
©1975 by United Feature Syndicate, Inc.
WHAP!
2-2
WHAP!
I DIDN'T INVENT THE DOUBLE FAULT... I MERELY PERFECTED IT!
SCHULZ

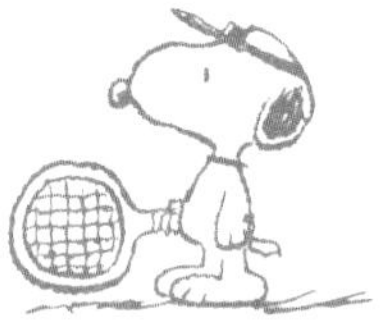

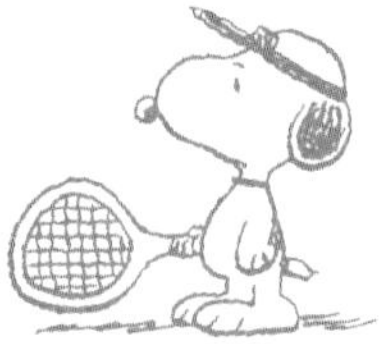

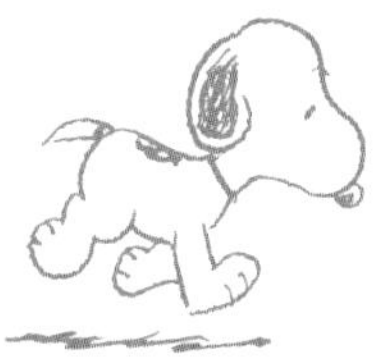

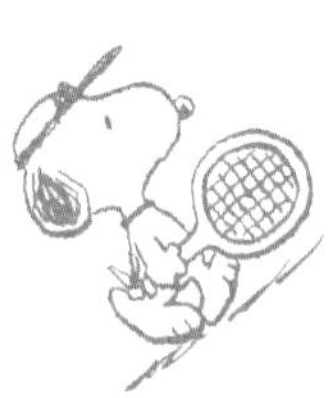

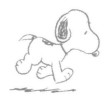

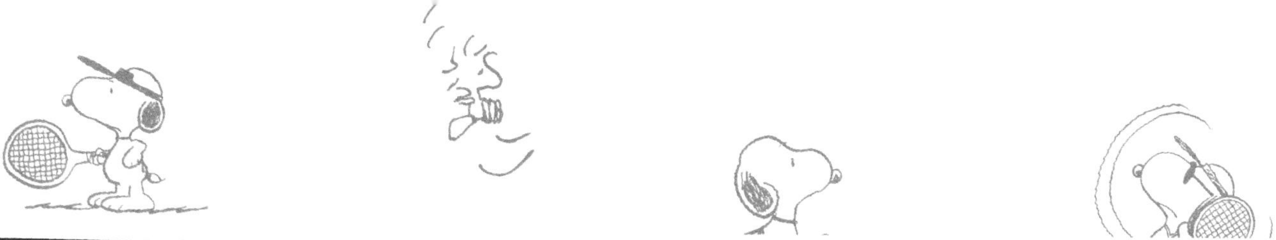

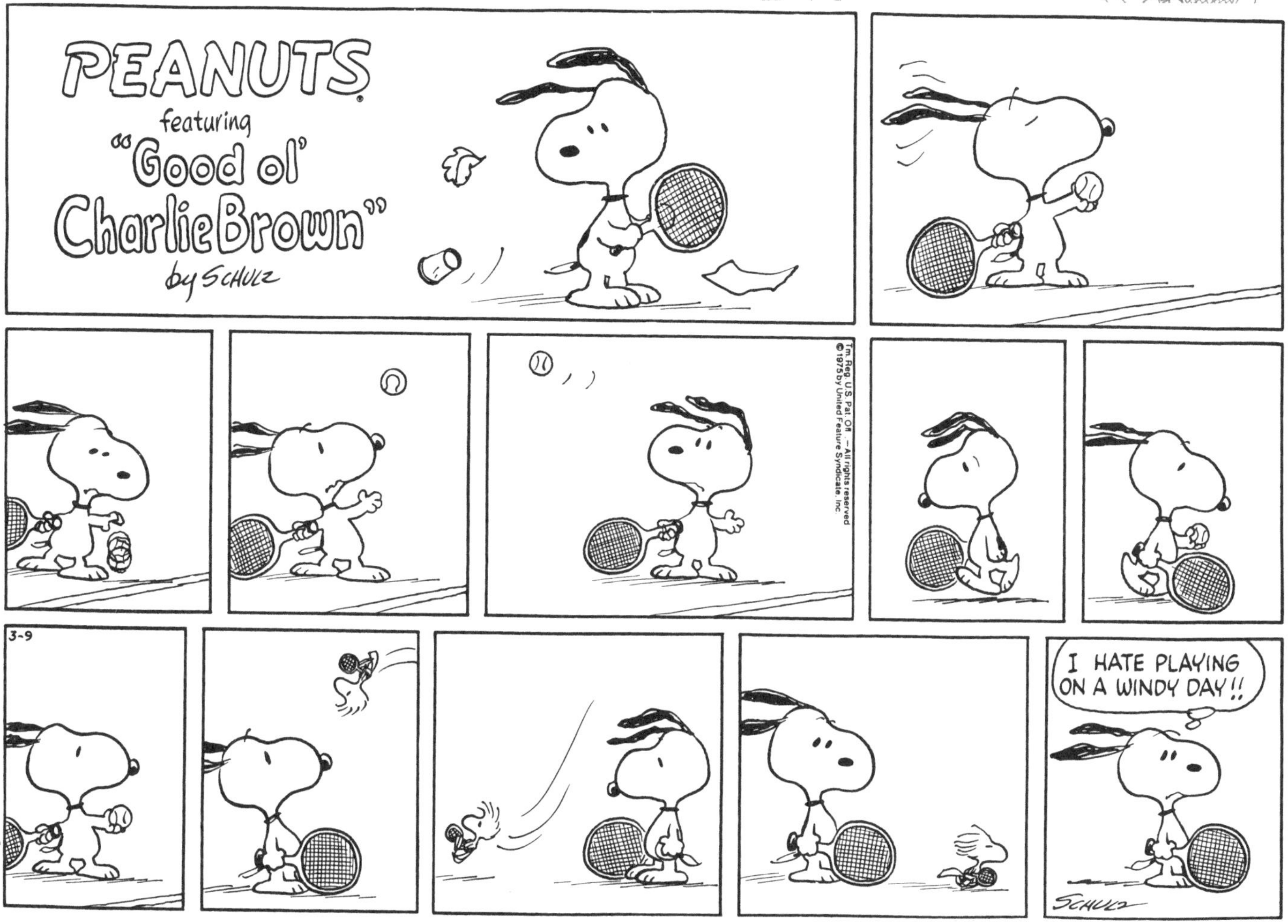
PEANUTS
featuring
"Good ol' Charlie Brown"
by SCHULZ
Tm. Reg. U.S. Pat. Off.—All rights reserved
© 1975 by United Feature Syndicate, Inc.
3-9
I HATE PLAYING ON A WINDY DAY!!
SCHULZ

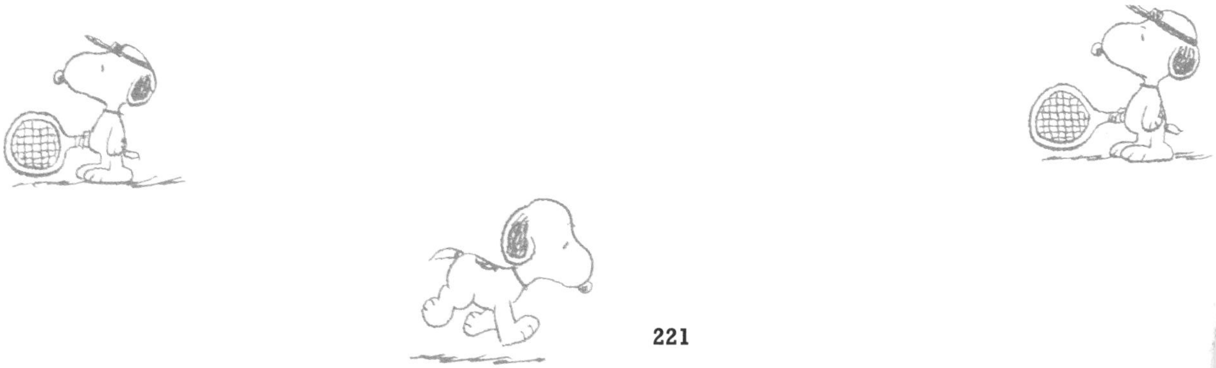

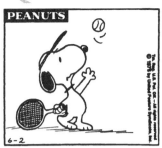

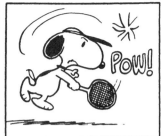

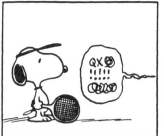

PEANUTS
6-2
POW!
ACED HIM AGAIN!

PEANUTS
HOLD IT! THERE'S A BUG CROSSING THE COURT!
6-3
HURRY UP, YOU STUPID BUG! DO YOU WANNA GET STEPPED ON? C'MON, YOU'RE HOLDING UP THE GAME!
WHAT?
LOVE-THIRTY... WE'RE FOUR-ALL IN THE FIRST SET!

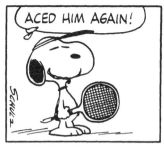

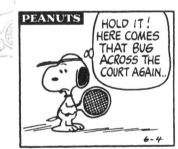

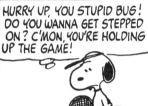

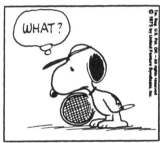

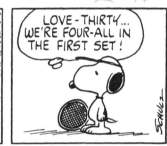

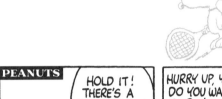

PEANUTS
HOLD IT! HERE COMES THAT BUG ACROSS THE COURT AGAIN..
6-4
WHAT? NO, THIS ISN'T HIGHWAY TWELVE...THIS IS A TENNIS COURT...
HIGHWAYS ARE BLACK... TENNIS COURTS ARE GREEN..
IT WAS THE STRIPE DOWN THE MIDDLE THAT CONFUSED HIM.......SERVICE!!

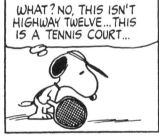

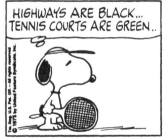

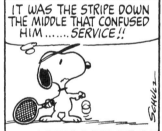

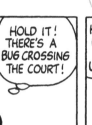

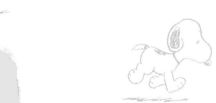

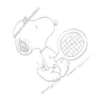

PEANUTS
OH, GOOD GRIEF... A LOB!
I HOPE IT GOES OUT! I HOPE IT GOES OUT!
I HOPED IT OUT!
6-5
SCHULZ

PEANUTS
AAUGH!! THIS GAME DRIVES ME CRAZY!
HAVE YOU EVER CONSIDERED SWITCHING TO A METAL RACKET?
NEVER!
A METAL RACKET HURTS WHEN YOU BITE IT!
6-6
SCHULZ

PEANUTS
WHAP!
AAUGH!
Tm. Reg. U.S. Pat. Off.—All rights reserved © 1975 by United Feature Syndicate, Inc.
I'M SERIOUSLY THINKING OF NOT TAKING MY TENNIS SO SERIOUS...
6-7
SCHULZ

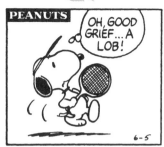

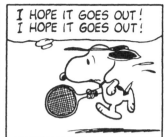

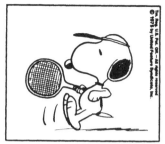

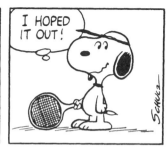

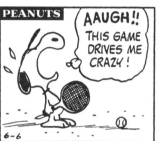

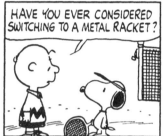

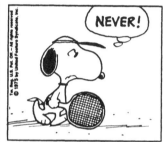

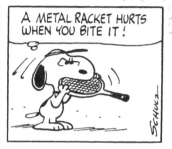

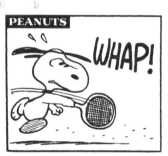

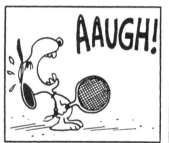

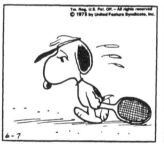

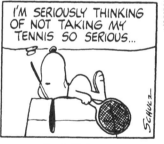

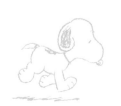

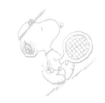

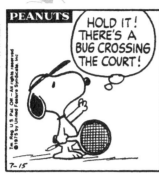

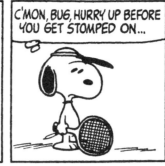

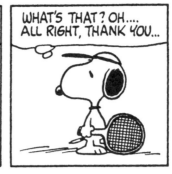

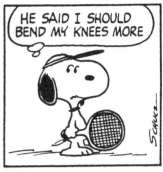

PEANUTS
HOLD IT! THERE'S A BUG CROSSING THE COURT!
Tm. Reg. U.S. Pat. Off.—All rights reserved ©1975 by United Feature Syndicate, Inc
7-15
C'MON, BUG, HURRY UP BEFORE YOU GET STOMPED ON...
WHAT'S THAT? OH.... ALL RIGHT, THANK YOU...
HE SAID I SHOULD BEND MY KNEES MORE
SCHULZ

PEANUTS
9-9
Tm. Reg. U.S. Pat. Off.—All rights reserved ©1975 by United Feature Syndicate, Inc.
HE'S BEEN HITTING BALLS AGAINST THAT GARAGE FOR WEEKS...
HE'S PRACTICING FOR A MIXED-DOUBLES TOURNAMENT
OH? WHO'S GOING TO BE HIS PARTNER?
THE GARAGE!
SCHULZ

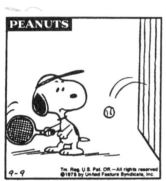

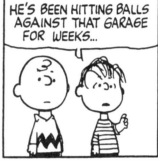

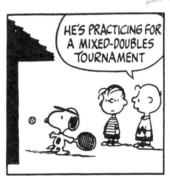

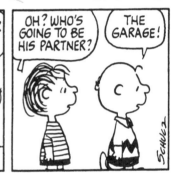

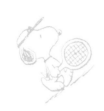

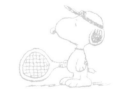

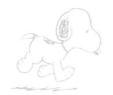

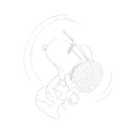

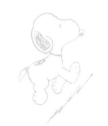

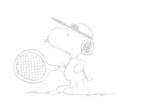

PEANUTS
I HEARD YOU AND THE GARAGE PLAYED IN A MIXED-DOUBLES TOURNAMENT
HOW DID YOU COME OUT? DID YOU PLAY WELL?
I PLAYED GREAT...
BUT THE GARAGE CHOKED!
Tm Reg U.S. Pat Off — All rights reserved ©1975 by United Feature Syndicate Inc.
9-15
SCHULZ

PEANUTS
HITTING BALLS AGAINST THE GARAGE AGAIN, I SEE...
I FIND IT INTERESTING THAT YOU SHOULD HAVE THE GARAGE FOR A PARTNER WHEN YOU PLAY MIXED-DOUBLES
9-16
I WAS ALSO WONDERING WHAT THE BEST PART OF HIS GAME IS...
HE NEVER FOOT-FAULTS!
SCHULZ
Tm Reg U.S. Pat Off — All rights reserved ©1975 by United Feature Syndicate Inc.

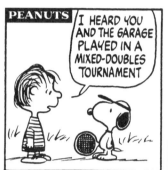

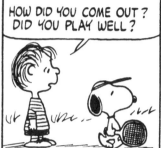

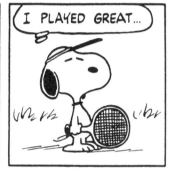

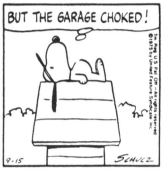

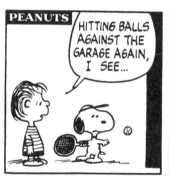

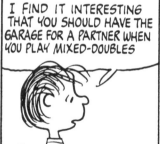

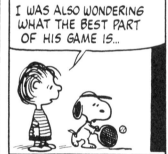

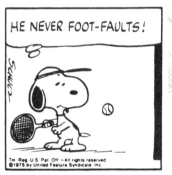

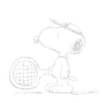

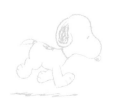

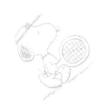

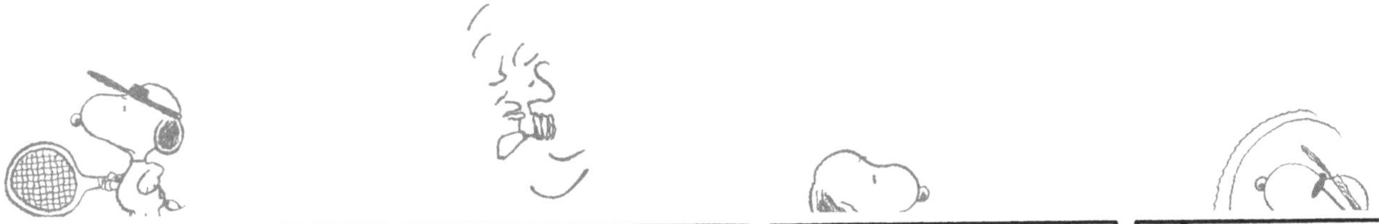

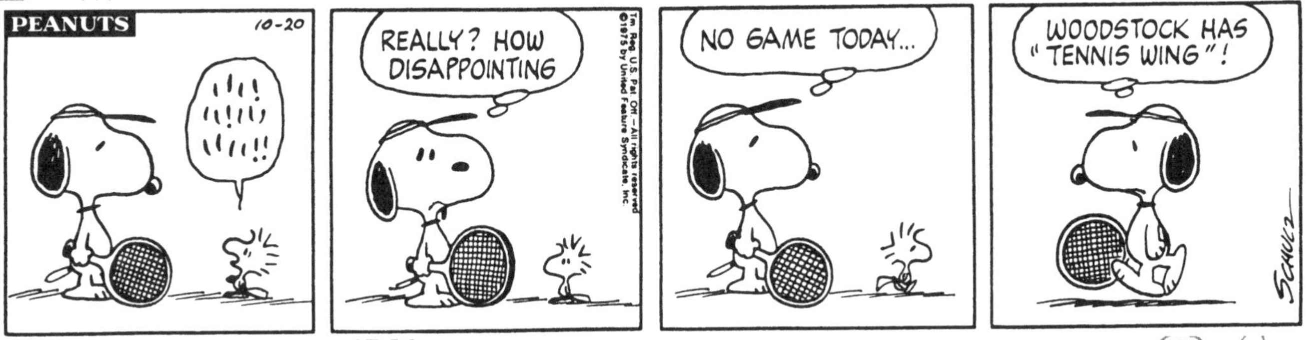
PEANUTS
10-20
REALLY? HOW DISAPPOINTING
Tm. Reg. U.S. Pat. Off.—All rights reserved ©1975 by United Feature Syndicate, Inc.
NO GAME TODAY...
WOODSTOCK HAS "TENNIS WING"!
SCHULZ

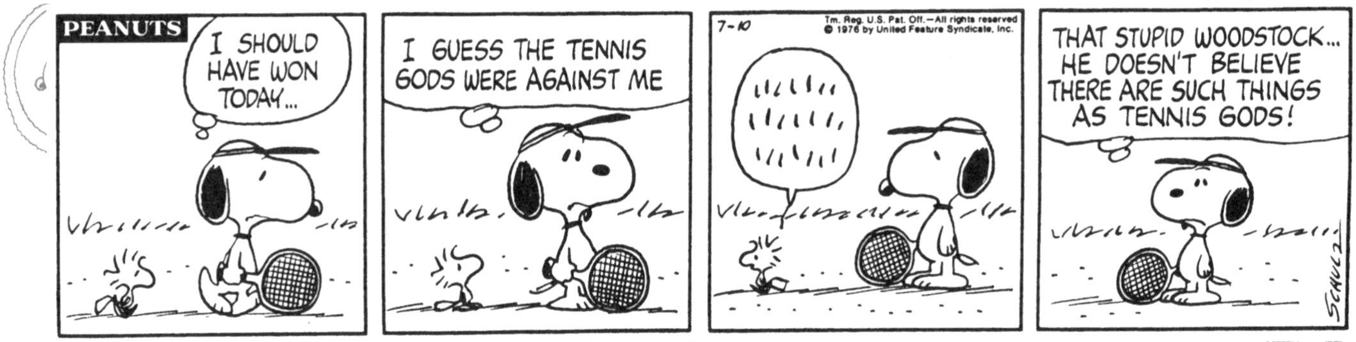
PEANUTS
I SHOULD HAVE WON TODAY...
I GUESS THE TENNIS GODS WERE AGAINST ME
7-10
Tm. Reg. U.S. Pat. Off.—All rights reserved © 1976 by United Feature Syndicate, Inc.
THAT STUPID WOODSTOCK... HE DOESN'T BELIEVE THERE ARE SUCH THINGS AS TENNIS GODS!
SCHULZ

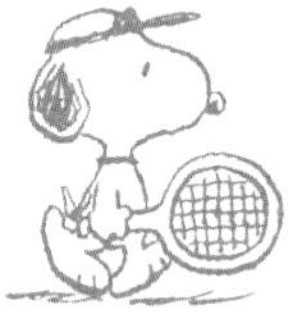

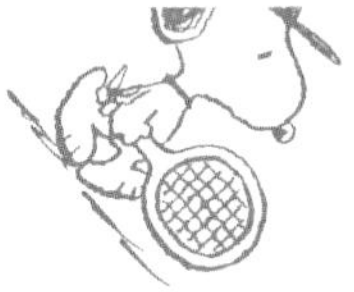

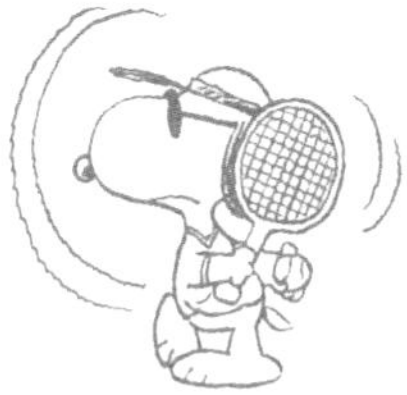

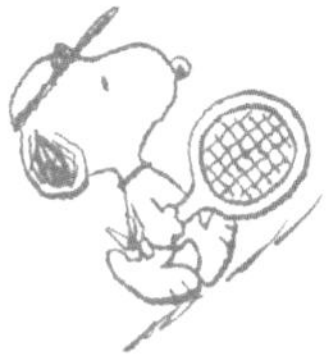

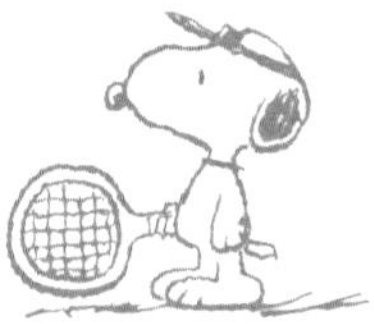

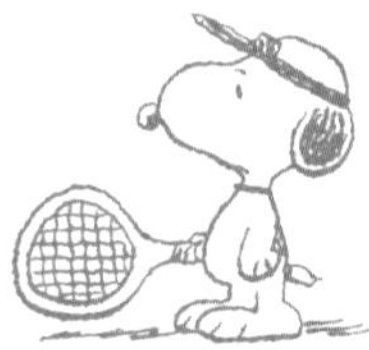

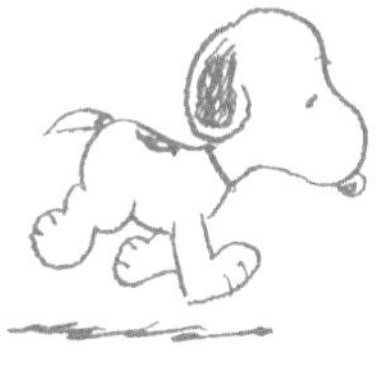

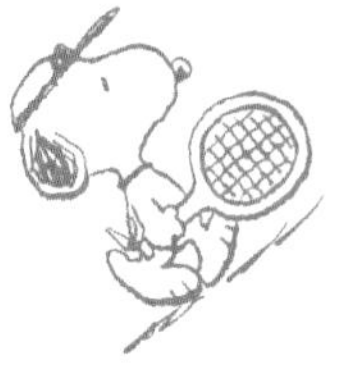

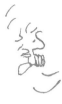

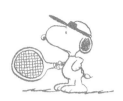

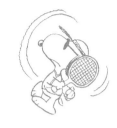

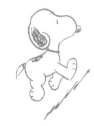

PEANUTS
Tm. Reg. U.S. Pat. Off.—All rights reserved © 1976 by United Feature Syndicate, Inc.
HERE'S A TENNIS TOURNAMENT YOU SHOULD ENTER...
AFTER THE TOURNAMENT IS OVER, THEY'RE HAVING A BIG BANQUET
7-14
I NEVER ATTEND TENNIS BANQUETS
IF I LOSE, I'M ALWAYS TOO MAD TO EAT!
SCHULZ

PEANUTS
Tm. Reg. U.S. Pat. Off.—All rights reserved © 1976 by United Feature Syndicate, Inc.
HERE'S SOMETHING YOU SHOULD THINK ABOUT WHEN YOU'RE PLAYING TENNIS
KNOW WHAT KIND OF BALL YOU'RE PLAYING AND WHAT NUMBER IS ON IT SO YOU WON'T GET MIXED UP WITH THE PLAYERS NEXT TO YOU
8-30
MINE HAS A LITTLE SNOWMAN ON IT...
THAT'S A NUMBER EIGHT
ANYONE FINDS A BALL WITH A SNOWMAN ON IT, IT'S MINE!!!
SCHULZ

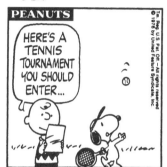

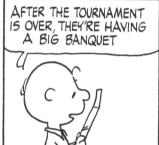

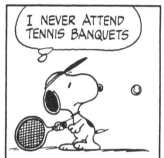

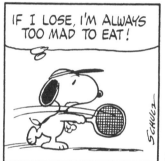

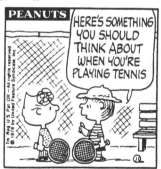

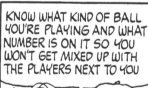

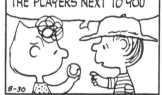

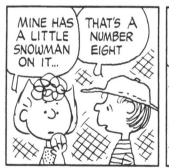

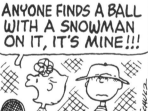

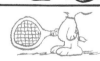

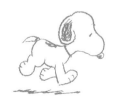

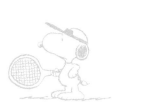

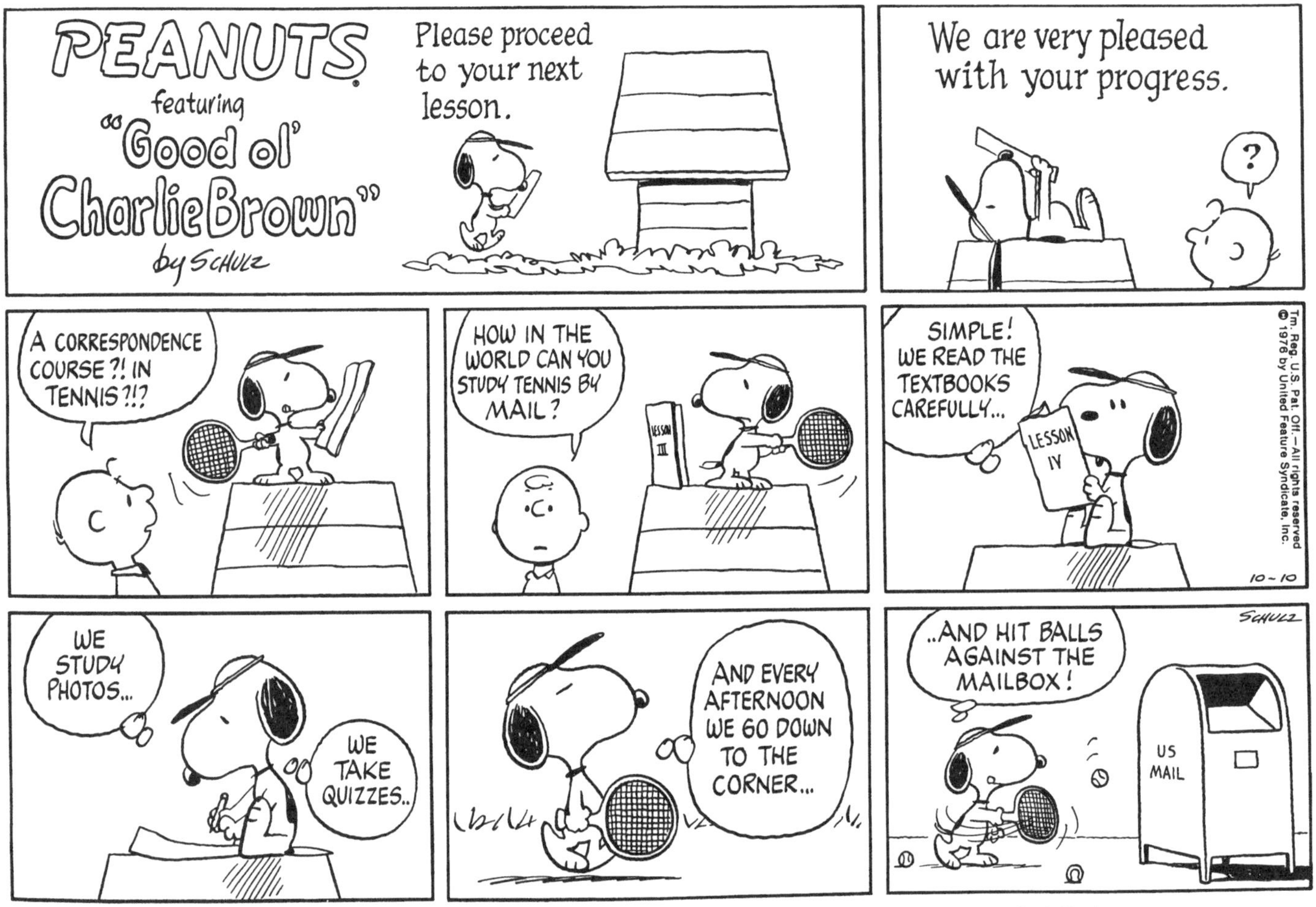
PEANUTS
featuring
"Good ol' Charlie Brown"
by SCHULZ
Please proceed to your next lesson.
We are very pleased with your progress.
?
A CORRESPONDENCE COURSE?! IN TENNIS?!?
HOW IN THE WORLD CAN YOU STUDY TENNIS BY MAIL?
LESSON III
SIMPLE! WE READ THE TEXTBOOKS CAREFULLY...
LESSON IV
Tm. Reg. U.S. Pat. Off.—All rights reserved
© 1976 by United Feature Syndicate, Inc.
10-10
WE STUDY PHOTOS...
WE TAKE QUIZZES..
AND EVERY AFTERNOON WE GO DOWN TO THE CORNER...
SCHULZ
..AND HIT BALLS AGAINST THE MAILBOX!
US MAIL

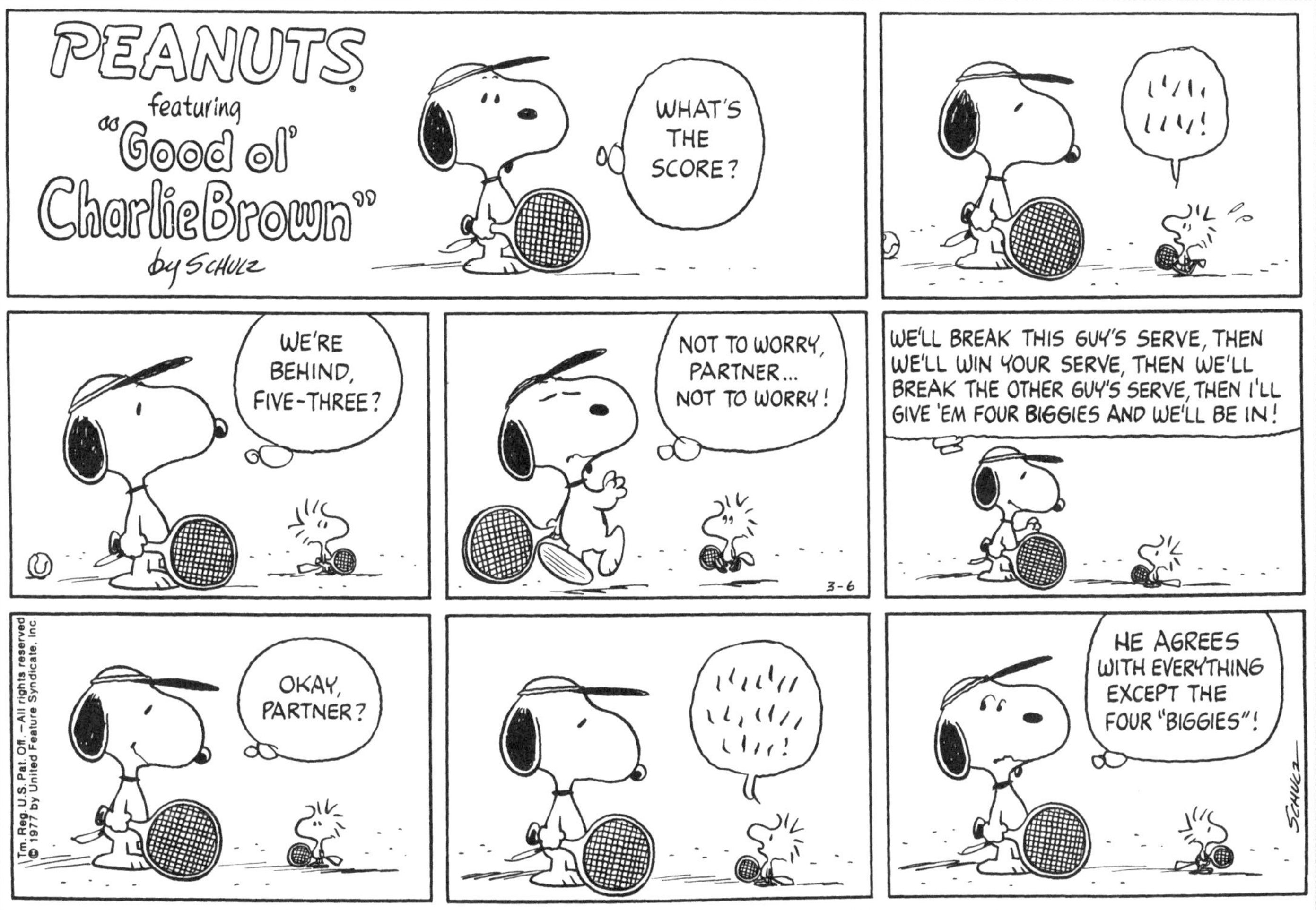
PEANUTS
featuring "Good ol' Charlie Brown"
by SCHULZ
WHAT'S THE SCORE?
WE'RE BEHIND, FIVE-THREE?
NOT TO WORRY, PARTNER... NOT TO WORRY!
3-6
WE'LL BREAK THIS GUY'S SERVE, THEN WE'LL WIN YOUR SERVE, THEN WE'LL BREAK THE OTHER GUY'S SERVE, THEN I'LL GIVE 'EM FOUR BIGGIES AND WE'LL BE IN!
OKAY, PARTNER?
HE AGREES WITH EVERYTHING EXCEPT THE FOUR "BIGGIES"!
SCHULZ

PEANUTS featuring "Good ol' Charlie Brown" by SCHULZ

TOP SEEDED

OKAY, PARTNER.. THE SECRET TO BEING A GOOD DOUBLES TEAM IS COOPERATION!

IF I SAY, "CROSS OVER!" YOU RUN TO THE OTHER SIDE IMMEDIATELY!

IF I SAY, "YOURS!" YOU TAKE IT...IF I SAY, "MINE!" THEN I'LL TAKE IT...

5-1

OKAY? LET'S SHOW 'EM HOW!

© 1977 United Feature Syndicate, Inc.

POW!

YOURS!

BANG
BANG
BANG

© 1977 United Feature Syndicate, Inc.

ALL RIGHT, WHO'S OUT THERE MAKING ALL THAT NOISE?

5-2

IT'S THE GARAGE

BANG BANG BANG BANG

HE KEEPS HITTING 'EM BACK!

© 1977 United Feature Syndicate, Inc.

HITTING BALLS AGAINST THE GARAGE MUST BE GOOD PRACTICE...

5-3

IT'S PROBABLY ALSO FUN, ISN'T IT?

UNTIL SOMEONE PARKS THE CAR!

PRACTICING FOR THE DOUBLES TOURNAMENT, I SEE...

I SUPPOSE YOU AND THE GARAGE WILL BE PARTNERS AGAIN...

5-4

I DON'T THINK SO

HE DOESN'T MOVE AS WELL AS HE USED TO!

© 1977 United Feature Syndicate, Inc.

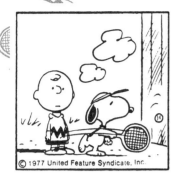

© 1977 United Feature Syndicate, Inc.
A TENNIS PRO ONCE SAID THAT YOU COULDN'T BE A CHAMPION UNTIL YOU HAD HIT TEN THOUSAND BALLS AGAINST THE GARAGE
5-5
THAT WASN'T A TENNIS PRO...
THAT WAS A GARAGE SALESMAN!
SCHULZ

© 1977 United Feature Syndicate, Inc.
GUESS WHAT..
THEY'VE POSTED THE TEAMS FOR THE MIXED DOUBLES TOURNAMENT
YOU KNOW WHO YOUR PARTNER IS? MOLLY VOLLEY!
5-6
MOLLY VOLLEY?
SCHULZ

© 1977 United Feature Syndicate, Inc.
SEE?
YOU DREW MOLLY VOLLEY FOR A PARTNER IN THE MIXED DOUBLES...
5-7
IN THE LAST TOURNAMENT SHE BEAT UP HER PARTNER, TWO LINESMEN AND A BALL BOY!
HERE SHE COMES NOW..
ALL RIGHT, WHERE'S MY PARTNER?
SCHULZ

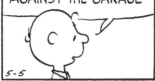

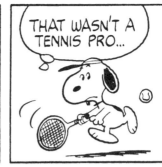

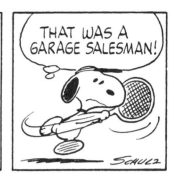

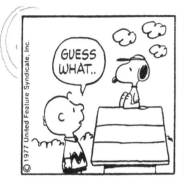

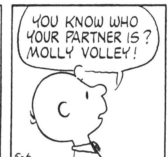

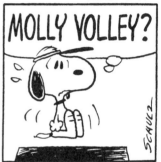

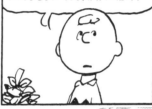

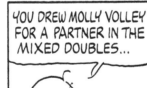

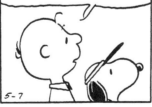

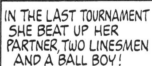

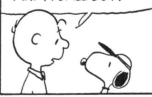

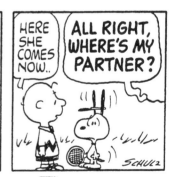

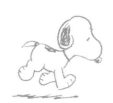

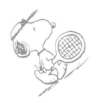

HI, I'M MOLLY VOLLEY!

HI, MY NAME IS CHARLIE BROWN

5-9

THIS IS SNOOPY...HE'S GOING TO BE YOUR PARTNER IN THE TOURNAMENT

I'VE HEARD OF MIXED DOUBLES, BUT THIS IS RIDICULOUS!

© 1977 United Feature Syndicate, Inc.

OKAY, "PARTNER.."

© 1977 United Feature Syndicate, Inc.

LET'S GET A FEW THINGS STRAIGHT... I HATE TO LOSE!

5-10

I'LL MAKE ALL THE LINE CALLS AND TAKE ALL THE OVERHEADS! ALL YOU HAVE TO DO IS GUARD YOUR ALLEY!

AND JUST ONE SMART REMARK ABOUT MY FAT LEGS GETS YOU A KNOCK ON THE NOGGIN!!

HERE'S SOMETHING TO THINK ABOUT, PARTNER..

THE FIRST TIME YOU DOUBLE FAULT, I'M GONNA HIT YOU RIGHT OVER THE HEAD WITH MY RACKET!

5-11

OKAY, GO AHEAD AND SERVE! AND DON'T BE NERVOUS...

© 1977 United Feature Syndicate, Inc.

© 1977 United Feature Syndicate, Inc.
OUT!
5-12
YOU HEARD ME!! I SAID IT WAS OUT!! YOU WANT ME TO SPELL IT FOR YA?!
EVERY BALL YOU GUYS HAVE HIT HAS BEEN OUT! EVERY BALL WE'VE HIT HAS BEEN IN!!!
HANG IN THERE, PARTNER, WE'RE GONNA WIN!!
SCHULZ

© 1977 United Feature Syndicate, Inc.
MINE!!
WHAP!
5-13
GOOD TEAMWORK, PARTNER! WE'RE GONNA WIN!
SCHULZ

OUT!
© 1977 United Feature Syndicate, Inc.
WADDYA MEAN, ARE WE SURE? WE CALLED IT OUT, DIDN'T WE?
5-14
YOU CALL YOUR SIDE, AND WE'LL CALL OURS! OUT IS OUT! QUIT STALLING! HIT THE BALL!
THAT'S TELLING 'EM, PARTNER!! WE'RE GONNA WIN!!
SCHULZ

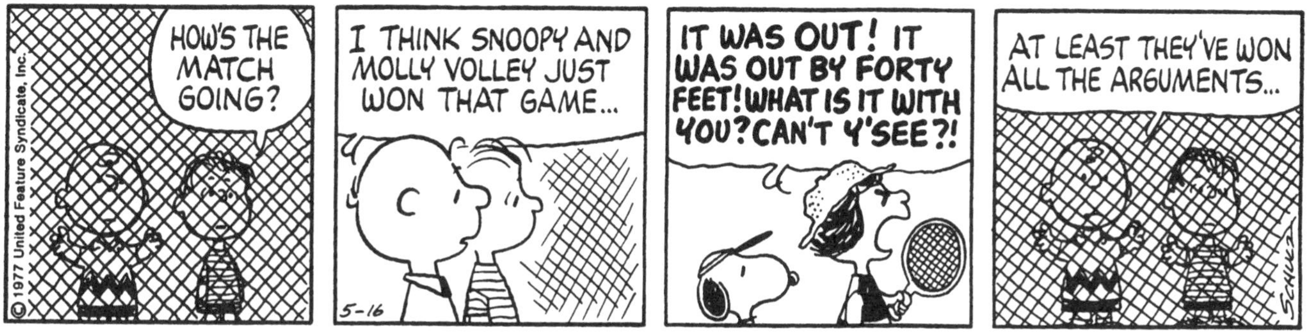
© 1977 United Feature Syndicate, Inc.
HOW'S THE MATCH GOING?
I THINK SNOOPY AND MOLLY VOLLEY JUST WON THAT GAME...
5-16
IT WAS OUT! IT WAS OUT BY FORTY FEET! WHAT IS IT WITH YOU? CAN'T Y'SEE?!
AT LEAST THEY'VE WON ALL THE ARGUMENTS...
SCHULZ

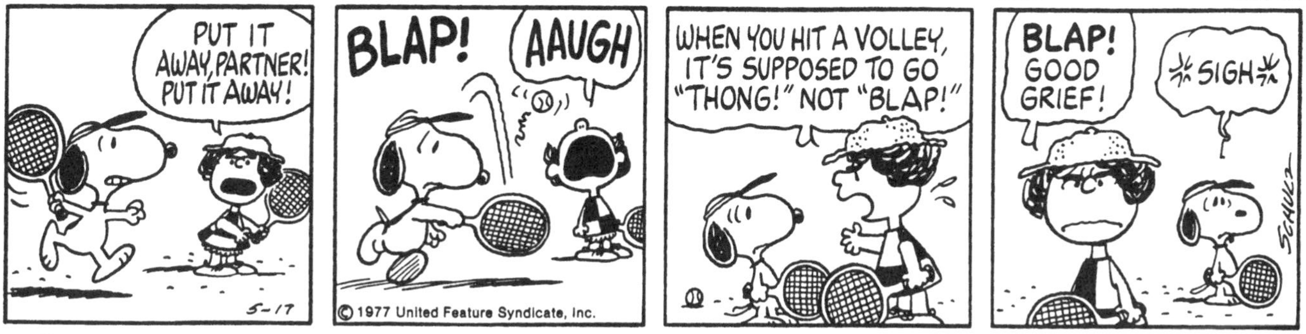
PUT IT AWAY, PARTNER! PUT IT AWAY!
5-17
BLAP!
AAUGH
© 1977 United Feature Syndicate, Inc.
WHEN YOU HIT A VOLLEY, IT'S SUPPOSED TO GO "THONG!" NOT "BLAP!"
BLAP! GOOD GRIEF!
SIGH
SCHULZ

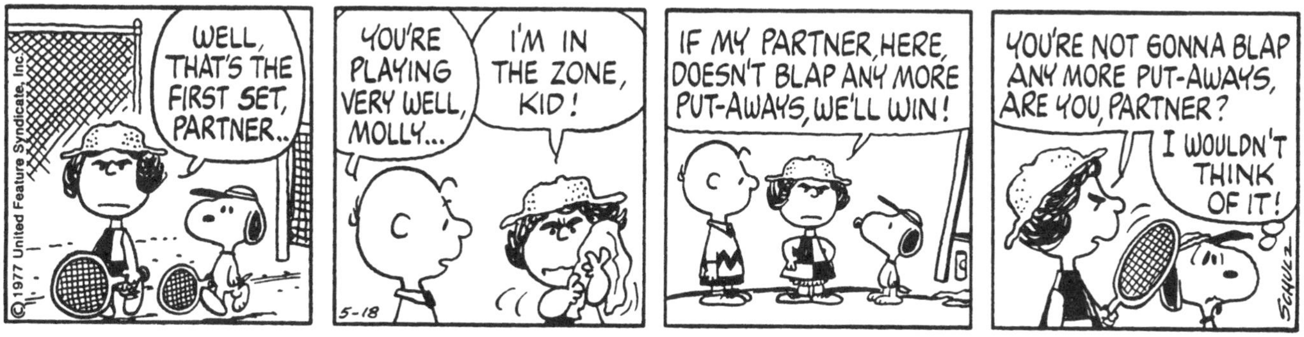
© 1977 United Feature Syndicate, Inc.
WELL, THAT'S THE FIRST SET, PARTNER...
YOU'RE PLAYING VERY WELL, MOLLY...
I'M IN THE ZONE, KID!
5-18
IF MY PARTNER, HERE, DOESN'T BLAP ANY MORE PUT-AWAYS, WE'LL WIN!
YOU'RE NOT GONNA BLAP ANY MORE PUT-AWAYS, ARE YOU, PARTNER?
I WOULDN'T THINK OF IT!
SCHULZ

© 1977 United Feature Syndicate, Inc.
YOU DON'T APPROVE OF ME, DO YOU, KID?
YOU THINK I TRY TOO HARD, DON'T YOU?
5-19
WELL, KID, LET ME TELL YOU HOW IT IS... YOU WANNA KNOW HOW IT IS?
I KNOW HOW IT IS WITH **ME**...I SHOULD HAVE STUCK WITH THE GARAGE!
SCHULZ

© 1977 United Feature Syndicate, Inc.
YOU KNOW WHERE CHAMPIONS ARE MADE?
WELL, THEY'RE NOT MADE AT WIMBLEDON OR FOREST HILLS, I'LL TELL YOU THAT!
5-20
THEY'RE MADE RIGHT HERE ON THESE DIRTY, BUMPY, MISERABLE COURTS WHERE YOU CALL YOUR OWN LINES AND KEEP YOUR OWN SCORE!
YOU GET WHAT YOU GO FOR, KID!
I'D LIKE TO GO HOME, BUT I THINK SHE'D KILL ME!
SCHULZ

© 1977 United Feature Syndicate, Inc.
SEE THAT FAT LADY OVER THERE?
SHE'S THE MOTHER OF ONE OF THE KIDS WE'RE PLAYING...
SHE COMES TO SEE THAT HER LITTLE DARLING GETS GOOD CALLS! SHE HATES ME
5-21
SHE KNOWS THAT WHEN I'M PLAYING, ALL THE CALLS ARE GOING TO BE IN CENTIMETERS!
SCHULZ

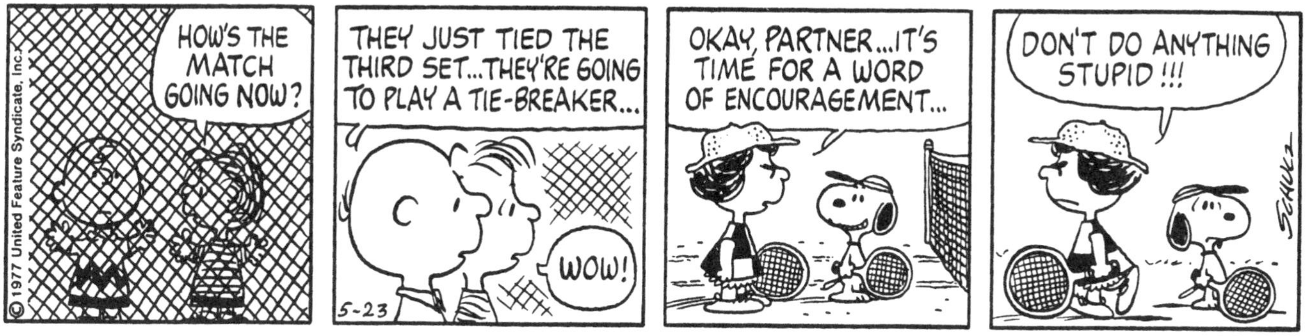
© 1977 United Feature Syndicate, Inc.
HOW'S THE MATCH GOING NOW?
THEY JUST TIED THE THIRD SET...THEY'RE GOING TO PLAY A TIE-BREAKER...
WOW!
5-23
OKAY, PARTNER...IT'S TIME FOR A WORD OF ENCOURAGEMENT...
DON'T DO ANYTHING STUPID!!!
SCHULZ

© 1977 United Feature Syndicate, Inc.
IT'S THREE TO FOUR IN THE TIE-BREAKER..
MINE!
5-24
WAP!
FOUR-ALL IN THE TIE-BREAKER!
SCHULZ

© 1977 United Feature Syndicate, Inc.
WHERE'S THE BALL?
I LOST IT IN THE SUN! WHERE DID IT GO? DID YOU SEE IT?
5-25
DID IT GO OUT?! WAS IT IN, OR WAS IT OUT? DID WE WIN, OR DID WE LOSE?
DON'T JUST STAND THERE! CALL IT IN, OR CALL IT OUT!!
SCHULZ

YOU CALL IT, PARTNER!
WAS IT IN OR OUT? DO WE WIN OR LOSE?
IN!
SORRY, PARTNER!
SMAK!
AAUGH!!
5-26
© 1977 United Feature Syndicate, Inc.
SCHULZ

MOLLY VOLLEY'S ON THE PHONE
NOW WHAT?
SHE WANTS TO KNOW IF YOU'D BE INTERESTED IN ANOTHER MIXED-DOUBLES TOURNAMENT ON SUNDAY...
I DOUBT IT...
I'VE HAD DISTEMPER, AND I'VE PLAYED MIXED-DOUBLES... I'D RATHER HAVE DISTEMPER
5-28
© 1977 United Feature Syndicate, Inc.
SCHULZ

6-11
DOUBLE FAULT!
JOE CHOKE
SCHULZ
© 1977 United Feature Syndicate, Inc.

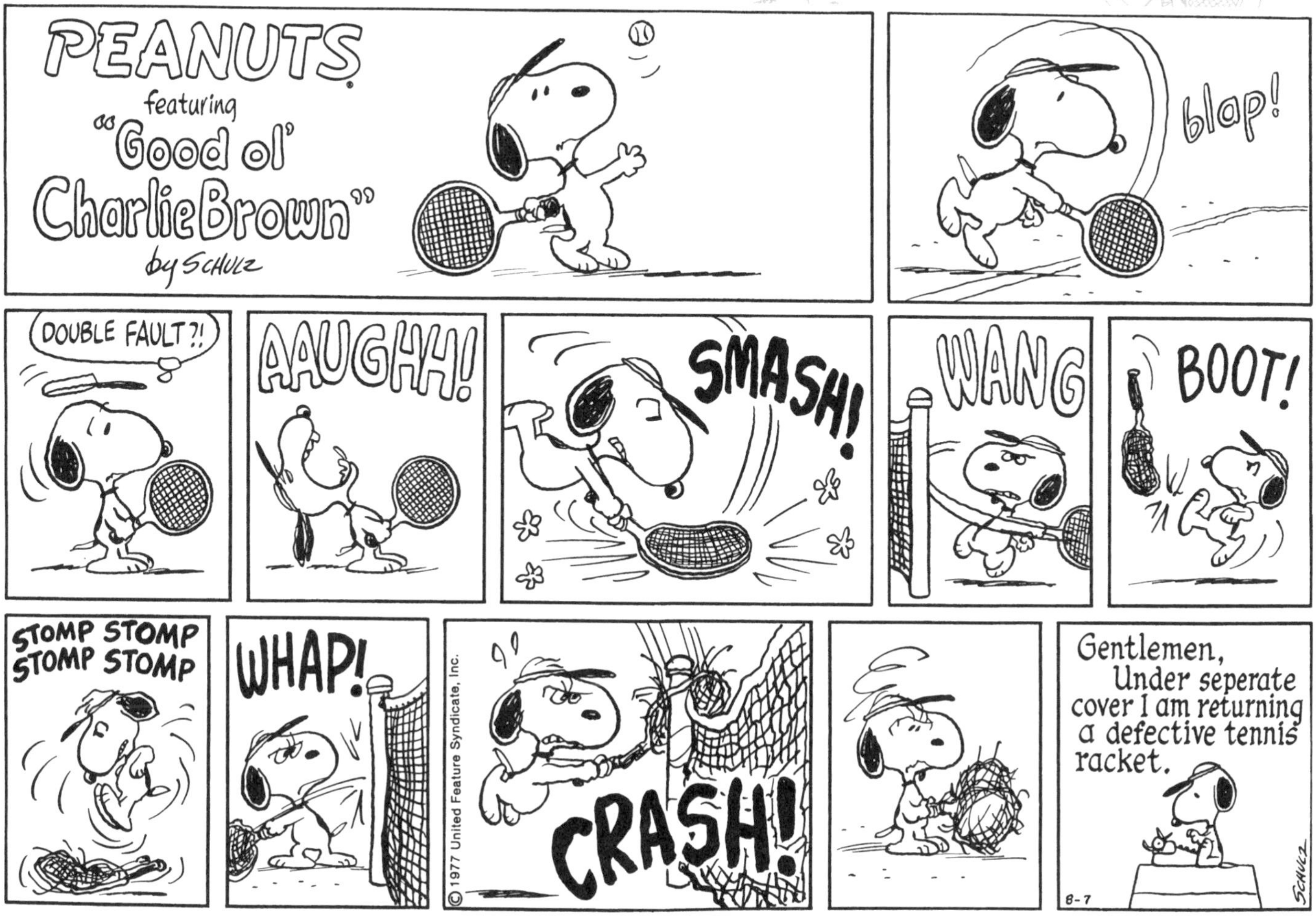
PEANUTS
featuring
"Good ol' Charlie Brown"
by SCHULZ
blap!
DOUBLE FAULT?!
AAUGHH!
SMASH!
WANG
BOOT!
STOMP STOMP
STOMP STOMP
WHAP!
© 1977 United Feature Syndicate, Inc.
CRASH!
Gentlemen,
Under seperate cover I am returning a defective tennis racket.
8-7
SCHULZ

Panel 1: ARE YOU READY TO PLAY?

11-7

Panel 2: OKAY...SPIN FOR SERVE!

Panel 3: © 1977 United Feature Syndicate, Inc.

Panel 4: THAT ISN'T EXACTLY WHAT I MEANT..

SCHULZ

242

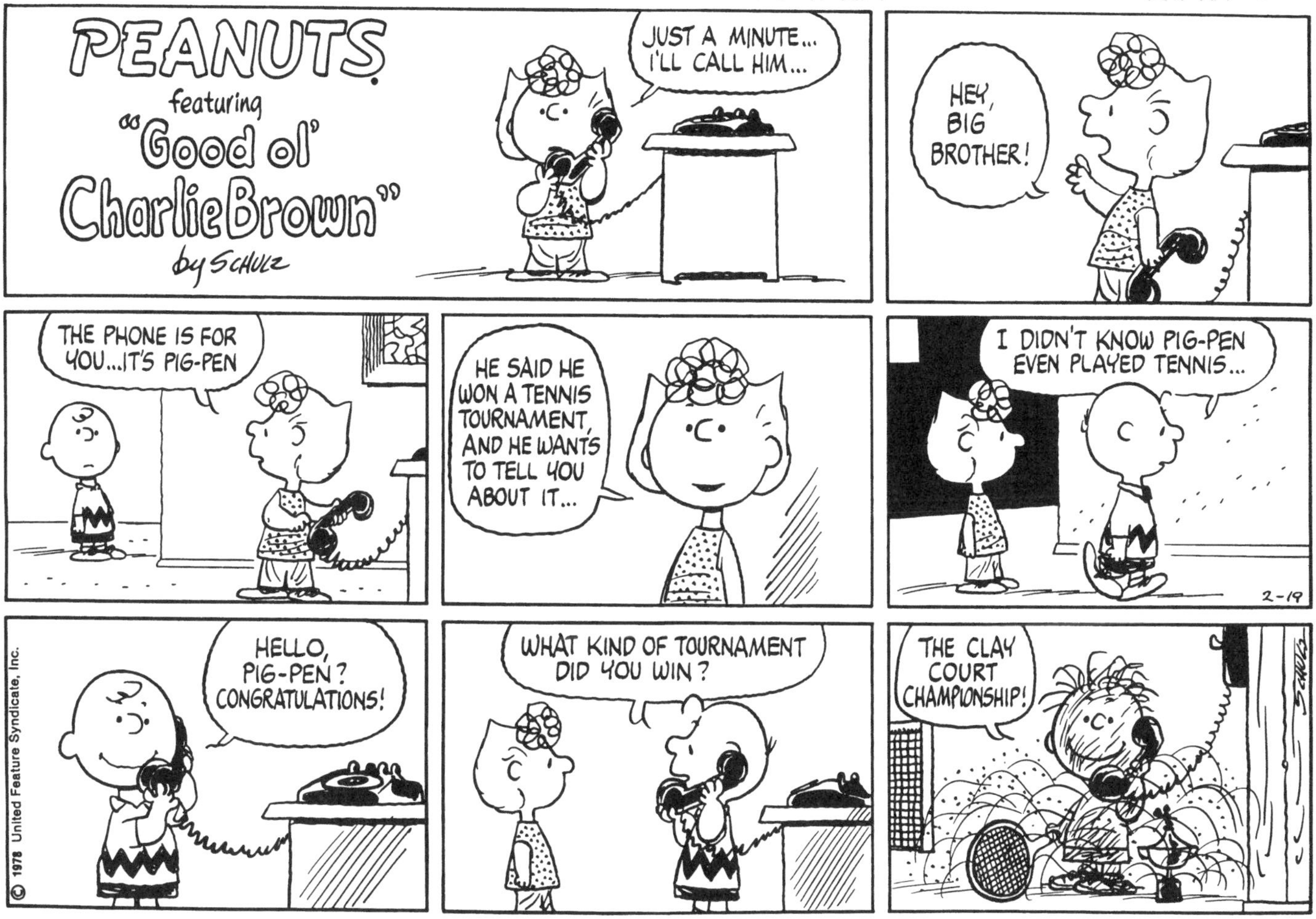
PEANUTS
featuring "Good ol' Charlie Brown"
by SCHULZ
JUST A MINUTE... I'LL CALL HIM...
HEY, BIG BROTHER!
THE PHONE IS FOR YOU...IT'S PIG-PEN
HE SAID HE WON A TENNIS TOURNAMENT, AND HE WANTS TO TELL YOU ABOUT IT...
I DIDN'T KNOW PIG-PEN EVEN PLAYED TENNIS...
2-19
HELLO, PIG-PEN? CONGRATULATIONS!
WHAT KIND OF TOURNAMENT DID YOU WIN?
THE CLAY COURT CHAMPIONSHIP!
SCHULZ

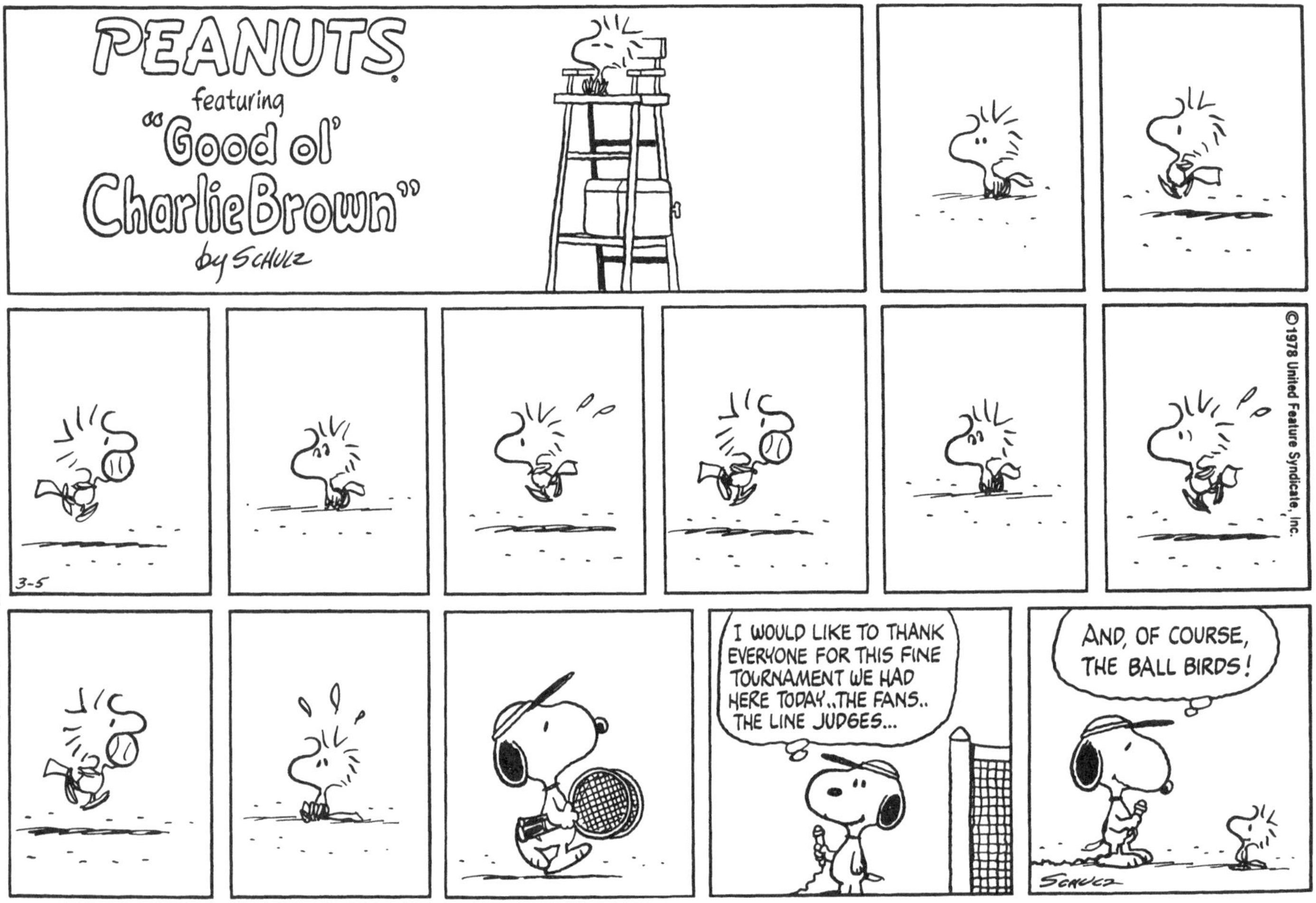
PEANUTS
featuring
"Good ol' Charlie Brown"
by SCHULZ
3-5
©1978 United Feature Syndicate, Inc.
I WOULD LIKE TO THANK EVERYONE FOR THIS FINE TOURNAMENT WE HAD HERE TODAY..THE FANS.. THE LINE JUDGES...
AND, OF COURSE, THE BALL BIRDS!
SCHULZ

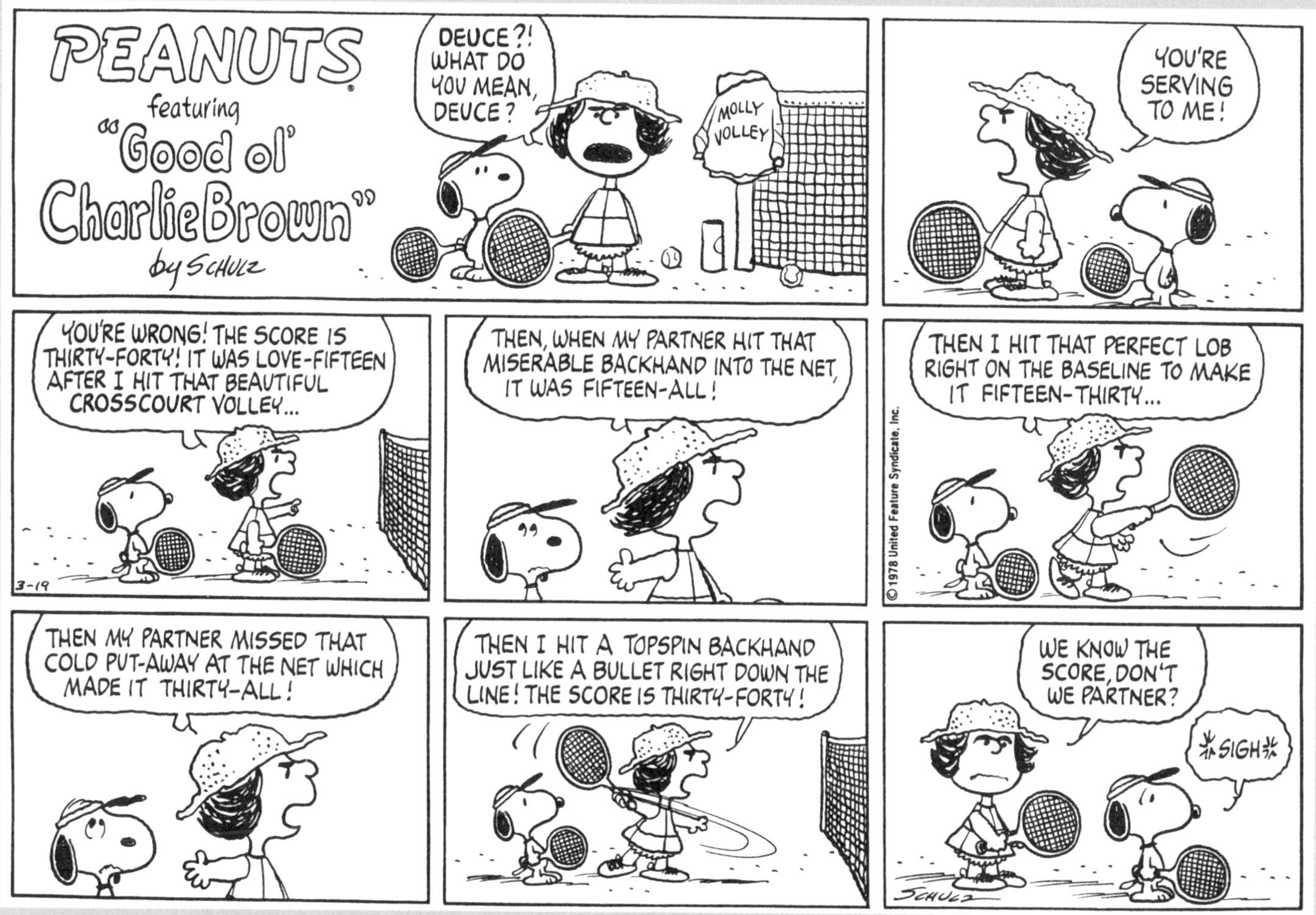
PEANUTS
featuring
"Good ol' Charlie Brown"
by SCHULZ
DEUCE?! WHAT DO YOU MEAN, DEUCE?
MOLLY VOLLEY
YOU'RE SERVING TO ME!
YOU'RE WRONG! THE SCORE IS THIRTY-FORTY! IT WAS LOVE-FIFTEEN AFTER I HIT THAT BEAUTIFUL CROSSCOURT VOLLEY...
3-19
THEN, WHEN MY PARTNER HIT THAT MISERABLE BACKHAND INTO THE NET, IT WAS FIFTEEN-ALL!
THEN I HIT THAT PERFECT LOB RIGHT ON THE BASELINE TO MAKE IT FIFTEEN-THIRTY...
© 1978 United Feature Syndicate, Inc.
THEN MY PARTNER MISSED THAT COLD PUT-AWAY AT THE NET WHICH MADE IT THIRTY-ALL!
THEN I HIT A TOPSPIN BACKHAND JUST LIKE A BULLET RIGHT DOWN THE LINE! THE SCORE IS THIRTY-FORTY!
WE KNOW THE SCORE, DON'T WE PARTNER?
SIGH
SCHULZ

HE HAS TENNIS ELBOW?

I HAVE A STRAP THAT MIGHT HELP

TELL HIM TO WEAR IT THE NEXT TIME HE PLAYS...

5-16

© 1978 United Feature Syndicate, Inc.

I HAVE MY DOUBTS, BUT I'LL TRY ANYTHING

YOUR SERVE AGAIN, PARTNER

THIS COULD BE GAME POINT

5-24

IT ALSO COULD BE SET POINT AND MATCH POINT...

© 1978 United Feature Syndicate, Inc.

HOW ABOUT CHOKE POINT?

PEANUTS
featuring
"Good ol' CharlieBrown"
by SCHULZ
© 1978 United Feature Syndicate, Inc.
7-2
IF YOU'RE GONNA FOOL ME WITH A DROP SHOT, YOU'LL HAVE TO DISGUISE IT BETTER THAN THAT!
SCHULZ

MOLLY VOLLEY JUST CALLED

SHE SAID THE MIXED DOUBLES TOURNAMENT STARTS TOMORROW

7-3

YOU GUYS PLAY "CRYBABY" BOOBIE IN THE FIRST ROUND

"CRYBABY" BOOBIE?!

© 1978 United Feature Syndicate, Inc.

I'VE PLAYED AGAINST "CRYBABY" BOOBIE BEFORE! IT'S AN EXPERIENCE!

© 1978 United Feature Syndicate, Inc.

HER BROTHER, BOBBY BOOBIE, DOESN'T SAY MUCH, BUT SHE COMPLAINS ABOUT EVERYTHING

7-4

JUST DON'T LET HER GET TO YOU....JUST LET IT ALL GO IN ONE EAR AND OUT THE OTHER...

THAT'S THE SPIRIT, PARTNER!

OKAY, WE'LL RECEIVE ON THIS SIDE
THAT'S NOT FAIR!
THAT MEANS WE HAVE THE SUN IN OUR EYES! WHY DO WE ALWAYS SERVE WITH THE SUN IN OUR EYES?!
7-5
© 1978 United Feature Syndicate, Inc.
SEE? DIDN'T I TELL YOU? "CRYBABY" BOOBIE COMPLAINS ABOUT EVERYTHING!
I THINK THE NET IS TOO HIGH! THESE BALLS FEEL DEAD! I CAN'T PLAY ON A SLOW COURT! THESE BALLS ARE TOO LIVELY! I THINK THE NET IS TOO LOW!
SCHULZ

HEY, "CRYBABY," WHY DON'T YOU SHUT UP AND SERVE?
THESE BALLS FEEL TOO LIGHT! MY SHOULDER HURTS! THE SUN IS KILLING ME! THE NET LOOKS TOO HIGH!
7-6
I SAID, "SHUT UP AND SERVE!"
© 1978 United Feature Syndicate, Inc.
NOW YOU'RE TRYING TO PSYCHE ME OUT!!
SCHULZ

FAULT!
FAULT?! THAT WAS A BAD CALL! THAT BALL WAS IN! HOW COULD YOU CALL IT OUT? YOU'RE CHEATING ME!
7-7
SHUT UP, "CRYBABY" BOOBIE, AND SERVE!
©1978 United Feature Syndicate, Inc.
THIS IS GOING TO BE A LONG DAY!
SCHULZ

HONK!
ALL RIGHT, "CRYBABY," TELL YOUR MOTHER TO CUT IT OUT!
SHE SITS THERE IN HER CAR, AND EVERY TIME YOU MAKE A GOOD SHOT, SHE HONKS THE HORN!
7-8
THE NEXT TIME SHE DOES THAT I'M GONNA TEAR OFF A WHEEL!
©1978 United Feature Syndicate, Inc.
I COULD HAVE STAYED HOME AND GOTTEN INTO A NICE GENTLE DOGFIGHT
SCHULZ

HOW'S THE TENNIS MATCH GOING?
"CRYBABY" BOOBIE AND HER BROTHER ARE LEADING
WHO'S HONKING THAT CAR HORN?
THAT'S "CRYBABY'S" MOTHER
7-10
©1978 United Feature Syndicate, Inc.
EVERY TIME HER DAUGHTER HITS A GOOD SHOT, SHE HONKS THE HORN
WILL YOU CUT THAT OUT?!
YOU DON'T LIKE MY MOTHER!
SCHULZ

ALL RIGHT, PARTNER, IT'S MATCH POINT...
WE HAVE TO CONCENTRATE! THAT'S THE SECRET, PARTNER! CONCENTRATE!
© 1978 United Feature Syndicate, Inc.
I GOT A LETTER FROM MY BROTHER, SPIKE, TODAY...
7-11
HAS ANYONE EVER NOTICED THAT THE PORTRAIT OF CARL SANDBURG ON A THIRTEEN-CENT STAMP LOOKS LIKE PANCHO GONZALES?
SCHULZ

"ACE!"
AAUGH!
7-12
WE WON!!!
©1978 United Feature Syndicate, Inc.
HONK! HONK! HONK! HONK! HONK! HONK!
I'M GONNA KILL SOMEBODY!
SCHULZ

IT'S MATCH POINT, AND YOU STAND THERE LOOKING AT A LETTER FROM YOUR STUPID BROTHER!
©1978 United Feature Syndicate, Inc.
NO WONDER YOU GOT ACED!
NOW WE HAVE TO GO AND CONGRATULATE "CRYBABY" BOOBIE! THIS IS GONNA KILL ME!
7-13
NICE MATCH, GUYS! LA DE DA DE DA DE DA
SCHULZ

BEATEN BY "CRYBABY" BOOBIE! WHAT A BLOW!

NOW I HAVE TO CONGRATULATE HER..

7-14

© 1978 United Feature Syndicate, Inc.

I DON'T KNOW WHY I PLAY THIS GAME..

CONGRATULATIONS, BOOBIE!

SCHULZ

HE NEEDS A HOME, YOU SAY?

© 1978 United Feature Syndicate, Inc.

WELL, I DON'T KNOW...

IS HE VICIOUS?

HE CAN BE IF HE GETS AHEAD IN THE THIRD SET!

SCHULZ

7-27

253

STILL HITTING BALLS WITH THE GARAGE, I SEE...
IT'S GOOD PRACTICE..HE GETS EVERYTHING BACK
8-7
I WAS SURPRISED YOU DIDN'T PLAY DOUBLES AT WIMBLEDON THIS YEAR..
THE GARAGE HATES TO FLY
© 1978 United Feature Syndicate, Inc.
SCHULZ

A PRESENT? FOR ME?
I LOVE GETTING PRESENTS
© 1978 United Feature Syndicate, Inc.
WOW! JUST WHAT I NEED...
8-23
A DOZEN FOREHAND VOLLEYS!
SCHULZ

PEANUTS
featuring
"Good ol' Charlie Brown"
by SCHULZ
DOWN THE CENTER STRIPE..
SERVICE!
ACE!
© 1978 United Feature Syndicate, Inc.
9-3
WHAT DO YOU MEAN, IT WASN'T AN ACE?
IF IT WASN'T AN ACE, WHAT WAS IT?
2 ♣
HEE HEE HEE HEE HEE
SCHULZ

Panel 1: TOURNAMENT TIME AGAIN, HUH?

Panel 2: I HEAR YOU'RE PLAYING IN THE THIRTY-FIVES...

4-5

Panel 3: YOU'RE NOT THIRTY-FIVE YEARS OLD

Panel 4: YEARS? I THOUGHT THEY MEANT INCHES!

© 1979 United Feature Syndicate, Inc.

SCHULZ

Panel 5: I'VE BEEN WATCHING YOU WHEN YOU'RE GETTING READY TO SERVE

Panel 6: ARE YOU SUPERSTITIOUS?

Panel 7: I NOTICE THAT YOU NEVER STEP ON THE BASELINE...

© 1979 United Feature Syndicate, Inc.

4-14

Panel 8: I DON'T WANT TO OFFEND IT

SCHULZ